SEX ON THE COUCH

SEX ON THE COUCH

What Freud Still Has to Teach Us About Sex and Gender

RICHARD BOOTHBY

Published in 2005 by
Routledge
Taylor & Francis Group
270 Madison Avenue
New York, NY 10016

Published in Great Britain by
Routledge
Taylor & Francis Group
2 Park Square
Milton Park, Abingdon
Oxon OX14 4RN

Routledge is an imprint of Taylor & Francis Group

Printed in the United States of America on acid-free paper
10 9 8 7 6 5 4 3 2 1

International Standard Book Number-10: 0-415-97413-5 (Hardcover) 0-415-97414-3 (Softcover)
International Standard Book Number-13: 978-0-415-97413-4 (Hardcover) 978-0-415-97414-1 (Softcover)

Library of Congress Cataloging-in-Publication Data

Catalog record is available from the Library of Congress

Taylor & Francis Group
is the Academic Division of T&F Informa plc.

Visit the Taylor & Francis Web site at
http://www.taylorandfrancis.com

and the Routledge Web site at
http://www.routledge-ny.com

Contents

Preface

Writing about sex can be a tricky business. The very images and acts that most excite in the heat of passion may seem grotesque, even comical, in the cool light of reflection. As a result, writing on sex tends to fall one way or the other, toward pornographic titillation or stolidly clinical description. And the reason is not hard to figure: sexual desire hungers for luridness, yet stuns sober evaluation. On the other hand, clinical discussion of sex tends to falsify its own object. The effect may be a definite turn-off, as if the act of speaking objectively of sex blocks our entry into it. Sexuality thus seems to face us with two mutually exclusive prospects. At one moment, we are swept up into the heated urgency of sexual excitement that turns every sensation into a new opportunity for stimulation. At another moment, we remain tied to the flat world of everyday practicalities in which the electric charge of sexual desire may seem an abstract, or even vaguely repugnant, possibility.

This dichotomy of the erotic and the everyday was familiar to Freud, who seized upon it as a defining structure of the human condition. For Freud, the divide between the mundane and the erotic arises from a split in our own nature, a war in which sober heads and faithful hearts are pitted against the crazed demands of swollen genitalia. Sex divides us against ourselves. The result is that we are never really whole, never able to engage ourselves as an uncompromised totality. Either we are claimed by the tasks and interests of the everyday world and remain at a distance from the maelstrom of sexual desire, or we are plunged into the swirl of sexual arousal and become the blissful slaves of Eros, oblivious to the call of practical responsibilities.

Yet Freud is not in fashion these days. Dogged by a varied army of detractors who disqualify his theories and the therapeutic practice he founded as unscientific, ineffective, misogynist, or simply irrelevant to contemporary concerns, Freud is now in some danger of being sidelined, an interesting but defunct chapter in the history of psychiatry. Already more than a decade ago, a cover story of *Time* magazine asked "Is Freud Dead?" and appeared to answer its own question by featuring a portrait of Freud, his head exploding in colored fragments. An exhibit of Freud's papers at the Library of Congress was delayed for five years and very nearly canceled altogether partly in response to a chorus of critics, outraged in one way or another by the thought of Freud receiving such positive attention. Can a renewed appeal to Freud be anything but a step backward?

Of course, there are some good reasons to be critical of Freud. His theories can readily seem reductive and mechanistic. Often borrowing his basic concepts from analogies to nineteenth-century physics and hydraulics, Freud's attempt to construct a general theory of the mind, what he called the "psychical apparatus," was like trying to do brain surgery with farm implements. In his great case studies, despite the ingenuity of his interpretations, Freud's efforts sometimes seem far-fetched, oversimplifying, or both. Like the social inept who tirelessly inflicts the same joke on everyone he meets, Freud often appears to force the complexity of psychological material into the cramped mold of a few crude themes. Perhaps it is no accident that some of his most famous cases, as Freud himself admitted, were botched and incomplete. Moreover, many of the clinical issues Freud faced are now out of date. In the frenzied atmosphere of the contemporary world, dislocation, aimlessness, and alienation have replaced the suffocating rigidity and social propriety that formed the background of the most characteristic forms of psychological distress in turn-of-the-century Vienna. The hysteria and anxiety neuroses familiar to Freud have given way in our time to depression, personality disorders, borderline psychosis, and anorexia.

Surely there is no shortage of grist for the mill of complaint against Freud. Yet if his work is now met with some justified criticism, we also ought to be suspicious of its wholesale rejection. Anti-Freud sentiment, frequently aroused as much by the character of the man as by the content of his ideas, often sounds shrill and vengeful. We ought to remember, too, that the context in which Freud is currently judged is far from neutral. Criticism of Freud and the time-consuming cure that he invented is sweet music to insurance companies anxious to cut costs for psychotherapy. The eagerness of pharmaceutical giants to profit from quick-fix remedies for mental illness is matched by popular demand for the perfect pill for every discomfort. In this way, corporate greed unites with the modern dream of pushbutton control to make the long and messy soul-struggle of psychoanalysis seem not only outdated but positively undesirable.

But perhaps the most troubling thing about recent attacks on Freud is how often they are made by people who seem to have read very little or nothing of his writings. And what is true in the university is even truer on the street. Test it for yourself: Find friends who roll their eyes at the mere mention of Freud and ask which of Freud's texts they have actually read. These days, we all seem to feel perfectly satisfied that we know Freud well enough to dismiss him. Why bother to read him? The most potent obstacle to understanding what Freud had to say about the unconscious is the thoughtless conviction that we already do.

However chilly the atmosphere that now surrounds him, Freud may well be the most influential thinker of the twentieth century. Freud? Surprising, isn't it? Yet it is a plausible claim when we consider the sheer range of disciplines upon which his theories have left their mark, fields that extend far beyond the boundaries of psychology: from anthropology and sociology to film and media studies, from literature, poetics, and aesthetics to history, biography, philosophy, and theology. Perhaps even more striking than the breadth of Freud's impact in the university is the enormity of his influence in the popular domain. Many of Freud's technical terms—*id*, *ego*, and *superego*; *repression*, *identification*, and *projection*—have become household words. But this very familiarity should make us pause. When we turn from the din of Freud's critics and settle more quietly into the pages of his writings, we realize how much of the received view of Freud's theories, now part of the common knowledge that we carry with us without a second thought, is grossly over-simple or downright wrong.

In this book, I want to ask what Freud still has to teach us about sex. Though interest in the topic is as lively as ever, our favorite metaphors for thinking about sex are now less psychological than biological. We have traded the Freudian arcana of family dynamics, childhood memories, and unconscious phantasies for the pleasingly simple-sounding language of genes and hormones. In reconsidering Freud's contribution, the point is not to deny the rootedness of sexuality in biology—Freud would be the last to make such a claim. Rather, the aim is to see how our animal nature is distorted by psychological factors to produce effects that are foreign to biology. We are animals, but with a twist. Kinky animals. And the kink makes all the difference.

In the course of revisiting Freud's theories, we will take a new look at some of his most basic concepts: the sexual drive, repression, fetishism, narcissism, and masochism. We will also reconsider his cardinal concept of the Oedipus complex, rescuing it from the tired banality of wanting to kill one's father and marry one's mother. Yet as we launch upon this rereading of Freud, it ought to be acknowledged that this book cannot pretend to be a mere presentation of Freudian theory, as if everyone in the broad field of psychoanalytic studies was in easy agreement. In fact, battles continue to rage among scholars about how exactly Freud's thought is to be interpreted. "Psychoanalysis," however much it is united around a battery of key themes and concepts, also embraces an array of disparate and contending perspectives. I have unfolded one such perspective, centered on questions of sexuality, that seems to me to be especially compelling and interesting. It is a perspective informed very much by the work of the French analyst Jacques Lacan, probably the most influential innovator in psychoanalysis since Freud himself, though a figure much better known in Europe and Latin America than in the United States. At the same time, my argument here is not narrowly "Lacanian." I have taken freely from Lacan what seems to me to be most useful and convincing without feeling the need to play the faithful disciple.

It ought also to be said that this book is not really a work of scholarship, at least in the sense that I have deliberately refrained from entering too deeply into particular arguments between competing schools of psychoanalytic theory. In what follows, I have tried to bring the main points vividly to light without getting entangled in a thicket of footnotes. Of course, this approach poses a risk of oversimplification. But it seems to me a risk worth taking if I can succeed in showing how the Freudian legacy still offers a fascinating and deeply meaningful vision of our sexual selves. For readers who want a more nuanced grasp of debates internal to psychoanalysis, I have appended a bibliography of some key sources. My immediate concern, however, is more elementary: Can we still accept Freud's teaching at all? Over a century after his invention of psychoanalysis, what does he still have to say to us? Do his theories even make sense?

In beginning, let us tackle that most notorious of Freudian preoccupations: the phallus.

Part I
Basics

1
The Phallic Code of Neckwear

Although attacks on Freud and his legacy have been mounted from many directions, probably nothing in psychoanalysis has roused more strident and perennial criticism than his treatment of gender. Here more than anywhere, we are told, Freud was blinkered by the sexist culture of Victorian Vienna. Nor can there be any doubt that the real bone of contention, if we can say so, has always been the phallus. Freudian insistence on the centrality of the phallus in the unconscious has always been something of a scandal. It spawned bitter disagreements during Freud's lifetime, but even after his death the issue has not gone away quietly. The battle lines have been redrawn most recently by the followers of Jacques Lacan, who take the phallus to be the privileged signifier, the cardinal element, in the workings of the unconscious. With Lacan, the old Freudian question—"What does a woman want?"—seems more inflammatory than ever.

Amid all of this phallic furor, it is instructive, and more than a little amusing, to consider the question afresh by focusing on an appropriately conspicuous example: the necktie. Can it be that this near-obligatory component of modern men's attire is a phallus? Can the evidence of phallic symbolism be so glaringly obvious? Has it been hanging under our noses all this time?

As a little reflection will show, the tie is unquestionably phallic, but there is more to it than that. The necktie is the pivotal element in an elaborate system of wordless communications, the key to a remarkably coherent, nonverbal lexicon for signaling gender. The necktie is the linchpin around which turns the contemporary code of neckwear. To see how this is so, we must borrow a few tools from semiotics, the science of signs.

Having to Stick Your Neck Out

The first semiotic concept that will be of use to us is that of *iconicity.* Unlike most verbal signs, which are linked to what they stand for by convention (a horse is a *cheval* or a *Pferd*, depending on which side of the Franco-German border one grows up on), iconic signs visibly resemble the things they signify. If a necktie is a phallic symbol, it is because that dangling silk tassel is shaped like a penis. The placement of neckties—hung along the midline of the body—only serves to underscore their iconic mimicry of the male organ.

The phallic iconicity of the necktie explains the most obvious feature of the neckwear code: Neckties are worn almost exclusively by *men.* The necktie echoes in the language of fashion what distinguishes the male in anatomy. It also allows us to recognize the necktie as the fashion successor of another great phallic icon: the sword. Traditions of costume have long required the man in charge to carry a big stick. In the early modern period, well after its function as a weapon was obsolete, the sword remained an important part of the elegant man's attire. For the well-dressed man on a state occasion, wearing a sword added that special something that put him a cut above the common herd. Those who find it far fetched to call the sword a phallic symbol need only to recall the Latin word for scabbard—*vagina.*

The necktie and the sword share a phallic shape but also a common function: the signification of power. In an unbroken lineage from the ancient world to the present, masculine power and prestige have been represented by all manner of columns, rods, staffs, and scepters. Homer tells us that the right to address the council of Achaeans was signaled by passing a special baton from speaker to speaker. The staff of Moses displayed his elevated authority (even without transforming itself into a serpent). From Trajan's column to the Washington Monument, great men have been honored by the erection of great phalli. That neckties continue this tradition is suggested by the fact that wearing a tie becomes increasingly obligatory as the context becomes more public and the role one is asked to assume becomes more official and authoritative. For a man to present himself as a full-fledged player in the public arena, a necktie is unquestionably *de rigueur.*

If neckties are basically emblems of power, all the more striking is the pecking order among ties themselves, some of which count as "power ties." Yellow was the power color of the mid-eighties, only to be edged out by red near the close of the decade. I have heard it said that it was Sam Donaldson's ties that first led us to red. True or not, it is an interesting possibility, as it suggests the male counterpart to the still-standard practice of female White House correspondents to appear at press conferences in a scarlet dress. What better way to signal one's burning desire to ask a question than to wrap it in red? In the Clinton era, men's ties turned to design as a power factor, opening up the power tie to a festival of swirls, paisleys, dots, expressionist splashes, even flowers. And how appropriate that George W. Bush, trumpeting his intention to restore decency and integrity to the White House, tended to shun passionate reds in favor of ties that were reassuringly cool, true blue.

But to fully understand the necktie as a phallic icon, we must pass beyond phallic representations of political power to the older, earth-bound tradition of the phallus as a fertility symbol. In ancient Greece, as in many ancient cultures, the male member was worshipped as the embodiment of the life-giving, creative force that animates all natural growth and generation. Symbolic phalli joined in celebration of the spring planting, an association that underlies the centuries-old poetic trope of the plow-phallus that parts the damp furrows of Mother Earth. Giant phalli were carried in sacred processions and revealed at the climactic moment of secret ceremonies associated with the Greek god of wine and rebirth, Dionysos, and with the later Roman diety, Priapus. Echoes of such phallic representations of fertility survived well into the early modern period in traditions like that of the Maypole and the "bride-stake," around which dance the celebrants of a wedding. Phallic power was also spectacularly manifest for the ancients in the mythical figure of the satyr. Closely linked with Dionysos and his drunken band, satyrs embodied everything raucous and randy. They were the very essence of the dark powers of nature in need of vigilant control by the forces of law and culture. Sporting an absurdly oversized erection, but also goat's horns, hooves, and a horse's tail, satyrs prefigured later Christian depictions of the devil.

By way of their ancient association with fertility, the male genitalia also came to be connected with representations of truth and authenticity. It is a connection that makes perfect sense. In a culture in which one's parentage was overwhelmingly the most important factor in determining social value and status, assurance of true paternity was a no-nonsense issue. Reference to the organs of procreation thus offered a ready model for truth-telling in general. The patriarchs of the Old Testament swore oaths by placing a hand on or near the genitals. Abraham, for example, secures the pledge of his eldest servant by asking him to "put thy hand under my thigh."

This tradition still echoes in our language, in which terms that connote a witness to truth—*testament, testify, testimony*, etc.—bear an unmistakable reference to the male seat of generation, the testicles. When asked to testify we are still required to lay a hand on something, though we now swear to the truth with a hand over a Bible rather than under a thigh. A similar etymology has been suggested for the word *genuine*, which can be traced to *genu*, literally "knee," a common euphemism in the ancient Middle East for "penis." The genuine is the true, and the true, in things as in persons, concerns what can be reliably traced back to its source, its parentage. Likewise, in Mesopotamia the word *birku* was taken to mean both *knee* and *penis*. In its later Latin transformation as *virtu*, it came to designate manliness and general worth or excellence. Etymologically, a *virtuoso* is a master of great phallic power.

The more archaic symbolism of fertility is directly connected to the later development of phallic emblems of military and state power. Roman versions of the Dionysiac festivals featured a huge mock-up of the erect phallus, referred to as the *fascinum*. It is from this origin that we derive the English word *fascinate*. This ritual phallus was in turn linked, by both name and shape, with one of the primary tokens of imperial power, the *fasces*. Carried by the Roman *liktors* as a mark of their authority, the *fasces* is a tightly wrapped bundle of rods topped off with the blade of a broad axe. The *fasces* neatly fuses the two kinds of phallic power, natural and political. It was a harvest symbol, the bundle of rods resembling a sheave of grain stalks bound together, but was also an apt representation of political power. In the ancient world, the strength of states was determined by dominion over expanses of cultivated land. The power of the battle axe was thus quite literally based on the sturdy foundation of the grain sheave. Centuries later the *fasces* was adopted by Mussolini as the symbol of his party and still sounds its name in the politics we call "fascist." The stiff-armed Nazi salute not only looks somewhat phallic. According to a long tradition of symbolism, it *is* phallic.

The *fasces* is still frequently found wherever state power has installed itself. The visitor to the U.S. House of Representatives will find two monumental *fasces*, one on either side of the Speaker's podium. A *fasces* also adorns the reverse side of the Liberty dime and reappears in a somewhat altered form, topped by a flame instead of an axe, on today's Roosevelt dime. Allowing for similar substitutions at the tip of the *fasces*, we recognize its descendants in many places. A soldier's memorial in downtown Baltimore presents an immense *fasces* with the axe appropriately replaced by the goddess of Peace. Just up the street at my own Loyola College, the Distinguished Teacher of the Year leads the annual Commencement procession carrying the Loyola Mace, itself essentially a *fasces*, the end of which has been equipped not with an axe but a lantern. This mutation from tomahawk to torch effects only a superficial shift in the symbolic function of the original. Power remains the fundamental issue; it is only the form of power that has changed. In our system of cultural values, it is the light of knowledge and truth, not the brute force of the battle axe, that holds pride of place.

Tying the Knot

This little history lesson is indispensable for our purposes because it highlights the way in which phallic symbolism comes down to us in two great streams, one associated with fertility, the other with political power. Like the *fasces*, the necktie participates in both. To see how this is so, we need only to observe that the necktie is more than just a phallic strip of silk. It is also *a knot*. After all, it is not for nothing that we call it a "tie" and it is the function of tying something up, of constraining and limiting something, that is the key to its meaning. What is bound up and contained by the tie is the procreative power of the natural phallus. The basic message of a necktie is: "I am a virile man, capable of performing a generative, sexual act … but not right now." Appearing in polite society means putting the raw force of sexuality aside. The more one needs to "pay attention to business," the more one needs to assume a detached and neutralized professional identity, the more such a bracketing of sexuality is called for. It is to serve notice of such that the proper man about town snugs up a necktie. Wearing a necktie marks the difference between a responsible male in society and a dancing satyr.

Of course, donning a necktie doesn't mean that a sexual liaison is out of the question; it only signals that sex has become subject to stricter rules of engagement. How the necktie achieves this impression of inhibition is not difficult to make out. In the first place, the necktie closes a man's clothing, it completes the "buttoning-up" of his attire. The tie also separates the head from the rest of the body. It chokes off access to the body below the neck and does so at an especially sensitive point, at which a range of natural functions—breathing, swallowing, shouting—might be threatened with strangulation. The necktie thus signals a shift from one form of phallic power to another: from private to public, from physical to spiritual, from natural to cultural.

But hold on! I began by taking the necktie as a phallic token of sexual identity, yet I now propose that the very function of ties is to communicate a suspension of sexuality. Isn't there a contradiction here? To see that there is no contradiction, or rather, to see that the contradiction is an indispensable part of the meaning of the necktie, we can again refer to a principle of semiotics: the idea that the sign is always in some measure *the negation of the thing it signifies.* The point was made startlingly succinct by the great German philosopher Hegel: "The word is the murder of the thing." It is this negative relation between the sign and the thing it signifies that lends to signs their almost magic power. I can use signs (in this case, words) to describe anything at all, from the events of my childhood (which no longer exists) to the end of the world (which hasn't happened yet), precisely because I know, and the hearers of my speech also know, that the words and the things they describe are not the same. The necktie is immensely useful for exactly this reason. It enables a man to signal both that he *is* a male sexual being (as his phallic tie quite clearly indicates) and that he *is not* a male sexual being, at least not right now (his tie is a mere *symbol*; literally speaking it is not a phallus at all). Because the tie both is and is not a phallus, it enables a man to communicate a measured distance from his own sexuality. He both shows and does not show his sex. The result is that his sexuality is shunted into the future; it is *deferred.*

We become more certain that tightening the necktie knot expresses a distancing of sexuality when we observe the effect of *loosening* it. For any member of our culture, that is, for anyone conversant with the current language of neckwear, the loosened tie eases the more guarded, public role and marks a new openness to private pleasures. It is the male equivalent of "slipping into something more comfortable." The relaxation connoted by the loosened tie signals a turning away from the propriety of the workplace. Note that we say "propriety" of the workplace, and not work itself. Loosening the tie and rolling up one's sleeves may be a gesture of really "getting down to work." But even in that case, the loosened tie tends to signify a certain suspension of the unwritten rules that govern the work world. It says, "anything goes to get this job done." The crucial point is that the loosened tie connotes a relaxing of social strictures and for that reason bears an unmistakable suggestion of greater sexual openness.

This effect of relaxation is so predictable that it can be used like a tool of seduction. Think, for example, of the Hollywood femme fatale who suggestively loosens the tie of the slow learner. She manipulates the code of neckwear so that the wearer himself might get the message. Not surprisingly, loosening the tie to the extreme of removing it altogether, perhaps leaving a few shirt buttons undone, creates an even more laid back and sexually available look. Continue this process far enough, unbuttoning right down to the beltline, and we have the stereotypical "Italian Stallion," the raw come-on of the motorcycle daddy or the disco king. It is an effect we could have predicted. When the phallic *symbol* is cast off, along with the hint of negation it carries toward the object it stands for, it is replaced with a palpable promise of the real thing.

Another experiment of variation yields a similar conclusion. Suppose that we alter the necktie, not by loosening the knot, but by tying it super tight. What is this but the bowtie? If "tying the knot" connotes a proprietous restraint of sexuality (as it also does in referring to other things besides neckties), then the more conspicuous knot of the bowtie quite naturally communicates an even more decided refusal, a more definitive turning away from sexuality toward other concerns. Not accidentally, then, the bowtie conjures the image of the natty professor, the proper lawyer, the meticulous curator of antiquities. There is something reassuring about this look, precisely because it suggests such a complete containment of male sexuality. The choice of the bowtie by Louis Farrakhan and his Nation of Islam is therefore an inspired one, because it offers an effective antidote, administered in the code of clothing, to the familiar racist stereotype of the over-libidinous black male. At the same time, of course, this strategy can backfire, leaving the man with a smart bowtie too little a man. Isn't this exactly what happened to Paul Simon's 1988 run for the presidential nomination? His ever-present bowtie gave off an air of goody-goody nerdiness that poor Paul could never fully dispel. No one could quite believe that this obviously intelligent, deeply dedicated public servant had what it takes to be Chief.

Here again we appreciate the balancing act performed by the necktie. It very effectively says two things at once: "I am a real man" (this phallic icon tells you that I've got the right stuff) but also "I am not playing a sexual role right now" (for the moment anyway, I'm well buttoned-up and under wraps). The problem with the bowtie is that it broadcasts the second message so much better than the first. Indeed, by subtracting the iconic reference to the phallus, the bowtie can suggest a positive emasculation. Consider, for example, the bowties (often conspicuously *small, plain* bowties) worn by a certain class of low-wage workers. For many fast-food servers—doormen, waiters, valets, busboys, the Maytag repairman—a bowtie signifies a real deficit of generative power. It designates a mere stand-by, a lackey. The meek bowtie of the service employee is the sign of the eunuch in our time.

Precisely because it tends to subtract the defining element of the real man, the bowtie can also easily suggest silliness or childishness. Thus we have the yuck-it-up look of Soupy Sales's comically enormous bowtie, or the perpetual-boy look of Pee Wee Herman's nifty little red one (the innocence of which only made Pee Wee's infamous movie theater escapade seem even more shocking). By combining a knot with a long silk tail, the necktie deftly avoids these pitfalls. While the knot communicates restraint and sociability, the shaft attests to the presence of the he-man underneath it all. The necktie successfully evokes the most charming position of yesteryear: it shows us a man who clearly has a sword but hasn't yet chosen to draw it forth.

Up Tight, Out 'a Sight

"Not so fast!" someone might now object. "You claim that the bowtie emasculates, but if that's true, what are we to make of the sexiness of black tie? It doesn't take a psychoanalyst to recognize the allure of a well-tailored tuxedo, crowned sharply with a tasteful bowtie. How does that square with your view of the wimpy bowtie?" The answer to this little riddle is not far off. The servant's bowtie emasculates because it is unmistakably worn *under someone else's order*. For the bowtie eunuch—the hapless hamburger flipper at the local fast food joint, the hotel bellboy who hops up whenever the desk clerk barks "Front!"—the absence of a phallic icon is combined with a clear implication about who is really in charge. Certainly not this guy!

The political meaning of black tie is just the opposite. Because black tie smacks of money, we judge the man in the tuxedo to be himself the one in control. If his garb bespeaks an extreme of control, an almost ascetic reserve that is appropriate for the observance of state occasions, for the enjoyment of high art, or for the receipt of august cultural recognitions, it also communicates that it is the wearer himself who has imposed that control. The impression is one of grand self-restraint, which, if we don't get the message from the discreet bowtie, is seconded by the button studs and cummerbund. Aside from the aphrodisial effects of sheer wealth, the sexiness of this ensemble derives in part from the tantalizing possibility that what the wearer himself has willingly done he might also willingly undo. The sexiness of black tie thus resides in the prospect of coaxing the knight of self-control to take off his armor. For the enterprising woman, the allure of such a seduction rests on the assumption that only a very powerful urge would require such elaborate containment. We find the masculine counterpart of this notion in the common male fantasy that the real tigresses are to be found among the most conspicuously straight-laced types—school teachers, nurses, librarians, even nuns. This fantasy trades on the idea, as Tolstoy says somewhere, that the surest sign of a passionate temperament is conspicuously rigid posture.

At this point, we easily see how the language of men's neckwear, like most symbolic codes, is structured around binary polarities: in this case, the polarity tight versus loose. The tighter and more constricting the knot, the more sexually restrained. The looser the knot, the more sexually open and available.

This idea seems amply confirmed by those occupations that require the most extreme self-control. For judges and priests, for example, even a well-cinched necktie is not enough. The high collar of a judge's black robe assures us that he will forsake his own desire in rendering his decisions, just as its somber color betokens their gravity. For the priest, who may himself be a kind of judge, a similar refusal of self-interest is required. What more perfect emblem of his renunciation of sexuality than the clerical collar? It shows no trace of buttons because there is (or ought to be) no possibility of its ever being unbuttoned. Its central white square, the point at which any possible opening appears to be welded shut, aptly attests that the priest's sexuality, assiduously gathered and focused, seeks its bliss only in union with God's pure light.

The soldier, too, must put the pleasures of the flesh aside, if only to steel himself in the face of danger. In contrast to the relative relaxation of the civilian sport coat, the military man's dress jacket typically multiplies the front buttons, often prefers the extra security of a double-breasted cut, and cinches things up tightly under the chin, perhaps even embellishing a stiff collar with crisscrossed swords or rifles. During the Second World War, when threat of death and danger was at a maximum yet the daily demands of war made formal dress impractical, many a GI would achieve a similarly severe effect by tucking the end of his tie in between the shirt buttons.

Even among the executive set for whom the strict rules of court, church, and parade ground don't apply, men are undeniably uptight about ties. Everything about ties seems to give cause for anxious concern. First, there is the daily trial of getting it tied right, neither too long nor too short. The rule of thumb is that the tip of the tie ought barely to touch the beltline, as if the knot above insists on communicating with the buckle below that is its functional cousin. Fully correct form also demands that the two ends be in fair proportion to one another. If the broad strip comes out too long, it creates a gawky and fumbling impression, not to mention forcing the vexing question of how to keep the stubby, short end from poking out at the wrong moment. And heaven forbid that one gets it the other way round, with the narrow, anemic end hanging down longer. Now there's a guy who doesn't know how to keep his equipment in order!

There's also the challenge of buying ties. How else are we to explain the trouble men go through to find exactly the right size, color, and design except to assume that the tie, more than any other element of dress, expresses who and what they are? In a fashion milieu where the standard for suits is still dominated by blues, browns, and grays, the necktie remains the one place where a man might "let it all hang out." Yet this very latitude poses a problem. Will a flowered pattern be too feminine? a bold, modish design too avant-garde? stripes too stodgy? Picking out a tie is a touchy business because the tie says something about the force of a man's impulses and the range of objects he will countenance to satisfy them.

The Ladies' Question: How Low Can You Go?

Having promised a discussion of neckwear in general, we need to consider women's fashions. Of course, the fact that styles of feminine neckwear communicate significant messages ought hardly to surprise us: In both men and women the neck and upper chest offer themselves as privileged areas for signaling personal identity and intentions. Stretched between the face and genitals, the upper thorax constitutes a special "signifying zone" of the body. An onlooker's gaze can comfortably linger in this zone while an inspecting look directed at the face or genitals would disconcert. Yet it was by no means arbitrary that we first dealt with the phallic necktie before turning to women's neck fashions. Contemporary women's neckwear is very usefully understood as a dialogue with the necktie. In the current language of neckwear, the tie tends to be the defining element of the code obeyed by both genders.

This situation would hardly surprise a student of semiotics, for it displays the characteristic of signs that linguists call "marked" and "unmarked." Symbolic codes are typically built around binary oppositions, which are themselves based on the presence or absence of some feature. So, too, the code of neckwear: the necktie present in men, absent in women. When linguists divide such oppositions between marked and unmarked, it is to indicate that one of the two positions, the unmarked one, is the "natural" position. Marked versus unmarked thus often expresses the opposition culture versus nature. Accordingly, the two pairs of oppositions discussed so far—tight versus loose and tie versus no tie—form a tidy pattern. The tightly knotted tie embodies the constraints of culture, while the loose collar with no tie stands closer to raw nature. In this way, the opposition tie–no tie echoes the age-old prejudice that associates men with the stability of culture and women with nature's fickleness and liability to change.

Of course, women *do* sometimes wear ties. Diane Keaton's wardrobe in the Woody Allen film *Annie Hall* is a famous example. Much of the charm of Keaton's character derived from her combining a very feminine manner with unmistakably masculine elements of dress: tweedy vest, rumpled hat, and tie. Yet if the *Annie Hall* look demonstrates the fun of a little cross-dressing, it also illustrates that the woman who wears a tie almost always does so in a way that signals that it is *borrowed* from a man. The tie is too loose, too long, too short, or askew. The narrow end is intentionally left much longer than the broad end. In one interesting variation, the tie is worn *inside* the shirt collar, as if it were a necklace. The impression is less one of really *wearing* a tie than of *playing* with it. The charming effect is akin to that produced by a young woman wearing a man's shirt: it is most piquant when the shirt is very obviously too big.

We also ought to admit that women do have their own ties, if any piece of fabric knotted round the neck is counted as a tie. But such feminine ties—including all manner of scarves, kerchiefs, shawls, and so on—are iconically related to the female genitalia almost as obviously as the necktie is to the penis. Women's "ties" tend to be soft, flowing things that offer an eye-catching swirl of tucks and folds at the base of the neck. Men's styles of neckwear are rarely so full and blooming, with the exception of the ascot, which, it can now hardly surprise us, often creates a distinctly feminine impression.

The word *blooming* immediately brings to mind another neckpiece not infrequently worn by women: the flower. For a swishy occasion, the neckline of an elegant dress can very effectively be graced with a flower. Once again, the iconic link to a woman's sexual parts is unmistakable. It is not by chance that we refer to the loss of virginity as "deflowering." Men, too, sometimes wear flowers, but *always* off to one side. Imagine the strikingly dissonant, almost alarming, effect that would be produced by a man wearing a flower, even a small one, precisely on the midline of his clothing.

Notwithstanding these options and exceptions in which women don a necktie or something vaguely tie-like, the classic and really defining style of contemporary women's neck fashions is unquestionably the open collar, and especially the "V" neck. To the extent that it communicates with the masculine necktie, this fashion poses no great difficulties, at least for the first stage of its interpretation. Obviously enough, the woman's open collar displays a lack: it bespeaks the absence of the phallus. But the feminine neckline doesn't confine itself to making a simple statement (I don't have it, period) but rather offers a range of responses to an ongoing conversation. If the basic question answered by a man's tie is about possessing the phallus, the essential message of a woman's neckline is about how willing she is to receive it from him. This message is delivered in an extremely straightforward way. The more open the neckline, the more open the invitation. A very high, closed collar gives a cooler, perhaps even prudish look. A more deeply plunging line, like a sort of inverted thermometer, almost unavoidably connotes increasing sexual heat. In the extreme case, a really deep-cutting neckline risks calling up the image of the slut or bimbo.

Now it is important to remember that the symbolic messages carried by clothing don't necessarily match the intentions of the wearer. The steaminess of a really low neckline may have little or nothing to do with the mood of the woman who wears it. Context, too, plays an important role. A provocatively revealing dress that is stunningly tasteful at a high-class party may seem cheap and tawdry atop a barstool. Yet clothes inevitably speak for themselves and lack of agreement between what a woman intends and what her clothes say for her can be a dicey business. When a woman puts on something extra sexy, it's usually meant for a limited circle of men with whom she wishes to have contact. Inevitably, however, the language of fashion calls out indiscriminately to every passerby.

Getting Beauty by the Throat

The feminine V-neck is a semiotician's field day. Aside from allowing a better peek at a woman's cleavage, the "V" mirrors the V of the legs, or even of the pubic triangle. Perhaps that is part of the reason the V-cut was considered so racy when it first burst on the fashion scene in the 1920s. The V-neck also prompts us to add the binary polarity high–low to that of tight–loose. Like tight versus loose, high versus low suggests the opposition culture versus nature. The buttoned-up look of a high collar bespeaks the primness of a cultivated and highly controlled person, where a low-cut bodice suggests a lustiness less restrained by convention. In this way, the V-neck participates in one of our culture's most pervasive metaphoric systems, according to which high is more intellectual, spiritual, and noble, while low is instinctual, earthy, and base.

Yet far more important than any metaphor is the way the V-neck shows the skin itself—and not just any patch of skin. If the open neck communicates a woman's erotic receptivity, there are few areas of the body better suited for the purpose. Many women show a blotchy "sex flush" over the throat when aroused, frightened, or embarrassed. The open collar of the V-neck offers an ideal space across which such physiological flags of emotion can be unfurled. So, too, the subtler clues of feeling betrayed by the rhythms of breathing can be spectacularly displayed by a low-cut bodice. Such a display was one of the main functions of the bygone fashion of décolletage, a marvelous example of which is offered by the costuming of Glenn Close in the film version of *Dangerous Liaisons*. Of course, corseting the bosom from beneath shows off the ampleness of a lady's mammary endowments. But it also presses the breasts into service as a kind of emotional message board upon which every sigh of sadness, every gasp of surprise, every flutter of excitement, is unmistakably registered in a quiver of flesh.

The necktie represents what a man *possesses* and what, as a result, he is capable of *doing*. A woman's neckline says something about how she *feels* and therefore hints at what she is willing to *undergo*. As John Berger has tersely put it, "*men act* and *women appear*." The brutal simplicity of this situation raises some problems. If the question answered by a woman's neckline is whether she is sexually willing or not, and if the terms of the answer are limited to the either/or of high and low, then women face a difficult task of balancing propriety with provocativeness. It is the fashion equivalent of a familiar double-bind that shuffles women between conflicting images of madonna and whore. The problem, of course, is that men so often want their women to play both roles for different reasons. Yet with only two options—high neck, low neck—women are condemned to fall too far one way or the other: too buttoned-up to be interesting, too unbuttoned to be respectable.

Styles of women's clothing therefore offer a range of ingenious devices for having it both ways. Imagine, for example, a very low cutting blouse, plunging well down between the breasts, but discreetly nipped in the middle by a single, tasteful button. At once racy and restrained, the effect is successful because it escapes the uncomfortable dichotomy of *mama–putana*. Lace can be very effectively employed to the same end, cooling down the excitement of a risqué neckline with a field of material that is almost transparent, but not quite. The result, once again, is qualified access, a charming balance of sassy display and social decorum.

Perhaps this is the place to add a note about the necklace. Like the lacy halter that both reveals and conceals, the necklace can provide a measure of closure for what might otherwise be too low and open a neckline. The necklace doesn't interfere with a good view yet punctuates it with a restraining band of metal and stones. At the same time, however, the necklace offers even subtler means for the delivery of a mixed message. Even today, when many women buy their own jewelry, the necklace continues to convey the palpable suggestion of having been placed there by a man. If diamonds are a girl's best friend, they also whisper that she has at least one other friend as well. This subtle indication of possession completes the signification of the necklace in the code we have been exploring. If a woman's neck flesh is a privileged area for signaling her sexuality, a necklace draped across it qualifies its openness in a general way, but also hints that the display is not equally open for all observers. The necklace permits a glimpse at a beautiful landscape, but may also help to mark it as private property.

That the throat is a special field for the registration of feeling in women is attested by the language not only of fashions but also of gestures. We will take just two. The first is that definitive posture of ecstatic pleasure in which, eyes closed, mouth slightly agape, the head is thrown back in an attitude of passionate transport. Much more characteristic of women than of men, this gesture of ecstatic swoon goes back to antiquity, where it is found in Greek statuary depicting the orgiastic flights of Dionysiac revelers. It is the primary gestural trope of Salvador Dali's dazzling photo-montage "The Phenomenon of Ecstasy." It is also fully contemporary. Flipping through any glossy fashion magazine will yield a trove of examples. The pose contains a suggestion of submission, reminiscent of an animal that signals its surrender by baring its neck to a rival. Yet in human beings, what is submitted to is less the social other than the otherness of desire itself. The thrown-back head is the quintessential gesture of willing abandonment.

The second gesture is also a typically feminine one. It involves placing one hand rather carelessly over the base of the neck, wrist cocked, with fingers just touching the skin. This is the paradigmatic gesture of coquettishness. Its feminine character is so pronounced that the male who mocks it can often create an immediately recognizable impression of homosexuality. It is especially interesting for our purposes, in part because it is parasitic upon the gesture of ecstasy we just discussed. Indeed, the two gestures are often found together and for good reason. The coquettish gesture of a hand poised over the bosom says two things at once. On the one hand, it covers the sensitive skin of the throat in an expression of modesty, surprise, or embarrassment. On the other hand, in covering that sensitive spot it also unavoidably announces it. What is this contradictory attitude but the very essence of the coquette? She is at the same time shy and seductive, retiring and exhibitionist. What is ultimately both dissembled and displayed is her own desire. Hovering self-consciously over the breast, the coquettish hand seems demurely to renounce an enjoyment that both she, and we, know very well is there.

Tie Die?

The psychoanalytic perspective we have adopted on neckwear could provide the basis for an interesting reflection about ladies' handbags. Dutifully toted by millions of women, these little sacks are absurdly misnamed "pocketbooks." More womb-like than book-like, and stuffed with who knows what sort of mysterious innards, aren't they the perfect feminine complement to men's phallic neckties?

But let us leave those matters aside in favor of some concluding remarks about the necktie. We might note, first, how my analysis of the neckwear code displays something crucial about the way unconscious symbolism works. Neckwear fashions for men and women function together in an integrated system. Neckwear thereby forms a *language* in the technical sense that semioticians give to that term, as an arrangement of elements each of which serves to define the meaning of the others. This conclusion is a valuable and interesting one, as it reveals how a highly articulate and precisely structured organization operates unconsciously to shape even the most mundane of everyday perceptions. In a sense, every increment of the preceding analysis (the loosened tie, the bowtie, the low-cut neckline, etc.) was already perfectly obvious and available to everyone. What was *not* so obvious was the way in which these elements work together in an ordered system of meaning. It is the *system* of meaning that is truly unconscious.

I also want to add a comment about the limits of the approach I have adopted. In the first place, the interpretation I have offered makes no claim to be completely comprehensive. My reading of the phallic necktie no more exhausts the meaning of everything people wear around their necks than clarifying the conjugation of a verb explains everything there is to poetry. Moreover, everything I have described is relevant only to a very specific constellation of recent history and culture—the reader will no doubt have noticed that many of my examples are somewhat dated. Fashion is a constantly changing phenomenon; indeed, its very existence depends upon change. I have focused only on a limited slice of the clothing system that we currently inhabit. Last, the fashion system I have described is immensely simpler than most. What makes it so simple is above all the iconic character of its key element, which serves to structure a number of quite primitive binary oppositions. Casting an eye over the larger history of fashion, such simplicity must be judged to be the exception rather than the rule. Most styles of costume are built around less crude distinctions, show less simple binary differentiation, and therefore comprise more complex codes.

Taken together, the historical specificity and simplicity of the current neckwear code leave us with a final, fundamental question: *Why the tie now?* After all, the contemporary necktie is barely a century old. If the necktie is iconically tied to the male genitalia and if the symbolic mechanism behind the necktie is therefore a relatively primitive one, why don't we find it popping up more frequently throughout the history of dress? In fact, the recent appearance of the necktie faces us with a double puzzle, for it presents the emergence of a symbolically primitive feature in what is otherwise the most complex and "civilized" period of history. How is all this to be explained?

The outline of an answer can be offered to the extent that the appearance of the necktie coincided very closely with a key development of industrial culture: the entry of unaccompanied women into the public space of the work-a-day world. Prior to the rise of urban capitalism, the division of gender fell neatly along the division of public and private spaces. But increasingly throughout the past century and a half, men and women have found themselves in the same social space, more and more competing for comparable jobs. Must we not imagine that this movement provoked a deep need for a redefinition of gender, a reassertion of masculine identity and prerogative? In that case, the masculine necktie would be exactly what the situation called for, providing an unambiguous indicator of who's who. This would explain how the necktie solves a specifically modern problem, but also why it relies on a relatively primitive means of doing it. The quasi-natural basis of an iconic symbolism would be just the thing to graphically buttress the boundary between masculine and feminine.

However tentative this explanation must remain, let us in closing venture a prediction on the basis of it. For if there is any truth to the thesis that the necktie answered to the special pressures of industrialized culture, it may pass away almost as quickly as it appeared. Indeed, don't we already see this process beginning? More and more frequently, one sees well-dressed men without a tie, sometimes with the collar buttoned up, as if to flaunt the deficit. Fashion watchers have even coined a term for it: the "Air Tie." For a Saturday evening at the symphony in, say, 1950, it would have been hard to find a single man without a necktie. These days, a visit to the same concert hall will find whole squadrons of sport jackets pulled on over polos, turtlenecks, open Oxfords, or even T-shirts.

Maybe the necktie really is on the way out, about to follow the codpiece onto the ash heap of costume history. It does seem that ties are losing the canonical status they have enjoyed for so long. The institution of the necktie is beginning to have the aura of something past. Then again, these developments may have nothing to do with a relaxation of the tensions that gave rise to the current code of neckwear. After all, ceaseless experimentation is one of the prime traits of our current cultural moment. Post-modernity erodes most everything except its own hunger for novelty. Will the tie die? Perhaps. But, with or without the necktie, men and women will likely continue the game of dressing gender and find new tokens to play it with. The theater of gender is still an immensely compelling and enjoyable one and we will no doubt find new languages with which to script it.

Critical Refrains

I've tried to show how phallic symbolism forms the key element of contemporary men's dress and, by extension, organizes a whole series of corresponding fashions for women. My aim was to demonstrate the continuing relevance of a cardinal Freudian concept at a time when psychoanalysis finds itself generally under attack. For those who find the analysis compelling—in fact, precisely to the extent that they are persuaded by it—the question might now be why they've never heard anything like it before. When I first began reflecting about the necktie, I asked myself the same thing. The more I investigated, the more obviously phallic the necktie appeared to me. So obvious, in fact, that in the end what astonished me most was that so few other people seemed to notice.

Freud himself more than once pointed to the phallic symbolism of neckties, yet his suggestion has not gotten much play among students of fashion. Even among writers friendly to a psychoanalytic viewpoint, the phallic character of the necktie receives surprisingly little discussion. J. C. Flügel echoes Freud's view in a couple of lines of his expressly psychoanalytic classic *The Psychology of Clothes*, but one can comb through a great stack of books on the symbolic value of clothing, from Roland Barthes's programmatic essay on *The Fashion System* to more specific works, such as Edmund Bergler's *Fashion and the Unconscious*, Susan Kaiser's *Social Psychology of Clothing*, Alison Lurie's *The Language of Clothes*, Fred Davis's *Fashion, Culture, and Identity*, or even Anne Hollander's *Sex and Suits*, and find virtually nothing about the phallic necktie.

How to explain this absence of remark? It is possible, I suppose, that students of fashion consider the phallic necktie to be too obvious, too easy (too comical?) to deserve further comment. But I suspect that the real reason lies elsewhere. It seems to me to be a case in which our very familiarity with Freud's ideas has prevented us from really applying them. The Freudian notion of phallic symbolism has become commonplace to the point of derisive banality. In ordinary conversation, to point out a phallic symbol may get a round of chuckles, but less because some object has been amusingly unmasked than because the Freudian theory of phallic symbols itself now strikes everyone as fairly laughable. These days, adopting a Freudian viewpoint tends to be something of a joke. Of course, if the preceding analysis of neckwear has any validity, then the joke is, quite literally, on us. Nevertheless, the question remains as to why, except among a circle of academic insiders, the psychoanalytic theory now finds itself in retreat.

The answer to this question is complex. As Freud said of the meaning of dreams, deriving as they do from various sources in memory and feeling, corresponding to multiple layers of the mind, the answer is "overdetermined." Yet perhaps the first and most important thing to be said is that Freud has been a victim of his own success. Freud is under attack these days in part precisely because his thought has enjoyed such enormous influence. Though I can't claim to have made a specific tally, I think it a safe bet that among Ph.D. dissertations written in the Western world during the second half of the twentieth century, the number devoted primarily or in significant part to Freud would eclipse any other single figure. His ideas have percolated far beyond the clinical consulting room in which they originated and have left an enduring mark over an astonishingly wide range of fields. Freudian theory has become part of the essential grammar of modern intellectual life.

Nor has Freud's impact been limited to the academy. Even more impressive is his hold on the popular imagination. Whether he knows it or not, the average Joe on the street now thinks and speaks in Freudianese. "It's good to get the anger out," says one person in an unwitting echo of Freud's early theory of emotional catharsis, "don't let it get bottled up inside!" "I can identify with that," says another, unaware that he or she is borrowing the term from the psychoanalytic theory of identification—a theory, incidentally, as subtle and complicated as anything in the whole of Freud's work. "Don't be so anal about everything," says a third, "you need to loosen up and enjoy life!" And so it goes with the litany of other analytic notions, from libido, repression, and the unconscious to the id, ego, and superego; from the Oedipus and castration complexes to projection and, of course, penis envy. In what other case has the technical vocabulary of a great thinker, a lexicon intended mostly for training a cadre of professional colleagues, been seeded so broadly in the field of popular consciousness?

But there are prices to be paid for such extensive notoriety. The first is a diminishment of real understanding. In reckoning the legacy of an innovative mind, one could almost assert an inverse proportion: the closer to being a mile wide, the more likely to be an inch deep. The second follows with equal necessity. Precisely to the extent that Freud's thought has exerted such enormous influence (enormous but not unprecedented: one thinks immediately of the long shadow cast from the nineteenth century upon the twentieth by Karl Marx), precisely to the degree that Freud's influence threatens to dominate our ideas too fully, we are virtually forced to cast off some of its weight. We *must* attack it, if only to reclaim some modicum of independence.

As we struggle to wrest from Freud some greater portion of our intellectual autonomy, it's bound to be somewhat deflating to realize that Freud himself predicted that we would. For what else is the meaning of the Oedipus complex if not the notion that assuming one's own identity, coming into possession of one's own voice, involves a kind of mortal struggle against the rule of some dominant father figure? The problem, however, is that this second consequence of Freud's influence mixes so badly with the first. When the battle for independence is combined with a fair degree of ignorance about what one is fighting against, the result is a deepening, general confusion. I'm probably more sensitive to this situation than most people. I bump into it whenever I teach Freud to otherwise smart and willing undergraduates. I not infrequently encounter students, for example, who've heard vague rumors about Freud's early investigations into cocaine, or even that he wrote a monograph about the drug, and who want to know how we can possibly accept the psychological speculations of a known user of addictive substances. Confusion, indeed!

Though the margin of separation is sometimes not as great as one might wish, there is, of course, a great distance between what is mouthed on the street and what appears in print, and it is obviously the latter that we have to take most seriously. Very roughly sketched, most serious critiques of Freud fall into one or another of three main categories, as they aim either at the theory, the practice, or the prejudices of psychoanalysis.

Matters of Theory

Many a professor has made tenure, or even staged a whole career, by attacking the scientific pretensions of psychoanalysis. And there is, we have to admit, a lot to question. Where, for example, is the measurable data upon which a science could be founded? Without reliable data that can be readily observed by more than one person, there can be no science. Yet the verbal exchange between analyst and patient is by nature a messy, private business. Scientifically speaking, things might be better if the analytic session were conducted by means of a standardized series of questions, or by some routine procedure—anything that would provide a benchmark against which variations between different patients could be measured. But the distinguishing feature of the psychoanalytic approach is a radical suspension of expectations. The "fundamental rule" of analysis, the only thing required of the patient, is to say whatever comes to mind, however absurd, embarrassing, or apparently irrelevant it may seem at the moment. The emphatically open and unstructured character of the analytic exchange, as well as its isolation and uniqueness (the fact that each session with each patient is idiosyncratic and unrepeatable), make data collection of the sort scientists usually insist upon very difficult indeed.

Along the same lines yet maybe even more damaging, how can the claims of psychoanalysis be verified when they concern an entity—the unconscious—that remains in principle invisible and unknowable? With everything in the analytic field referred to the inaccessible black box of the unconscious, what is to prevent the analyst from wholly fabricating its contents? What is there to prevent psychoanalysis from being merely a license for unrestrained myth-making?

All of which recalls an old joke:

Q: What is science?
A: Looking for a black cat in a dark room.

Q: What is philosophy?
A: Looking for a black cat in a dark room where no black cat exists.

Q: What is psychoanalysis?
A: Looking for a nonexistent black cat in a dark room and finding one anyway.

There are meaningful responses to these dilemmas, one of which can be laid out with the brevity required here. We might remind ourselves, for example, that psychoanalysis is by no means the only domain in which the object of inquiry cannot be directly examined. The black holes of astrophysics come immediately to mind. Though predicted on the basis of pure theory, black holes are in principle invisible for the reason that their gravitational field is so strong that even light seeking to escape from them is sucked back into their super-dense mass. However, this intrinsic invisibility does not put black holes completely beyond the reach of science. Impossible to see directly, their existence is detected by observing their influence on objects around them that we can see. In similar fashion, the unconscious, in principle unavailable for direct inspection, can be discerned by its effects in speech and behavior: in slips of the tongue and unintentionally loaded phrases, in meaningfully bungled actions, in dreams, and in symptoms. The evidence lies both in the *fact* that such distorted communications and behaviors occur but also in the way that they display *patterns* relevant to one or another personality type or neurotic style.

It is with reference to such indirect evidence that we can return to the first objection about lack of data. Of course, the details of a psychoanalytic case report cannot offer the sort of neatly quantifiable data that is demanded, say, by physics. And this means that there will always be a margin of uncertainty accompanying all psychoanalytic interpretations. But this lack of unimpeachable certitude should not lead us to discount the validity of psychoanalysis altogether. History, too, is an interpretive inquiry in which masses of complex and ambiguous evidence must be sifted to produce provisional hypotheses about past events that in principle cannot be directly inspected. Yet no one would think of throwing out history because it cannot duplicate the standards of certainty enjoyed by the laboratory sciences.

Matters of Practice

Several major currents of criticism, though rooted in theoretical debates, have taken aim at psychoanalysis primarily as a mode of psychotherapy. A great many of these critical voices can be gathered into two main camps. Let's call them the anti-reductionists and the pro-medicalists.

Among the anti-reductionist crowd, there are those of a religious, existentialist, or humanistic bent, to whom Freud's theories appear crudely mechanistic or determinist. The problem with psychoanalysis, they say, is that it fails to appreciate the spiritual essence of the human being, the core of personal subjectivity that grounds freedom, choice, and responsibility. Freud talks as if everything were reducible to the influence of unconscious complexes or, worse yet, to animal instincts. Under the analytic microscope, the human being no longer seems human at all.

Another group, anti-reductionist in another sense, faults Freud for sacrificing the subtler and more complex aspects of human beings not so much to a crude mechanics of libido as to the battery of shopworn themes that psychoanalysis has invented for itself. The real problem with psychoanalysis, then, is the tyranny of its own categories. Everyone has to be pressed into the same Procrustean bed of the Oedipus complex or stretched on the same, tired, three-cornered rack of id, ego, and superego. Some of these critics, whether they are willing to admit it or not, simply want to replace what they regard as the rigid and unyielding frame of psychoanalytic thematics with some equally fixed approach of their own (behaviorist, cognitivist, gestaltist, transactionalist, etc.). Others just want a more flexible and eclectic clinical practice, unconstrained by any one conceptual or ideological bias.

The pro-medicalist camp attacks psychoanalysis from exactly the opposite direction. Inspired by biological explanations for psychopathology and flushed with enthusiasm for new generations of psychotropic drugs, this group faults Freud for overemphasizing the psychological and humanistic. The result, they charge, is a kind of misplaced moralism. By failing to acknowledge the organic causes for conditions such as schizophrenia, for example, psychoanalysis invites us to blame the victims of mental illness, or maybe their parents and loved ones, for what should be recognized as errant biochemistry. The cure for these unfortunate sufferers is not endless rehashing of dreams and childhood memories but swift administration of the right medication. Pharmaceuticals, not philosophizing! It is a perspective that is frequently operative without being explicitly stated—informing the limitations imposed by health insurance providers on coverage for varying sorts of treatment, for example. Indeed, its basic motive hardly needs energetic promotion, if only because it lines up so neatly with the fondest hope of our modern, technological culture, namely, that there ought to be a pill for every ailment.

In surveying this range of critiques, with the humanists in one corner and the pharmacists in the other, the striking thing is that Freud gets it from both ends. Psychoanalysis is alternately accused of being insufficiently humanistic or of being too much so. It overlooks the role of a freely choosing subject or it invents one where there really isn't any. While it certainly doesn't resolve the relevant debates on either side—indeed, these are debates that raise some important and difficult questions—it is worth noting that this critical crossfire is not at all accidental. On the contrary, it indicates something essential about the psychoanalytic perspective, a consequence of the paradoxical character of the unconscious itself. The humanist complaint is that Freud reduces the free and conscious human individual to the mere mechanics of repression, to the automata of the animal instincts, or to the blind repetition of infantile complexes. The medicalist advocate of drug treatment attacks from the opposite quarter, claiming that Freud inserts a choosing subject where we need to respond on the level of neurochemistry. Yet the very concept of the unconscious requires something of both these perspectives while fully agreeing with neither. If there is any part played in our behavior by unconscious motives, the paradox is that such motives are simultaneously *attributable* and *not attributable* to an individual subject. The unconscious is at one and the same time *me* and *not me.*

To treat this point with any real adequacy would plunge us too deeply into philosophical complexities. We can readily get a sense for what is at stake, however, simply by reflecting for a moment on the nature of desire. By *desire* we mean something more subtle that the pressure of bodily need, yet more substantial than the temptations of passing fancy. Desire has to do with the force of longings that I may hardly know how to name, yet which stir me most deeply and define my outermost aspirations. Desire may be what fires my most absorbing hobby, what draws me to my favorite novel, what prompts me to quit my job and look for something else more stimulating, what leads me to marry *this* person, with his or her unique mix of strengths and weaknesses. What could be more *mine,* indeed what is there that more directly defines me, than desire in this sense? I am marked and distinguished by the pattern of my desire as by a fingerprint. And yet, isn't it obvious that I myself am not the author of my desires? I can't simply *decide* to have desire for something. In a certain crucial sense, desire comes to me from beyond myself. I am its receiver, its servant. Indeed I may feel my own desire to be a burden or a curse. I may even feel the need to rebel against its iron law as against a tyrant or a slave master. Is this not the meaning of the biblical injunction to cut off the hand that offends me, or to pluck out the unruly eye? What is it but the swerve of my own desire that moves my offending hand or that leads my wayward eye astray?

The psychoanalytic concept of the unconscious is centered precisely on this inner ambiguity of desire, at once the heart of my identity and yet strangely and stubbornly foreign to me, a force that drives me beyond myself. And it is for this reason that Freud can be neither pure humanist nor pure medicalist. What interests him most, in fact, is precisely the way in which the human being, a creature of desire, is a walking paradox, a kind of impossible mixture between freely choosing subject and fatally determined object. It is a paradox that is built into the very structure of the psychoanalytic process. That process unfolds in strict accordance with what the patient him- or herself says. The patient always has the lead, taking a free and active role in telling the analyst what comes to mind to say. Yet the patient, too, must wait for what comes. To be sure, it is the patient's own dream that must be recounted, the patient's own memories or associations and the patient's own emotional reactions that need to be shared. But the patient, too, must learn to listen for these elements of his or her own inner life as if they were the contents of a long-range radio broadcast from a foreign country, perhaps audible only intermittently above the crackle of static. In psychoanalysis, the patient who speaks is also in a certain sense a pure auditor. The result is indeed a paradox. The patient needs to be both active and passive, both openly willing and also forced to accept the dictate of something not freely chosen.

Matters of Prejudice

Surveying the range of attacks to which psychoanalysis has been subject, it is hard to avoid the conclusion that the most strident and most broadly influential criticisms, both inside and outside the academy, have been directed at Freud's own character and personality. They are attacks aimed less at the technical difficulties of either theory or practice than at the prejudices of psychoanalysis, the ways in which Freud's legacy remains prisoner to built-in biases and blind spots. There have been a number of such waves of critique. For one of the lesser known, decisive in the former Soviet Union, the bugbear was a class issue. Freud's theory was condemned for ignoring social and economic realities and his method rejected for being perniciously individualistic. The apple does not fall very far from the tree: in the end, psychoanalysis must be denounced for being as petty bourgeois as the middle-class Viennese Jew who came up with it.

More recently, attacks on Freud have sharpened their focus on allegations of his personal dishonesty. A number of detractors have roundly called him a liar and a charlatan. He is variously charged with failing to properly acknowledge sources, with hiding or withholding evidence contrary to his desired conclusions, or with simply falsifying the clinical record when it was in his interest to do so. Combing through archival material of various sorts and researching the biographies of some of Freud's more famous patients, for example, critical sleuths have revealed discrepancies between the historical facts and Freud's presentation of them in his published papers. The conclusion to be drawn, it seems, is to impeach the scientific credibility of Freud's theories by showing their source to have been contaminated from the start.

At the risk of appearing to dismiss such critics with a facile comment, many of these Freud detectives may be said to be right in their facts but wrong in their verdict. By that I mean that their objections tend to hold Freud's writings to a standard that is inappropriate to them. It is possible to find details in Freud's clinical reports that are not in perfect alignment with the facts—mostly, it must be said, because he takes such extraordinary care to respect the anonymity of his subjects. Yet it needs to be remembered that, for all Freud's insistence on the scientific relevance of psychoanalysis, his works more resemble art than science for the reason that his prime objective was less geometric proof than pedagogical demonstration. To accomplish that end, he produced highly crafted presentations that, while certainly intended to be truthful, were less interested in legalistic accuracy than in rhetorical effectiveness. To damn the whole on the basis of the details is to miss the forest for the trees.

For many critics of Freud's honesty, however, the most damning suspicion is that Freud's work is distorted by the pressure of his own prejudices. As Gore Vidal sums things up, Freud's psychoanalysis is "a crackpot religion that would never have got off the ground had it not been for his personal brilliance and imperturbable megalomania.... Certainly he never saw anything in human nature that he himself, rather like an absent-minded god, had not put there." And there can be no doubt as to which of these megalomaniacal prejudices has been found most objectionable. No strain of Freud critique has been as heated or, probably, as convincing to so many people, as the assault on his conception of gender.

Around the issue of gender, Freud's legacy has repeatedly sparked a general conflagration. And in one way or another, the flashpoint has always been the centrality to psychoanalysis of the Oedipus complex and the way in which the Oedipal theory appears to be modeled on the experience of boys, not girls. The particularly ambivalent hunger for the mother's love and the aggressively tinged rivalry with the father—how can these features of the Oedipus complex be attributed to the experience of the little girl? How, indeed, can psychoanalysis avoid the charge that it has forced feminine psychology into the disfiguring mold of the masculine? In fact, doesn't Freud admit as much, claiming that women are merely castrated, dismembered men? Doesn't this make a woman something *less* than a man?

Moreover, the critics ask, mustn't we now acknowledge that Freud was simply wrong about certain basic facts of feminine sexuality? One thinks especially of his botched conception of female orgasm, in which he asserted that maturity in women means that a so-called vaginal orgasm displaces an earlier form of genital satisfaction centered on the clitoris. A gathering sense of skeptical reservation bursts fully into flaming outrage when it comes to the notorious

Freudian concept of penis envy. Semester by semester, my students give me ample evidence that it is a notion especially galling to contemporary American women. Many of them react to it with a visceral contempt that far outstrips anything that a simply implausible idea would elicit. Perhaps the reason is that for these career-aspiring young women, the Freudian theory comes infuriatingly close to a limited measure of truth. Struggling to win parity in a traditionally man's world, these women might well feel a sense of envy for the advantages enjoyed by men. But envy for those few ounces of wrinkled flesh? Guess again!

The very outlandishness of the theory of penis envy invites us to suppose that here, if anywhere, Freud was played upon by his own preoccupations. It is a supposition that is hard to resist, even for thoughtful people who have read Freud carefully. Consider, for example, Gloria Steinem's *Moving Beyond Words*, in which, half humorously, half seriously, she reverses all the gender signs in Freud's work. The result is Dr. Phyllis Freud, that intrepid female explorer of the deep psyche who, heroically willing to buck the psychiatric establishment of her time, discovers the womb envy of her male patients and builds a whole psychology around it. By means of this playful construction, Steinem invites us to suppose that the symbolism of the phallus would never have come to occupy such a privileged place in the theory of the unconscious had Freud been a woman. Only a man could have come up with the fairy tale of penis envy.

Steinem's angle of view is enormously convincing for a great number of people, especially those for whom the quotes she provides are the only snippets of Freud's own words that they have ever read. In fact, whether it be the culpably deliberate bias of an old-style Victorian or merely evidence of the way even great minds are limited by their cultural and historical contexts, Freud's alleged sexism has become an article of faith among American feminists. To be pro-woman and pro-Freud now seems like a contradiction in terms. In reconsidering what Freud may still have to teach us about sex, there is no greater obstacle than that posed by this popular perception of Freud as a nineteenth-century male chauvinist. How are we to respond to this challenge?

It is one of the main objectives of this book to provide an answer. It is a daunting task, if only because it will mean getting many readers to reconsider a point on which they have already made up their minds. It is my suspicion that, even among those who are still inclined to take a sympathetic view of Freud, a substantial majority, including a great many professional psychotherapists, have simply decided to accept the fact that Freud's own jaundiced attitude toward women distorted his views of feminine psychology. They may be willing to grant that there are other aspects of Freud's discoveries that remain of enduring value, some of which even bear the stamp of genius, but his theory of gender is not among them. Short of throwing him out altogether, the only recourse is to save Freud from himself. His account of gender must be cut away from the rest of the psychoanalytic theory the way a tumor is removed from an otherwise healthy body.

But there's a big problem with this operation. Malignant or not, Freud's theory of gender is inseparable from the heart of psychoanalysis: the theory of the Oedipus complex. Freud always insisted upon the centrality of the Oedipus complex; indeed, that tireless insistence precipitated the most violent battles of the early psychoanalytic movement, including Freud's falling out with three of his closest followers, Alfred Adler, Otto Rank, and Carl Jung. The real challenge, then, is to revisit Freud's theory of gender in a way that reveals it to be interesting and useful, especially to a contemporary audience that has absorbed the lessons of the women's movement, while at the same time showing how it is intimately bound up with the Oedipal drama that Freud regarded as the indispensable core of psychoanalysis.

But can it be done?

2
Drive You Crazy

I offered an analysis of neckwear to suggest the enduring usefulness of a psychoanalytic perspective. Yet even if my discussion succeeded in detecting a pulse, it is far from bringing Freud back to life. We have yet to learn very much about the real substance of Freud's theories or about what they may have to teach us about sex. In this chapter, let us take a further step by asking a crucial question: What exactly did Freud mean by "sex drive"?

It's probably not what you think.

Whatever Turns You On

Sometime around 1920, a young man entered Freud's office with a peculiar problem. He had, Freud tells us, "exalted a certain sort of 'shine on the nose' into a fetishistic condition." In other words, this fellow could find a woman attractive only if she were graced by a special glint of light on the nose. The oily sheen that most women struggle to leave in the powder room was for him the ultimate turn-on. It was this odd detail that lit the pathway to the fulfillment of his desire. Without it, he remained indifferent.

Freud tells us tantalizingly little about the meaning of this strange fetish. The ensuing analysis traced it to a verbal slippage in which an English phrase from the patient's childhood found its way into the German of his adult life. What emerged in German as a "shine on the nose"—a *Glanz auf der Nase*—was originally spoken in the patient's mother tongue: a *glance* at the nose. The fetish was thus constructed around a wrinkle of language.

Though we know nothing more about the details of the case, even this fragment opens a useful window on Freud's clinical work. The result is a typical one for the way that it traces an unconscious mechanism to a play of symbols. The perverse fixation of the fetish took shape around a conjunction of signifiers, the ambiguous *Glan(z)ce.* At the same time, the case displays a key aspect of Freud's view of human sexuality: the triggers of sexual desire may have no obvious biological value. From the point of view of the natural aim of sexuality—the reproduction of the species—the peculiar object that excites the fetishist may be utterly irrelevant. In fact, the artificial and apparently useless character of the fetish object, far from diminishing its appeal, seems only to enhance its power to excite. Feathers, rubber, lace, fur, sheer stockings, high-heeled shoes—the characteristic objects of fetishistic interest conspicuously lack any natural meaning or function. Fetishes are grandly superfluous.

As such, fetishism suggests something paradoxical about human sexual desire. Human desire may be most electrified by objects at the greatest remove from brute animality or biological necessity. Sexual response may be most intensely charged by purely symbolic stimuli.

Implicit in Freud's analysis of the fetish is one of his most basic working assumptions. The bizarre details of pathology hold clues for understanding perfectly familiar, everyday behavior. In Freud's view, the fetishist's strange choice of love object is not so far removed from "normal" human sexuality as it might first seem. If the biological end of sexuality is reproduction and all deviation from that aim is, technically speaking, to be considered perversion—etymologically a kind of swerving or veering off the track—then the entire sexual field in the human being must be seen to be tinged with perversity. A very great share of human sexual behavior has very little to do with procreating. Biologically speaking, human sexuality is rather conspicuously "off road."

Of course, Freud's point is not wholly to collapse the distinction between pathology and normalcy. There remains an important difference between pathological perversion and the perverse quality of human sexuality in general. A perversion becomes pathological when it assumes the character of fixation and becomes the exclusive point of the subject's sexual interest. In this way, Freud's conception of pathology rejoins the older psychiatric definition of madness as being dominated by an *idée fixe.*

But isn't all of this a bit too hasty? By taking the fetish as his clue in styling human sexuality as unnatural and perverse, doesn't Freud overestimate the distance between human and animal? After all, isn't the sexual behavior of many animals stimulated by fetish-like displays of extravagant feathers, brightly colored patches of skin, flowing manes, jutting horns and tusks? Are human beings really so different? To take a first step toward answering this question, consider the kiss. Like the curious "shine on the nose" that so excited Freud's patient, the kiss is completely irrelevant to the act of copulation that defines the biological aim of sexuality. Nevertheless, for most people kissing is an almost indispensable part of lovemaking. So what is the function of kissing?

Despite our fondness for thinking that animals, too, indulge in kissing, the kiss remains a uniquely human act. We enjoy sending one another cute greeting cards in which bears appear to nuzzle, penguins to peck, and fish to greet one another pucker to pucker. But the fact is that only human beings take contact of the mouth and lips as in itself a source of sexual pleasure.[1] The reason is

[1]I am aware of only one possible exception to this rule: the bonobo, a chimp-like higher primate thought by some authorities to be our closest animal relative. The most highly promiscuous and sexually active of the apes, bonobos spend enormous amounts of time in a wide variety of free-for-all sexual activities, including open-mouth kissing. See Frans de Waal, *Peacemaking Among Primates*, Cambridge, Mass.: Harvard University Press, 1989.

that only the human being lives in a world of symbols. Particularly when the tongue assumes the role of a penetrating organ, pressing with all the urgency of passion between the lover's lips, kissing becomes the oral analogue of intercourse. The whole drama of the sexual act is rehearsed in the kiss: a hesitating, tentative approach is followed by a brushing caress of lips, increasing pressure of flesh on flesh, the warm and slippery entry of one into the other, and, finally, the tender parting at the end of the kiss, with its momentary withdrawal and relaxation. It is as if, before actually copulating, we must perform it symbolically in another zone of the body. Unlike the strokes and caresses that prepare desire for intercourse by direct stimulation, the kiss performs its role in foreplay by providing a figurative representation of what is to come. It stimulates because it *simulates.*

The erotic effect of kissing is more psychological than physical. What excites us above all is the *idea* of a kiss. No wonder, then, that the particular quality of a kiss is the best barometer of the emotional tone of a sexual engagement. A wet and sloppy grinding of lips cries out for more. A light and tender peck, the labile equivalent of a pat on the head, may make a sexual liaison seem even more remote than not kissing at all. If the kiss symbolically mirrors the mechanics of love—or rather, precisely *because* it symbolizes those mechanics—it also provides an arena in which we can measure the meaning of love. The kiss is a key term—perhaps *the* key term—in the language of love. As Cyrano de Bergerac said of it, "a kiss is a secret that takes the mouth for an ear." Understood in this way, the kiss is a product of art, not nature. That it seems so natural is less a matter of biological necessity than of cultural habit. Indeed, there exist some cultures in which kissing remains virtually unknown. We kiss not because we are motivated by an instinct to do so, but because kissing belongs to a long tradition of lovemaking, retold over centuries of poetry, painting, literature, and film. We learn about kissing in a manner that recalls the famous quip of La Rochefoucauld: "Some people would never have fallen in love if they had never heard of love."

The chasm that separates human sexuality from the behavior of animals is spectacularly displayed by the tradition of courtly love. Celebrated in the songs of medieval troubadours, the rules of courtly love governed a game of passion played between knights and ladies. The basic formula was a simple one. A brave and able chevalier, often abroad for long stretches, was bound by a love of excruciating intensity to a captivating lady who, usually by virtue of being married to someone else, remained largely unattainable. This very unattainability appears to have been the key feature of courtly love. For all the urgency of its passion, therefore, courtly love was very little concerned with sex. The fevered devotion of the knight to his lady was erotically charged in the highest degree. Yet in the ideal case this white heat of desire remained deliberately unconsummated. The summit of excitement was achieved in the vigil, the long and sleepless night in which the knight and his lady lay naked in the same bed, but foreswore the ultimate consummation of his passion. In this paroxysm of erotic transport, the very thing that most defines the objective of sex for the animal, the moment of fertilization, was deliberately refused.

The ideals of courtly love purified the sexual act of everything animal. It was all buildup and no climax. The aim was maximally eroticized chastity. Which is to say, the entire drama of courtly love was strictly confined to the domain of the symbolic. Everything pointed toward a consummating act that remained forever deferred. It is not by accident that the knight's passion came to focus on some relatively trivial token his lady might bestow upon him—her glove, say, or her handkerchief. This snow-white hankie symbolized the purity of his love and of his lady's virtue. It was the only thing upon which he could lay his hands, as if substituted for the silky skin of the lady's body.

Why You Are Not an Animal

How, then, to conceptualize the difference between animal and human sexuality? Freud's answer is the distance between "instinct" and "drive." Sexual behavior in animals is hardwired with respect to its objects, aims, and stimuli. It is this immutable pattern that constitutes "instinct"—the same unvarying response to predetermined stimuli that prompts birds to make nests or to fly south for the winter. An arctic tern will mate only with another of its kind, and only when stimulated by the prescribed mating dance with its fixed pattern of bobbing and pecking. The human being, by contrast, can be sexually aroused by a range of objects, some of which only incidentally involve a fellow human being and which may have little or nothing to do with the act of heterosexual copulation that is the biological *telos* of sex. It is for this reason that Freud describes the human sexual impulse as *Trieb*, or "drive." What distinguishes drive from any instinctual behavior is its variability and plasticity. Drive is pure urge or impulse, decoupled from any naturally specified object or end. Drive is the sheer force of instinct that has wandered off the path of its natural destiny and become available for new and unfamiliar engagements.

Pure drive, Freud says, is "polymorphously perverse." It is omnivorous, ready for anything. Or at least it is so on the level of the unconscious. In Freud's view, the primary task accomplished by psychological development, the process of becoming a well-adjusted adult, is that of assigning to the sexual drive its preferred and acceptable objects. In the unconscious domain of dream and phantasy, the drive remains immeasurably more promiscuous, willing to imagine for itself a much wider range of objects and acts. The bottom line is that the scope of our true desires is far broader and more varied than we can tolerate.

If we first glimpse the distance between animal and human in the variability of the drive, even more striking is the way human desire passes beyond mere variety toward hunger for the unknown. The drive is at its purest in longing not only for an object that isn't there (the absence that makes the heart grow fonder) but for an object that remains as yet to be determined. The sexiest thing is the shadow of something as yet unseen. What I mean can be illustrated fairly easily. We need only to reflect for a moment about quite commonplace phenomena. Who doesn't know, for example, that a half-clothed torso is often sexier than a fully naked one? Something is revealed, but even more importantly, something remains concealed. The space of this concealment offers a field for the free play of imagination. What remains hidden beneath the veil is inevitably more alluring than what is already exposed.

For the same reason, the most erotically compelling women's fashions display some skin, yet tastefully and tantalizingly withhold a fuller view. A highly slit evening dress may therefore be much sexier than a miniskirt. With each step, the slit opens and closes, affording a brief glimpse of thigh only to snatch it away again. Or consider that intensely erotic scene in Bernardo Bertolucci's film *The Last Emperor*, in which the young Chinese emperor makes love with his wife and a concubine beneath an enormous silk sheet. Shot from directly above the imperial bed, the shimmering coverlet pulses and undulates with the movements of the bodies hidden under it. What gives this scene its charm is less what we see than what we don't see. The scene succeeds in arousing us precisely because it evokes an unseen dimension in which the drive can luxuriously contemplate its own outermost possibilities.

By contrast to the animal instinct that is satisfied by a narrowly specified object or act, there is something infinitely restless about the drive. The drive tends to seek an object beyond every object. It always wants more. This point is illustrated by an example from pornography—an example that seems at first glance to prove the contrary. I have in mind the favorite pose of a certain genre of soft core pornographic magazines: the so-called spread shot. The centerpiece of this shot is the woman's vulva spread wide for the camera to inspect. Seeking to explain the appeal of this defining image we might naïvely suppose that the spread shot satisfies insofar as it "shows all." It leaves nothing to the imagination. The viewer has finally won unimpeded visual access to the inner secret of the feminine. From a Freudian point of view, the conclusion is exactly the opposite. What attracts the scopic drive to the vaginal spread shot is precisely what it doesn't show, what in fact cannot be shown. The result of the "show all" strategy is to create even more intense hunger for something that cannot be imaged. The more you see, the less you find what you are really looking for.

The Freudian view is that the lust for pornography is excited less by what is revealed than by what remains unseen. Desire is stimulated by something that perpetually eludes the lecherous gaze. How is this Freudian interpretation to be justified? One "proof" is the compulsion that shuttles the consumer of pornography from one girlie image to another, and another, and another. If the spread shot really succeeded in "showing all" then presumably one image would be enough. But the sexual drive engaged by pornography shows its real essence less in the satisfaction created by any one image than by the perpetual craving it generates for *yet another one.* The enormous commercial potency of pornography derives in large part from this mechanism of re-created desire. Porn continually restimulates the very hunger it promises to satisfy.

The allure of pornography depends on the viewer's relation to something that forever escapes the roving lustful eye, some moment of ultimate satisfaction that is continually promised but never fully given. In this sense, pornography demonstrates very well the open and indeterminate quality of the sexual drive that prompts Freud to call it perverse.

With this background in mind, we can return to the distinction Freud makes between cases of pathological perversion and the perversity he attributes to human sexuality in general. A Freudian point of view forces us to invert the age-old moralism that condemns the behavior of the clinical pervert as unnatural. On the contrary, compared with the wider latitude of normal human sexuality, the fixated interest of the pathological pervert more closely resembles the unvarying repetition of animal desire. Like the animal whose sex response is fixed by instinct, the clinically perverse individual tends to want just one thing. From a purely formal standpoint, therefore, the pervert should seem quite "natural." The wider range of sexual tastes and behaviors in perfectly normal human beings, on the other hand, along with the variety of contexts that may trigger arousal, contrast markedly to the unwavering preferences of the animal. By this route, Freud leads us to the surprising conclusion that the most truly unnatural acts are those of normal human sexuality.

The wild and wandering, anything-but-animal, character of human desire is a key part of Freud's concept of "phantasy." In the Freudian lexicon, "drive" and "phantasy" thus form a kind of couplet. What does Freud mean by *Phantasie*? The British tradition of psychoanalytic theory often retains the ph-spelling in order to distinguish Freud's intention from the more everyday "fantasy." In the ordinary sense, we think of fantasy as something unreal or merely imaginary. We also think of it as something definite, having a specific and concrete object. Bored at the office, we imagine a fantasy vacation at the beach. Salivating with hunger, we indulge a fantasy about a juicy filet mignon with truffle-mashed potatoes.

But the psychoanalytic sense of phantasy is something different. Energized by the unconscious, the Freudian phantasy is something even more unreal, even more distant from actuality than common fantasy because it always contains an aspect of something unknown and unknowable. At the heart of the phantasy discovered by psychoanalysis there is something vague and indeterminate. It is this elusive I-don't-know-what, this object of longing that paradoxically refuses to come fully into focus, that defines the most characteristic feature—the most truly *human* feature—of human desire.

Perhaps we can glimpse a bit more of what is at stake in phantasy, especially its character of harboring a kernel of something unknown and unimaginable, by risking a little experiment of introspection—usually, it needs to be said, not a very useful window on the unconscious. For a moment, make the experiment of indulging your own sexual phantasies. Try to picture your dream of the most uninhibited and satisfying passion. What sorts of things come to mind? Perhaps a grab-bag of fleeting and fragmentary images. These days we hear a lot of talk about sexual fantasies, and for most of us the idea of sexual fantasy probably calls up a certain number of stock images, perhaps modeled on one or another vaguely pornographic scenario. To this extent, the domain of our sexual desire has been colonized by fantasy in the more or less ordinary sense of the term. Our sexual desire might thus appear to be pretty straightforward. Perhaps it is even as banal and stereotypical as the porn images it feeds upon.

But in trying to glimpse the shape of your wildest sexual desire, you may also experience a certain subtle inability to get the picture. At some point in the process of trying to imagine the apogee of desire, the play of images trails off. You may sense that something else is there, some even more compelling image, urge, or act. You may feel quite certainly the tantalizing presence of something delicious. Yet this "something more," this summit of rapture, hovers elusively at the furthest horizon of desire. It remains ungraspable, like a distant object shimmering in the far-off welter of summer heat waves. The ultimate object of desire refuses to appear in the theater of imagination. It is this very absence that is interesting. We may quite surely feel the force of desire, yet we cannot completely see its object. In fact, precisely where we sense that the pressure of sexual hunger might reach its maximum, we may be unable to bring anything clearly into focus. *This* is the point at which the more properly Freudian sense of phantasy kicks in.

From a psychoanalytic point of view, this failure to be able to see clearly to the end point of the trajectory of desire, this inability to imagine complete fulfillment, to fill the space carved out by our own impulses, is absolutely crucial. It means that human desire, energized by the movement of what Freud called *Trieb*, is always after more than it can specify. We lust after something more than we can imagine. In a certain sense, therefore, phantasy always falls short of itself, and the reason is that the motive force of the drive that animates phantasy always wants something more than any particular image can provide. It is this excess energy of the drive that gives phantasy its most compelling power. The restless hunger of phantasy is ultimately rooted less in what the phantasy shows to us than in what remains to be seen.

It is this virtual dimension of phantasy, the way in which phantasy is pregnant with more than it can imagine, that separates human desire from mere animal rut. And with this distinction between animal and human sexuality in mind, we begin to see more clearly how far the popular reception of Freud's work has strayed from its true meaning. We are all too familiar with the image of Freud as the champion of the animal in all of us. As the title of one scholarly book has it, Freud is a "biologist of the mind." The real situation is more nearly the opposite. The genuine Freudian teaching stresses the *unnatural* character of human sexuality, the way in which human desire stands at a distance from everything animal by virtue of being shaped by a symbolic universe. In misreading Freud as a biologist, we press him into the mold of our current penchant for interpreting most everything as an effect of genetic and hormonal influences.

A prime source of this confusion is a gross error in the translation of Freud's German into English. James Strachey, the general editor of the twenty-four volume *Standard Edition* of Freud's works, chose to render the Freudian notion of *Trieb* as "instinct." "Instinct" is precisely what *Trieb* is *not. Trieb* would have been much better translated, as I have done here, with the term *drive*. The mistake should have been clear from Freud's own text. He does occasionally use the word *Instinkt*, but always to refer to the genetically predetermined behavior of animals. *Trieb* is something much more mysterious. To understand it correctly is not to ignore altogether an organic contribution. The pure energy of the drive, like a rush of water welling up from the depths of a spring far below the earth's surface, is rooted in the innateness of the body. Sexual response—we ought not to lose sight of this basic point—can never be fully divorced from its organic sources. Nevertheless, the drive comes into its own only when it is partially cut loose from its biological basis and regrafted onto a new supporting framework, the trellis of a symbolic architecture. It is for this reason that Freud reserves a special name for the energy of the sexual drive—*libido*—and conceives of the drive as a border concept, halfway between the somatic and the psychical. Toward the end of his life, Freud again stressed the unnatural indeterminacy of the drives, describing them as "mythical entities, magnificent in their indefiniteness."

Baby, Oh Baby!

To appreciate more fully Freud's concept of the drive, and especially to underline its distance from any natural, biological function, let us turn to his theory of infantile sexuality. It is there, in the famous oral, anal, and phallic stages, that the drives are first formed.

Freud poses the three stages against the background of two key features of child development. The first, now widely accepted by embryologists, is the prematurity of human birth. Due to the relative enormity of the human head and the limits of the pelvic canal through which it must pass, the human being is born long before its fetal development is complete. To remain in the womb any longer than nine months would make vaginal birth impossible. The human infant is thus dropped into the world in a sadly unfinished state. For many months after birth, it will be completely dependent upon its mother for its every need. It will be a full year before it can walk. The consequence is that instinctual mechanisms that might otherwise regulate the neonate's behavior are not yet consolidated. The human baby is a jumble of uncoordinated impulses. It is like a car that has been rushed off the assembly line: the engine is up and running but there was no time to hook up the transmission or the steering wheel.

Even more significant is the second factor: the prolonged delay between birth and the onset of puberty. The human child must wait more than ten years for the maturation of its reproductive system. And yet, Freud insists, the energy of the sexual drive is present from the start. The result is that the sexual drive becomes a kind of orphan. Unable to inhabit the organ system designed for it by biology, it takes up residence elsewhere. The sexual drive is piggy-backed upon the organ systems of other drives, particularly those of nutrition and elimination.[2] The function of sucking, itself motivated by a genuine instinct (like the "rooting" reflex that turns the infant's head toward the breast), thus becomes infused with an energy that is foreign to it. The act of sucking and the mucous membranes of the mouth that perform it become sexualized.

The evidence for supposing this sexualization of the mouth and lips is based first of all on direct observation. The nursing infant displays all the physiological markers of sexual arousal—increased rates of breathing and heartbeat, sweating, blood engorgement of erectile tissues, as well as the cycle of excitement and relaxation, that are so typical of sexual satisfaction. "No one," Freud remarks, "who has seen a baby sinking back satiated from the breast with flushed cheeks and a blissful smile can escape the reflection that this picture persists as a prototype of the expression of sexual satisfaction in later life." Even more striking than such physical indicators is the way in which behaviors of thumb sucking, kissing, eating, and drinking suggest an enduring erotic charge. From the child who reassures itself in an anxious moment by greedily sucking its thumb to the stressed-out co-ed in her first year of college who spends Friday night curled up with a double fudge sundae, putting something in one's mouth can be a welcome substitute when other satisfactions remain out of reach.

If the Freudian notion of the oral drive is relevant in the first place to physical gratification of the lips and mouth, the fuller dimensions of Freud's idea come into view by asking what it is that the infant seeks to take into itself. For the desire to suck seeks something more than the mother's milk. The oral drive transcends mere need for food. This something-extra that the child hungers after is the mother's love. The developing human being increasingly relates itself to the question of whether and with what degree of love and acceptance it is recognized by its nurturer. But here the child's hunger knows no limit. What the oral drive wants most profoundly cannot be fully possessed. By this route, the longing of oral phantasy becomes formally infinite. It

---

[2]Freud's term for this "piggy-back" function of the sexual drive is *Anlehnung*. According to the literal meaning of the word, the sexual drive is "leaned upon" other systems and functions.

thirsts after a truly ultimate satisfaction. It is therefore no accident that the mystic's desire for the touch of the divine has more than once been compared to the nursing infant's desire for the breast. It is with precisely this analogy that St. John of the Cross begins his *Dark Night of the Soul*, comparing the soul's restless search for God to the child's confused response to the mother who weans it by blackening her breast.[3]

Few examples of this insatiability of the oral drive better illustrate the psychoanalytic view than tobacco smoking. The point, of course, is not simply to reduce the smoker's urge to an infantile desire to nurse. Obviously enough, addiction to tobacco is largely a matter of chemical dependency. Nor is the psychology of smoking unrelated to its chemical aspect: the cycle of anxiety and relaxation repeated with every cigarette is both induced and gratified by the effects of nicotine. Yet precisely when we consider the cigarette as a drug delivery system there is room for a psychoanalytic supplement. If mere nicotine delivery were the sole factor, the pressing question would be why tobacco use is not confined to that other, very efficient manner of extracting its narcotic effect: chewing it. The riddle that remains unanswered on the purely chemical level is about why we go to such lengths to turn tobacco into something that can be sucked. Cigars, cigarettes, or pipes—the result is the same. We administer nicotine through something nipple-like.

The psychoanalytic conclusion is thus not to deny the role of a narcotic but to suggest that the power of chemical addiction is augmented by a deep psychological satisfaction, a repetition of the most archaic act of infantile gratification. Contrary to Freud's famous remark—indeed, as Freud knew better than anyone—a cigar is never just a cigar. To which we can add a last note about the way in which the oral drive seeks a surplus satisfaction, the "something more" than milk. For it cannot fail to strike us that the moments when the desire for a cigarette is felt most urgently are exactly the moments when the smoker has already been satiated. As any smoker can tell you, the perfect time for a cigarette is just after eating or after having sex. How can we not suspect that these after-dinner and post-coital cigarettes pertain to a desire that remains unfulfilled by food and sex? They seek to provide that elusive and indefinable something that one *didn't* get at the table or in bed.

What Only a Mother Could Love

The distance between animal instinct and human drive is especially clear in what Freud called the anal stage. The animal rejects its feces in accordance with a powerful instinct. The dog on a walk will show a good deal of interest in other dogs' scat, but will unhesitatingly walk away from its own, often with a backward kick of the hind legs, as if to emphasize its contempt for what has

[3]It was not uncommon in centuries past for a weaning mother to discourage her baby's attachment to the breast by smearing it with black and bitter substances.

been left behind.[4] It is this instinctual retreat from its own excrement that trainers rely upon to housebreak dogs. Instinctually programmed to avoid defecating in its own den, the puppy will not soil the floor of its training crate. Once the puppy comes to associate elimination with the newspaper pad laid *outside* the crate, the trainer can steer the puppy just about anywhere by moving the newspaper.

By contrast with the natural animal rejection of excrement, the developing human being becomes aware from a very early age that its excrement gets infinitely fussed over by other people. A full diaper elicits meticulous attention on the part of the mother or caretaker—attention that is clearly marked by anxious concern. How can the infant fail to conclude that this otherwise worthless substance is mysteriously valuable, indeed that it is the most valuable stuff in the world? And how can the infant fail to realize that the zone of the body that produces excrement links the infant to the mother in a particularly intimate way? Over a period of years, the mother returns thousands of times to the task of fastidiously cleaning, powdering, and diapering it. The long struggle of toilet training, a struggle in which the stakes are nothing less than the introduction of the child into the rule-governed world of polite society, impresses upon the child that good bowel habits are among the surest means of winning the mother's love.

Signaled by the mother's attention as something important to her and thereby taken up into the love relation with her, the infant's feces are freighted with a significance that is utterly unlike any animal attitude toward excrement. The feces may even become privileged tokens in an exchange of love. The two-year-old is jubilant over its most recent production. Parents may be invited into the bathroom for a triumphant exhibition. Excrement has become a gift, offered enthusiastically to the mother who appears to demand it. In my own family, the story is told about the day that my parents, then still in the first years of their marriage, wallpapered the dining room. Exhausted at the day's end, they collapsed in the adjoining room. When they returned to the dining room they were horrified to find that my brother had added his own special touch to the job. Drawing upon his well-loaded diaper as a palette, he had spread great swathes of his own dark paint over the newly papered walls. Though surely not appreciated by his parents as such, my brother was offering his most valued contribution.

Of course, the enthusiasm of the two-year-old for its excrement will not last. The first flowering of pride in its own productions results from the child's correctly perceiving that its excrement is of special interest to the mother. But eventually the effects of toilet training overtake even the most enthusiastic young fingerpainter. Even if they continue to relish a certain symbolic echo of

[4]The biological function of this backward kick no doubt has more to do with spreading the smell trail of the dog's feces than with any act of rejection, but the basic fact remains that the dog, while keenly attentive to other dogs' scat, turns its back on its own.

their former glory in making sandbox mud pies, school-age children will come to share the unhesitating judgment of proper society that excrement is something disgusting and despicable. In this respect, it appears that the human child has rejoined the animal that rejected its feces from the start. But the similarity is deceptive. The end result seems the same, but the process by which it is arrived at is completely different. Where the animal responds to instinct, the human child takes its cue from the reactions of its fellow human beings. It is love and the inscription of love in symbols, not mere instinct, that shapes the human attitude toward excrement.

A parallel point can be made about human heterosexuality. The statistical majority of heterosexuals tempts us to think that, in humans and animals alike, the heterosexual norm is simply a biological fact, a result of genetic programming. But the statistical regularity masks a fundamental difference. The human being may arrive at a similar destination, but it takes a different route to get there. Unlike the animal, sexual identity in the human being is in large part a psychological construction, the achievement of a process that is mediated by symbols. Whatever the role played by biology—and surely there is one—human sexual desire and its preferences bear the impress of psychological, social, and cultural factors that no animal has to contend with.

By linking love with what is most naturally worthless, the anal stage extends the range of possible objects of human desire to include potentially even the most abject and revolting content. It accomplishes a radical reversal of all natural values. While for the oral stage it is still possible to think of the emergence of the drive as a kind of supplement or add-on to naturally occurring organic strivings, the unfolding of the anal stage and the inscription of the excremental object in the unconscious inaugurates a profound denaturalization of human desire and of the relation to one's fellow human beings.

The result is thus completely contrary to the commonplace judgment that finds in excrement the point at which our human reality touches most closely on what is crudely natural and animal. The true state of affairs is more nearly the opposite. There is no naturally occurring analogue to what psychoanalysis calls the excremental object. In a certain crucial sense, the animal knows nothing about what we call "shit." And we can readily recognize the ground of this break with all naturally determined value: unlike the mother's milk whose symbolic value as an index of love remains bound up with its value as food, the value of excrement is entirely a function of its being signaled as such by the caretaker, as something that needs to be produced and disposed of in very particular ways. The human significance of feces is founded entirely on its being subject to the demand of the other.

In this way the excremental object might be said to be the first truly human symbol. The first human symbol and, in a sense, the most pure and perfect. Why? Because in taking what is most worthless (the fecal waste) and linking it with what is most valuable (the mother's love), excrement becomes the most extreme embodiment of the basic characteristic of all symbols, the feature that we noted earlier in our discussion of neckwear: there must always be a distance or negation between the symbol and the thing it symbolizes. In the case of excrement, that distance is effectively infinite. What is lowest and most vile becomes a token of what is most precious and sublime.

The symbolic potential of excrement is all the more powerful for the fact that there remains something essentially unknowable and unimaginable about it. Shit presents us with a kind of stubborn opacity, a barrier to thought. It is, we rightly say, a pure *mess*. It is this unthinkability of excrement that is the true ground of its horror. Our reaction of disgust, our sense of something intolerable and unapproachable, is therefore the affective measure of something imponderable, something that resists understanding. Shit embodies something we-know-not-what. This unthinkability is related to the fact that excrement never fully rises to the status of an object. Lacking the discrete and bounded character of an identifiable thing, it remains not object but *abject*.

With this unthinkable dimension of excrement in mind, we find ourselves back in the characteristic domain of phantasy. Indeed, excrement must be counted as one of the really central tropes of phantasy—it occupies its negative pole, as it were, the very embodiment of everything vile and repellent. A choice term of profane speech, the importance of which may escape our notice only because it is used so frequently, *shit* is an almost universal metaphor for foulness and evil. But what we need to notice is that shit is able to perform this symbolic function exactly because it harbors something unimaginable. *Shit* is such an effective, all-purpose cuss word precisely because it names something beyond words, something that isn't just bad, but is in some sense infinitely base and degraded, a kind of consummate evil. Earlier, in speaking of the unlimited character of the oral drive, we remarked upon the presence of oral phantasy in Christian mysticism. Excrement, too, figures prominently in Christian imagery, at least in its more unofficial expressions. Martin Luther, for example, was especially drawn to scatological metaphors. In some of his more impassioned orations, rejecting the devil's temptations or excoriating the corruption of the popes, he gave full vent to such metaphors. As William Manchester has pointed out,

> again and again, in recalling Satan's attacks on him, Luther uses the crude verb *bescheissen*, which describes what happens when someone soils you with his *Scheiss*. In another demonic strategem, an apparition of the prince of darkness would humiliate the monk by showing his "arse" (*Steiss*). Fighting back, Luther adopted satanic tactics. He invited the devil to "kiss" or "lick" his *Steiss*, threatened to "throw him into my anus, where he belongs," to defecate "in his face" or, better yet, "in his pants" and then "hang them around his neck."

"But I'm confused," someone will now say. "First you talked about feces as a gift, something signaled by the mother as valuable and therefore elected as a token of love. But now it's appearing as the symbol of what is most dirty and disgusting. Which is it?"

It's both, and that's precisely the point. As the mediating token in the archaic relation between child and mother, excrement will exert an unconscious influence on all future relations to others by serving as a kind of symbolic switch point between what is most valuable and most worthless. Shit is the most primitive object of the radically mixed feeling that psychoanalysts call "ambivalence."

Excrement is perfectly destined to embody such ambivalence, first, because its status between self and other is ambiguous. It strangely belongs to both. My own excrement is the most personal substance, the stuff which utterly singles me out and identifies me, like a kind of primitive accusation. Yet excrement is simultaneously the most impersonal and anonymous substance, the substance most utterly devoid of ownership or identity. As soon as it leaves my body, excrement is almost immediately disowned. Whatever *that* is, it has nothing to do with me!

Suspended between self and other, excrement also founds an unstable oscillation between good and evil, attraction and repulsion. The mother first appears to demand it and to reward its production, but increasingly she teaches the child to condemn and reject it. This mixed message will tend to color all subsequent experience of love with a profound two-sidedness. In the heart of the love relation is something that may at any moment reveal itself to be repulsive and worthless. Jokes about the sexual function thus become "dirty jokes." Love is perpetually haunted by the deeply rooted suspicion that it is "much ado about nothing."

Something similar can be said about the way in which the drama of toilet training establishes an ambivalence concerning the entirety of human social life and the institutions on which it is based. In a very real sense, the human being enters into civilized life by way of an unnatural investment of interest in the functioning of its bowels. The edifice of civilization is founded upon the unconscious libidinalization of excrement. Perhaps it is not wholly without significance that the ancient code of Hammurabi, among the most primitive establishments of law in all of human history, is inscribed on a great black cylinder of slightly irregular but smoothly hewn stone, an object that is less phallic than fecal in its symbolic resonance. Quite literally, the most fundamental human law, the first of all laws, is the one that tells us where it is permitted to defecate and where it is prohibited.

This deep link to the excremental means that everything having to do with law (yes, including lawyers) threatens to arouse a primitive sense of repulsion. Just beneath the surface of civilized propriety, the order of cultivated values that defines acceptable and unacceptable behavior, there lurks a hateful disgust for the entire regime of rules and regulations that governs the social world. The words of a popular song—"Take this job and shove it!"—express the point with perfect accuracy: working for the boss is really nothing but being forced to accept shit that ought to be shoved back where it came from.

If the anal stage colors relations with others with ambivalence, it also leaves behind a lasting trace of mixed feelings for one's own creations. Artists and writers may feel a powerful sense of disappointment at the moment when a work is finally completed, as if in detaching it from themselves, the work suddenly appears vaguely repulsive. To the extent that the artistic creation echoes the first infantile "creations," the artwork assumes the taint of something excremental. It is said that in his old age St. Thomas Aquinas suddenly turned on his life's work, the *oeuvre* that we now value as among the most monumental achievements of the Western mind, and declared that it suddenly seemed to him to be "mere straw." From a psychoanalytic point of view, all human creations hark back to that most original production, the effluent of the body itself. It is, of course, a connection that remains almost completely unconscious. Indeed, to call attention to it would spark a special shock of outrage. One wonders whether this wasn't exactly what happened when some Senate conservatives caught wind of the stage act by the performance artist Karen Finley in which she smeared her body with chocolate syrup while waxing eloquent about the symbolic meaning of feces. The resulting scandal, a veritable bonfire of national outrage, was a virtual deathblow to funding for the National Endowment for the Arts.

The toddler takes a conspicuous pleasure in its own feces but will later greet it with disgust. And a good thing, too, every nanny will say! But is this shift from enjoyment to revulsion merely a matter of developing manners? Once again, the first thing to note is the distance between the animal and the human. Animals don't exhibit disgust. Dogs routinely do the most revolting things—eating another dog's vomit or feces, for example—without the slightest trace of disgust. In fact, the most disgusting thing about dogs is their very lack of disgust. Its uniqueness to humans already suggests that there is nothing "natural," nothing purely instinctual, about disgust. Disgust is something we learn. In this respect the two-year-old child and the family dog have something in common: both are oblivious to disgust. The implication is that the line between the acceptable and the disgusting is a product of psychology, not biology. Even more suggestive of the psychological origins of disgust is that disgust can replace desire. What the two-year-old relished, the seven-year-old will energetically reject. The seventeen-year-old may positively gag over it. What has happened in the interim?

What's happened is that the child has grown up. And what does that mean but that the child has succeeded in winning a new measure of independence from the mother? If the toddler's enthusiasm for its excrement is a reflection of its mother's attention to it, then the later victory of disgust signals a shift in the child's relation to the mother. During infancy, the smelly stuff of excrement was a key part of the bond between mother and child. The duties of hygiene provided no end of shared moments, delicious for their privacy and intimacy. But later on, the maturing child must take a distance from its mother and lay claim to its own independence. A growing disgust over everything excremental is the understandable complement to this movement of increasing independence.

The experience of adolescence offers some confirming evidence. Revulsion at excrement and at all things "gross" generally reaches a high-water mark during adolescence for the reason that nowhere in the life cycle is the question of independent identity more sensitive. Everything that previously linked the child to the mother is now rejected. The adolescent is scandalized to have to walk beside the mother, to be called away from a circle of friends for dinner, to hear her voice break in on an important phone call. Teenagers seem embarrassed to have anyone know they even have a mother. It is immediately tempting to generalize this result and to take attitudes toward excrement as an index of relations with other people. How perfectly appropriate that we express our indifference to others by saying that we "don't give a shit"!

The insertion of the feces into the love bond between the mother and infant also profoundly affects the child's relationship to its own body. Toilet training attests that the mother is intensely interested in the most primitive functions of the infant's physiology. The anus and its ring of musculature become invested with deep emotional value. It is the site at which the most elemental body functions, the rhythmic movements of peristalsis, are entwined with the most subtle psychological and interpersonal dynamics, laid down by the infant's experience of love or rejection. In toilet training, the anus is infused with concern for the other and above all for the other's good or bad judgment. Throughout the future life of the individual, the contractions and relaxations of the anal muscle may call up immensely more global connotations of mastery or submission, independence or dependence, triumph or disgrace.

For these reasons, surprising though it may sound in view of the repugnance we generally attach to everything excremental, the anal sphincter ought probably to be considered the most profoundly social organ of the body. Though it is the last part of the body that we want others to see, it is probably the spot at which our relations with others, and particularly our wish to please them, has been most viscerally registered. No wonder the anus and the buttocks that frame it mark the site of our greatest vulnerability to shame, the point at which we may feel most deeply and most acutely the sting of others' condemnation. It is not by accident that we deliver a particularly virulent insult by calling someone an "asshole." Nor is it by mere chance that we specially reserve this part of the body for punishment. When all else fails in the effort to train a rambunctious youngster and the annoyed and impatient parent is driven to blows, it is the buttocks that are struck. And how can we fail to recognize the significance of this choice? Of all the body's parts and functions, the anus is most deeply regulated by obedience. Spanking a child on the buttocks therefore achieves something more than a mere infliction of pain. It also serves to reannounce the whole history of the child's training. It is like reminding the child that here more than anywhere else the child has already submitted to the wishes of the other. In effect, a spanking delivers the message, "You will obey now just like you have learned to obey in the past."

The particular meaning of excrement varies from one culture to another, but the underlying dynamics are nevertheless easily recognizable across the lines of cultural difference. In Chinese, for example, there is no precise equivalent of the English insult of calling someone an asshole. There is, however, another expression, that of cursing someone by wishing them to have a child born without an asshole. The apparent implication is that such a child will grow up to be a helpless and pathetic coward, good for nothing. Yet in this case, too, we can glimpse the way in which the excremental object and the aperture from which it is expelled are intimately bound up with the symbolic matrix of relation to the other. It is tempting, that is, to suppose that the Chinese curse exploits the symbolic potential of shit as a tool of aggression. Unable to express itself, the child without an asshole will spend its life incapable of self-assertion, doomed to be helplessly shit upon by everyone else. A parallel metaphoric usage exists in English: to "give people shit" means to mistreat them, to give them a hard time.

A Note about Analytic Interpretation

All this talk of excrement and anality may leave many readers skeptical. No, worse than that. A certain amount of disbelief is almost unavoidable. Why? If we allow the skeptical impulse to speak for itself, it would lodge a familiar complaint about psychoanalytic interpretation that "reads too much into things." Isn't it psychoanalysis itself that "makes much ado about nothing"? The skeptical voice wants to protest that "sometimes a shit is just a shit!" These objections need to be answered, not least because they are bound to come up again.

We ought first to admit that there is something almost unavoidably unsatisfying about psychoanalytic interpretations. The first reason is that a psychoanalytic perspective never explains everything. Unconscious dynamics of the sort that interest the psychoanalyst always function along with a host of other factors, adding a supplemental push to something that is already in motion. Phallic symbolism, for instance, is by no means the only reason men wear neckties. Nor is winning independence from one's mother the sole reason excrement smells bad. The first thing to remember about any analytic interpretation, therefore, is that it makes no claim to being exhaustive.

This point is especially important with respect to the drive's independence from biology. Each day we become aware of new ways in which the behavior of human beings is puppeted by biological influences. Freud doesn't wish to deny that influence but insists that there is another, denaturalizing factor—the swerve of the drive. Human behavior might therefore be compared to a baseball pitch. Biology supplies the basic momentum, the pure thrust that will put the ball over the plate. But psychological factors distort the straight line of biological causes with a variety of spins, drops, slides, and curves. When the game is over and the score is tallied, it may be hard to say which of these two causes—sheer force or trick motion—was the more decisive in determining the outcome.

If a psychoanalytic perspective is never total, never explaining everything, neither can it be securely based on unambiguous observations. The researcher of the unconscious must be satisfied with a web of indirect evidence, a tissue of minor details and anomalies that suggest a conclusion without fully certifying it. To accept this sort of incomplete and tentative conclusion can be taxing in the extreme as it runs counter to the demand of common sense to see the objects of knowledge clearly in the light of day. Seeing, as we say, is believing. Partly for that reason, to enter upon psychoanalytic reflection is to resist the insistence of common sense. Not an easy task. Nothing flatters our accustomed sense of everyday reality more reassuringly than the idea that things are basically simple and obvious. We almost instinctively recoil from the complications and hidden meanings revealed by psychoanalysis. The more Freud rubs our noses in them, the more deeply we feel resentful and violated.

What is at stake is not merely a challenge to our usual habits of thinking but a threat to the stability of the familiar, everyday world and of ourselves in that world. To encounter the unconscious is to be confronted with something uncanny and threatening about ourselves. It is to be forced to realize that we remain unknown to ourselves. Our first impulse, quite naturally, is to turn away and to take refuge in simple pieties and platitudes.

Last, there is the sense in which psychoanalytic interpretations often seem less traumatizing than simply ridiculous. And, let's face it, the results of Freud's researches can often seem to border on the ludicrous. Yet here we must remind ourselves that if Freud is right that key aspects of our inner life remain largely unconscious, then the most accurate analytic interpretations, the ones that reveal the truth of the unconscious most nakedly, are bound to strike us as unbelievable or even silly.

Which returns us to the theme of anality. For what is more distant from our ordinary awareness than the anus? Though we must daily attend to our own bowel exit, often with a fair amount of effort, and though street slang is well larded with references to shit and the orifice that produces it, most of us are utterly unaccustomed to paying any attention whatsoever to the anus. No wonder so many family doctors complain about patients who ignore for too long the wide variety of ailments that may afflict the rectum and anus. It is something of a project even to lay eyes on this part of our body. And our inability to see it is matched only by our lack of desire. The anus and its function is the unconscious of the body itself. To raise it for careful and explicit discussion, as we have done, runs counter to our general obliviousness about it and tends quite naturally to arouse a sense of disbelief. Yet psychoanalysis insists on rooting around where angels fear to tread. With that in mind, perhaps we ought to be a bit suspicious of our first reaction to many psychoanalytic interpretations of behavior—suspicious, that is, of our immediate temptation to dismiss them as so much "bullshit."

Stick Shift

The key point that we ought to take with us from these notes on the oral and anal stages concerns the role of the mother's love. What began for the nursling as a service of pure need for the mother's milk becomes more and more a search for her attention and affection. In the anal stage, too, the mother's love plays the pivotal part. The toddler's sensitivity to the mother's attention can elevate even the worthless refuse of excrement into something precious. Milk and feces thus become objects of exchange in an unfolding economy of love.

Looking back over the early development of the human child, we therefore see a deepening interest in the mother as something more than a mere provider of physical satisfactions. The infant is profoundly affected by the emotional tone and quality of the mother's nursing. In the later anal stage, the child shifts from being the happy recipient of the mother's love to being an active pursuer, increasingly caught up in the effort to please her. The question becomes what the mother wants. The feces that had earlier bound the mother to the infant by reason of simple hygiene then offer a primitive answer to the question of the mother's desire. It assumes the status of an offering, a gift, or a trophy. In the phallic stage, the period from roughly age four to six during which the Oedipus complex will come to full flower, the underlying question receives a new answer. What the mother most wants is the phallus.

Why the phallus?

With the issue of the phallus we arrive at the core of the Freudian theory of the Oedipus and castration complexes. But how to understand it? On the most basic level, it is comprehensible from one point of view only: that of a child. The child's imagination seizes upon the phallus as what differentiates the father from the mother, but does so by way of a mistake that few adults would make. In at least two different ways, the child creatively *misperceives* the situation. In the first place, the child assumes that there is something missing in the mother. The fact, of course, is that there is nothing missing in the female. She is fully whole and lacking nothing. The female is not incomplete but simply different from the male. But that's not the way a child sees things. For the four- or five-year-old, the presence of the penis in the father and its absence in the mother means only one thing: he's got something she doesn't. The reason is that the four-year-old thinks in concrete terms. It cannot yet manage abstractions, nor can it easily relate to things that aren't clearly present in plain sight. It is more than a matter of "out of sight, out of mind." What cannot be seen doesn't exist at all.

My son's attempt to understand sex difference is a good illustration of this childish misperception. Trying our best to behave like parents who had read Dr. Spock, my wife and I explained that Daddy has a penis (like you do, too!) and that Mommy has something of her own—a "vagina." We were well pleased with this enlightened program until a bath-time discussion at around age four revealed how completely my son had misunderstood. Obviously proud of having at last solved a great riddle, he triumphantly announced that "Mommy has a vagina" while "Daddy has a penis … and a vagina!" Hmmmm. It took some minutes to disentangle the crossed wires, during which time I received a simple but important lesson in how children view the world. While my wife and I had been congratulating ourselves on having explained that Mommy has her own special something, my son had quite logically assumed that we were speaking of what is visibly present in the crucial spot: pubic hair. If a vagina is pubic hair, then Mommy has a vagina and Daddy has a penis *and* a vagina. My son's reasoning had proceeded on the purely concrete level of what he could see.

The thought process of the typical four-year-old is governed by a perceptual literalism that is hard for many adults to imagine. The child assumes that the mother is missing something because there's nothing there to be seen. But the child makes an additional leap of illogic that is almost as irresistible as it is invalid: something is always better than nothing. Take two children and give one of them something—it could be an ice cream cone or a tarantula—and the child who has been left empty-handed will beg to be given one, too. This reflex assumption that "something is better than nothing," or, said otherwise, that "having is always better than not having," supplies the final premise for the conclusion: Mommy must want what she doesn't have. The phallus marks what the mother lacks and what the father possesses. And of course the mother wants what she lacks. The psychological dynamics of the phallic phase are set in motion by this chain of infantile reasoning.

So what are the implications of this infantile logic? What exactly is the phallic stage? It is the period during which the four- to six-year-old displays a new self-assertiveness the aim of which is to place itself in its spotlight of the parent's desire. Put in the most brutal (and no doubt over-simple) terms: The little boy wants to seduce the mother and the little girl wants to bear the father's baby. That is to say, the child wants either to *be* the phallus (as the boy wants the mother to see how strong, clever, and daring he is) or to *have* the phallus (as the girl cradles her dolls, plays house, etc.). What the phallus represents in these little dramas of seduction is not so much the male member itself, but the ultimate object of desire, the apogee of all longing, the summit of fulfillment. What the child wants is somehow to offer itself in the place of what it imagines to be the object of the parent's desire. It is during this period, then, that the child will for the first time seize upon certain key aspects of the parent's interests or activities and imitate them. The young boy will be seen toting his father's tools about the house or trying on his father's hat. The little girl may pore over her mother's jewelry and serve tea with miniature cups and saucers.

Inevitably, however, there is some question about what exactly the parent wants. There is an obscure dimension of the other's desire because there is a limit to the child's ability to imagine the parent's yearning. In psychoanalytic terms, the phallus represents this mysterious dimension. The phallus is the unknown and unknowable something, a pure "X," not so much itself a dream as the goal at which every sweet dream aims. It is the ultimately satisfying object, the thing that will finally and once and for all do the trick. As such, the phallus is something forever sought and never attained. It symbolizes what is most characteristic of human desire, namely, that there is no end to it. The phallus remains perpetually out of reach. Dedicated to the pursuit of the other's desire, the child is destined ceaselessly to chase this elusive prize.

The phallus is the symbol of the limitlessness of human desire. To see a little better how this is so, and why the male member in particular is elected to serve this function, consider the contrast between the phallus and the breast. We are no strangers to the breast as a metaphor for contentment. We speak tenderly of the milk of human kindness. We are happy for the prodigal child who is taken back, as we say, into the bosom of the family. And no wonder. The infant's most archaic experiences of bliss were derived from direct contact with the breast. From its great, soft mass flowed the most primitive satisfactions. What better emblem of complete gratification could be imagined?

And yet the breast cannot compete with the phallus as a privileged element in the lexicon of human symbols. Columns, pillars, obelisks, towers, steeples, rods, staffs, pikes, scepters, batons, wands, swords, even neckties!—across different cultures and over many millennia, the phallus and its derivatives have eclipsed all other symbolic references to the human body. Why? Because the only thing more compelling to the human imagination than the dream of contentment is the pure restlessness of desire. And for *that* the best symbol is precisely what the mother doesn't possess. The symbolism of the phallus points beyond the mother and whatever she was able to provide. Indeed, the phallus indicates not only what she could not provide but what the child could not provide to her. It designates a third point, off the original, dual axis of mother and child, to which the mother looks for the fulfillment of *her* desire.

This third point is, of course, the position of the father, the third point of the Oedipal triangle. Awareness of it faces the child with the realization that it cannot enjoy a monopoly on the mother's attention. In its infancy, the child felt itself wholly enthralled by the mother. The mother was the world. But as time goes on, the child comes to recognize that there are other things that attract her. There are other enticements with which the child may have to compete. How can the child avoid the conclusion that winning the mother's love will henceforth require doing, saying, or being something extra? In this way, the phallic phase opens the child's relation with the mother to a larger sphere of activities and involvements, skills and accomplishments.

The trajectory of the three stages—oral, anal, and phallic—thus forms a progressive development of the child's awareness of the world and its relation to the other. The three stages unfold a kind of rigorous logic of loving and giving. In the oral phase, the infant's position is essentially passive. It awaits the mother's attention like *manna* from heaven. When the mother is present, there is bliss. With her absence comes misery. The anal stage raises the possibility of a more active role in which the child can participate in some give and take. For the first time, there appears to be something of its own that can be offered in exchange for the mother's love. Where the nursling remained a helpless recipient, the toddler may strive to please the mother with its productions or, later on, with its mastery of toilet etiquette. In the phallic phase, however, the child must reckon with the possibility that the mother has some wants that the child cannot satisfy. The circuit of exchange is thus extended to include an indefinite number of objects and activities in the larger world, many of which remain beyond reach or which can be attained only by considerable time and effort. The progression of libido through the three infantile stages thus coincides with an ever-expanding circle of the child's consciousness of the world around it.

Surveying the oral, anal, and phallic stages as a whole, we see that the unifying factor is less any natural impulse of the child (to suck, to defecate, to urinate or masturbate) than concern for the love and interest of the caretaker (a longing for her love, a desire to please her, a question about what it is that she wants). It now remains merely to link this observation to our earlier remarks about phantasy. For psychoanalysis, we said, there is always something unimaginable at the heart of phantasy. We can now recognize that this unimaginable kernel of the phantasy is inseparable from the child's relation to the other. This kernel of unknowability is nothing less than the finally unanswerable question of the other's desire. The desire of the other ultimately eludes me and remains beyond my grasp. Try as I might, the other remains a closed book, a room behind a curtain. It is this unknown and unknowable dimension of the other's inwardness that is at stake in the drive and in the play of phantasy that is set in motion by it.

The drive and its phantasies are thus always bound up with an intersubjective dimension. In this respect, too, the psychoanalytic sense of phantasy is wholly different from the ordinary sense of fantasy, which we tend to think of as a selfish indulgence, perhaps even as the very definition of purely egoistical satisfaction. By contrast, phantasy always contains an implicit reference to the other human being. What psychoanalysis discovers at the core of the unconscious is not merely that I am a mystery to myself, that the sources of my own motives remain unavailable to my awareness, but that I am myself always, intimately, and enigmatically related to some other outside myself, that my own desire is obscurely bound up with the dark and unknowable horizon of the other's desire. From this point of view, we begin to sense the meaning of Lacan's question, a kind of summing-up of the cardinal riddle of psychoanalysis:

"Who, then, is this other to whom I am more attached than to myself, since, at the heart of my assent to my own identity, it is still he who agitates me?"

Phallic Phantasy or Fantastic Fallacy?

These first forays into Freudian theory may yet leave many people troubled by pesky questions, many of which cluster around the concept of the phallus. It is, we might say, the real sticking point of psychoanalytic theory. Before moving on to new topics, it will be worthwhile to examine it a little further.

We have seen how the pivot between infantile and adult sexuality is located by Freud in the phallus. What appears to be missing to the mother comes to represent the privileged object of desire. But with this notion a handful of doubts and hesitations immediately arise. How, for example, could the unfolding of the child's development depend on such chance factors as seeing the parents' genitalia? Surely that doesn't always happen, right? And what about the case of a single-parent family, in which the child may have no opportunity for making an enlightening comparison?

The answer to these questions offers an opportunity to be a little more precise about how the Freudian unconscious is formed and how it functions. While the child's experience of its parents is surely the most decisive influence in laying the foundations of the unconscious, the ground is already well prepared by the child's perceptions of a larger social world. The cultural domain is everywhere saturated with unconscious phantasy. We have already elaborated just such a saturation in the neckwear code and could easily supply other examples. As a result of being bathed in the symbolic representations of the phallus and of sexuality in general, by the time most children actually see their parents' genitals the sight has been rehearsed countless times in subtle symbolic hints that are virtually ubiquitous. From this consideration a general principle can be drawn: the unconscious discovered by Freud is not just in our heads, nor is it confined to the bedroom and the nursery; it is everywhere in the world around us. The effects of the unconscious are present wherever human beings use symbols.

It is worth lingering a moment longer on this point. One of the prime obstacles to understanding Freud's treatment of the phallus is the demand we almost inevitably feel, here and elsewhere, for simple explanations. If we are to accept the idea that the phallus plays a privileged role in the unconscious, we naturally want to know how and why it does, and we expect there to be a simple answer to what seems to us a perfectly straightforward question. But the problem is that, from the very nature of the case, there isn't a simple answer. The unconscious is intrinsically complex. It is both individual and collective, both a matter of personal psychology and of cultural symbolism. In fact, the unconscious is precisely the relation between the two, a relation that is dialectical, with each side, the individual and the collective, influencing the other.

There may also be a question about what the phallus really symbolizes. After all, isn't the phallus more a symbol of power than of desire? The truth is that it is both, and is so because power is ultimately reducible to desire. At bottom, there are two basic forms of power: the power to control enjoyment of the object of desire, or the power to resist it. The first form is the more familiar one. It is the power of the tyrant to hoard wealth and goods for his own use and to deny access to competitors. It is the outward power of domination over others. But there is also the inward power of self-control. Such was the principle discovered by the ancient Stoics. The best way to avoid the agony of powerlessness is to minimize one's expectations of satisfaction. The person who desires nothing cannot be disappointed, nor can he or she easily be dominated. Opposed to the brute intimidation of the despot, then, there is the quiet potency of the saint. But in both of its forms, power is measured by desire. The powerful person possesses either the resources to satisfy desire or the will to say no to it.

The unity of power and desire in the symbolism of the phallus is well illustrated by the example of the trophy wife. No doubt she bolsters her older husband's sense of power, but does so only because she radiates a general force field of desirability. The aging male in midlife crisis is flattered by the notion that this dramatically younger and strikingly attractive woman finds him desirable. She also certifies that he is himself still capable of desiring. She is the visible display of his virility (or at least a plausible pretence of it). Of crucial importance, however, is that these effects are staged in front of other men. The trophy wife empowers her husband only insofar as she incites desire in others. The real value of the trophy wife, as the very name implies, resides in being seen with her. Such a woman can be worn on a man's arm at a cocktail party the way some men display the crest of an upper-crust prep school on their blazer pocket. All of which means that the trophy wife *is* the phallus for the man who lays claim to her. The effect of power created by this beautiful woman is largely dependent on the degree to which other men find her attractive and impressive. She enhances one man's power by cultivating the envy of others.

Which brings us to the infamous "penis envy." This Freudian concept has probably stirred up more controversy than any other. In making a first approach to it, let us right away dispense with the common assumption that penis envy is something that only a woman can have. Not at all! It is quite true that Freud's primary intention was to point to a difference in the way men and women relate to each other. Women tend far more than men to buttress their identity by linking themselves to a powerful spouse. The example of the trophy wife makes the point neatly: Can we imagine this beautiful young woman wedding a man who is not only significantly older but also poverty-stricken and socially outcast? It is this project of prestige by association that Freud called penis envy.

But the man, too, is looking for the phallus, as *his* interest in the trophy wife shows very well. The marriage of the tycoon and the trophy wife is a relatively simple contract in which youth and beauty are traded for money and status. In psychoanalytic terms, what each gives to the other is an incarnation of the phallus—what she *is* for what he *has*. Women therefore have no monopoly on penis envy, but only a different way of living it. Where women traditionally look to a man to supply the hook on which they will hang their sense of power and prestige, men continue to enjoy a wider range of options, from professional success to a litany of phallic toys—sports cars, cigarette boats, motorcycle crotch-rockets, etc. Of course, the game of sexual identity is changing somewhat in our own time—we hear more often of older women marrying younger men, for example—but in turn-of-the-century Vienna the rules were stark indeed. Freud can hardly be blamed for making them explicit.

The Really Prickly Question

But all of these preliminary questions are incidental to the really basic one: Doesn't the Freudian theory of the phallus take the masculine position as the norm, thereby pressing women into the mold of male desire? Even if it makes sense to speak of a privileged object of desire, a kind of dream-object that would fulfill the most extravagant human longing, what justification is there for identifying it with the male member? Isn't this Freudian doctrine merely a pseudo-scientific form of male self-congratulation?

While a fully satisfactory answer to these questions probably isn't possible in a brief compass, let us at least make a beginning by clarifying a key misconception, then offering a general comment. The misconception is that *phallus* is simply a fancier-sounding word for *penis*. It is quite true that Freud locates the origin of the unconscious symbolism of the phallus in the anatomical difference of the sexes—the presence of the penis in the father and its absence in the mother. But once set in motion, the symbolic value of the phallus has very little to do with the penis. What a woman desires is less related to the penis than to the man who is attached to it. Strength, intelligence, virility, competence, creativity, influence over others—combined, of course, with desire for her—these are among the qualities that will arouse her. And it is these qualities, as traits that set one man apart from the common lot, that Freud calls "phallic."

Then the crucial point that completes the picture: The man, too, desires the phallus. He does so in (at least) two ways, first as it is incarnated by the woman he loves, and second as he himself embodies it in the sexual act he performs with her. With regard to the first: For the masculine lover, sex is very typically a two-stage drama in which a man is first lured by the woman as a captivating object. Her hair, lips, and eyes, her breasts, legs, and hips—everything about her body is an occasion for arousal. In Freudian terms, her body is an embodiment of the phallus. The artist Hans Bellmer makes this point with special force:

> In all probability no one has to this point seriously enough considered to what extent the image of a desirable woman is dependent on the image of the man who desires her, so that in the end it amounts to a series of phallic projections which progress from one segment of a woman to configure her entire image, whereby the finger, the arm, the leg of the woman, could actually be the man's genitals—that it's the male sex organ in the woman's firm, stockinged leg, the thigh swelling over—or in the pair of rounded buttocks out of which, arching backwards in tension, the column of the vertebrae extends—or in the double breasts, that hang down from the extended neck or freely from the body—so that the phallus is finally the entire woman, sitting with hollow spine, with or without hat, standing erect.

But this first phase of a man's fascinated attraction with the woman as a phallic object may give way in the heat of lovemaking to a second form of phallic enjoyment that consists in a kind of flattery of his own prowess. A man assumes the role of the phallus to the extent that he experiences his capacity to please his woman, to dominate her, to penetrate and possess her. He becomes himself the phallus, not just as the bearer of the erectile organ of copulation but as a total ensemble of qualities to which a woman responds.

How, then, are we to pin down the definition of this more general, non-penile sense of the phallic? The difference between penis and phallus is reflected in the etymology of the two words. Both derive from ancient Greek but signify quite different things. *Penis* is from the Greek *peos*, or "tail." It is the word from which we derive "pencil" and also "pendant" or "pendulous," as things that hang down. The penis is therefore named for what it looks like—a tail. And the meaning of the Greek *phallos*? It bears a reference to the penis, of course, but only as it is flushed and swollen with desire. *Phallos* is the penis risen to special prominence and conspicuousness, less the organ itself than the state of its engorgement. *Phallos* is erection. By extension, *phallic* may connote anything that announces itself as especially significant, as having exceptional value or interest, anything—we say it only half jokingly—that really stands out. *Phallic* can thus refer perfectly well to things that do not look at all penile. What is at stake is not so much the way something looks as the degree to which it commands attention.

With the emphasis on this aspect of what draws our attention, we're reminded of the *fascinum*, the paraded phallus of Roman festivals we earlier remarked upon. The phallus is what fascinates. Given this sense of what is phallic, we can better see what it means to say, as in the example of the trophy wife, that a woman may embody the phallus while displaying no literal reference to the penis. In the tradition we have inherited, women are objects of visual attention much more so than men. Women dress, make up, and present themselves to be seen. By contrast, men traditionally command attention less by looks than by wealth, achievement, position, and status. We have already had occasion to quote John Berger's brutal assessment: "men act, women appear." In art and in fashion, the female form, adorned or not, represents the phallus by being a lure for the eye.

Even beyond their greater tendency to be taken as visual objects, women can play a phallic role by virtue of being an object possessed by a man. As such, women serve as markers of value to be recognized by other men. To possess a woman functions for the man who claims her to send a signal to others about what kind of man he is. Think, for example, of the role played by first ladies in helping to define the identity of presidents. Whatever or whoever these women might be by themselves, their public role is that of providing a flattering accompaniment to their husband's image. Stepping too far beyond this accompanying role in the direction of independent action or identity, as Hillary Clinton did in the health care reform fiasco of 1993, is to risk a particularly virulent form of rejection.

In this respect, the psychoanalytic theory can be linked to the anthropology of Claude Lévi-Strauss, which takes account of the way in which women may function as objects of exchange. Kinship systems in various societies present a range of different means for accomplishing exogamy, the practice by which women are drawn by marriage out of their family of origin and into the family of a husband. Exogamy strengthens the general fabric of society by stabilizing relations between kinship groups. But in the process, women become tokens of kinship identity that are circulated between families. Women become the means by which men signal their identity to other men.

The phallus thus refers to the penis while being not at all limited to it. All the same, however—and here we come to the general comment promised a moment ago—doesn't all this talk of the phallus contain a prejudicial reference to the masculine? In taking the phallus as the symbol of desire, doesn't psychoanalysis hopelessly taint itself with a vestige of patriarchy? Doesn't Freud's insistence on the centrality of the phallus merely show how deeply his theories have been influenced by a male-dominated culture?

Of course! And that is precisely the point! It is with respect to this issue that a feminist sense of outrage over Freud's preoccupation with the phallus goes astray. From Freud's own viewpoint, such outrage simply shoots the messenger. Freud's battery of concepts, and especially that of the phallus, inevitably appears sexist because it is drawn directly from a culture that is itself sexist. If Freud is correct, the unconscious function of the phallus is not only inseparable from the patriarchal order of European culture, it is the psychological linchpin of patriarchy. The dominance of the phallus in unconscious phantasy is a reflection of the dominance of men in political, social, economic, and cultural life.

Not everyone sees this point. Many critics of psychoanalysis, put off by Freud's "phallocentrism," insist on tracing the problem back to Freud's own misogyny. So Gloria Steinem would have it, whose imaginative invention of Dr. Phyllis Freud, founder of the theory of womb envy, we noted earlier. If only Freud had been a woman, Steinem supposes, then everything about psychoanalysis would have been completely different. But the supposition is a bogus one. For all the ingenuity of Steinem's reconstruction, at points illuminating as well as entertaining, the stubborn reality remains that phallocentrism is not the private fantasy of a quirky Viennese psychiatrist but rather a cultural fact to be interpreted. Freud's intention, as Juliette Mitchell has aptly reminded us, is not prescription but description. Freud did not *invent* the symbolic value of the phallus. Nor was his attention to phallicism a product of his own sexist attitudes. Rather he *found* the symbolism of the phallus in the culture around him, as we can do in our own, and sought to ask what it meant. His aim was not to endorse phallic culture but to explain it. The theoretical challenge is not simply to bemoan the asymmetry of sexual politics and to dream about utopian alternatives, but to understand how those politics came into being in the first place. Freudian talk about the phallus doesn't justify the sexist culture it describes but merely aims to call it by its right name.

Let us linger another moment on this point. Freud's insistence on the pivotal significance of the phallus offends many feminists because it appears to ignore the specific character of women's desire. The assumption is that women have been the victims of an age-old male conspiracy and that Freud's theories merely reinforce that victimization by celebrating the key symbol of masculine power and prestige. But aside from the tendency just noted to mistake Freud's *description* for a mode of *prescription*, this point of view must reckon with what is for many feminists an uncomfortable thought: Women's desire very often tends to flow in the channels prescribed for it by the phallic regime of traditional Western culture. The black leather machismo of the motorcycle daddy, the bulging crotch of the guitar-pumping rock star, the rippling muscle beneath the construction worker's T-shirt—these days we cannot avoid a smile at these clichés of masculine sexiness. Yet their appeal as erotic stimulants for a great number of women remains stubbornly alive and well. To the consternation of many feminists, the best argument for the predominance of the phallus——not the penis, but the *phallus*—is the desire of average women. Indeed, it can readily seem that the most fervent wish of many feminists is less an impulse to rewrite Freud than to reform the behavior of other women.

Must Freud then be counted among the enemies of feminism? Must we accept an inevitable conflict between feminism and psychoanalysis? On the contrary! Criticism of Freud by feminists in the United States contrasts markedly with his reception by many European feminists. For them, Freud remains among the most deeply insightful theorists of gender. Freud is a resource and an ally precisely because he maps so provocatively the psychological structure that underlies the traditional regime of masculinity and femininity. Far from being inimical to the women's movement, a Freudian perspective is deeply consonant with it, so long as we hold fast to the fact that Freud's effort is to *recognize* the dynamics of gender difference, not necessarily to *recommend* them. From a Freudian point of view, the whole phenomenon of gender is inseparable from the sexist order of patriarchy, an order not merely skewed by the privilege of the phallus but founded upon it.

The Prime Cut

Having given some account of the psychoanalytic notion of the phallus, it now remains to say something about the successor to the phallic phase, the Oedipus complex, and about its pivot-point, the so-called castration complex. How exactly are they related? In Freud's classic formulation, the answer was quite straightforward. The little boy must give up access to the mother under threat of castration by the father. Love of the mother is then replaced by identification with the father. Of course, this theory had its drawbacks. On the one hand, it appeared to tie castration fear too closely to an actual threat by a parent or nanny. What if no such threat was ever made? On the other hand, it wasn't easy to see how the experience of the little girl could be fit to this model. Maybe little boys are edgy at the idea of losing their swizzle-stick but what warrants the assumption that little girls ever think about such things? One of the great advances of the French analyst Jacques Lacan was to clarify this problem, revealing the way in which Freud had correctly intuited the unconscious significance of the phallus and castration though failed to give them their proper significance. To see what is at stake here, we need for a moment to go back to the basics.

To recap the upshot of the preceding discussions: Like the first object exchanged between the infant and the mother—the excrement—the value of all objects in the human world is based at least in part on the degree to which others appear to desire them. Here, the Freudian perspective parallels that of Marx, for whom *use value* (the worth of an object for satisfying a practical need) is very often less important than *exchange value* (a measure of the object's attractiveness to others, regardless of its utility). Objects signal status and prestige to a community of others in whom they incite desire. *Phallus*, we might say, is merely the term by which the theory of the unconscious designates that general function of desirability.

The phallus is an especially apt choice to perform this symbolic function by virtue of its link to the penis, first of all because it is absent in the mother and present in the father, but also and more generally because it refers to a part of the body. That a bodily organ is taken to symbolize the general possibility of desire suggests that desire always remains tied to some other human being whose attention and interest singles out something as valuable. There is also the erectile function of the penis, which serves so dramatically to mark the presence of desire. Erection is desire made visible. Objects in the world may unexpectedly be recognized as valuable and become extra-conspicuous in somewhat the same way that the penis, flushed with the pressure of the sexual urge, announces itself in becoming erect. At the same time, however, the real meaning of the phallus is precisely its distance from the penis. As the signifier of the ultimate object of desire, the phallus stands for what no mere object, and surely no mere body part, can provide. The phallus represents what is insatiable about human desire, that aspect of desire that passes beyond all possible objects of satisfaction.

Freud was surprised and puzzled by the frequency with which he encountered phantasies of castration in his patients' dreams and reveries. Even more conspicuous were the castration fears that cropped up in his work with children, most famously in his analysis of Little Hans, the boy whose phobia of having his "whittler" bitten off by a draft horse made him for many months a virtual prisoner of the household. The meaning of these phantasies of castration becomes clearer against the background of the symbolic meaning of the phallus we have been unfolding. If the phallus represents the ultimate object of desire, then the loss of one's own penis, however pathetic a stand-in for the grander dimensions of the object symbolized by the phallus, signifies that the "real thing" is henceforth and forever something possessed by someone else. Castration is the symbolic admission of not having what it takes. It confesses an inadequacy of self and a dependence on the other that are irreversible. The phantasy of castration involves coming to terms with the painful realization that the satisfaction of desire cannot be guaranteed. The wherewithal of gratification is not under one's own control and cannot be hoarded or secured but circulates uncertainly in the space between one human being and another.

It is this view of castration that is put forward by Jacques Lacan. Castration becomes less a threat of punishment than a symbolic task, less a fear of something to be avoided at all costs than a reimagining of the child's relation to others. In passing through what Lacan calls "symbolic castration," the child comes to realize that it does not possess the supreme object of desire. Loved though it may be by the mother, the child is not all that she loves. Castration thus spells the end of narcissism. It fractures the infantile dream of forever remaining the center of the mother's attention. The child is no longer His or Her Majesty the Baby.

It is in this sense that Lacan associates castration with the child's entry into language—admittedly an association that is not easy to understand. In relinquishing the dream of fully controlling the fulfillment of desire (relinquishing, that is, the dream of being able to satisfy the desire of the other at will), the child becomes anxiously dependent on the uncertain response of the other. The child is suspended in a new way before questions about what it is the other really wants and what the child might have to be or do in order to live up to the other's expectations. Not only must the child now listen to what the other says, but it must allow for a significant margin of difference from what it might like to hear. This gap between what one wants, expects, fears, or hopes to hear, and what is actually said (or what goes unsaid), then becomes the zone of real intimacy between human beings. It is the no man's land across which the effort to understand must labor to connect. To give up the phallus in symbolic castration is thus to acknowledge that there is no shortcut to genuine relationship. There is no magic wand, so to speak, that will establish perfect rapport between self and other. There is only the boundless resource of language itself, the treasury of symbols with which we offer our love and seek the love of the other in return.

This Lacanian view marks at least two key changes from the classical Freudian account. First, Lacan's approach makes it easier to see how castration is an issue for both sexes. Every human being, boy or girl, must face the limit of his or her capacity to fill the void of the other person's longing. Every person must suffer the wound to his or her own narcissism that is required to enter genuine society with others. In this sense, the magnetism of the phallus and the fear of losing it are shared by everyone. Second, the Lacanian view puts the dynamics of castration more decisively into the unconscious. The phantasy of castration emerges not from angry nannies' threats of punishment but from the most primitive strata of the child's own imagination. The drama of castration anxiety derives from the child's encounter with its own limits.

But wait! How do we know that any of this castration anxiety really exists? We have been talking about castration fear for some time now as if the evidence for it were perfectly plain. But nothing could be further from the truth. If Freud is correct, becoming aware of the unconscious symbolism of the phallus is a little like trying to hear oneself snore. If penis envy exists at all, the person who suffers from it will, by definition, be the last to know it. So, too, castration anxiety, precisely as *unconscious*, is anything but obvious. What evidence can be offered in support of the Freudian theory?

A Little Slice of Heaven

The only really adequate answer to this question is to be drawn from the analytic couch—the stuff of dreams, phantasies, archaic memories, slips, symptoms, etc.—but discussion of that sort of clinical detail would take us too far afield of our main concerns. We can usefully take a second-best approach, a path already well worn by Freud himself, by way of examples from the cultural domain. And in this instance the example most ready to hand is as nuanced as it is impressive for the central role it has played in the history of Western culture. It concerns nothing less than the founding myth of the three great monotheisms, Judaism, Christianity, and Islam. I have in mind, of course, the story of Abraham's covenant with God.

We are told in Genesis that God wished to make a covenant with Abraham. For his own part, God was prepared to give a great deal. He promised to multiply Abraham's seed, seeing to it that Abraham would become "father of many nations." Should Abraham agree to the terms of the covenant, he would hit the jackpot of all jackpots. What, then, must he do in return? Surely some very considerable feat. Hercules, after all, had to perform twelve enormous labors, each one a veritable theater of the impossible, in order to receive from the gods his immortality. What must Abraham do to get the earthly equivalent of the same? Astonishingly, God asked only that he cut a flap of skin from the tip of his penis. God wanted Abraham's foreskin. If the story is familiar, it ought not to strike us as any less bizarre. On the level of a contract in which goods are exchanged, the biblical covenant is obviously ludicrous: God gives the world for a useless scrap of skin. Even more curious, a scrap to be culled from the nub of the penis. Were it not God himself making it, the demand would seem not only absurd but also distinctly perverse. What are we to make of this strange transaction?

There are many ways to interpret this famous episode. One needn't be a biblical exegete, for example, to recognize in the story of Abraham's covenant an echo of older traditions of blood sacrifice. Yahweh demands a symbolic blood-letting just as other deities of the ancient Middle East required the ritual slaughter of rams, goats, cattle, and so on. Abraham's sacrifice by circumcision also foreshadows his later trial when God will ask him to sacrifice his son Isaac. For our purposes, however, the salient question centers on the object of sacrifice. Why is it precisely the genitals that are put to the knife?

From the psychoanalytic perspective that we have opened up, what may otherwise appear to be nonsensical becomes transparently clear. God's demand for circumcision is a form of symbolic castration. In accepting to undergo it, Abraham signals his acknowledgment that he does not himself possess the privileged object of desire, nor does he lay claim to the ultimate power to produce or satisfy desire. This means, among other things, that he is not himself the source of the progeny begotten by him. Abraham not only willingly spills his own blood, voluntarily taking upon himself the mark of death, but does so in the very seat of his own reproductive power. His gesture thus betokens his awareness of a higher power. His children come through him but are not his own creation. Their true father is Yahweh. If a great nation is brought forth through the seed of Abraham, it is the power of Yahweh that makes it possible.

Far from being a nonsensical or arbitrary detail of the story, therefore, Abraham's acceptance of circumcision is profoundly appropriate for the purpose of binding the covenant. What else has Abraham to offer God? He has only his devotion and obedience. Only his acknowledgment that all power and all glory come from God. Abraham's circumcision symbolizes his posture of pious submission and does so in its acknowledgment of this crucial point: all true paternity belongs to God. This way of looking at the biblical story repeats the point we have been at pains to make: the phallus is not the penis. Indeed, the purpose of Abraham's circumcision is to establish the distinction between the two. His penis is symbolically wounded in order to signify that the true power of generation resides elsewhere.

To the extent that Yahweh promises to multiply the seed of Abraham, Hebraic monotheism might be said to echo the pagan worship of the phallus. Like earlier religions centered on fertility worship, the power of the Hebrew God is linked to the procreative power, symbolized by the male organ of generation. But by requiring that Abraham "sacrifice" his own organ, marking it with a sign of finitude, Yahweh establishes an entirely new order of generative power, a phallic power beyond any mere spawning of the penis. This new phallic power cannot be imaged. It is this invisibility of the new power that will distinguish it from the idol worship of Baal and other local deities of the ancient Middle East. In this way, we recognize how the Judaic condemnation of idolatry is connected with the founding story of the Abrahamic covenant. Abraham does not castrate himself in order then to bow down before a gigantic phallic image in the manner of Dionysiac revelers. The religious purpose of the circumcision is rather the opposite; it symbolizes a measured negation of the sexual metaphor in favor of an invisible power of divinity. It is this invisible power that will overthrow the pagan world of images.

Once we recognize the dynamics of psychoanalytic castration in Abraham's circumcision, a subsequent chapter in the history of the Jewish religion—its transformation in the birth of Christianity—becomes interpretable in a parallel fashion. The Hebrew prohibition of idols kept open and protected a certain gap between the earthly domain of images and the unimaginable power of the divine. For the Judaic tradition, only the sacred Word could spark this gap. But with Christianity the Word was made flesh. The gap between mortal and divine was filled by a living, breathing human being. With the coming of Jesus, although Christianity retained the Hebrew condemnation of graven images, the chasm between heaven and earth was bridged. The almost inevitable result was a new tendency toward idolatry, a kind of renewed temptation of the image. It is a temptation around which some of the bitterest struggles in the history of the Christian church have been waged. The debate over iconoclasm led to the schism between Roman Catholicism and the Byzantine Eastern Orthodox Church and played a less direct but still potent role in the Protestant Reformation.

Against the background of the Hebrew wariness of idolatry, the rise of Christianity provided the opening for a resurgence of an image-worship akin to that of pagan culture, mostly in the form of the image of Christ himself. The tabernacle that enclosed the sacred scripture in the Jewish temple now housed the Host of Holy Communion, the symbolic representation of the body of Christ. The crucifix adorned the space above the altar as an object of particular veneration. Does this veneration imply that the figure of Christ sometimes became in itself a phallic icon? The idea becomes more plausible when we take account of the hundreds of Renaissance churches that claimed to house the Holy Prepuce, the foreskin of Christ. At least thirteen of them are reputed to survive today. These especially potent relics were relied upon to enhance women's fertility exactly in the manner of ancient phallic icons in Greece and Rome. One of the most well known of them, watched over by the monks of the Abbey Church at Chartres, has been credited with thousands of miraculous pregnancies.

Or consider the frequency with which the altars of Christian churches were built to contain hidden pagan phalli. While surveying the damage done by World War II bombing to an old English church, Professor Geoffrey Webb, a member of the Royal Commission on Historical Monuments, was amazed to find a large stone phallus hidden within the altar. Subsequent investigation revealed that roughly 90% of English churches built before the 14th century possessed similar concealed phalli. These phalli attest with particular clarity to the way in which Christianity did not simply replace paganism, but subsumed many pagan rituals and symbols, repackaging them in its own idiom.

3
Why Sex Is Such a Touchy Subject

A frequently heard question about Freud asks why he chose to focus his theories so exclusively on sexuality. Surely sex is only one among many dimensions of our lives, yet Freud seems to have been downright obsessed with it. It was this issue more than any other that led to the break between Freud and his gifted protégé, Carl Jung, at one time the undisputed heir-apparent of Freud's legacy. Jung complained that the master's overemphasis on sex obscured other key aspects of the human condition, not least spiritual and religious life. Freud's own answer to this challenge is audible in an old story that I first heard from the Harvard psychologist Henry Murray, who claimed to have it from Jung himself. When asked the reason for his preoccupation with sex, Freud replied that early in his career his search for the origins of human motivation led him to three main candidates: sex, power, and aggression. Why seize upon sex? Because when he would talk to people about power and violence, they would nod thoughtfully, retain a proper academic demeanor, and murmur guarded expressions of curiosity or skepticism. But whenever he spoke about sexuality, there was hell to pay. The mere raising of the topic sparked outbursts of passionate indignation and vigorous protest. Freud took this rise in temperature as a sure sign that he was on the right track.

Murray's story illustrates Freud's penchant for deliberately cutting against the grain of prevailing opinions (and hints at the enjoyment he took in the commotion it stirred up). It also recalls Freud's clinical procedure of pursuing analysis most insistently precisely at the point of the patient's resistance. But the story frames a deeper question: Why is sex such a ticklish business? Across widely varying cultures and throughout different epochs of history, sexuality has very conspicuously been subject to elaborate restrictions and taboos. Sex is surrounded by a special sensitivity. It is the object of our most ready embarrassments, our most familiar guilt, our most biting sense of shame. Why? What is it about sex that gives us so much trouble? The question was to occupy Freud throughout his career.

How We Look to Martians

Human attitudes toward sex are truly something of a mystery. Imagine the reaction of Martian visitors to Earth. Reporting back to their fellow Martians, they would describe a strange race of two-legged creatures, members of the dominant earth species, the majority of whom regard the attainment of physical pleasure as the primary aim of life. At the top of the list is the pleasure of copulation. So great is the satisfaction afforded by it that the words most associated with supreme pleasure—ecstasy, bliss, rapture—tend to be tinged with sexual overtones. A great deal of time is spent by earthlings in contemplating the prospects of sexual enjoyment, exorbitant effort is expended in making themselves attractive to potential partners, and enormous risks may be taken in the accomplishing of the act.

But then comes the really astonishing thing. Despite the cardinal place of sex in the pantheon of human pleasures and despite the intensity of the hunger it stimulates, sex is, of all human pleasures, the most subject to restriction. Our Martian visitor would thus be forced to report this curious paradox: Where the pleasure derived from sex leads one to expect that human beings would seek to maximize their opportunities for it, the reality appears to be precisely the opposite. Sexual activity seems everywhere to be hemmed in by a host of controls and limitations. Indeed, the field of partners, potentially as wide as the species itself, is generally whittled down to a single person, contact with whom requires both religious authorization and legal sanction.

Even with this solitary partner, indulgence in sexual behavior tends to be tightly circumscribed. Sex is usually confined to a single room of the household, so much so that the word *bedroom* can often pass as a synonym for sex. Sexual contact also tends to be relegated to the particular time of day just before going to sleep, the erotic equivalent of the "happy hour," though perhaps not as frequently enjoyed. Moreover, for most mating pairs, sex is limited to a number of fairly routinized actions and is completed in an amazingly brief time. According to Kinsey, the average couple completes intercourse in less than two minutes. Viewed from above, as a Martian would see them, human cities present a striking picture of sexual segregation in which the dwelling places of the vast majority of people are separated from ghettos of erotic hunger where sex is sold in lurid little corners—the "red light districts." In Boston, it's called the "Combat Zone." In Baltimore, it's "The Block." It is difficult to escape the impression, as Freud remarked, that society "will only permit sexual relationships on the basis of a solitary, indissoluble bond between one man and one woman, and that it does not like sexuality as a source of pleasure in its own right and is only prepared to tolerate it because there is so far no substitute for it as a means of propagating the human race."

From a Martian's point of view, it would be hard to see why we behave so differently with sex than we do with eating. Both are important bodily functions, motivated by powerful forces. Both are activities required for the survival of the species and both are rewarded by an intense yield of pleasure. Moreover, while satisfaction in both can be taken alone, both become immensely more enjoyable in the company of others. For the Martian, then, the question would be why we don't share sex the way we share pizza. Why is eating promoted to the status of public ceremony while sex is closeted away in shameful secrecy? Martian visitors would likely leave Earth scratching their heads over those funny humans for whom sex is such a problem. What, they'd be asking, is all the fuss about? The overall impression left by these circumstances is paradoxical indeed. Sex is at once the fondest dream of human pleasure and the point at which pleasure is most conspicuously refused. What are we to make of this conundrum?

From one vantage point, of course, the battery of legal, religious, and cultural restraints on sexual expression can be interpreted as the means for maintaining certain forms of social power and domination. By restricting access to satisfaction, one group lords it over another. Minors are prohibited from touching themselves or each other, women are removed from the company of men or may even be forced to undergo surgical removal of sexually sensitive tissue, homosexuals are isolated and persecuted. But this explanation in terms of social control can't tell the whole story, for limitations placed on sexual behavior, while surely greater for some people than for others, are nevertheless fairly universal, affecting pretty much everybody, even those at the top of the heap.

A similar objection can be made to another promising approach. Surely an important part of the answer to the riddle of sexual repression concerns the fact that sex leads to babies, and babies raise the sensitive question of inheritance. If property-owning males are to control the handover of their worldly goods and power to the next generation, then they will require some proof of their own paternity. What better way to vouchsafe one's own lineage than carefully to restrict the sexual behavior of women? Lock them up in the household, prohibit them from uncontrolled public exposure, perhaps even hire a cadre of eunuchs to guard them. It's been done. It's still being done. Yet it is hard to see how control of sexual pleasure can be reduced solely to control of insemination. If women suffer greater sexual restriction, it can hardly be said that men enjoy unfettered license. Gauged in relation to the force of their desire, the majority of men around the world are almost as constrained in their sexual opportunities as women. Then again, there is homosexuality. If sexual repression were merely a matter of regulating fertilization, then homosexual behavior ought to pose no problem at all. Far from being condemned, same-sex relations would presumably be, as they were in ancient Greece, a welcome and even highly prized alternative to heterosexuality.

The stubborn fact is that just about everyone is subject to constraint when it comes to sex. But why? Is there something in us that turns aside from too much pleasure, something that cannot tolerate too much happiness? Is there perhaps something about the very nature of sex that invites repression? "Sometimes one seems to perceive," Freud speculates at one point, "that it is not only the pressure of civilization but something in the nature of the [sexual] function itself which denies us full satisfaction and urges us along other paths."

Unknown to Ourselves

Perhaps it is worth noting in passing that sexual repression is not the only paradoxical aspect of human happiness. A little reflection reveals some curious things. Consider, for example, how frequently we respond to a typical greeting —"Hi, how are you?"—with a curt and innocent "Fine!" Are we always so fine? It is not hard to suspect that this "Fine!", this reflex of public politesse, is very often nothing but a graceful mini-fib, a socially necessary lie. But what is its function? In part, of course, it is an appropriate answer to the question. An answer that tells us almost nothing is the perfect rejoinder to a question that is not really a question. When we ask "How are you?" we are not seriously interested in an answer. Were someone to respond with a lengthy exposition of the day's little triumphs or disasters, we would have to think that person had misunderstood our customs of greeting. Far from being an invitation to authentic exchange in which two people would actually discover something about one another, the "How are you?–Fine!" routine actually serves to sidestep any real encounter. While appearing to be an effort to learn something about another person, its real function is almost precisely the opposite. The quick and easy exchange "How are you?–Fine!" greases the cogs of social intercourse and allows us to slip past one another with a minimum of genuine interaction.

But there is something else to be said about such thoughtless greetings. When we wave aside another's pseudo-query with a flippant "Fine!" we excuse the other from the burden of our lives' gritty details, many of which are less than agreeable. Social grace requires that we hide our troubles from others. Yet we also hide them from ourselves. Indeed, perhaps this is the most gratifying thing about vapid social banter: We lose ourselves in it. In midst of the most routine and familiar chitchat—the weather, the neighborhood gossip, the box scores—we become momentarily oblivious to our private miseries. Let's face it: The tissue of mundane social life is carefully cultivated in no small part for the purpose of shoring up a falsely inflated sense of well-being. The fact is that most people will say they're fine when asked, including (and maybe especially) a great number who aren't fine at all. But this implies an odd disjunction between our real state of well-being or lack thereof, and what we are willing to admit about it, even to ourselves. We are very often not as happy as we claim to be.

And with that, we're firmly back on Freudian ground. The disjunction I'm pointing to between our everyday unhappiness and our usual understatement of it is ultimately related to the rift between consciousness and the unconscious. We may be living one thing, but we'll say another. It is no accident that the point at issue concerns the level of our general sense of satisfaction. If Freud is right, repression is precisely what allows us to misrecognize our own desire and the degree to which it has been fulfilled. Repression hides us from ourselves. Nor should we be surprised that an effect of the unconscious shows itself on the plane of such mundane interaction. Where better to work its trick of self-deception? The Freudian unconscious and its mantle of repression is hardly an exotic and exceptional occurrence. On the contrary, the greatest unconsciousness may be maintained by the most banal and familiar activities.

"Give me a break!" the skeptic may now say. "After hearing you go on about it these last pages, I'm more than ever convinced that Freud was overboard about sex. Not everybody is going around with an unsatisfied case of the hots. Most people aren't panting after the wild sex that Freud imagines and, by the way, they're pretty happy as they are."

One of the main problems with this objection concerns its own image of sex. It implicitly supposes, as many of us do, that when Freud speaks of sexual repression, what he has in mind is prohibition of the most flagrant and juicy acts of copulation. And so he does, but not only that. When Freud wrestles with the meaning of sexual repression, he is referring to bodily pleasures that we might grant to one another that are by no means limited to raw copulation. Especially in later works like *Civilization and Its Discontents*, sexual repression is thought to affect a good deal more than explicitly erotic behavior. It includes, for example, the sort of body contact that other members of the primate family enjoy every day. As Jane Goodall and others have shown, the higher apes spend extravagant amounts of time in close physical contact with one another—grooming, cleaning, patting, stroking. Such contact plays an indispensable role in the health and happiness of individuals and in the cohesion of the group.

A sidelong glance at our jungle relatives helps remind us how very little physical contact we have with one another. Indeed, by the standard of physical intimacy enjoyed by our closest animal kin, we are virtually starved for touch. Even to touch knees under the table or to accidentally brush against a colleague in the hallway generally triggers a mild but electric sense of transgression, an immediate recoil, and a hasty, awkward, and fumbling apology. If we define sexuality in the larger sense to include everything that might be called emotionally significant touching of skin to skin, we have a more accurate idea of what Freud means by sexual repression.

We also see better why he thinks that it is a problem. For unless we suppose ourselves to be very different from our primate cousins, we can only conclude that our own deficit of touching constitutes an immense and painful deprivation. It is precisely such a deprivation that Freud has in mind when he ties civilization to inevitable "discontents." Entry into civilized life requires renunciation of many sorts of gratification, prime among them a greater degree of physical intimacy with one another. In fact, far from it being the case that the human beings need less body contact than other primates, isn't it more likely that the need for reassuring touch in the more intelligent and emotionally volatile human being is, if anything, even greater?

From a Freudian point of view, it is a measure of the effectiveness of sexual repression that what might otherwise be a natural predisposition to touch has become an occasion for anxiety and repugnance. For most people, the idea of rubbing skin to skin with a relative stranger, or even with someone with whom they are fairly familiar, is distinctly uninviting. One reason is that in the absence of a controlling context in which contact is explicitly authorized and limited—in a doctor's office, a barbershop, a shoe store—any sort of touch is liable to be construed as erotic. It is as if, once subject to the strictures of repression, the pleasure of physical contact cannot be reapproached without unleashing the full force of a pent-up need. Any touching threatens to set loose a little flood of erotic longing. It's all or nothing. Isn't it for the same reason that the word "sex," rather than evoking a range of touching from the caring and affectionate to the fully sensual, tends immediately to call up images of intercourse? The hungry imagination skips the foreplay and goes for the climax. Which returns us to the skeptic's objection of a moment ago. Ironically, the common concept of sex, dominated by X-rated images, is itself a product of the culture of sexual repression.

For Freud, the reaction of anxiety elicited by unexpected touch is in itself an indicator of the presence of repression. Were we not at some level restraining ourselves against our own desire to touch and be touched we would not be, well, so "touchy" about it. But Freud also thinks that there is another, more indirect, but equally telling evidence of the toll exacted by repression: the pervasive use of drugs. In Freud's view, the renunciation of basic animal satisfactions that is required by civilization leaves us with a kind of pleasure-debt to our own bodies. Reliance on the numbing effects of drugs is one of the primary means by which human beings compensate themselves for the sacrifices demanded by civilized life.

These days, amid the din of the much-trumpeted "war on drugs," we are liable to forget that the use of various intoxicating agents has always played an immense role in human life. In fact, drug use is so central a part of human existence that chemically induced intoxication could plausibly compete with two-leggedness, the gift of speech, or awareness of death as a good definition of the human animal. We know of virtually no human culture for which the ingestion of mood-altering substances is not routinely practiced, often sanctified by religious ritual. Moreover, the quantity of drugs consumed appears to increase in fairly direct proportion with increasing social organization and complexity. From prehistoric times, human beings have turned to a great litany of intoxicating herbs, fruits, fungi, and their derivatives. Then there was ethyl alcohol, the production and distillation of which was among the most archaic human achievements.

With the emergence of the modern age, however, the appetite for drugs seems to have exploded. In the seventeenth and eighteenth centuries Europeans discovered the gratifications of coffee (caffeine) and tobacco (nicotine). At the same time, they vastly increased the consumption of processed sugar, the mood-altering effects of which ought not to be underestimated. Chocolate, anyone? The nineteenth and early twentieth centuries saw the creation of an ever-lengthening shelf of analgesics and anesthetics, the miracle pain relievers that are increasingly part of the daily life in every industrialized nation. And with the dawn of the new millennium, the age of Prozac, a new generation of expressly psychological drugs has burgeoned forth, promising an unprecedented capacity to create an artificially induced sense of well-being. In contemporary society, most people habitually use multiple intoxicants, rotating their effects from morning to night. Collectively, a country like the United States consumes a veritable mountain of intoxicating substances each day. The enormity of drug consumption, Freud contends, matches the level of frustration and alienation imposed by the process of "civilization."

Higher Love

How, then, does Freud answer the riddle of why human beings so severely limit and distort the satisfaction of their sexual needs? Given the magnitude of unhappiness inflicted by sexual repression, it might come as something of a surprise that Freud declares it to be an absolute necessity. The reason, he says, is "economic," by which he refers to the requirements of psychical energy. To accomplish the myriad tasks called for by civilized life, enormous quantities of energy must be marshaled. But from what source is it to be drawn? Freud's answer is sexuality. The sexual response must be dammed up by repression to provide a reservoir of energy available for other purposes. The energy that might otherwise be expended in the satisfaction of the erotic drive is thus siphoned off and redeployed elsewhere in nonsexual activities that are indispensable for the social and intellectual life of a human community. In constraining the sexual life of its members, therefore,

> civilization is obeying the laws of economic necessity, since a large amount of the psychical energy which it uses for its own purposes has to be withdrawn from sexuality. In this respect civilization behaves towards sexuality as a people or a stratum of its population does which has subjected another one to its exploitation.

The energy of libido is redirected by repression into the desexualized employments necessary for civilized life. Freud calls this process "sublimation." It implies an almost infinite plasticity of the sexual drive, such that it is capable of radical transformations. We have already seen how such transformation is possible. The potentiality for sublimation is prepared for in the displacements of the sexual drive in infancy. Unable to discharge itself in the organ system and function for which it is ultimately destined, the sexual drive is poured into other, already existing channels of need and satisfaction—primarily those of nutrition and excretion. Libido is from the very outset a nomadic force, happy to pitch its tent in foreign territory. Sublimation merely exploits this original dislocation of libido, assigning to it ever new objects and aims.

Under the influence of sublimation, the energy of the sexual life is pressed into the service of desexualized ends, chief among them the pursuit of intellectual interests. In this way, Freud explains the double meaning of the word *passion*, a word by which we refer not only to erotic obsession but also to any consuming interest or concern. The classical example is that of the artist whose libido is satisfied in crafting an erotic image rather than actually having sex. But sublimation is equally operative in the mathematician who is fascinated by the solution of an equation, the aircraft engineer who loses track of the time while engrossed in designing a better propeller, or the architect who wakes up in the middle of the night having dreamed the design of his or her latest construction—in all of these instances the ardor of creative endeavor is drawn from the sexual drive. In sublimation, sexuality in repression provides the animating fuel for absorbing and inventive vocations.

In one respect at least, Freud's theory of sublimation is by no means completely novel. A very similar view is put forward by Plato in his *Symposium*. In this dialogue, the priestess Diotima tells the young Socrates that the power of Eros may take either of two forms, physical or spiritual. On the level of the physical, Eros is attracted by corporeal beauty. It seeks the coupling of bodies with one another and issues in the production of children. Yet Eros is also the animating power of the soul. It is Eros that moves the soul toward increasingly abstract forms of beauty and brings to birth the spirit-children of art, literature, religion, and philosophy.

If Platonic Eros is unmistakably akin to the shape-shifting of Freudian libido in sublimation, the Freudian outlook is nevertheless separated by a great chasm from the Platonic one. For Plato, there is a natural if not quite inevitable progression from the physical to the spiritual, from the material to the intellectual. It is a progression that is suggested and even prodded along by the process of physical aging. With the passage of years, the body weakens and withers, stripping the soul of its earthly sheaf. In the course of aging, the soul is weaned away from its bondage to the body. Like a space capsule, launched into orbit atop rocket boosters that will burn out and fall back to earth, the soul is eventually spun free from its corporeal husk and hurled into a transcendent dimension. In this way, Eros arranges for its own graduation from the body.

The Freudian prospect is not nearly so optimistic in reckoning of the ultimate destiny of human life. Nor does it suppose that body and soul work so harmoniously toward the same end. For Freud, the life of the mind is possible only on the basis of a deep alienation in which the animating vigor of sexuality is enlisted in purposes that are essentially foreign to it. In this way the body is ultimately pitted against itself as its own vital energies are seized upon and pressed into the service of vast labors that no animal would ever undertake. Freud thus envisages the spiritual flowering of sublimation only at the price of a splitting of the human being against itself.

In sublimation, the energy of repressed libido is reinvested in desexualized objects and activities. However, repression also transforms relationships to persons. In what Freud calls "aim-inhibited libido," the originally sexual link of each human being to others of its kind is converted into a range of entirely new forms of emotional relationship. In fact, this alchemy of repression is the origin of many of the heart-skipping, tear-wrenching waves of feeling that we call "emotions." Sentiments of affection, tenderness, friendship, loyalty, and sympathy are traced by Freud back to their roots in sexuality, or better, to the sexual feeling *we would have experienced* were it not for the influence of repression. If he is correct, then we would expect to find the greatest effusion of emotion in those relationships where sexuality is most completely refused. And something of the sort does indeed seem to be the case. Nowhere are sensations of affection and tenderness more pronounced than in the bosom of the family, where the prohibition against incest utterly rules out sexual relationship.

The transformation of sex into affection takes place with special force in the relation to the mother. Understood psychoanalytically, the unique tonality of lump-in-the-throat emotion that often surrounds the memory of one's mother is the result of the fact, not only that a sexual relation with the mother is prohibited, but that it was once a reality. A reality? This, of course, is the core postulate of Freud's theory of infantile sexuality: the idea that the infant's relation to the mother is essentially sexual. And given the preceding qualifications about the meaning of the term *sexual* we can see better what he means. "Sex," again, need not be limited to copulation, but includes a whole range of emotionally significant touching. That we tend to think of sex in narrower, more "explicit" terms says more about us than about mothers and infants. What Freud has in mind when he claims a sexual bond to the mother, aside from the way that libido is invested in the satisfactions of suckling, is that the infant enjoys a blissful access to the mother's body. The infant is tied to the mother by an emotionally charged flesh-bond of a sort that will not be enjoyed again until marriage, and then only in an enormously reduced and compromised form. An archaic memory of this flesh-intimacy with the mother will be unconsciously carried forward into every subsequent love relation. The bond to the mother is thus the hidden heartbeat of all love. Mother love is the very archetype of nostalgia.

Freud's notion of aim-inhibited libido opens a window on the hidden dynamics of family feeling, but also on special kinds of relationship outside the family. Team spirit is a good case in point—the sorts of camaraderie and fellow feeling that bind together members of an athletic team, a platoon of soldiers, members of a string quartet, or any cadre of people working in close coordination toward a common purpose. Sexual abstinence is famously associated with such groups. Simple abstinence, however, is not the only means for producing the effect of group bonding that Freud has in mind.

An extension of Freud's idea in this instance is the way in which team spirit may coalesce for a same-sex group by means of degrading the opposite sex. It is a phenomenon that is especially clear in the case of young men for whom sexist jokes and stories of sexual conquests (many no doubt greatly exaggerated) help to solidify an emotional link between them. Something similar can occur in the strip bar, where the patrons' enjoyment of each other's company is enhanced by the presence of the stripper. In these cases, a quantity of erotic energy is withdrawn from the opposite sex and enlisted in a fraternal bond. Less obvious is the way the same group of young men may be bonded together by the transmutation of unacknowledged homosexuality. Less obvious except for anyone who, like me, has survived the locker room antics after a high school boys' swim team victory: the ceaseless bouts of arm punching and towel snapping, prankish clothes thievery, and "wedgies" (a favorite trick among adolescent boys, named for the embarrassing condition that results when an unsuspecting victim's underpants are yanked up from behind).

The theory of aim-inhibited libido also sheds some interesting light on the controversy over gays in the military. The current atmosphere of disapproval contrasts very markedly to legends from the ancient world about armies composed of pairs of lovers, legends that probably have at least some basis in fact. As we learn from Plato and others, it was thought that homosexual couples would make ideal soldiers, each seeking to impress his lover with displays of strength, courage, and sacrifice. Ironically (in view of the fact that I suspect very few modern colonels have made much study of Freud), current objections to gays in the ranks are, at least from one point of view, a fair application of Freudian principles. The most common complaint is that the presence of gays damages *ésprit de corps* (the French term seems to be a favorite in this context). This is exactly what the Freudian concept of aim-inhibited libido would lead us to expect. A particular kind of chumminess between men—a chumminess that is tinged with an undercurrent of aggression, that opens the door for abuses like the "hazing" of recruits, but that also allows for considerable displays of loyalty and group solidarity—can only be maintained by keeping utterly at bay all question of homosexual desire. The Freudian point is that this chummy bond *is* homosexuality, though altered under the influence of repression. From this point of view, the Clinton policy of "don't ask, don't tell" was particularly ingenious. It enabled gay men to remain in the ranks while also keeping awareness of the whole issue of homosexuality sufficiently unconscious.

Of course, none of this is to say that greater acceptance of gays would lead to the sort of breakdown of morale that the generals fear. On the contrary, it might eventually lead to an easing of aggressive tensions and to a new form of group feeling. What is produced by the current regime of repression is not the only possible group cohesion, but merely a particular form or inflection of it.

Who Needs an Ego Anyway?

Freud insists upon the necessity of sexual repression, but it remains to be determined how exactly such repression happens. A common misconception holds that repression is solely a product of social sanctions, internalized by the agency of conscience that Freud called the "superego." Were it not for the killjoy influence of puritanical society, it is supposed, we would have no trouble in expressing the full range of our desires. While there is no doubt some truth in this view, it tends to obscure Freud's more original and far-reaching insight, namely, that the greatest obstacle to the fulfillment of desire is not other people but we ourselves. Whatever the repressive influence of the superego, at least as great is that of the ego. In fact, the repressive potential of the superego, which will submit the tormented ego to the punishing voice of outside authorities, is built upon a foundation of self-alienation, a split internal to the subject itself, the cleavage between the ego and the id.

What, then, are ego and id? Freud's original German gives a better clue than James Strachey's latinized translation. Ego and id are *Ich und Es*—I and it. The function of the ego is to distinguish between what is me and what is not me. Put roughly, the ego is my self-image. It is what gives me a unifying sense of agency for action, and what enables me to separate in perception what is familiar and reassuring to me from what is foreign and threatening. As such, the ego is partly conscious; indeed, consciousness is essentially an ego function. However, a great portion of the ego remains unconscious. A very considerable part of what makes us who we are, our sense of character and identity, remains outside our awareness and control, the product of long-engrained and thoughtless habit.

If part of the ego is unconscious, there are also parts of myself that are even more deeply inaccessible to consciousness and which deserve a separate designation—those aspects of ourselves that Freud calls "id." The id, says Freud, is that archaic reservoir of impulses out of which the ego originally grew as a separate structure serving special purposes. The ego functions to categorize things and persons in the outside world (those with whom I identify versus those with whom I conflict), but even more importantly the ego discriminates between contending forces of my own desire (those of my impulses on which I will act versus those that I will refuse and repress). Fundamental to this conception of psychic structure is Freud's assumption that we are animated by a great heterogeneity of impulses. We are, at some basic level of ourselves, a chaos of conflicting urges. Ego thus refers to the restricted economy of impulse that grounds my feeling of having a stable and predictable identity. The ego selects from a range of impulse energies and leaves the others behind.

"Id" names that remainder of my own urges and incipient acts that have been excluded from the ego and held in repression.

So what sorts of repressed impulses are we talking about? Freud identifies two main classes: aggressive and sexual. It is by definition not easy to be more specific—we are, after all, dealing with impulses that remain *unconscious.* To get a rough sense, take a scene from Jean-Paul Sartre's classic novel of existentialism, *Nausea.* The novel's protagonist, Roquentin, is seated at a café with a rather nerdy and obnoxious companion. Roquentin is bored and sickened by the fellow's idiotic babbling. Suddenly, weary to death of this annoying nebbish, he feels that he might plunge a cheese knife into the man's eye. Now, here's something most people haven't done! Something most people would be incapable of doing. But is it something we are incapable of *wanting to do*? Freud's contention is that there is in all of us a deeply sadistic streak, a cruel and vengeful brute who would gleefully gouge out an eye with a cheese knife. But we have buried that monstrous self beneath a layer of repression. What is unusual about Roquentin (and what makes him emblematic of an existentialist sensibility) is the margin of freedom he has in the moment, a freedom borne partly of boredom, partly of despair, that enables him to have access to an outrageous impulse that would not ordinarily have risen to consciousness.

What is the nature of the barrier that usually keeps such impulses from becoming conscious? What is the agency of repression? Part of it, surely, is the voice of conscience, the activity of the superego. But another very significant part is the ego itself—the whole machinery of our everyday image of ourselves, composed of a long-habituated pattern of feelings, perceptions, judgments, and responses. If the superego is the punishing voice of guilt that torments us for a violent outburst or that gnaws at our guts for even being tempted, the ego is the timeworn sense we have of ourselves that prevents us from even becoming conscious of our own desires for violence. Of the two, the ego is the more primitive and fundamental structure of repression. The superego kicks in, we might say, when the more basic controlling influence of the ego fails to keep our impulses in check.

The impulses of the id also include sexual urges, and the repressive influence of the ego can be seen with special clarity in sexual orientation. Most people feel sexually disposed either toward men or toward women, but not both. Yet one of the cardinal postulates of Freud's psychoanalytic theory is that the vast majority of us are, at bottom, much more bisexual than we are willing or able to acknowledge. This means that somewhere between our deeper, bisexual nature and our everyday sense of our sexual selves the distorting force of repression has intervened. For Freud, the primary evidence for this assumption of an underlying bisexuality was supplied by his patients' dreams, symptoms, and associations. He was also impressed by the fact that some individuals undergo changes in sexual orientation, sometimes in response to changes in their life situation, sometimes spontaneously. Then again, there was the evidence of cultural variation in sexual mores. Particularly striking were the homosexual practices of ancient Greece—more accurately called *bisexual*, for most of the men involved in homosexual contact were also sexually active with women. The fact of such cultural differences strongly suggested the sexual orientation is not a biological given, but is largely a product of social and psychological factors.

A psychoanalytic perspective does not deny that sexual orientation may have some biological determinants. Having begun his career as a neuroanatomist, Freud was very far from believing that personality and character are wholly independent of biological factors. Nevertheless, in theorizing about the nature of the ego, Freud's real interest centered on psychological factors, the ways in which our biological disposition may be constrained, distorted, or derailed altogether by psychological needs. Prime among those needs are the demands for stability, consistency, and predictability. The structure of the ego is an attempt to answer to those needs.

When the ego fails in its regulatory task, the result is an outbreak of anxiety. Freud's most basic definition of anxiety is the felt experience of repressed impulses threatening to reenter the ego that has excluded them. What is felt as anxiety is therefore nothing other than the force of desire itself, but desire that has been submitted to repression. Here we can see an intersection between psychoanalysis and existentialism. For the existentialist tradition, too, the human experience of anxiety and its meaning are absolutely central. What Freud theorizes as the upsurge of repressed urges, Sartre depicts as the dizziness of freedom in the face of unlimited possibilities. Both result in anxiety. As Roquentin leaves the café after having contemplated stabbing his companion, he is afflicted with a deepening sense of panic and disgust. He feels himself increasingly cut off from other people, increasingly a stranger, even to himself. He has committed no crime. He has *done* nothing at all. His only transgression was to have violated the strictures of his own ego. Merely by imagining himself capable of something radically contrary to his own image of himself, he is plunged into anxiety.

> I get up, everything spins about me.… As I am leaving, I notice that I have kept the dessert-knife in my left hand. I throw it on my plate which makes a clinking noise. I cross the room in the midst of total silence.… I don't know where to go, I remain planted beside the cardboard chef. I don't need to turn round to know that they are watching me through the windows; they are looking at my back with surprise and disgust; they thought that I was like them, that I was a man, and I deceived them. All of a sudden, I lost the appearance of a man and they saw a crab escaping backwards from that all too human room.

Described psychoanalytically, Roquentin's anxiety was triggered by the upsurge of a murderous impulse that he had up to then managed to keep at bay. Anxiety may similarly result from a threat to the ego's sexual organization. For many straight men, to enter a gay bar or to be sexually propositioned by another man would provoke an immediate attack of anxiety. Here, too, anxiety results from the way in which the well-worn mold of the ego has been violated by the approach of something foreign to it. The key point, however, is to recognize that the "foreign invader" in this case is not the homosexual who makes the proposition. He is just the occasion for the real "invader"—the straight man's own homosexual desire. Were there nothing at stake for him, were it not for the internal pressure of his own disavowed homosexuality, he would presumably deal with the approach of a gay man as casually as he would a request for a cigarette. His anxiety is a measure of the strength of his homosexual impulses and the severity of his own effort to repress them. Psychologically speaking, the worst dangers faced by the ego come from within.

In explaining these points of Freudian theory to my students, I often have recourse to the example of a little cross-dressing. I invite them to imagine what it would be like for me to come to class with some gender-bending alteration of my familiar professor's garb. How about if I were to show up wearing pink tights and a nifty tutu? Or, perhaps being a little more discreet, I could reveal, just under my tweedy jacket, a lacy brassiere. My first point in such examples is to get the students to imagine my own anxiety in arriving on campus in this sort of get-up, an anxiety that would be only partly related to the certainty that I would soon afterwards receive an invitation to visit the Provost's office, or the University Counseling Center, or both. Along with the anxiety of scandalizing other people would be that of being a scandal to myself. By violating my accustomed profile of gender identity, I would have precipitated a crisis for my own ego.

There are some other things to be learned from my little scenarios. As you can imagine, my examples invariably elicit from the students a round of distinctly edgy laughter, a reaction that, however "natural" it may seem to be, is nevertheless very interesting. It teaches us two things, the first one related to the laughter itself. Such laughter is a release of anxiety. Indeed, from Freud's point of view, laughter is quite typically related to anxiety. In one of his most neglected works, his 1905 book on *Jokes and Their Relation to the Unconscious*, Freud argues that a certain discharge of anxiety is always an ingredient in comedy. Why? Because the mechanism of most jokes depends in one way or another on the ambush of expectations. Puns, for example, short-circuit a play of meaning between words, replacing one expected meaning by another, unexpected one. So, too, in my cross-dressing example, the laughter is provoked by the appearance of something totally unanticipated and incongruous. Such violations of expectation are inevitably violations of the smooth functioning of the ego. In fact, the regular and predictable management of expectations is the most basic function of the ego. In a certain sense, ego identity is nothing but behaving according to expectation.

The other thing we learn is something about the social nature of the ego. By that I mean the way in which maintaining the identity of the ego is always a cooperative enterprise. Other people act toward me in more or less predictable ways, and I, in turn, am expected to perform my accustomed role. In this way, we reinforce each other's ego. Ultimately, in fact, the ego cannot be considered as an isolated structure that belongs merely to one person. What Freud called "ego" is rather the structural effect in me of a tissue of social relations that includes pretty much everyone else I live, work, and play with. The good regard of other people constantly buttresses my sense of who I am. Likewise, my looks and behavior help stabilize for others around me their own well-worn sense of themselves. For me to appear in class dressed like a drag queen therefore breaks an implicit set of rules that binds us all to one another. It constitutes a kind of breach of contract, not just internally, between my behavior and my own ego, but also externally, between myself and my students, all of whom are doing their best to keep their own ego intact.

The Fictive Self and Its Objects

By functioning as a distorting barrier between my conscious sense of myself and the chaos of my unconscious impulses, the ego is a falsification of my own inner reality. The ego is a kind of lie I've told to myself. Or better, the ego rehearses to me a lie about myself that I continually accept as true. The ego constantly generates two main illusions. The first is that of denying its own character as a psychological construction. Call it "the illusion of subjective necessity." It is the reassuring illusion that I am not an arbitrary, piecemeal, and improvised being, liable to change at any moment, but rather a firm and stable necessity. The ego acts like the leader of a bogus religious cult who convinces his followers that his own scribblings ought to be taken as Holy Writ. In somewhat similar fashion, one of the main effects of the ego is that of convincing me, as if the ego were a sort of internal hypnotist, that the particulars of my character are perfectly natural and unchangeable, that they are brute and simple givens, like my height or my shoe size. The purpose of the ego is thus to provide a regulation of impulses that requires no thought or deliberation. The payoff is an internal regulatory system that "runs by itself," like a kind of psychological autopilot. The ego predefines the patterns of my behavior and enables me to feel that I am a stable and consistent being, that I am a coherent unity and not a chaos. Having an ego signifies that I am a person, and defines what sort of person I am, without my ever having to think about it.

The ego's illusion of subjective necessity is well illustrated by the phenomenon of gender identity. Most people immediately and unreflectively feel themselves to be masculine or feminine. There is no sense of having *chosen* a gender. Gender rather appears to be something merely given, something we simply *are*. Yet it is not difficult to suspect that this sense of my gender as a natural necessity is trumped up. When we review the countless behaviors in which gender is expressed, some grand and obvious, others so minute and fleeting as to be almost undetectable, it is hard to escape the impression that masculinity and femininity are like different dance steps. Sexual identity is defined in large part by a repertoire of gestures and patterned responses, many of them culture specific. The different way men and women typically look at their fingernails is a familiar, almost clichéd, example. Men tend to look at their fingernails by turning the palm uppermost and curling the fingers into a half fist, often drawing the hand somewhat closer to their face as if to get a good inspection. Women, by contrast, look at the back of their hand with the fingers fanned out flat, typically moving the hand away from their face slightly, the way older people who have forgotten their reading glasses might look at a menu. Gender-typed patterning of this sort could be cataloged for thousands of behaviors—masculine versus feminine ways of getting into a car, picking up a glass, taking a bite of a sandwich, brushing hair, etc. There are times when we deliberately exaggerate such gender-identified behaviors for some effect, comic or otherwise.

With these sorts of behavior patterns in mind, we are led to conclude that gender is something like an actor's performance. Being masculine or feminine is merely a matter of *miming* the right role. The point of such performance is to signal our gender to others, but also to ourselves. Indeed, perhaps it is we ourselves who need to get the message more than anyone. Yet the fact remains that in being masculine or feminine we don't feel ourselves to be playacting. Ninety-nine percent of the time we are wholly unaware of any sort of posing. Why? In Freudian terms, the answer is the ego. It was in part for this reason that Freud claimed that the ego is largely unconscious. The ego is the sedimented history of my choices, yet is so in such a way that I have forgotten my own role in making them. The ego is a structure that I myself have built, yet which now appears to me as given by nature.

Theoretically, the ego thus faces us with this paradox: On the one hand, the ego is not something we are born with, it is not a biological given, but is open to the shaping influences of culture, family structure, and idiosyncrasies of personal history. On the other hand, the ego is able to form the central framework of our personal character and affords us the sense that we are not continually improvising ourselves, that we are not merely *acting* but really *are* someone, precisely because it is not something we are free to alter willy-nilly, at any moment. Getting rid of such a sense of contingency and thus closing the space of possibility for acting differently from the way I have in the past is the most basic function of repression.

Coordinated with this first illusion of the ego is a second one—what we might call, in tandem with the first, the "illusion of objective reality." To recognize it, we can return to sexual orientation. By virtue of ego structure, an underlying bisexuality is channeled into this or that sexual orientation. It is therefore the structure of my ego that will establish the basic parameters of my desire, defining the objects toward which I will gravitate and the acts from which I will derive gratification. The objects of my love are mirrors of my own psychological structure. Yet we are continually subject to the illusion that desirability and repugnance are merely features of the objects themselves. Who or what we love seems to us a matter determined by the intrinsic qualities of things in the world. Such is the illusion of objective reality created by the ego. The ego is like an eye that sees everything except itself. I always have the certainty that it is the object itself that draws me by virtue of some attribute(s) of its own. This illusion is particularly powerful in the case of love and sexual attraction, in which the face and body features of the beloved become so magnetic.

In accordance with the ego's "objective" illusion, objects that conform to and reinforce the structure of the ego appear to me as lovable objects. The illusory effect is even clearer in the case of objects of hate. When people or things in the world arouse the repressed passions of the id, they may elicit a virulent hatred. This is the phenomenon Freud called "projection." In projection, I find in others what I have repressed in myself—and despise them for it. To illustrate, we can return to the man propositioned by a homosexual. The gay man's approach triggers a flood of anxiety, caused by the way in which this unexpected situation calls upon the straight man's own homosexuality. One strategy for managing that anxiety is therefore to make sure that all homosexuality stays in the other. In effect, the straight man now uses rejection of the homosexual other as a means to reinforce his own barriers of repression. The homosexual now becomes a vile and disgusting thing: a queer, a fairy, a dirty faggot. By hating some vile thing outside itself, the threatened ego keeps any trace of the subject's own homosexuality at arm's length.

To eliminate all ambiguity, to show how utterly he rejects everything homosexual, it may even be necessary for the homophobic man to buttress verbal abuse with physical violence. In some cases the response can be positively murderous. So it was when Steven Mullins and Charles Butler led Billy Jack Gaither out of an Alabama bar in 1998, drove him to a remote country road, and beat him to death with an axe handle. When Gaither was dead, they burned his body atop a pile of cast-off tires. According to the sheriff's deputy in Coosa County, Mullins and Butler killed Billy Jack Gaither because he was gay. According to the psychoanalyst, they killed him because they couldn't bear acknowledging their own gayness. Gaither became the screen onto which his murderers' own homosexuality was projected. So intense was the anxiety Gaither aroused in them that the only escape appeared to be his destruction.

In projection, the other person is used as the repository for everything that cannot be accepted in the subject him- or herself. Projection demonizes the other. It is the primary mechanism of bigotry and prejudice. That its virulence can lead even to murder should not be surprising. The underlying issue for the threatened ego is one of life or death—its own. To lose one's ego is to lose one's self. The weak and defensive ego desperately needs objects of hatred over and against which it can establish itself as uncontaminated by the hateful substance of the other. Thus the Nazi walks taller in the face of cowering Jews, the Ku Klux Klansman bolsters his own sense of himself by persecuting blacks, the homophobic straight man feels himself to be more of a man by despising gays. Through it all, however, what is vilified in the other is an aspect of oneself. Hitler was haunted by the possibility of his own Jewish blood and insisted on being repeatedly tested. From this point of view, the horror of the Final Solution was a gigantic exercise of self-purgation. For Steven Mullins and Charles Butler, beating Billy Jack Gaither to death was a desperate attempt to secure their identity as straight men. In killing Gaither, they were, quite literally, trying to beat the homosexuality out of themselves.

Murderous though it may become, the hatred of projection is not at all an expression of mere brutishness. Projection has an inner structure that stems from its relation to enjoyment. What the bigot despises in the other—without ever knowing it as such—is their enjoyment. We can reread the history of persecution with this point in mind. Thus the pagan is condemned by Christians for continuing to indulge in pleasures that the pious have given up. The witch hunter seethes when he imagines the orgiastic Black Sabbath in which witches dance around a blazing fire and revel in fornication with the Devil. When the Jews are accused of being greedy and scheming, the charge conceals a secret envy of their wealth and intelligence. When the gay man is denounced for being promiscuous, his antagonists may be telling us less about homosexual cruising than about the frustrated state of their own sex lives.

To clarify a final point: Freud doesn't intend his theory of projection as a comprehensive account of human hatred. His claim is not that the energy of all hatred is somehow to be traced back to unconscious desire, repressed in oneself and attributed to the despicable other. Rage and hatred are the fruits of human torment, the bitter harvest of injustice and abuse. What Freud's theory does help to explain is how such hatred becomes attached to the familiar target groups of racism, sexism, or homophobia. The unconscious mechanism of repression and projection acts to provide objects even for feelings of rage that may not have their source in repressed desire. The object of projection—the Jew, the black, the gay—gathers and focuses hatred like an old sock that attracts to itself all the lint in a load of laundry.

Subversive Sexuality

"I detest you! I spit on you!" With this outburst, we have the quintessential expression of hatred—an expression whose form is by no means accidental. According to Freud, spitting has a special place and function in the psychology of hatred. Anger and frustration tend almost inevitably to assume the form of a compulsion to spit. Why? The reason follows from Freud's definition of the ego as formed around the body image. "The ego," says Freud, "is first and foremost a bodily ego; it is not merely a surface entity, but is itself the projection of a surface." The psychological function that will define the boundary line between what is me and not-me is modeled most primitively on the physical boundary between the interior and exterior of the body. The border between ego and id thus echoes the line that separates inner and outer. In consequence, what I take into myself and make my own by swallowing versus what I refuse by spewing it out of my mouth assumes a special psychological significance. Love and hate, tied to what the ego takes to be acceptable and consonant with itself versus what challenges and threatens it, become symbolized in the most primitive way by the opposition between taking in and spitting out. Spitting becomes the perfect emblem of projection. Something literally ejected from one's own body comes to signify the most abject and revolting substance.

In taking account of the role of the body image in the formation of the ego, we recognize more fully the aptness of calling the ego a self-image. We also see more deeply why Freud compared the formation of the ego with the Greek myth in which Narcissus was condemned to fall in love with his own reflection. Jacques Lacan makes this point with special clarity in his concept of the "mirror stage," the psychologically formative period in which the infant recognizes its own body unity. By means of the body image the infant realizes its own unity, but also its separateness from the mother with whom it was originally fused. The development of an ego is therefore the birth of psychological autonomy, the first declaration of independence from others.

To avoid anxiety, the ego needs to maintain a degree of relative constancy. It is a need that we see reflected in clothing. Each day, we rehearse a more or less familiar image of ourselves in the second skin of clothing. Continuous with the underlying function of the ego, the purpose of this carefully managed ensemble is not only to present a predictable impression to others, but even more importantly to present it to ourselves. As we have already seen, to depart too radically from our established style releases a discomforting anxiety, as if we had allowed the question to be reposed in the language of dress: Who am I really? What am I really capable of?

Like the body image on which it is modeled, the ego requires a semblance of unity and coherence. This means that anxiety, the signal of a threat to the ego, may be provoked in an especially direct way by phantasies of bodily violation or dismemberment. The fear of castration is one such phantasy. So, too, the toddler may develop anxious concern for the loss of its feces, as if the passing of its excrement raises the disturbing specter of losing a piece of itself. For the same reason, retaining the feces can become a means of psychological reassurance, a project of maintaining basic security.

The young child will continue to show signs of a special anxiety around violations of the body image well into grade school. Who hasn't seen an eight-year-old boy burst into the house after falling off a bicycle? A bleeding cut on the forehead has him whimpering but not yet crying. Until he catches sight of himself in the hallway mirror. He then erupts into a fit of all-out screaming. For a school-age child, the sight of the injury can be worse than the injury itself. Said otherwise, an injury to the body may be less painful than an injury to the ego. This view helps to explain the comfort children take from a Band-Aid. Its prime value in "making it all better" is merely to hide the site of violation. A Band-Aid replasters the rent surface of the body, making it merely *appear* better. The strategy works nevertheless because for the young child the ego is mostly a matter of appearances. Such judgment by appearance may endure well into adulthood. Many adults retain a horror of hypodermic needles, for example—another instance in which it is less the actual pain than the *idea* of bodily violation that is so hard to take.

The ego's need for unity and coherence also illuminates the reaction of disgust, itself a form of anxiety. Consider, first, the way in which disgust tends to be elicited by things that have no unitary contour. The typical objects of disgust tend not to be really "objects" at all but rather messy, amorphous blobs, puddles, and smears. Imagine some disgusting substance that has been neatly formed into a regular geometrical solid—say, a perfect sphere or cube. Is it not immediately less disgusting that way? From a psychoanalytic viewpoint, this means that things become disgusting when they symbolize, even in a purely formal sense, something contrary to the ego's ideal of unity.[1]

We ought also to note how the prime stimulants of disgust are substances emitted by the body—feces, urine, vomit, sweat, saliva, blood, pus, hair, even fingernail cuttings. Of course, such bodily exuviae are especially liable to provoke disgust when they are other people's. They threaten to violate the boundary that separates my ego from the body-ego of the other. We are disgusted when something belonging to the other, especially some intimate and private part of the other's substance, comes too close. But bodily fluids and wastes may be disgusting even when they are our own. Why? Because disgust may be elicited by anything that blurs the dividing line between the interior and the exterior of the body, the most primitive line separating me from what is not me. Vomit, feces, mucus, and so forth are obvious examples. Yet even food may become disgusting in this way. Held in one's mouth and chewed long enough—which means held long enough at the very threshold of inner and outer—even one's favorite food becomes nauseating. Disgust thus perfectly fits the Freudian definition of anxiety: it is the emotional consequence of a threat to the integrity of the ego.

[1]This discussion should recall the account of the unthinkable character of excrement in Chapter 2.

It is significant that the high-water mark for anxiety over bodily injury—a shot at the doctor's office, for instance—occurs in middle childhood. Before that time, the infant has not yet developed a sufficient ego-image to be anxious about a shot (it will react merely to the pain inflicted by a stranger). Later, the teenager will likely find the primitive anxiety over bodily integrity to be less pressing than the social anxiety that requires "cool" (they would rather be dead than be seen crying like a child). Most young adults will have graduated from both anxieties (he or she may still hate needles but will bear up bravely rather than give in to a fear now recognized as irrational). This evolution of attitudes reflects the maturing of the ego.

When the first sense of self begins to coalesce in the latter half of the infant's first year, the beginnings of the narcissistic stage, the contours of the ego are at their most primitive. This infantile distinction between self and other and the corresponding capacity of the infant to discriminate internally among its own feelings will tend toward crude, either–or alternatives. The young child will continue for some years to live in a world of all or nothing, black or white contrasts of good and evil. It is for this reason that the universe of children's fairy tales and cartoons is populated so conspicuously by heroes and villains. The child will vacillate between love and hate, jubilation and wailing. The adult, by contrast, will become increasingly capable of managing shades of gray. With maturity, the ego evolves greater complexity and becomes more capable of conceiving ambiguity and tolerating ambivalence.

Mindful of this background sketch of the relation of ego formation to body image, we are in a position to grasp more fully the profound opposition that Freud postulates between the ego and sexuality. One of the key premises on which Freud's view is founded is the developmental perspective we just examined. The point is that human attitudes toward sexuality carry with them an enduring kernel of infantile thinking. At a very fundamental level of ourselves, we continue to regard sex as the six-year-old does.

And how is that? Sex poses a threat to the infantile ego because it involves a transgression of the boundaries between self and other, and does so in the most electrifying way by raising the specter of a physical interpenetration of bodies. From the point of the view of the infantile ego, sex is almost unavoidably scandalous. By its very nature, sex tends to undo the labor of ego-consolidation that is the primary task of early childhood, breaching the newly closed contours of the ego. Sex is inevitably a primitive form of violation. It is not for nothing, therefore, that the school-age child will greet the facts of life with a decisive "Gross!" The child quite naturally finds the prospect of such body intermixture to be disgusting. No doubt this sense of disgust arises in part because the child has absorbed social taboos about sexuality from its general environment and is repeating them in its rejection of sex. But the child's anxious reaction is not merely a matter of parroting other people's attitudes. On the contrary, the child's revulsion over sex is a spontaneous response to what it correctly recognizes as a challenge to the bodily integrity upon which the archaic ego has been modeled.

For the young child, all sex has essentially the character of rape. It is therefore the six-year-old in all of us that understands how a grave insult can be delivered by the phrase "Fuck you!" For many adults, the idea of getting fucked might seem in some contexts to be not such a bad idea. Nevertheless, to be told by someone else that we ought to "Get fucked!" is demeaning because, at some level of ourselves, we persist in assuming that being fucked is inevitably a matter of being violated. When we generalize the principle in saying simply "Fuck you," we implicitly suppose that fucking means losing something. What is lost is the self-contained integrity of the ego, that sense of self-possession that has, since toddlerhood, been based on the idea that my bodily integrity is what makes me *me*.

Of course, the sense of revulsion felt by the six-year-old at the thought of sexual intercourse will in time give way to a growing curiosity and interest. Then begins the long struggle during which the closed circle of the ego contends with the necessity of opening itself to what is foreign to it. And it is not difficult to see why this struggle is destined to occur. The reason is that what has been excluded from the ego is not just other people, but some portion of the subject's own desire. We can see the results of this internal battle on the schoolyard playground as single-sex flocks of girls and boys chase one another, each taunting the other for having "cooties." Do they want to get away or be caught? They want both, of course, and the deliciousness of the game consists in the constant alternation between the two opposing wishes. In adolescence, this inner war of ambivalence will reach its peak as interest in sex begins to gain ground against inarticulate fears of losing of oneself. The adolescent is torn between the demand for independence and the desire for fusion—thus the great contradiction of adolescence, at once the most rebellious and most conformist period of life.

With the flowering of sexual activity in adulthood, the ego will have accommodated in part to the challenge of sex. But only in part. Most adults, even those who understand themselves and are understood by others to enjoy a fully functioning sex life, are able to experience only a limited portion of sexual possibility. The average adult ego establishes only a slim beachhead on the dark continent of sex. A more or less stable sexual role is established, like a secure base of operations from which the erotic self will make modest forays. Experimentation and variety of behavior generally wane, to be replaced by fairly routinized patterns. The result is that the ego takes into itself a finite quantity of sexuality and tames it in the same way that a very small dosage of a microbial pathogen may be injected for the purpose of inoculating the body against a full-scale infection. The walls of ego-identity are then re-sutured around this limited opening upon the sexual domain. Sex has become something desirable, but only within carefully controlled parameters. Beyond those bounds, sex retains its power to traumatize the ego, to remain a threat to its project of self-definition. Even in "well adjusted" adulthood, sex remains a potential source of an anxiety-producing loss of control.

Sex and Intimacy ... or Maybe Not

When I say that even a mature adult experiences only "a limited portion of sexual possibility," I don't mean merely some residual prudishness, or some lack of freedom to enjoy sexual exotica (strange positions, forbidden acts, etc.), though self-restrictions of that sort surely exist for most people. Rather, what I have in mind is the emotional potential of sexuality. The first and most basic thing that the Freudian tradition has to teach us, so basic that it is often overlooked, is that sexuality presents a privileged opportunity for human intimacy. It does so because the sexual relation inherits the traces, however unconscious, of the infant's experience in the mother's embrace. Sex is a unique path of return to the most archaic experiences of our lives and a unique avenue of access to the most profound level of our emotional being. However, an equally crucial point of Freud's teaching is that, even among copulating individuals, it tends to be a path not taken. Sex is often anything but an experience of intimacy. In fact, sex can frequently involve a minimum of real connection between partners and can readily be more alienating than it is affiliating.

To remind ourselves of the link between sex and intimacy recalls for a last time the riddle of sexual repression. Up until now we've considered that riddle mostly, we might say, from an "extensive" point of view. We've been mostly concerned with questions of frequency and kinds of sexual activity, choice of object, number of partners, and so on. But there is also the "intensive" question, centered on the depth and quality of the emotional satisfaction derived from sex. This emotional dimension primarily concerns the degree of openness or connectedness to the other person. And here, too, there is a something mysterious, indeed perhaps ultimately even more mysterious. If we grant that sex is a privileged path to human intimacy, and if we presume that intimacy is something we want and need, then we're left wondering not only why we don't have more sex but also why we don't have sex that is more intimately satisfying.

From a psychoanalytic point of view, it's not merely a matter of bad luck. On the contrary, the lack of more emotionally gratifying sex is finally to be traced to the source of sexual repression we've been examining: the nature and functions of the ego. If there is an obstacle to satisfaction in sex, it is often we ourselves, in the most literal sense of the term *selves,* who are to blame. To see why, we need only to retrace the Freudian theory of the ego with the emphasis on its defensive relation to the other. To summarize our discussions so far, sex tends to be inimical to the primitive ego for two interrelated reasons:

1. The ego, particularly in its immaturity, provides a stable and unifying sense of self only at the cost of excluding a whole range of disparate currents of desire.
2. The ego is formed around the image of the body's unity and is consequently threatened by violation of that unity.

In view of these two factors, sex challenges the ego both in the diversity of its appetites (what Freud called "polymorphous perversity") and for the way in which it inevitably breaches the body's unity (the fact that sex involves physical intercourse).

To which we can now add that the regulatory function of the ego, seeking always to establish a regular and coherent economy of impulses, is anything but neutral in relation to the other person. On the contrary, from the earliest period of its development, the ego opposes intimate connection to the other. At the time of birth and for some months afterwards, the infant remains fully fused with the mother. No ego function has yet detached itself from her and established itself as an independent entity. With no differentiation yet established between mother and infant, the nursling floats in a sea of sensations, unable to conceive of its own separateness. The original achievement of the infantile ego is that of defining a self distinct from the mother. The purpose of this development is essentially defensive. The fundamental demand of the unitary ego is for separateness, autonomy, and self-subsistence.

What does it mean that the ego is established in a defensive relation to the other? The answer is that the ego develops essentially as a response to pain. The psychological process that produces the ego unfolds like a kind of scar over the site of loss, frustration, and disappointment. In this sense, the biblical verse is correct: we are born in suffering. Imagine a miraculously efficient mother who so completely anticipates her infant's every need that the baby never feels any delay between need and satisfaction. The baby never knows the pain of privation. Indeed, it never even becomes aware of its own needs, so immediately are they satisfied. Such an infant would never come to realize that the mother is a separate being. It would forever think that the mother is a part of itself. It is the experience of the mother's absence, the experience of *lack* of satisfaction, that will prompt formation of a separate ego-identity, the primary aim of which will be self-protection and self-sufficiency.

The ego is what we hold onto when the other fails us. To this extent, therefore, the very existence of the ego is opposed to intimacy. It functions to repress a great portion of my own impulse-life, but it also, by its very nature, puts the other person at arm's length. The ego confirms and even creates the distance between me and other people. It is a fact well illustrated by the toddler who, in the process of discovering its own separateness from the mother, goes through that trying stage of self-assertion called "the terrible twos." It is a period of foot-stamping and tantrum-throwing during which the child takes a special pleasure in saying "No!"

We can confirm the opposition between the ego and other people in a particularly suggestive way by returning for a moment to the example of disgust. For most people, smell is, of all the five senses, the most likely to produce the nauseated reaction of visceral disgust. And of all smells, it is bodily odors that tend to be most offensive. Yet for most other species of mammals, smell is the primary stimulant of sexual activity. Dogs and other higher mammals communicate with each other sexually by means of odors. In Freud's view, the contrast here between human and animal is perfectly fitting. Having been distorted in the human being by the influence of repression, the sense modality that is naturally most liable to arouse desire becomes the sense most likely to provoke the most visceral loathing. But equally striking, according to Freud, is the fact that virtually identical odors may provoke totally different reactions depending on the circumstances. Particularly telling is the fact that people are generally not disgusted by the smell of their own odors and excretions, but only by those of other people. This means that the human reaction of disgust is really at a double remove from any natural or animal response. The most sexually stimulating sense has been transformed into the most ready trigger of repugnance, but it has also become subject to an involuntary discrimination between self and other.

In some ways, of course, the hard edge of the line separating the ego from others will soften over the course of development into adulthood. Yet Freud insists that psychological structure will forever retain some features of the most primitive stages of its formation. Indeed, the pressure of conflict and competition may even deepen the moat around the defensive ego. It is for this reason that sexuality is bound to be experienced as a challenge to the ego. Sex threatens the integrity of the ego by raising the specter of bodily interpenetration, but it also compromises the ego's hard-won emotional independence. Sexuality is opposed to the self-containedness of the ego by virtue of bringing about a renewal of connection, exchange, and relationship to the other. Sex revives the archaic memory of fusion with the other. Yet this prospect of fusion is the stuff of both dream and nightmare. It is on the one hand the core of the fondest wish of romance, a hope that two might become one, that the individuation of the ego might be undone in favor of a return to a blissful state of indifferentiation. On the other hand, drawing too close to the other threatens to erase the fragile borders of the ego, as if the newly created island of the ego were to be swallowed back into a great, dark, and shifting sea. In sex, the self becomes vulnerable to becoming lost in the other, exposed to the wounding influence of the other's caprices, enslaved to a renewed dependence. The fear of being re-engulfed by the other is thus the very prototype of anxiety.

Given this psychological danger posed by the sexual relation, it is no accident that human beings have sought to detach sex from interpersonal connection. The most familiar form of such detachment is that of the oldest profession. Prostitution is an attempt to maximize genital satisfaction while minimizing emotional consequences. For the prostitute, sex is transformed into a mere commodity, a market value. For the john, it is physical satisfaction largely devoid of emotional content. The advantage of this arrangement is a reduced danger of emotional connectedness with the other. Psychologically speaking, prostitution is sex for the ego alone. The payment of money might therefore be looked at in either of two ways. By paying for the prostitute's sexual services, the john buys access to the prostitute's body. Prostitution is body rental. But the exchange of money also frees the john to retain his own sense of control. In paying a prostitute, the john pays the mortgage on continued possession of his own ego.

Paying for it is not the only way to have sex while keeping a psychological distance from the partner. The example of prostitution is valuable for showing us one extreme among a range of options. Another means of maintaining a similar detachment from the other is to allow the sexual relation to be tinged in one way or another with sadism. Mixing sex with a measure of aggression, degradation, or exploitation serves to immunize the ego against the danger of too intimate a connection. There is, for example, what a college acquaintance of mine rather brutally called the "hate fuck," a sort of kinder, gentler cousin of outright rape, in which competitiveness or personal dislike may actually enhance the sexual charge. Alternatively, the autonomy of the ego can be protected by having sex with a partner who is significantly different in age, social or economic status, looks, or who is in some other way relatively disempowered. What these examples show is that sex, once partially taken into the ego and made its own, can be used for defensive purposes. Indeed, sex can be drawn upon not to deepen intimacy but to avoid it.

The technological revolution that has given us the video camera and the Internet also promises to open up vast new means for divorcing sex from interpersonal entanglements. *Sex* is by far the most frequently searched subject-word on the Net and chat rooms already abound in which users can enjoy cybersex relationships that are completely anonymous. But imagine the future possibilities. The time is not far off when streaming video will be combined with robotic appendages (operated perhaps—the term now comes into its own—by a "joy stick") that will allow people who have never met, who remain nameless and perhaps faceless, to survey and stimulate each other's bodies via computer link.

Few readers will fail to see that the psychological dynamics I am describing here tend, like prostitution, to be conspicuously gender-typed. The strategies I've mentioned for protecting the threatened ego in the passage through the sexual relation are predominantly masculine. A psychoanalytic perspective explains this fact by referring to the differences in ego structure between masculine and feminine personalities. We say "masculine" and "feminine" here, and not "men" and "women," because we are dealing not with anatomy but with psychological makeup. Masculinity is characterized by more definite, rigid, and exclusive ego boundaries, a trait that leads many men to feel easily threatened by too much contact with others.

More defined ego boundaries lend to the masculine subject a greater freedom from other people's influence, a characteristic that has been shown experimentally in tests of what psychologists call field dependence and independence. Field independence is the ability to judge objects in isolation from their surrounding contexts. Imagine, for example, a vertical rod enclosed by a rectangular frame. If the frame is rotated slightly to one side, an observer who is field independent will continue to perceive the rod as vertical. The field-dependent observer, on the other hand, will be misled into thinking that the rod has itself tipped to one side. The reason is that the field-independent observer is able more effectively to disembed the figure from the influence of its context. From a Freudian perspective, this capacity for perceiving objects independently of their surrounding background is related to, and ultimately derives from, a greater independence of the ego itself. It is a capacity that is more prevalent among men than among women and suggests that the masculine ego has firmer, more rigid, and defensive boundaries.

Behind the question of gender-related ego structure stands the cardinal Freudian issue of the Oedipus complex. That the masculine ego needs to define itself more rigidly and defensively reflects a greater need for autonomy from the mothering figure. We can even say that masculinity is actually *constituted* by a more energetic and decisive insistence on autonomy. The underlying reason is that the heterosexual man will take a sexual partner of the same gender as the mothering figure of his infancy. This means that for the majority of men the sexual relation inevitably recalls the experience of infancy in a way that it doesn't for women. In effect, heterosexual men must perform the psychological feat of first pushing away the maternal figure and becoming independent of her, then reuniting with a sexual partner of the same sex, someone who therefore inevitably draws him back into close relation with the very person from whom he struggled to free himself. Accordingly, the masculine ego needs additional protections. The more fortified masculine ego defends against the danger of regressing to an infantile position when a man enters intimate proximity with a woman.

This psychoanalytic view might seem to confirm the familiar stereotype that "men are only interested in one thing," that they avoid commitment because they really want sex without emotional connection. But this is a superficial impression. If men appear to be allergic to commitment, if they seem to pursue "just sex" while avoiding more meaningful emotional entanglement, the reason from a Freudian point of view is not that they don't want intimacy with a woman. The reason is precisely the opposite: *they want intimacy too much.* Taking account of the unconscious in this instance means looking past the cliché of crusty, unfeeling males who don't cry, who deride sentimentality, and who prefer to appear as though they have no emotional needs whatever. This leathery exterior, the shell of an embattled masculine ego, serves to conceal and to defend against exactly the feelings that it appears to lack. Somewhere inside every macho guy is an injured little boy. And little else makes the tough guy more anxious than being loved.

We have defined danger to the ego in two ways: first in relation to the repressed impulses of the id, then in relation to the other person whom the ego seeks to keep at a safe distance. It can now be seen that these two dangers are really one and the same. For what threatens the ego about the other person is ultimately the way in which the presence of the other may evoke impulses in the subject himself or herself. It is no accident that the two great classes of repressed impulses—the aggressive and the sexual—concern feelings for and about others. The ego is the very matrix of self, the id is the internal other. It is thus through the figure of the other outside myself, for good or for ill, that I am confronted with the repressed of my own id. What I fear most about others is the feelings that they may arouse in me.

Part II
Genders

4
Love You Madly

Contrary to the popular view of Freud's thought that sees sexual repression solely as a function of the punishing, self-denying superego, repression of sex must finally be traced to the tension between sex and the ego. On this more basic level, constriction of sexual life is not merely a matter of internalizing the voices of nay-saying killjoys but is rather the price to be paid for a stable and coherent psychological identity. The denial of Eros therefore reflects a profound paradox about the human condition: repression is that form of alienation from ourselves that is required in order to be a self. Repression is what makes it possible to be a separate and independent being, distinct from others. The "discontents" visited upon us by civilization are ultimately rooted in the fact that we are civilized "selves" at all.

A detail from one of Freud's most famous cases, the so-called "Wolfman," provides a perfect emblem of this tension between sexual desire and ego identity. Many of the Wolfman's inner conflicts surrounded especially intense sexual compulsions. Among the most electrifying was the phantasy of a woman's legs opening and closing like the wings of a butterfly, a movement that he associated with the Roman letter V. In a particularly meaningful dream, he saw a man pulling the wings off a wasp (in German, a *Wespe*), but in later recounting of the dream he omitted the initial letter (the W, or double V). The insect of the dream had been, he said, an "*Espe*." By dropping the initial W, the wing-like letter that conjured up the image of the opening legs, he had eliminated the reference to the sexual phantasy. "But *Espe*," he then realized, "why, that's myself: S.P." In Austria, "*Espe*" and "S.P.," the initials of his own name, would be pronounced exactly alike. The dream thus presented an elegantly compact expression of the way in which the foundations of the ego are constituted by repression of sexuality. The wasp wings of sexuality having been torn away, what was left was … himself.

It is impossible to understand Freud's view on this point apart from a developmental perspective, or better, apart from Freud's insistence that the core structures of personality are formed around certain *failures* of development. It is not for nothing that Freud called the Wolfman's case "An *Infantile* Neurosis." The conflict is not so much between sex and the ego as it is between sex and the *immature* ego, some traces of which always survive into adulthood. Freud allows that the ego becomes more complex, more flexible, and more inclusive with maturity. The well-adjusted adult has graduated from the cartoon world of the eight-year-old in which perfect superheroes battle diabolical villains and the self is neatly separated from the other. At least on a good day. Stressed by a family death, a job loss, a lover's quarrel, or maybe just a traffic jam, many an adult will revert to older and more primitive patterns of emotional life. Whatever the growth and change that occurs with age, something of the archaic and infantile structure of the ego always remains, ready to receive the embattled ego back into its embrace.

This primitive level of psychical structure is crucial for Freud's entire outlook. It is the remainder of infantile organization that underlies the viciousness of projection, the unrestrained panic of phobia, and the lure of fetishism. It lies hidden beneath the surface of more developed and elaborated psychological formations in somewhat the same way that the path of even the most enormous canyon system was originally cut by a relatively tiny stream, carving a primeval channel that continues, many centuries later, to guide the flow of water in the hidden depths of the chasm. The opposition proposed by Freud between sex and ego is unintelligible without reference to such a prehistoric layer of mental structure. It is also this archaic layer of the personality that grounds Freud's theory of gender. Our discussions of the last chapter were haunted by the unresolved issue of gender. In this and the following chapter, we turn more directly to this question. The objective—and this qualification needs to be emphasized—is not to provide an exhaustive accounting of the phenomenon of gender, nor to exhaust what Freud has to say on the subject. The aim is more limited: to sketch one or two of the main lines along which Freud traces the dynamics of gender back to their infantile roots.

Gender is a tricky issue for more than one reason. First, there is the question of terms. Even at the crudest level, three pairs of categories pop up in discussions of sex: female–male (a matter of anatomy), feminine–masculine (a psychological identity), and homosexual–heterosexual (a choice of erotic object). And while the class of "male" obviously shows a significant degree of overlap with the category of the "masculine," the two are by no means the same thing. Sexual orientation is still another question altogether. It is thus quite possible to mix and match categories of sex, gender, and orientation to get any combination. We can easily imagine a masculine homosexual woman, a feminine heterosexual man, and so forth.

Yet even the most cautious treatment of terms can't blunt the sense of outrage generated by some of Freud's more inflammatory claims. In the next couple of chapters, we'll focus on two. Women in love, Freud says, tend to be (1) narcissistic and (2) masochistic. Now there's throwing down the gauntlet! No wonder Freud has brought down upon himself such storms of indignation. How can we avoid the impression either that Freud simply had it in for women or that he grossly misunderstood them?

But how well have we understood *him*? To read Freud's theory of gender with any care is to realize that men don't fare any better under the lens of his analysis. In fact, maybe the most disturbing thing about Freud's view of love is that both men and women are shown to be entangled in motives that are equally infantile, and that the passions of Eros for both sexes are revealed to be fatefully caught up in the coils of dark and mysterious forces. The first task is to resist a rush to judgment, which means resisting the ready sense that we have already understood Freud well enough to dismiss him out of hand. The challenge is to pause long enough give him a fair hearing.

Through the Looking Glass

So what did Freud mean by saying women are narcissistic in love? His essay "On Narcissism" doesn't make it easy.

> Women, especially if they grow up with good looks, develop a certain self-contentment which compensates them for the social restrictions that are imposed upon them in their choice of object.
>
> Strictly speaking, it is only themselves that such women love with an intensity comparable to that of the man's love for them. Nor does their need lie in the direction of loving, but of being loved; and the man who fulfills this condition is the one who finds favor with them.

Freud quickly assures us that "this description of the feminine form of erotic life is not due to any tendentious desire on my part to depreciate women." To which he adds the caveat that between men and women "differences are of course not universal" and that "there are quite a number of women who love according to the masculine type." But no doubt for many readers the damage is already done. The problem is to see how it can possibly be undone.

To grasp what Freud has in mind it is helpful, as it sometimes is in psychoanalytic research, to look first to patterns in society at large. On this level, one need not be tendentious to assert that women spend a good deal more time, energy, and worry over their appearance than men. Can there be much doubt about which member of the average couple, preparing for an evening on the town, primps longest in front of the medicine cabinet? It is not for nothing that over centuries of art history the mirror has provided a ready symbol of the feminine. Indeed, the history of art amply testifies to the fact that women, especially unclothed women, tend far more than men to become objects of purely aesthetic contemplation. From the Venus de Milo to Manet's "Olympia," women's bodies have been reserved for special appreciation, not because they are depicted in the act of doing anything in particular, nor because they focus a tribute to fame or achievement, but merely because they offer a sumptuous spectacle to the eye. The female form is the art object par excellence.

Consumption of cosmetics is another obvious indication. A truly ancient form of beauty enhancement, cosmetics date at least to the time of the Egyptian empire, credited with the invention of lipstick. Today, of course, the cosmetics industry is a multibillion-dollar business, almost exclusively supported by women anxious to paint themselves to best advantage. Among some college co-eds of my acquaintance, even to show up for mid-morning class requires "putting one's face on." Most of the men in my classes, by contrast, seem almost to insist on looking like they just rolled out of bed. A parallel point could be made in considering the usages of jewelry. While these days men increasingly deck themselves out with bracelets, studs, earrings, and chains of various sorts, most men's bauble collections fall far short of the contents of the average woman's jewelry box.

Then there is hair. No one would claim that men don't make a fuss over their hair—especially when it begins falling out! But it is interesting to note the difference between men's and women's hair care. For a man, the proper look is generally one of discreet and controlled grooming. But it should never look like he spent more than a minute or two dealing with it. A particularly winning effect is achieved by a sort of rough and ready, slightly tousled, or wind-blown look that suggests a life of action. Perhaps he's just back from the tennis court or has just stepped off his yacht. The really crucial message delivered by this sort of casual look in men's hair is that he's got more important things to think about. The man who worries too much over keeping every fiber in place risks appearing unmanly because we tend to measure masculinity by a degree of active engagement with things outside oneself. The real man must never allow himself to sink to the level of being a mere object. He needs to be an active agent, involved in a world of external things over which he exercises his skill and prowess. Isn't this why there is always something dangerous about toupees? Sporting a hairpiece is too self-conscious, too fastidious. The guy with a rug is forever on the edge of becoming the sort of man who can't be taken seriously precisely because that carefully poised hair-mat hints that he devotes to much attention to his own appearance.

A woman, on the other hand, can get away with a far more studied look. Of course, women, too, can be flattered by casual tresses, though mostly because some fly-away hair suggests that there is still something a little wild and untamed about the woman who wears it. But for the most part, a woman runs very little risk of a negative judgment by others when her hairstyle announces that she has lavished an hour or two on getting it just right. In fact, giving the impression that she has devoted a good deal of attention to her hair assures us that she is playing a truly feminine role. The reason is that a woman's hair is supposed to be an eye-catching object in its own right, almost a kind of gift, like a cake or flowers, that she offers for the appreciation of others. The term *hairdo* thus tends to be really applicable only to women. Indeed, in the presence of a luxuriant overflow of feminine waves and ringlets, we can almost forget that it is hair at all. Women's hair is something more like a suitable ornament, a striking and tasteful headpiece, that echoes the drapery of the dress below.

It is tempting to interpret these differences between men's and women's hair as merely a matter of cultural convention and, of course, to a very large extent they are. There have been many periods of history during which men's hair styles were at least as extravagant as women's. The powdered wigs of the European eighteenth century are only one example. Moreover, we have to be alert to the way in which the different standard now applied to women's hair contributes to the general disempowerment of women. As Shulamith Firestone argued in *The Dialectic of Sex*, the expectation that women devote inordinate amounts of time and energy to their appearance serves very successfully both to reinforce their status as mere objects instead of agents and to distract them from other, more publicly productive and significant pursuits. Naomi Wolf has more recently made a similar case in *The Beauty Myth*.

Freud's notion of feminine narcissism certainly doesn't deny the truth of these claims. He is not unaware of the cultural relativity of varying forms of self-adornment or of the uses to which they can be put as means for signaling social status and prestige. Nor is he trying to argue that women's greater degree of self-consciousness about their appearance is to be chalked up solely to psychological factors. He does, however, want to insist that there is a psychological issue at stake, grounded in the different regard that men and women have for the body-image. To get a rough sense of what he means, consider for a moment what difference it would make if men's penises were as visible from outside the veneer of clothing as are women's breasts. Far more than men, women are conscious of their bodies as objects seen by others.

Here, too, there are social and cultural factors to be taken into account. Cultural fashion has sometimes made up for what nature has not provided, whether in the form of an aboriginal penis sheaf or an Elizabethan codpiece. Moreover, little girls are powerfully socialized to be aware of their visual impression. Entering a room of adults, a little girl is almost certain to be met with a comment about her *appearance*—"How cute she is!"—where the little boy will hear something relevant to his *activity*—"Just don't knock over Grandma's lamp!" Nevertheless, Freud argues that the greater concern women show for their bodily appearance is not merely a matter of cultural convention or socialization. There is something in the psychological structure of femininity that prepares women to assume the roles that culture assigns to them.

What, then, is its basis? In the essay "On Narcissism," Freud relates women's predisposition toward narcissistic self-consciousness in part to the distinctive experience of the little girl at puberty. The passage through puberty inevitably reminds the growing girl of her body image in a way that has no counterpart in the budding young man. Before the onset of puberty, the little girl and little boy may be equally absorbed in outward activity—running, jumping, climbing trees, and so on—in a way that affords the luxury of being fairly oblivious to their own bodies. But the adolescent swelling of female hips and breasts spoils this democracy of childhood innocence. The pubescent girl becomes subject to a self-consciousness about her own body-image that will leave an indelible mark on her sense of herself. She will forever after be disposed toward that consciousness of being seen by others that is so typical a part of narcissism.

Far from contradicting Firestone's claim that women are enslaved by social expectations concerning their appearance, a Freudian perspective further illuminates it by revealing the sensitive point in feminine psychology at which such expectations gain a foothold. Women's greater degree of narcissistic body consciousness, the sense of being an object for the other's gaze, exposes many women to particularly painful and crippling forms of humiliation. In this way, Freud helps us to better recognize the insidiousness of the most recent trend in the social control of women: the preference for ultra-thin fashion models. Since the 1960s, advertising aimed at women has been dominated by images of near-anorexic female bodies. The average fashion model now weighs a whopping twenty-three pounds less than the average woman.[1] This enormous discrepancy serves the interests of advertisers who hope to sell a host of products, from clothes and cosmetics to diet plans and weight reduction surgery, by creating in women an equally enormous sense of self-doubt and inadequacy. Freud helps us to see how deep this sense of deficiency goes. The standard of feminine beauty with which women are continually bombarded is, quite literally, an image of nubile prepubescence. The current canon of beauty is bound to hit women where it hurts most. Indeed, it is hard to imagine a more effective means for arousing in women an enduring sense of shame and self-hatred.

A recent *Time* magazine cover story shows perfectly how women are now rip-sawed by media images of nearly impossible body ideals (see Fig. 4.1). The article was ostensibly an appreciation of feminine physical prowess, reviewing the various ways—certain forms of physical stamina, disease resistance, greater longevity, and so on—in which women excel over men. The text of the story thereby appeared to celebrate the promise of a newfound pride in women's bodies. But the magazine cover image featured a female torso so lithe and sinewy as to appear almost anorexic. The combination of text and image thus formed a perfect contradiction: The physical superiority of femininity touted on the inside of the magazine was belied by the almost emaciated form on the cover. The contradiction was in fact all the more unbearable for the fact that many of the physical benefits explored in the article directly or indirectly derive from the extra layer of fat that distinguishes the female form, yet it was this very feature that was thoroughly eliminated in the cover image.

There is, of course, another way to read this cover image, less as anorexic than as simply masculine. Apart from the absence of body hair, the image chosen

[1]This statistic may be a bit out of date and thus understate the case. I take it from Jean Kilbourne's excellent documentaries about images of women in advertising, "Killing Us Softly," "Still Killing Us Softly," and "Slim Hopes."

Fig. 4.1 *Time* March 8, 1999.

by the editors of *Time* to illustrate "The Truth About Women's Bodies" is unmistakably more male than female. Either way, however, the result is a debilitating contradiction. On the first reading, women are presented with the impossible choice between biological femininity (including the greater percentage of overall body fat naturally carried by women) and an artificial ideal of waif-like thinness. What makes this double-bind especially pernicious is that health is equated with such thinness—an equation now mightily exploited by the advertising juggernaut of diet regimens and fitness boutiques. On the second reading, femininity is not so much redefined as it is simply eliminated in favor of masculinity. The ideal for women then becomes, as it seems to be in the recent craze for body-building and weight-training for women, to do their level best to look like a man.

In one way or another, the strategy of many advertisers is to inflate women's greater concern for body-image into a crippling self-consciousness, available for a variety of manipulations and product pitches. To take one example, consider the functions of the so-called cover-girl image that adorns fashion magazines such as *Vogue, Elle, Glamour,* and *Redbook.* Especially during the 1980s, these dazzling images were recognizable on the newsstand from a hundred yards away.

Two things immediately strike us about these cover-girl faces. On the one hand and most immediately, they present objects of uncommon fascination. Extraordinary care is taken, formerly by airbrush and now by computer retouching, to produce an epiphany of uncannily flawless beauty. The result is a magical image of mesmerizing power. On the other hand, the cover-girl face typically looks directly back at the viewer with an almost unbelievably intense gaze. Here, too, very deliberate care is taken to achieve the effect. Reflective highlights in the eyes are strategically placed in order to produce an electrifying stare. Whatever the captivating attractiveness of the rest of the face, the glittering, jewel-like eyes stand out with such unmistakable brilliance that they exert an arresting effect all their own.

The question is: Why put these faces on the cover? How do they help sell magazines to the women at whom they are targeted? The question is a challenging one when we reflect that the jaw-dropping beauty of the cover girl must also make many women feel inadequate by comparison. Mustn't the cover-girl image call up a painful anxiety in the average woman who so little resembles her? Why, even the model herself doesn't really look that good! She needs the help of makeup, lighting, and careful retouching to achieve such blemishless perfection. But if that is so, how the anxiety of the hapless passerby must be intensified by the way in which the cover-girl stares back at her! That piercing gaze communicates an implicit judgment as it reflects threateningly back upon the viewer the prospect of an unflattering comparison. Indeed, the more the cover-girl face is inflated with the value of the beautiful, the more commanding and dangerous its gaze becomes.

So how does such heightened anxiety help peddle magazines? The answer to this riddle, I suspect, is to be related to the double aspect of the cover-girl face, both an arrestingly beautiful object and a condemning gaze. How can we not imagine that the result is an unstable oscillation in which the viewer is shuttled back and forth between fascination and shame? A psychological seesaw of this sort would provide the perfect mechanism for selling magazines to women anxious about their own appearance. At the same time that the cover-girl gaze excites a feeling of self-doubt it also promises an escape from doubt and shame by providing a marvelous, remobilizing image upon which the threatened ego can feed, the wherewithal to mimic what is available for sale within the pages of the magazine. Does the penetrating gaze of this gorgeous face make you a little uncomfortable about your own looks? Not to worry, we've got a whole warehouse of cosmetics and beauty tips that will help you to catch up. You, too, can look like a showgirl with a little help from Revlon, and Clairol, and Lancôme, and Pantene, and ....

In the nineties, the cover-girl face that had virtually defined the genre of the fashion magazine gave way to a new cover image that has become almost as slavishly adhered to as the full-face image that it replaced: the cleavage shot. It features a gorgeous woman, shown from the waist or knees up, with the emphasis on the flesh cleft between her breasts. She still looks out at us with a decidedly intense gaze, but the hotspot of the overall tableau is the cleft between the breasts. A quick survey of examples in the supermarket checkout rack (*Cosmopolitan* appears to have been the trendsetter here) easily reveals the salient feature: The models who sport all this breast flesh are otherwise true to type—pencil thin. Lean and lanky, but with big breasts. This discrepancy gives some evidence of the current prevalence of breast augmentation surgery but it also points us toward the hidden function of the cleavage-bedecked cover-girl. It generates a contradiction not unlike the one in the *Time* magazine article. Traditional concern for fashion and glamour has recently been countered by concern over health and fitness. Or better, fitness has itself become fashionable and glamorous. There was a brief period, during the late seventies and through the eighties, when it almost seemed that the mania for big-breasted women, the Jayne Mansfield look of the fifties and sixties, was becoming positively déclassé. Dolly Parton would still turn heads but not without a certain hint of derision. Now it appears that women must have it both ways—thin *and* busty. Today's ideal demands a woman who runs marathons but *also* wears a double-D cup. Once again, women are caught in a double-bind, the crossfire of conflicting expectations. The foundation of that double-bind, the reason women become susceptible to it in the first place, is that they remain painfully sensitive to the way in which their physical appearance is perceived by others.

Every One a Boy

It is quite true, then, that Freud discerns in femininity a lingering narcissism. Before condemning that conclusion as a product of misogyny, however, it is crucial to note that he finds men prey to an infantile fixation that, while perhaps less obvious, is even more elemental. Feminine narcissism is an attachment to the first flowering of narcissism in toddlerhood, the moment when the child first models its nascent ego on the unity of its own body image. Prior to that phase, the libidinal life of the child is almost entirely occupied with the mothering figure who nurtures and cares for it. It is to this even more primitive stage, the phase of what Freud calls "attachment" or "anaclitic love," that the masculine subject remains bound. His erotic life will forever be haunted by the dream of returning to the mother. His deepest longing will tend to revolve around the lodestar of the nursing caretaker.

We have already had occasion to remark on the reason. Unlike women, who (if they pursue a heterosexual choice of love-object) will shift their love from the female nurturer of their infancy to a member of the opposite sex, the heterosexual man will take a lover whose body inevitably recalls that of his first significant physical and emotional attachment. Sexuality thus tends to draw him back to the most primitive orbit of his psychological make-up: the nursling's dependency on the mother.

At this point, psychoanalysis contacts the inner truth of the old adage that the way to a man's heart is through his stomach. At the most basic level of their psychology, men remain in thrall to the dream of regaining the blissful union with the mother's nursing embrace. It must immediately be added, however, that this tendency sets up an elemental tension between the deep longing for return to the mother and the need to sustain independence from her. It is a battle between the pressure of a man's most primitive emotional needs and the imperative of autonomy. And as we have already seen, this tension gives rise to a series of defensive formations, the firmer boundaries of the ego that are characteristic of masculine psychology. The masculine personality is more resistant to the call of its own emotional life and more wary of intimate connection with the other.

Like the Freudian theory of feminine narcissism, Freud's view of the masculine tie to the mother can be drawn upon to augment a feminist critique. In fact, it is precisely this view to which Simone de Beauvoir appeals in her classic work of feminist theory, the book that might well be considered the founding text of the feminist movement, *The Second Sex*. The keynote of de Beauvoir's outlook is the profound ambivalence displayed by men toward the feminine other. Woman is the embodiment of the primeval forces of nature upon which man is dependent, yet against which he must define himself as an independent being. She is the fertile source of regeneration and birth, the very substance of fecundity. But for the same reason, woman is a figure unavoidably associated with death. She is the earth-bosom from which life springs and to which it must eventually return. As such, woman represents to man a vulnerability to his own needs, the disturbing reminder that he can never fully establish his separateness.

After brilliantly cataloging the history of this ambivalence in religion, art, literature, and philosophy, de Beauvoir concludes with a reference to the Freudian Oedipus complex. She insists that Freud's idea must be reformulated, not so much as a rivalry with the father for the mother's love as a rivalry with himself, the struggle between his desire for reunion with the mother and the unrelenting requirement of self-sufficiency. It is a struggle that is repeated each time he finds himself again longing to be enfolded in a woman's arms. At bottom, however, de Beauvoir's view is less a reformulation of Freud's theory than a restatement of it.

> Man finds it repugnant to come upon the dreaded essence of the mother in the woman he possesses.… The Oedipus complex—which should be redescribed—does not deny this attitude, but on the contrary implies it. Man is on the defensive against woman in so far as she represents the vague source of the world and obscure organic development.
>
> The Oedipus complex [is] considered too often as being produced by a struggle between instinctual tendencies and social regulations, whereas it is first of all an inner conflict within the subject himself. The attachment of the infant for the mother's breast is at first an attachment to Life in its immediate form, in its generality and its immanence; the rejection by weaning is the beginning of the rejection by abandonment, to which the individual is condemned once he emerges as a separate being from the Whole. It is from that point, and as he becomes more individualized and separate, that the term *sexual* can be applied to the inclination he retains for the maternal flesh henceforth detached from his. His sensuality is then directed through another person, it has become transcendence toward an object foreign to him. But the quicker and the more decidedly the child realizes himself as subject, the more the fleshly bond, opposing his autonomy, is going to become harassing to him. Then he shuns his mother's caresses; and her authority, the rights she has over him, sometimes her very presence, all inspire in him a kind of shame. In particular it seems embarrassing and obscene to be aware of her as flesh, and he avoids thinking of her body; in the horrified feeling aroused by his father or stepfather or a lover, there is not so much a pang of jealousy as a sense of scandal.

What, then, becomes of men's narcissism? After all, the little boy, too, passes through the ego-formative stage of primary narcissism. The answer brings us to a key point of Freud's theory of relations between the sexes. For the masculine position, narcissism is not fully extinguished in the course of maturing but rather gets transferred from himself to the object of his love. It is this process that leads to what Freud calls the "overvaluation of the love object." He is thinking of the particular form of jaw-dropped adoration that afflicts the love-sick fool, the fever of love in which the love-struck man can't take his eyes off his beloved. In the throes of this febrile state, the masculine ego is buttressed by its fascination with the image of the other. The sense of self is paradoxically strengthened by being utterly absorbed in eroticized contemplation of the face or body of the beloved. It is a form of externalized or projected narcissism, a kind of narcissism by proxy. Its power and attraction is strikingly evoked by Nietzsche in a passage devoted to "Women and their action at a distance."

> When a man stands in the midst of his own noise, in the midst of his own surf of plans and projects, then he is apt also to see quiet, magical beings gliding past him and to long for their happiness and seclusion: *women*. He almost thinks that his better self dwells there among the women, and that in these quiet regions even the loudest surf turns into deathly quiet, and life itself into a dream about life.... Oh, what ghostly beauty! How magically it touches me! Has all the calm and taciturnity of the world embarked on it? Does my happiness itself sit in this quiet place—my happier ego, my second, departed self?... As the boat with its white sails moves like an immense butterfly over the dark sea. Yes! To move *over* existence! That's it! That would be something!

Freud's notion of erotic overvaluation as externalized narcissism and his association of it with masculinity are not to be taken to mean that women are incapable of doting preoccupation in love, but rather that men's style of loving tends more predictably to gravitate toward the specific character of infatuation with the beloved *as an object*. On its more masculine side, libido emphasizes its attachment to an object, and particularly to its visual aspect. The typically feminine manner of loving, Freud contends, shows a greater degree of attraction to less tangible qualities of the beloved—competence, wit or humor, gentleness, social grace, and, of course, the deeply gratifying sense of her lover's regard for her. The woman in love tends to be aroused less by a pretty face than by strong character, less by objects than by situations.

From a similar vantage point, we can understand why Jacques Lacan characterizes masculine enjoyment in love as "phallic" and can further clarify the psychoanalytic meaning of the phallus. The phallus, we've said, is by no means equivalent to the penis, but rather designates the privileged object of desire. We need to put sufficient stress on the word *object*. What is most salient about the phallus is precisely its status as an object. And it is this function of object-focus that psychoanalysis associates with the distinctively masculine posture in love. The genuine psychoanalytic view is thus ironically the opposite of what is commonly supposed by people who hear the Freudian talk about castrated women, penis envy, and so on. When the phallus is considered in its symbolic status as a stand-in for the object of desire, and when this phallic function is seen in its elemental tendency of focusing and directing desire by relating it to a desirable *object*, the surprising conclusion is that the love life of men is even more conspicuously organized around a chase for the phallus than that of women.

The Battle between the Sexes

Having made some further progress in outlining the dynamics of masculine psychology, locating its roots in the longing for the mother's embrace and the defense against that longing, we can now return for a moment to the little girl, whose emerging narcissism we earlier traced to the transformations of puberty. It is now possible to see how the self-consciousness of the pubescent girl, her anxious awareness of the way her body appears in the eyes of others, has been prepared for much earlier in her relationship to her father. That is to say, we can now take note of the difference between mother-love and father-love. As Erik Fromm famously pointed out in *The Art of Loving*, mother love is unconditional. One need not deserve this love, nor win it, but merely finds it bestowed, like sweet rain that falls freely and spontaneously upon parched ground. The mother's love is given, not for what I do, nor what I have to give in return, but merely for the fact that I exist at all. The mother loves her child for simply being. The father's love, on the other hand, is less given than granted. There is in the relation to the father a distance that must be crossed, some requirement that must be met. The father loves conditionally. His love must be gained by pleasing him.

We can immediately see what sense this makes in terms of the actual relation the child has with mother and father. The child is tied to the mother by a physical bond, the contact of flesh and the flow of milk. The link to the father, by contrast, cannot rely upon such physical immediacy but must jump like a spark across a gap of separation. The mother is there from the start; indeed, mother and child begin as one flesh. By contrast, the father is something of a stranger. He is bigger and smells different, his voice lower and more gravelly, the skin of his hands and face feels rough and scratchy. As a result, the history of mother-love and father-love will have almost opposite trajectories, the one passing from fusion to qualified independence, the other seeking to establish a linkage that overcomes an original separateness. Mother-love is always already there, life's point of departure. Father-love, like the far shore of a river, must be reached by traversing a distance.

These differences have dramatic consequences for the shaping of gender. To the extent that the little girl becomes caught up in the eroticized relation with the parent of the opposite sex, her deepest longing toward the father becomes a quest for recognition and approval, a longing to be "the apple of his eye." Underlying this quest (and motivating it) will be a nagging sense of being unacknowledged and underappreciated. The degree of her self-satisfaction will thus depend on the degree to which she deems herself to be satisfactory to others. In this way, the feminine disposition toward narcissism is cemented into place in relation to every successor to the father. Femininity becomes a quest to please others, to be the center of their attention, to bask in the sunlight of their approval.

All of which requires more than one emphatic note of caution. First, though I have fallen into speaking of masculine and feminine as roughly parallel to male and female, the parallel is not at all an equivalence. The underlying intention at this point of Freud's theory is to define two basic orientations to love, those of narcissistic and object libido (self-love and other-love), and to align them—very approximately!—with feminine and masculine styles of loving. But there are no absolute or exclusive lines of demarcation here. Not only are men sometimes closer to the feminine type and women more masculine, but some admixture of narcissism and object love is always to be found in every individual. A whole range of erotic character structures is therefore to be envisaged along the continuum between the two poles.

A second cautionary reminder is that Freud's analysis of these points makes no pretense of fully covering the field of human loving—very far from it! Nor do my brief comments here exhaust what Freud himself has to say about love. His distinction between anaclitic and narcissistic libido, what amounts to a distinction between loving and being loved, merely highlights two facets of a much more complex phenomenon. Before turning to some other factors involved in love relations between the sexes, however, it is worth pausing a little longer to see better how things look even from this limited angle of view. Within this compass, love tends to organize itself along one or the other of two axes: the narcissistic axis of adoring and being adored, and the anaclitic axis of nurturing and being nurtured. The result is a system of four positions shown in the diagram (see Fig. 4.2).

This system of crisscrossing axes describes an almost inevitable tension because the narcissistic woman wants to occupy the position of the adored, while the man who longs for return to the mother seeks to be nurtured. The problem, of course, is that the two axes tend to be mutually exclusive. While the man who is captivated by the beauty of his beloved may enjoy the ecstatic transport of his devotion to her, his desire to be nurtured by her is frustrated. On the other hand, the woman who allows herself to play the caretaker, and who admittedly may take considerable satisfaction of her own in doing so, must renounce the dream of being the object of a man's erotic infatuation. Caught in this nexus of conflicting desires, the two sexes work at cross purposes. The arrestingly gorgeous woman before whom the masculine lover

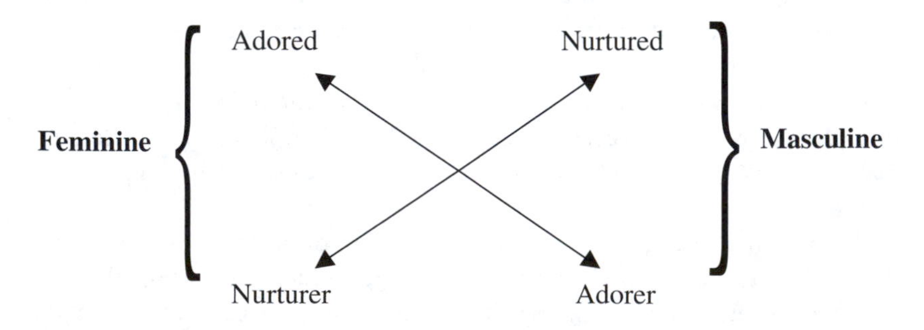

Fig. 4.2 Narcissistic axis of adoring and being adored, and the anaclitic axis of nurturing and being nurtured.

prostrates himself may finally appear to him as cold and withholding. Even as he continues to be lured by her beauty, the man in love may feel inexplicably empty or lonely. Then again, the man who looks to refind in his lover the infantile bliss of his mother's love risks disappointing the woman who cares for him by appearing to her as a needy little boy. Many a mother of three comes to feel that she has four children, the three kids and her husband.

With this chart of the two axes in view, we immediately recognize something about the typical course of a love relation. Love almost always first blossoms on the narcissistic axis. The opening gambit is a matter of a man's being attracted by a woman's physical beauty, and the woman being flattered by his attention. Later on, the gears of love shift and the stakes of attachment love come increasingly into play. The established housewife may shear off her luxuriant mane of hair and leave her high heels in the closet. Her man brings her fewer flowers and begins to fatten on her cooking.

Confronted by this dreary prospect, we see with a wince another expression of Freud's famous pessimism. We may take some small comfort in reminding ourselves that it is a picture crudely drawn and that not every couple, thank goodness, is doomed to reproduce it. Nevertheless, Freud takes his analysis to illuminate underlying tendencies to which many of us are liable. Moreover, there is a further wrinkle that can make matters even worse: the arrival of children. For many women, Freud contends, the love they feel for a baby offers the only occasion on which a woman's narcissism is transferred to an object outside herself in the manner of a man's adoration of feminine beauty. She now comes to occupy the position of the adorer. She gazes at her child with a rapt infatuation comparable to that of the man in the grips of the first flowering of romance. This situation faces the man with an especially painful problem, for he can now occupy neither of the positions outlined for him by the dynamics of narcissistic and anaclitic love. He can no longer play the star-struck lover in thrall to his woman's beauty, if only because she is less invested in presenting herself as the object of such attentions. At the same time, he cannot enjoy the warm embrace of the nurturer because those arms are now filled by another whose needs are far more extravagant than his own. The prediction to be made on psychoanalytic premises thus coincides with the observation of common knowledge: the temptation for a man to become involved in a love affair is at a maximum when his wife is tending infants.

"Aha!" the critic of Freudian sexism will exclaim. "Now he's going to tell us that it's a woman's fault. The marriage may go on the rocks because she's not playing by the rules of the game." Such might well be the complaint felt by the hapless husband we've pictured. But that wouldn't be Freud's view. From a psychoanalytic standpoint, it must be said that the whole system of conflictual dynamics that we have charted above owes more to the defensive requirements of the masculine personality than to any selfishness of women. To see how, consider again the shift from the narcissistic to the anaclitic axis in the history of a love relation. According to Freud, this shift puts a man where he most wants to be—back in his mother's arms. But the reason love first takes fire fueled by a woman's beauty is due not only to her narcissistic bent but to a man's need to hold his own deepest longing at a distance. Mesmerized by a woman's attractions, he is conveniently oblivious to his own emotional needs. The sexier the woman, the less she appears in the role of his mother. In effect, the masculine investment in adoring a beautiful woman can thus function as a defense against a deeper yearning for reunion with a mothering caretaker. The quadrangle of love relations is thus tensed by an underlying dissymmetry. The conflicting axes of narcissistic and anaclitic love are structured at the most basic level by the masculine need to manage this impossible task: to be happy in love a man must refind some echo of his mother's embrace, yet feeling himself to be once again a helpless child is the one thing that he cannot tolerate.

We can supply some other, indirect evidence for the leading part in love relations played by masculine defensiveness. The two positions assigned to women are those of the Adored and the Nurturer. How can it fail to strike us that these two positions describe exactly the two basic genres of women's magazines? On the one hand, there are fashion serials such as *Vogue, Glamour, Elle,* or *Mademoiselle* that bombard women with ideal images of feminine beauty, the means to imitate which are advertised in their pages. On the other hand, there are the household manuals such as *Good Housekeeping, Woman's World,* and *Family Circle,* with their endless parade of recipes and homemaking tips. The two main categories of women's magazines thus rehearse for women the two parts they are expected to play in the quadrangle of love relations we've outlined: the beauty queen or the hearth goddess.

And what about men's magazines? There are plenty of them that appeal to his role as the adorer of feminine comeliness. From time-worn standards such as *Playboy* and *Penthouse* to more recent arrivals such as *Maxim* and *FHM,* a wide shelf of men's magazines presents a cavalcade of eye-catching models. Even magazines that cater to other masculine interests often ornament their pages with pin-ups. The most spectacular example, of course, is the swimsuit issue of *Sports Illustrated,* the best-selling single issue of any magazine in the world.

But what's out there in the way of magazines that address themselves to the last of the four positions, that in which the man assumes the role of the nurtured child? Absolutely nothing at all! This result might seem a bit strange. If Freud is correct that this position corresponds to man's deepest longing, shouldn't we expect to find an even more extensive array of media that caters to it? Of course not! And the reason is that, of all four positions, it is the most decisively girt about by a defensive perimeter of repression and denial. Glamorous or homey, a woman can feel herself to be genuinely a woman, just as the lascivious man who whistles at a passing hourglass figure may feel himself to be very much a man. But to be needy and childlike is to be no longer a man at all, and all of his forces, at least in public, must be marshaled to prevent it.

If we want to put a finger on the most decisive motive that lies concealed beneath the sound and fury of the battle between the sexes, we must find it in this masculine defensiveness. In this way, the underlying conflicts of love can be traced back to the Oedipus complex. Rules of the game there are indeed, and they tend to be stacked against the woman because she generally arouses in the man who loves her an ambivalence more intense than any she may feel about him. This Freudian conclusion is once again in line with an astute observation of Nietzsche. Not long after the passage quoted above about "women's action at a distance," Nietzsche offers the following little story.

> Someone took a youth to a sage and said: "Look, he is being corrupted by women." The sage shook his head and smiled. "It is men," said he, "that corrupt women; and all the failings of women should be atoned by and improved in men. For it is man who creates for himself the image of woman, and woman forms herself according to this image."
>
> "You are too kindhearted about women," said one of those present; "you do not know them." The sage replied: "Will is the manner of men, willingness that of women. That is the law of the sexes—truly, a hard law for women. All of humanity is innocent of its existence; but women are doubly innocent. Who could have oil and kindness enough for them?"
>
> "Damn oil! Damn kindness!" someone else shouted out of the crowd; "women need to be educated better!" —"Men need to be educated better," said the sage and beckoned the youth to follow him. —The youth, however, did not follow him.

These reflections about the difference in what men and women look for in love prompt me to risk a final remark about romance. There is some truth to the cliché that women are more interested in romance. Romance flatters a woman's sense of being the object of a man's doting attention. She craves candles, soft music, and flowers, especially if they provide a more effective staging for her to be the admired focus of a loving regard. Psychoanalytically speaking, the reason is not far to seek. If her body consciousness is stimulated by the transformations of puberty, a woman's narcissism is also directed from an early age by the desire to be her father's darling. For many women, the deepest longing is for recognition, the sense that she is paid attention to by others. Ultimately, it is a longing that far transcends any desire to be a beautiful object and that animates the yearning to be listened to and understood, to be appreciated for her true self. And if that cannot be had completely, then the standard rituals of romantic love—having a man open doors for her, carry her things, fuss over her with a protective umbrella, step in to pay the bill—may offer a workable second-best.

Nor is it difficult now to see why men, however willingly they may be enlisted in the first blossoming of romance, tend fairly predictably to lose interest in it as time goes on. Aside from the enjoyment it might give to a woman, from which a man admittedly might benefit, for most men romance is not in itself a compelling source of pleasure. The reason is that romance is essentially a spark that flies across a certain gap. Romance requires a certain experience of distance. There are few things as surely stimulating to romance as a physical separation—when lovers are forced, say, to live in separate cities for a period. Absence, as the saying goes, makes the heart grow fonder. Such distance is the natural element of women's longing for love, because it echoes the margin of distance that characterized her relation to her father. Not so for men. To the extent that men in love seek to regain the embrace of a woman in the place of the mother, to the extent, that is, that men seek not recognition but recontact, not mere acknowledgment from the other but actual reunion with her, the distance that feeds romantic longing is bound to become not only burdensome but downright unsatisfying. In his heart of hearts, he wants more than anything to abolish all distance and to curl up contentedly in a refound bliss of fusion.

The problem, the thing that dooms relations between the sexes to be a perennial struggle, is that men simultaneously tend to find such reunion intolerable. Too close a proximity raises the fear of being engulfed and suffocated. The psychological dynamics to which men are subject thus shuttle them restlessly back and forth between two poles, the ultimately unfulfilling position of the romantic lover and the unbearable position of the cared-for little boy.

Adam and His Rib

The keynote of the psychoanalytic understanding of the masculine relation to women is ambivalence. Passage through the Oedipus complex leaves the little boy in a deeply conflicted position. On the one hand, he longs for reunion with the reassuring embrace of the mother. On the other, he must find his own way in the world as an independent and autonomous being. It is a tension of mixed feelings that is played out countless times in the course of every boy's life, as when the Little League third baseman takes a bouncing line drive smack in the face. As he crumples in a sobbing heap, what he most wants is his mother's arms around him, her calming whisper in his ear—not his father, not his coach, not his big brother, but his mother. But gathering himself sufficiently to sniff back the tears, he will look up anxiously from the shelter of his mother's hug, as if suddenly reminded of the others who are watching this little drama of humiliation. He may then jump up, turning away from his mother as if brushing away a clot of mud still clinging to his uniform, and rejoin his companions in the field, desperately pretending that nothing at all has happened. To remain tied to his mother's skirts is to remain a kind of cripple, a lesser being, unable to hold his head up among the peers of his tribe.

With the focus on the ambivalent tension that underlies men's relation to women, a tension rooted in the drama of the boy's separation from his mother, we can shed some new light on the alleged masculinist bias in Freud's work. Untold numbers of critics have seized upon this bias as the most objectionable feature of Freud's legacy. In fact, Freud's failure to understand feminine psychology is now in many circles assumed without further ado. There might be some things of value in Freud, we hear, but clearly he knew nothing about women. For these critics, Freud's theories appear to be arbitrarily and illegitimately based on the example of boys. Feminine psychology is cut to fit this masculine mold with the result that women appear in psychoanalysis as incomplete or defective men. The reason, it is often supposed, is that Freud was himself a man.[2] No wonder his psychology is skewed in favor of boys, men, and everything masculine.

I earlier tried to answer this criticism by showing ways in which the underlying issues at stake in castration and the Oedipus complex affect both boys and girls. And yet, having now seen a bit more of the way Freud maps the relation between the sexes, we can return to the criticism and admit that there is something absolutely crucial to be retained in it, though not what the critics themselves want to assert. By that I mean that the initial point of the criticism contains an indispensable grain of truth, though the reasons adduced for it and the implications drawn from it are faulty. The twin epicenters of Freudian psychology, the castration and Oedipal complexes, *are* more directly relevant to the little boy than to the little girl. But the reason is no mere matter of chauvinism. Rather, Freud wants to shed light on the ways in which masculine psychology is based upon a fundamental defensiveness in relation to the feminine.

And then the really crucial point: This defensive posture of the masculine personality is the decisive factor in establishing the very phenomenon of gender and in determining the implications that follow from it. Femininity positions itself in relation to that masculine defensiveness; indeed, Freud understands femininity as being largely *constituted* in this way. There is, we might say, no neutral ground upon which masculine and feminine can meet, no free space in which the sexes can encounter one another in an unbiased way. In entering the field of relations with the other gender, woman must somehow reckon with the fact that she always arrives after the first move has been made. Masculine psychology is always already postured defensively against her. The best she can do is to find a suitable counter move, to place herself in relation to men in a fashion that one hopes makes the best of a compromised situation.

[2]Among the first to level this charge was Karen Horney, herself a psychoanalyst and one of the earliest members of the Freudian school.

The masculinist bent of psychoanalysis is no mere quirk or personal preference of its founder. But neither does it somehow favor men. On the contrary, as we have begun to see in this chapter and will see further in the next, the legacy of the Oedipus complex, if it leaves the little girl with a stubborn sense of vulnerability and insecurity, is arguably even more problematic for boys, who tend to take with them into later life a rigid and inflexible character shell that tinges their relations to others with aggressiveness. Far from being an unqualified advantage, masculine psychology saddles men, and the women connected to them, with a range of psychological and interpersonal challenges that often work to the detriment of everyone.

"Not so fast!" the critic will protest. "You've presented a picture of masculinity and femininity that turns Freud's classical theory upside down. Freud asserted that the path of women's development is the more difficult and perilous, for at least two reasons. First, unlike the little boy who can retain the love of his mother with a substitute in later life, the maturing little girl must transfer her original love for the mother to a wholly new object, the father. It is a transfer that is made easier by her discovery of the feminine lack of a penis, for which she blames her mother, but it also leaves her with a permanent scar to her self-esteem. Second, Freud thought that the growing girl must switch the zone of her genital enjoyment from the clitoris to the vagina. In early childhood, the little girl's clitoris may be a pleasure zone exactly like the penis, but the grown woman learns to enjoy stimulation of the vagina. You, by contrast, pose the masculine path as the more difficult, as it requires a tricky mix of separation and connection to the mother. The legacy of this more difficult task is permanent ambivalence toward woman. What for Freud seemed a challenge you thus turn into an advantage: the destiny of feminine loving avoids such intense ambivalence by seizing upon a love object in later life that doesn't recall the original, caretaking other. Strictly speaking, your account isn't really 'Freudian' at all!"

In one sense, the critic is precisely right. I have indeed inverted a key point of Freud's classical account. Where Freud emphasized the little girl's difficulty in switching objects, I have put the accent on the challenge faced by the little boy in keeping the same one. The young man must return in maturity to the female Other from whom he has gained a hard-won measure of independence. But must this revision be disqualified as wholly un-Freudian? I think not. In the first place, the essential terms are Freud's: The fundamental issue in personality formation, masculine or feminine, is the psychological tension between early and later formations of libido. The attachments of infancy continue to reverberate in adulthood, but with mixed results. Second, my account reiterates the most basic point of Freud's theory of femininity, the point on which he disagreed with many of his own followers, Karen Horney and Ernest Jones among them. That point is to insist that there is no original, inborn, or *sui generis* femininity. In her early development, the little girl's love life is basically parallel to the little boy's. Only later does she develop specifically "feminine" characteristics. And why? Precisely in response to the requirements of the masculine other (the father) whose love she seeks. The traits of femininity are developed in response to the masculine. Far from being a natural state, "femininity" is something that men require women to be. Femininity is a kind of mask that women are required to wear.

The third reason the view I have offered can claim to be Freudian is that Freud's own account is not monolithic. Though he sometimes portrays it as a kind of advantage that the little boy may carry his love for the mother forward into his adult life, he nevertheless stresses repeatedly the profound ambivalence that animates the masculine regard for women and everything feminine. One of the most interesting and useful of Freud's ideas about love can be located at this point. Masculine ambivalence toward the feminine, rooted in the tensions that animate the Oedipus complex, issues in a defensive splitting of the libido into two currents, the affectionate and the sensual. While sometimes palpable in women as well, this split tends to be exaggerated in men and becomes an especially prominent feature of their emotional adjustment to the challenges of loving. In effect, the masculine personality defends itself against the specter of fusion with the mother by separating the sexual from the affectionate. In this way, the entire sphere of sexuality tends to be defined in opposition to the emotional bond that tied the little boy to the mother.

This split between affectionate and sensual currents of libido favors a division of women into two categories. There are women for whom a man feels a tender affection and respect, more or less devoid of sexual attraction, and those who stimulate an intense sexual charge, but without a sympathetic connection. This dichotomy of the tender and the torrid corresponds to the distinction between madonna and whore, the division made in Mediterranean countries between *mama* and *putana*. It is a distinction that is reflected in the biblical pair of women, Mary and Eve, or again between Mary, mother of Jesus, and Mary Magdalene, the prostitute. Yet even such a partitioning between women of different orders cannot save those men whose divided libido has given rise to it. Their love life is everywhere haunted by impotence. Women who are viewed affectionately are unavailable by virtue of the prohibition against incest, while women who well represent the sensual pole offer little or no emotional gratification. Freud's terse assessment of such men is dreary indeed: "where they love they do not desire and where they desire they cannot love."

Rooted in the same ambivalence is the tendency, noted by Simone de Beauvoir and others, for women to symbolize both the summit of human aspirations and the depths of human depravity. "Woman," as Tertullian famously said of her, "is a temple built over a sewer." She is stretched impossibly between angel and animal, between saint and strumpet. "If she agrees to deny her animality," de Beauvoir remarks, "woman—from the very fact that she is the incarnation of sin—will be also the most radiant incarnation of the triumph of the elect who have conquered sin." The result for most women is necessity of a difficult steerage between the poles of men's conflicting expectations. She is constantly in danger of falling to one side of a painful double-bind: being too prudish to be interesting, or too loose to be respectable.

Yet the sensual and sexualized side of the masculine relation to woman is subject to a further defensive elaboration: the tendency toward an aggressive debasement. It is as if the separation of the affectionate from the sensual requires an additional and decisive gesture of rejection, in accordance with which the sexual object is not only stripped of emotional significance but is also painted with the black brush of a hateful devaluation. For many men, Freud observes, the debilitating effects of sexual impotence are avoided only by demeaning and humiliating women.

As we will see in the next chapter, it is a tendency that has far-reaching and destructive consequences for relations between the sexes.

A Touchy Question

Freud's claims about feminine narcissism have to be read in tandem with his theory of the anaclitic tendency of the masculine personality and the defenses arrayed against it. When we do so, what may at first appear to be an affront to women is revealed to be anything but a misogynistic slander. On the contrary, the Freudian theory on this point underscores and supplements many feminist views of gender difference. But what of Freud's other claim that women in love are masochistic? Here, one suspects, it may be a good deal more difficult to get Freud off the hook. Yet here, too, many people, outraged by what they have heard of Freud's theories, understand neither his conclusions nor the underlying intention that animates them.

So why does Freud accuse women of being masochistic? What he has in mind first of all is the deferential tendency of femininity, the many ways in which being feminine requires putting the powers and prerogatives of others ahead of one's own. The properly feminine woman is reluctant to speak too loudly for fear of appearing to demand too much. When tempted to act on her own, she thinks first of the effects of her choices on others. Demurely keeping her own light under a bushel, the acquiescent woman provides the perfect complement for a man whose confidence needs bolstering. In the extreme case, we have the prostitute who submits to her pimp though it may not be in her interests to do so, or the long-suffering wife of the abusive husband who continues to stand by her man even in the face of ongoing emotional or physical mistreatment. It is with these self-effacing or even self-destructive tendencies in mind that Teresa Brennan has argued on Freudian grounds that femininity amounts in itself to a kind of pathology.

And immediately we see one of the main objections to psychoanalytic talk about feminine masochism. Mustn't any claim about women's masochism amount to saying that whatever the abuse a woman may suffer, she ultimately brings it upon herself, that she really wants it? Doesn't such an appeal to masochism merely blame the victim? Moreover, doesn't the Freudian view overlook the social and economic factors that contribute to the enslavement of women? No sophisticated psychology is needed to see that the realities of a man's world are organized to the disadvantage of women. The 7th Avenue hooker may be forced to rely on a male pimp to protect her from the dangers of life on the street. The battered wife who returns to her abuser may not be economically free to leave. Perhaps she refuses to testify against him for fear of further mistreatment to herself or her children. And Freud would have us believe that these women are motivated by some obscure impulse to embrace their own afflictions? What could be worse?

There is no question that Freud stands here on very dangerous ground. Why, then, does he persist? The case is an exemplary instance of a point we have made several times before that is central for a psychoanalytic perspective. Freud is not at all interested in denying the existence of external factors—social, economic, legal, and otherwise—that shape psychological reality, in this case factors that contribute mightily to the social and political disempowerment of women. Nor is he saying that women simply bring down upon themselves the abuse that befalls them in a world in which violence against women is a sadly pervasive reality. He does want to argue, however, that the psychological dynamics of feminine personality subtly predispose it in the direction of self-denial and self-punishment. These more hidden, psychological dynamics provide fertile ground for the operation of other, external forces.

In making this point about how internal, psychological factors prepare for and supplement the effects of external ones, we are dealing with the tricky question of how exactly the individual unconscious interacts with a larger world of other kinds of social, cultural, or economic forces. In some ways the two can and should be considered separately. In other ways, they may work together or be intertwined with each other in an ongoing dialectic. An analogy might be made to the inner workings of an old-fashioned pendulum clock. The movement of the clock is powered primarily by the swing of the pendulum, to which we can compare the external forces of economy and society. High up in the clock mechanism, however, there is a tiny rocker arm that contributes a minute impetus to each swing of the pendulum. This rocker arm is connected by gear wheels to the clock weights that must be wound up periodically. With every oscillation of the pendulum, the rocker arm borrows a tiny quantum of force from the descending weights and kicks back ever so slightly against the motion of the pendulum arm. Without this additional increment of force, the pendulum would fairly quickly come to a stop. Though its actual contribution of force is relatively small, the function of the rocker arm in the overall movement of the clock is therefore indispensable. In a somewhat similar fashion, psychological predispositions participate with forces impinging upon the mind from outside it, strengthening and supplementing their influence. In Freud's view, aspects of external reality are crucially augmented by the dynamics of a hidden, inward, but decisively important "psychical reality."

It is with such a notion of psychical reality in mind that we can disentangle some recent flaps of Freud criticism. There is, for example, the stir created by the publication in 1984 of *The Assault on Truth: Freud's Suppression of the Seduction Theory*, a book whose authoritativeness appeared strengthened by the fact that its author, Jeffrey Masson, served for a time as the curator of the Freud Archive and edited a comprehensive volume of Freud's letters to his friend Wilhelm Fliess. Early in his clinical experience, Masson argues, Freud repeatedly traced the psychological distress of his patients to childhood sexual abuse and came to believe that neurosis is the psychological consequence of real-life trauma. The result was Freud's so-called seduction theory of neurosis. So far, Masson is perfectly correct. He is also correct that Freud came to reject the seduction theory and that this rejection was intimately bound up with the breakthrough that led to the psychoanalytic theory. Where Masson goes wrong is in his attribution of motive. According to Masson, Freud came to deny the role of childhood sexual trauma, proposing instead that neurosis is triggered by the child's own phantasies of abuse, because the truth was just too hard to swallow. Masson invites us to imagine that, faced with the outrage of male colleagues who refused to believe in the prevalence of childhood seductions by fathers, uncles, and brothers, Freud recanted his original theory in a cowardly bid for professional acceptance. The whole edifice of psychoanalytic theory is thus condemned by Masson as nothing more than a cover-up, an attempt to forge a psychology that would flatter the self-denials of a sexist culture.

Masson's sensational charges sound impressive, but they don't stand up to scrutiny. In fact, even a fairly casual reader of Freud can discern that it is Masson, not Freud, who willfully suppresses the evidence. Over the course of his career, Freud repeatedly reminds us that the frequency of childhood sexual abuse is commonly underestimated and he continues to insist upon its psychologically disastrous consequences. Two decades after abandoning his seduction theory, Freud reiterates that "phantasies of being seduced are of particular interest, because so often they are not phantasies but real memories." In one of his last papers, Freud returns again to "the sexual abuse of children by adults" and "seduction by other children (brothers or sisters)" in order to say that while they "do not apply to all children … they are common enough." In alleging that Freud turns away in horror from the reality of childhood sexual abuse, Masson is simply wrong.

But there is a larger issue at stake between Masson and Freud. Behind Masson's critique lies the assumption that only real experiences count as psychologically effective. Only actual abuse can precipitate psychological illness. This assumption was the real core of Freud's own seduction theory. So why did he give it up? Not because he wanted to avoid the censure of the psychiatric establishment. His subsequent development of psychoanalysis offered no shortage of other opportunities for professional attack and institutional ostracism. Rather, Freud became increasingly aware that even children who have suffered no direct or explicit abuse may still develop debilitating neurotic symptoms in later life. He was thus driven to consider the part played by forces internal to the psychological subject that may operate on their own, independent of traumatic experience.

But that's not all. Ironically, given Masson's critique, Freud rejected the seduction theory precisely in order to explain how and why experiences of real trauma have such lasting effect. In Freud's view, the real riddle is not understanding why trauma leaves a psychological wound, but why the traumatized individual so typically returns again and again to the traumatic experience, re-creating its painful impact. Freud's problem, addressed in the following brief passage to the example of a sexually abused little girl but equally applicable to boys, is to understand why "a little girl who was made the object of a sexual seduction in her early childhood may direct her later sexual life so as constantly to provoke similar attacks."

Freud rejects the seduction theory, first because it cannot account for psychological disturbances for which no real abuse ever occurred, but also because it cannot explain the persistence of neurotic complexes even when they can be traced back to some actually experienced trauma. Against Masson, Freud maintains that the mind is no merely passive receptacle but is an active, integrating power of its own. This initiating and constructive activity Freud calls phantasy. In phantasy, the psyche is not only responding passively to the world around it but is actively anticipating experience, pressing it into molds of the mind's own making. The pendulum swing of experience is always subject to an additional push from the psychical rocker arm of phantasy.

The key to grasping the real meaning of Freud's rejection of the seduction theory thus lies in his discovery of the existence and effects of unconscious phantasies. In fact, appreciation of the role of such phantasy in psychical life forms the very foundation of psychoanalysis. Yet with respect to the psychoanalytic concept of phantasy, it seems to be a matter of "damned if you do and damned if you don't." If Jeffrey Masson faults Freud for overlooking real abuse in favor of phantasies, other critics have assailed Freud for the opposite sin of leading us to mistake mere phantasy for actual events. Frederick Crews, an English professor at the University of California and an outspoken critic of psychoanalysis, has made something of a cottage industry of this form of Freud bashing. He focuses on the so-called repressed memory movement, under the influence of which scores of patients, many of them children, have been guided by therapists to recover false "memories" of abuse. This testimony has then been used to bring criminal actions against parents, nannies, teachers, and pastors who are innocent of the charges against them. In one respect, Crews is right. It is quite true, as he says, that "a number of parents and child-care providers are serving long prison terms, and others are awaiting trial, on the basis of therapeutically induced 'memories' of child sexual abuse that never in fact occurred." But Crews then goes on to point the finger of blame at Freud. "Although the therapists in question are hardly Park Avenue psychoanalysts," Crews argues, "the tradition of Freudian theory and practice unmistakably lies behind their tragic deception of both patients and jurors." Is Freud really the culprit here?

Setting the record straight on this issue is not entirely simple, if only because it can fairly be said that the Freudian tradition *has* contributed something to the rage over repressed memories. It was Freud, after all, who taught us to look back into the mists of childhood experience to find the keys with which to unlock our present distress. Yet the irony remains that it was also Freud, more than any other theorist of the mind, who warned us against taking everything reported in memory as a literal record of actual events. On the contrary, the very essence of the Freudian concept of phantasy is to define a register of psychical reality that is crucially separate from reality per se. The psychological reality that determines so much human misery routinely outstrips the influence of actual experiences of trauma. That Freud is now held accountable for the excesses of the repressed memories movement is thus a crude distortion of the facts.

If Frederick Crews were really interested in stemming the tide of false claims of childhood sexual abuse—allowing, of course, that such abuse is often real enough—then Freud could quite reasonably be counted upon as an ally. The reason is that Freud so clearly warns us that young children, encouraged by the barest minimum of suggestion, will very readily inflate their memories to assume the proportions of astonishing crimes, losing in the process all capacity to discriminate between fact and phantasy. The real lesson to be drawn from Crews's attack on Freud is thus, as it is in so many other castigations of psychoanalysis, an appreciation of the degree to which Freud's legacy is now pervasively present in the popular domain, but very often with little or no understanding of the real meaning of his thought.

But we have already strayed some distance from our objective. How to return to the theme of feminine masochism? To handle it adequately we will have to consider the darkest and most mysterious of Freud's theoretical formulations, the notion of the death drive. It is to that topic that we must now turn in the next chapter.

5
Love You to Death

The enigma of feminine masochism is best approached by way of Freud's more general concept of masochism. Over the course of his career, masochism increasingly emerged at the very heart of the mystery of the unconscious. We have already glimpsed the point at which Freud first encountered it: the compulsion of his neurotic patients to repeat the painful experience of trauma. But what he first noted in the behavior of genteel Viennese *Hausfräuen* became much more striking among the home-coming veterans of World War I. Reeling from the mortal horrors of the trenches, many of these men remained for years afterwards prisoners to recurrent dreams of wartime atrocities. Here, too, there was evidence of the way in which psychic reality could trump any actual occurrence of trauma. The worst cases of war neurosis were to be found among soldiers who merely witnessed death and dismemberment—soldiers who actually suffered physical wounds often fared better. These instances of traumatic repetition were stubbornly difficult to explain, especially for a theorist of the unconscious who well appreciated the power of the mind to block painful thoughts from awareness. Why did these war survivors so compulsively return to traumatic memories that might otherwise have been repressed?

The answer allowed Freud to link attachment to trauma with the underlying riddle of all neurotic distress: Ultimately, the sufferings of the neurotic must be counted as self-inflicted. The neurotic is his own worst enemy. The debilitating symptoms of neurosis—the overpowering terror of the phobic, the sleeplessness of the insomniac, the paralysis of the hysteric, the self-defeating preoccupations of the obsessional—all appear to be various forms of self-punishment. Equally telling for Freud were the many instances in which a patient, poised on the edge of making some positive movement in therapy, would inexplicably abort the process, fomenting a blow-up with the analyst or disappearing from treatment altogether. This all-too-familiar occurrence, what Freud came to call the "negative therapeutic reaction," suggested a deep attachment to the patient's own suffering, a mysterious unwillingness to feel better. Wrestling with these puzzling phenomena, Freud felt driven to hypothesize the existence of an obscure impulse of self-destructiveness. This deep strain of masochism appeared to violate the eminently reasonable expectation that every creature naturally seeks pleasure and avoids pain. Freud seemed faced with a force operating "beyond the pleasure principle" and contrary to it—a *Todestrieb* or "drive toward death." As we will see, the solution to the problem of feminine masochism lies in this most profound and puzzling of his hypotheses.

Love and Death

Rejected outright as ludicrous by Freud's detractors and found dubious even by many of his closest adherents, the theory of the death drive nevertheless continued to enjoy a privileged place in Freud's thinking during the last twenty years of his life. Indeed, he more than once referred to its discovery as the summit-achievement of his theoretical work and he centered his most far-reaching speculations upon it. In one of his last papers, he insisted again on the value of the dual drive theory of Eros and Death. "Only by the concurrent or mutually opposing action of the two primal instincts—Eros and the death instinct—never by one or the other alone," he said, "can we explain the rich multiplicity of the phenomena of life." To understand his view, it is helpful to refer it to the earlier dualism that had informed Freud's thinking before 1920. In many ways, the opposition between Eros and Death was a transposition and radicalizing of his earlier theory of the tension between the ego and sex. And it is for that reason that the theme of the death drive will be of such relevance to the questions before us about gender and sexuality.

But immediately we seem to encounter an obstacle. In drawing a parallel between Freud's two great dualisms—ego and sex, then Eros and Death—the part played by the ego in the original theory, associated with the interests of self-preservation and stability, later comes to be linked with Eros, the power that gathers things together into unities. But that would leave the sexuality of the original scheme to be paired with death. How exactly does all of this fit together? Is the later dualism somehow contradictory to the first? Given the original *opposition* between ego and sexuality, how and why does the mature theory throw the ego together with Eros?

We have already anticipated the answer in noticing that the maturing ego comes to claim a certain measure of sexuality for itself.[1] Indeed, it is along those lines that we gave a first indication of the definition of gender from a Freudian point of view. The determination of the ego as masculine or feminine, as well as its choice of sexual object in homosexuality or heterosexuality, both reflect the sexualization of the adult ego. Unlike the infantile ego for which the entire sexual domain is *terra incognita*, there is virtually no adult for whom some aspect of sex has not become part of their conscious identity, even if it is only to inform a choice of celibacy. The interests of the ego thus come to coincide with the erotic, or at least with some portion of it.

But as we have also seen, there always remains an excessive and potentially overwhelming aspect of sexuality, belonging to those dimensions of sex that

---

[1]See especially the last paragraph of the section devoted to "Subversive Sexuality" in Chapter 3.

are excluded from the established identity of the ego. In this sense, sexuality retains the possibility to destabilize the ego. The effects of the death drive, what Freud calls the "mysterious masochistic trends of the ego," therefore echo the potential of sexuality to traumatize the immature ego. Sex forever retains its power to scandalize us, to appall, horrify, and *mortify* us. In this way, sex plays a role on both sides of the divide between the two great Freudian drives of Eros and Death. On the one hand, sex belongs to what Freud calls Eros and furthers its aims of unity and stability. Sex can flatter and reassure our sense of self, helping us to know ever more certainly who we are and where our limits lie. On the other hand, the threatening and destabilizing power of sex is rightly associated with the death drive. Sexual desire can be the imp that tempts us to step beyond the safe and the familiar, the troublemaker that prompts us to scandalize ourselves, the force of inexplicable attraction that lures us toward acts in which we are no longer recognizable to ourselves.

The relevance of the death drive to sexuality is hinted at in the poetic French term for orgasm: *la petite mort*. In "the little death" of orgasm, the boundaries between self and other may seem to disappear in a flood of overwhelming sensation. Psychoanalytically considered, orgasm effects a momentary eclipse of the self, an ecstatic death of the ego, brought about by the blurring of separation between self and other. From the point of view of the id, struggling under the mantle of repression, this mortification of the ego could not be more welcome. For the ego itself, however, seeking to maintain itself as a stable and coherent structure, the eruption of the repressed energies of the id may trigger the outbreak of anxiety. The anxiety-arousing potential of sexuality is especially acute for the psychotic, whose fragile ego is already deeply destabilized.

Freud speculated about the rootedness of the death drive in biology, wondering whether its psychological manifestations might someday be traced to the most primitive tendency of organic matter: that of reverting to the inorganic. Perhaps, he thought, masochism is the psychological counterpart of the built-in self-destructiveness that leads to the death of every organism, the biological equivalent of automakers' "planned obsolescence." In that case, the *Todestrieb* would be an "instinct" in the properly biological sense. But the logic of the death-seeking impulse can clearly be discerned on a purely psychological level in terms already familiar to us as a function of the tension between ego and id. The death at stake is none other than the death of the ego itself, and the motive force behind its destruction is the alienating effect of repression. Divided against itself by the organization of the ego, the psyche seeks to reintegrate what the ego has excluded. In this way, the self-destructive tendency emerges not as an instinct but as a *drive*, a function not of biological determinism but of psychological structure. The death drive can thus be identified with the deepest strivings of the id against the strictures imposed upon it by the ego.

Aside from clinical facts that cried out for explanation, the hypothesis of the death drive served Freud's purposes in helping to answer another of the most basic questions raised by his evolving theory, that of the punitive virulence of the superego. For a child to fear the sting of an angry parent's spanking required no great leap of theoretical imagination. But what motivates the guilty individual to become his own judge and jailer? The urgency of the question lay in its connection with the central mechanism of neurosis as a self-inflicted agony. By assuming the existence of an internal motive of attack on the ego, Freud could provide an answer to this vexing enigma. The superego is animated, as he put it, by "a pure culture of the death drive." In effect, the punishing voice of conscience joins forces in common cause with the obscure, self-destructive trends of the death drive to attack the ego. In this way, Freud could explain both the universality of the tendency toward guilt and also the viciousness with which it could be inflicted upon the neurotic ego. The superego draws its motive energy from sources deep in the id. Thus Freud suggests that "the superego is always close to the id and can act as its representative *vis à vis* the ego. It reaches deep down into the id and for that reason is farther from consciousness than the ego is."

With the theoretical construct of the death drive in hand, it becomes clear that it is ultimately we ourselves who desire the "death" of the ego. What most opposes the ego is the force of desire itself. Under the influence of Jacques Lacan, the French school of psychoanalysis has evolved a term for the anxious enjoyment aroused by the activity of the death drive, the paradoxical satisfaction that is beyond or even contrary to the pleasure principle, the basic law of psychical functioning as laid down by Freud prior to his discovery of the death drive. Lacan called such paradoxical pleasure, this strange pleasure taken in the very antithesis of pleasure, *jouissance.* Derived from the French word *jouir,* its slang usage meaning "to come," *jouissance* refers to an ecstatic enjoyment that involves a certain loss of control, a suspension of the ego's watchful guardianship. The appeal of *jouissance* is what lures us to the edge of a precipice despite its terror, or better, *because* of it. The thrill of *jouissance* is motivated by an urge to test the limits of the ego, an impulse to breach its protective envelope.

No wonder, then, that *jouissance* very typically takes the form of a fascination with violation of the body image, the original template upon which the infantile ego is modeled. *Jouissance* is that curious mixture of fear and delight a child feels at hearing the grisly details of many fairy tales, as in the story of the ogre who bursts apart when he plummets to the bottom of Jack's beanstalk or that of the wolf who eats Grandma and Little Red Riding Hood, only to be hacked open by the woodsman, stuffed full of stones, and sewn up again. Likewise, it is a certain taste of *jouissance* that motivates passing motorists to gawk at a bad car accident. What is it that they hope to see there but the very thing that would most horrify them? Plato remarks on this enigma in the *Republic* when a certain Leontius, passing the place of execution on his way back into the city, cannot take his eyes off the corpses laid out there. "With wide staring eyes, he rushed up to the corpses and cried, 'There, ye wretches, take your fill of the fine spectacle.'" Seven centuries later, St. Augustine will wonder again: "What pleasure can there be in the sight of a mangled corpse? Yet people will flock to see one lying on the ground simply for the sensation of sorrow and horror that it gives them." In many cultures and in virtually every epoch of history the execution of criminals has been a festive occasion in which whole communities have enjoyed the exhibition of death and dismemberment, the bloodier the better.

Viewed from the perspective of psychoanalysis, such fascination with the spectacle of the mangled body, a fascination that irresistibly attracts even as it horrifies, betokens the activity of that enigmatic and primitive impulse that Freud called the death drive. It signifies an anxious desire to look beyond the boundaries of life itself, a desire that is rooted in the need to escape from the confines of the ego. It is the surfacing of something in us that is more than us, something of us yet beyond us, something that we ourselves *are* that remains utterly other to our everyday sense of ourselves. The force of the death drive, the transgressive satisfaction of *jouissance*, is the pressure of the id seeking to crack open the cramped and puny shell of the ego.

In an earlier chapter, I was at pains to show how the Freudian notion of drive is intimately linked to the desire of the other. Over the unfolding of the oral, anal, and phallic stages, the child is caught up in a formative dance with the mother, motivated first by a search for her love and later by the question of what it is that will satisfy her. The vicissitudes of the drive are therefore always oriented to the position of the other and the unknown quantity of the other's desire. We can now see how the theory of the death drive, far from being unrelated to this issue of the other, is a radicalizing of it. The death drive, we might say, is the gravity of the other in its purest form, the force that decenters the ego and draws it into the orbit of something radically other to itself. In the grips of the death drive, the human being becomes subject to a centrifugal pressure by which it is continually spun beyond itself. The death drive is the attractive force of the Other as such, a force so primal and ultimately so irresistible that its satisfaction may well demand the literal death of the individual.

But there is an obvious problem with this theory. Taken straight on and without qualification, Freud's claim is that our deepest longing is for our own annihilation. As he puts it at one point, the deepest aim of all life is death. Yet how can such a theory possibly convince us? Even if we resist the temptation immediately to throw out Freud's hypothesis of a death drive for being nonsensical or self-contradictory, what evidence do we have that such a thing exists at all? Risky or even self-destructive behavior is familiar enough, but surely that is the exception. Far more prevalent and conspicuous than acts of suicide are those of desperate self-preservation. How can we possibly agree with Freud that our most primitive and elemental motivation seeks not life but death?

A large part of the answer to this question lies in Freud's supposition that the force of the death drive is almost never directly expressed, mainly because its self-destructive fury is transformed into other, more manageable expressions. Among the most common and effective of these transformations is outward aggression. In aggression, the self-corrosive potential of the death drive is "turned outwards" under the influence of the ego's struggle to maintain itself. It is as if the ego manages to turn the death drive to its own advantage, using the threatening energy of death to declare war on something outside itself. In the process, the ego is strengthened by means of violence directed toward some object in the world. In this way, Freud seeks to explain the inner secret of the human disposition to savagery and destruction. The longing for death that issues from the tension between ego and id may assume the form of a crude and brutish hunger for violence, the magnetic attraction of murder and mayhem. The dynamics of cruelty and violence are thus seen by Freud to be rooted in conflicts internal to the human psyche. Destructiveness is directed to external objects by means of a turning outwards of an originally self-destructive impulse. Human aggression has therefore nothing whatever to do with the violence of animal predators. Human hatred ultimately derives from self-hatred. Human aggression has its origins in a psychological conflict that is a purely human burden.

The force of the drive toward death may also be discharged in more benign ways. In the enjoyment of the rubbernecker, for example, what Freud refers to as the "primordial masochism" of the ego is relished from a safe distance. In the security of being a mere spectator, the ego continues to assert its rights. In such cases, the death drive is again blended with the self-preservative influence of Eros. It is the delight of looking over the edge without actually being in danger of falling. It is the thrill of feeling oneself to be in the presence of mighty and terrifying powers—the deafening rage of thunderstorms, the pounding of towering surf, the immensity of awe-inspiring mountain ranges—yet able to savor their enormity without risk. Immanuel Kant, the great eighteenth-century German philosopher, described it as the experience of the sublime, a term that happily anticipates the Freudian concept of the same coinage. In sublimation, the achievement of great art, for example, something of the otherness of unconscious desire is tasted without unbearable threat to the ego.

When it is circuited by symbols, the death drive is "tamed" by a process of sublimation. By this means, the death drive may assume a productive, almost lyrical, aspect. The primordial masochism of the death drive comes to energize the lure of the unknown. It is the hidden motive that presses the mind to pass beyond the horizon of the familiar. In this, its more sublime employment, the death drive becomes the engine of the scientist's research or the explorer's hunger for uncharted territory. The death drive draws the human being toward the challenging confrontation with what lies beyond itself.

But, the impatient reader now asks, what has any of this to do with the question before us about feminine masochism? The answer is that, aside from the soul-enlarging path of sublimation (a path at least in principle open equally to men and women), there are two alternative destinies for the violence of the death drive, one that tends toward internalization in the form of self-punishment (the more familiar dynamics of masochism), and another that externalizes the self-destructive drive in aggression and violence. Among the implications of the Freudian view of gender that are most far-reaching, if seldom remarked, is the way in which that view invites us to align femininity and masculinity with these two alternative means of discharging the death drive. In what follows, let us make the experiment of applying our account of the Freudian death drive to an explanation of gender difference.

The Riddle of Masculine Aggression

How, then, are we to clarify the linkage between gender and the death drive? Our path into this problem begins with a simple but enigmatic fact: The overwhelming preponderance of violence in the world is perpetrated by men. How are we to explain it? Of course, there are factors involved in the phenomenon of male violence and aggression that stand apart from any psychoanalytic consideration. Perhaps prime among them is the hormonal basis of aggressiveness, the effects of male testosterone. Recent research in endocrinology has clearly pointed to the role played by this powerful substance. What, then, can Freud add? Once again, the pendulum swing of nonpsychological causes is augmented by the rocker arm of psychical reality. The psychoanalytic solution to the mystery of male violence takes us back to the point that has guided our discussions of gender from the start: differences in ego structure between masculine and feminine. What most characterizes the masculine personality is a greater rigidity of the boundary that separates self from other, ego from id. At bottom, it is a matter of a more definite gulf between the sense of oneself as a stable and coherent identity and a deeper stratum of emotional need that is held at a distance. And we have already seen that this more decidedly defensive orientation tends to exaggerate the distinction between self and other. It disposes masculinity toward the dynamics of projection, in which what is repressed in the self is attributed to the other, then degraded and despised.

From a psychoanalytic point of view, it is this dynamic that animates the impulse to rape. The rapist regards his victim not as a feeling person but as a debased and humiliated object, a mere thing. It is an attitude that is shockingly evidenced by the transcript of "The Winter Soldier Investigation," a panel of inquiry into atrocities committed by American troops in Vietnam. The following exchange occurred between a panel moderator and Sergeant

Scott Camil, who served with the 1st Battalion, 11th Marine Regiment, 1st Marine Division from March 1966 to November 1967. Camil later became a leader in Vietnam Veterans Against the War.

Camil: The main thing was that if an operation was covered by the press there were certain things we weren't supposed to do, but if there was no press there, it was okay. I saw one case where a woman was shot by a sniper, one of our snipers. When we got up to her she was asking for water. And the lieutenant said to kill her. So he ripped off her clothes, they stabbed her in both breasts, they spread her eagle and shoved an E tool up her vagina, an entrenching tool, and she was still asking for water. And then they took that out and they used a tree limb and then she was shot.

Moderator: Did the men in your outfit, or when you witnessed these things, did they seem to think it was all right to do anything to the Vietnamese?

Camil: It wasn't like they were humans.... They were a gook or a Commie and it was okay.

In the course of his research of the My Lai massacre of 1968, Seymour Hersch recorded the following conversation with a squad leader concerning rape and rape-murder of Vietnamese women by American GIs:

> That's an everyday affair. You can nail just about everybody on that—at least once. The guys are human, man....
>
> Did you rape, too?
>
> Nope.
>
> Why not?
>
> I don't know. I just got a thing. I don't—of course it got around the company, you know, well, hah, "the medic didn't do it."
>
> Did anyone report these incidents?
>
> No. No one did. You don't dare. Next time you're out in the field you won't come back—you'll come back in a body bag. What the hell, she's only a dink, a gook, this is what they think.

Whatever its hormonal determinants, male violence is also predicated upon psychological dynamics that favor dehumanization of the other. In order for rape to be possible, the masculine ego must cut itself off from all sympathetic connection to the other. A dink, a gook, a filthy Commie. Better dead than Red. A bitch, a whore, a cunt. You can use them, abuse them, then lose them. To be sure, not every man is a rapist. Nor is every rapist a completely heartless monster, incapable in other contexts and relationships of acting upon a sympathetic and concernful connectedness to others. Nevertheless, the defensive perimeter that defines the masculine ego, the repressive cordon that keeps a man's own deeper emotionality at bay and enables him to assert himself in the world as an independent being, makes it easier to relegate another human being to the status of an inanimate thing.

This greater power of severing the emotive connection to others does not mean that the rapist fails to see the tortured reactions of his victim. Indeed, the pain and panic of the victim serve to reinforce the sense of his own prowess. In the terrified eyes of the woman he abuses, he sees his own power reflected. The rapist becomes a god in the most primitive sense: He becomes a commanding, dominating agency who measures his power, indeed his very reality, by the fear of his awestruck worshipper. The rapist's enjoyment derives in no small part from this display of fear. In this way we can explain the fact, as deceptively simple and obvious as it is horrifying, that in the double crime of rape-murder, rape *precedes* murder of the victim, not the other way round. There is little thrill to be had from the violation of a body that no longer resists. There is no satisfaction without the other's living reaction to being brutalized.

Contrary to what one might suppose based on a superficial understanding of the Freudian theory, or based on the utter savagery of many acts of sexual violence, rape is less a crime of the id than of the ego. Rape is an act by which the threatened ego re-armors itself by debasing and dehumanizing the other. It is a means of reasserting an embattled masculine identity. In this way, rape is an extreme instance of the way in which sex, far from opposing the ego, may be deployed as one of its most potent defenses.

It is in this sense that rape is rightly said to be a crime not of sex but of power. In forcing another person to submit against his or her will, the rapist enjoys the other as the mirror of his own mightiness. But in appreciating the way in which rape flatters the potency of the rapist, we run the risk of overlooking the degree to which the masculine position in the sex act may routinely afford a man the enjoyment to be derived from the assertion of his own ego. Even the most loving sexual exchange may at some point be significantly tinged with aggression. In fact, to the extent that the masculine ego is threatened by the approach of the woman who recalls to him the embrace of his mother, to the extent, that is, that the intimacy of the sexual relation tends to draw him back into the emotional orbit of his infantile self, the integrity of his ego may benefit from being braced by a tincture of aggressiveness.

The psychological situation of warfare inevitably exaggerates the longing for mother-comfort and correspondingly elicits extraordinary means of defending against the prospect of emotional hemorrhage that it poses. There is a profound truth in the cliché about wounded soldiers who cry for their mothers. The conditions of the battlefield constitute a psychological challenge quite apart from the very real threats of bodily harm. The psychical trial of warfare, borne of fear, faces every soldier with the danger of an inward collapse, the threat of being overwhelmed by the frightened little boy that hides in the heart of every man. Confronted with this inward peril, the masculine subject rescues his own ego by familiar means: He projects the conflict outward onto the other. He reinforces the integrity of his own ego by placing before himself an external ego-object that must be dominated, humiliated, violated, crushed.

It is in this sense, then, that masculine violence is rooted in the Freudian death drive, as the basis of the obscure impulse in all of us that seeks the loss of the ego, the drive to overcome our separateness and to undo the effects of individuation. Masculine aggression is *a defense against that loss.* According to Freud's classical theory, aggressivity is a turning outwards of a primordial masochism of the death drive. The keynote of masculine character, of what might be called the masculine style, is precisely such a turning outwards, the tendency to relate itself to an object or objects outside itself. The threatened ego lashes out against the other in a desperate attempt at self-preservation.

The crucial point of this account concerns the way in which external dangers awaken an internal one. The experience of warfare displays these dynamics with particular clarity. The trials of war, what Homer's Agamemnon called the "battle-test that brings honor to men," presents physical dangers, but also psychological ones. The soldier must resist the temptation not just of retreat to the physical safety of his tent but, much more primordially, of retreat to the psychological haven of the mother's embrace, the retreat that abandons the autonomy of the ego itself. Beset by threats from the world outside it, the masculine personality thus becomes ever more intensely menaced by what it otherwise desires—to reenter the fusional bond of security and comfort that tied the infant boy to his mother. He wants more than anything to abandon the lonely outpost of his own individual ego and to be reabsorbed by the caretaking other. Aggression directed upon a demonized and degraded other forms a check against this regressive slide. By means of aggressiveness, the masculine psyche sandbags itself against the overflow of its own deepest longing. What emerges is a crusted and over-armored ego, an ego ever more violent and intolerant.

Of course, the atrocities committed by soldiers are often inseparable from the psychology of groups. Participation in a group leads many men to commit acts of brutality that they would never contemplate alone. Commenting upon the mass rape committed by American soldiers at My Lai, veteran George Phillips remarked that "they only do it when there are a lot of guys around.... You know, it makes them feel good. They show each other what they can do—'I can do it,' you know. They won't do it by themselves." In gang rape, men use women's bodies less as a source of enjoyment in themselves than as a means of signaling their prowess to other men. "I hate gooks," another My Lai veteran said, "and of course the only way you could determine who hated them the most was how many times you beat them or killed them or raped them or something like that."

Atrocity thus becomes a measure of each man's competition for the respect of his comrades. Or a means of marking his victory over his enemies. Wartime rape of women becomes a means of attacking other men—the fathers, brothers, husbands of the victims. Flying over My Lai after the massacre, door gunner Ronald Ridenhour spotted a body lying in the field below. "It was a woman," Ridenhour later emotionally testified, "she was spread-eagled, as if on display. She had an 11th Brigade patch between her legs—as if it were some type of display, some badge of honor." Anthony Wilden reports a particularly grisly evidence of this usage of rape as a strategy by which one group delivers a message of conquest and domination to another. "In El Salvador women tortured and then murdered by government forces or freelance death squads have been found with the husband's or boyfriend's head sewn up inside them."

Yet the greater liability of men to rape in groups does not detract from our basic point that rape serves to resolidify the shaky ego. On the contrary, it reinforces that point once we recognize that the group comes to function as a kind of collective ego, a source of security and coherence to which the threatened individual ego clings. Derided by comrades' jeers of "chicken" or "queer," the conscience-stricken hold-back may join in a vicious gang rape. Whatever his later horror or remorse at his own act, he is rewarded by feeling himself enfolded in a new sense of belonging, fortified by his place in a group solidarity. The group is cemented together in common cause against a definite enemy, bonded by a shared participation in atrocity.

In her classic study of rape, *Against Our Will: Men, Women, and Rape*, the book from which the preceding examples of wartime rape are taken, Susan Brownmiller makes the claim that rape "is a conscious process of intimidation by which all men keep all women in a state of fear." One man's rape serves the interests of all men by establishing all women as vulnerable to rape. It is a point with which we can agree precisely to the extent that there is always a collective dimension of the ego. To be a man inevitably means comparing oneself to other men and defining oneself in relation to other men's actions (just as being a woman involves measuring oneself against the standard of femininity established by other women). In this way, every rape contributes something to the very definition of masculinity. Every actual rape retraces the lines of what is possible: every man is potentially a rapist, and every woman potentially a victim.

We should again stress that the circumstances of war and the psychological dynamics they set in motion, extreme though they are, are not as distant from those of ordinary life as it might appear. The pressures of battle are not wholly dissimilar to the competition men routinely face in the workplace, in school, or in the social sphere, in which they often feel themselves measured painfully against demands on their performance and comparisons with other men. In each case, men must find ways to buttress their sense of themselves as competent, confident, and controlling, and they frequently use women as a means to that end. Thus the man who is unemployed, who has been humiliated by co-workers or by his boss, who shortly expects another bill for the rent that he cannot pay, may find himself flying into a rage at his wife or his children. "Why aren't the dishes done?" "Why are you wearing that ratty old dress again, you know I hate that dress." "Why is there no peace and quiet around here?" To defend himself against the force of his own self-hatred, to fend off his own impulse to beat himself for being a wretched failure, he beats his wife. Caught in a cycle of despair that threatens to reduce him to a crying child, he remobilizes himself as a man by degrading and humiliating a woman.

She Loves to Be Beaten?

What of the woman's part in all of this? Does Freud's conception of feminine masochism amount to a claim that the rape victim secretly desires her violation or that the battered wife brings the abuse upon herself? Does the Freudian view authorize the self-justification of the rapist that "she asked for it, she wanted it"? Of course not. The violence visited upon women by desperate men is as deplorable from a Freudian point of view as it is from any other. In fact, as we have just seen, among the most valuable of Freud's contributions in this instance is the window it opens on the psychological dynamics of masculinity that underlie the brutalization of women.

What, then, does Freud mean by feminine masochism? It refers primarily to the readiness of many women to take on the roles assigned to them by men, even when it is very clearly not in their interest to do so. We have already evinced a prime example in feminine narcissism. The greater disposition of the feminine personality toward bodily self-consciousness is itself a form of being attuned to the regard of the other. Many women willingly volunteer themselves as artificially enhanced objects of beauty in part because they know that men like them that way. If men want and need them to function as dolls, many women jump unhesitatingly to fulfill those expectations.

To play the part of the beauty-object is not without power satisfactions of its own. Feminine beauty can be a potent means of manipulating men who hunger for it and the dazzlingly decked-out woman who turns heads in a room full of men may enjoy a distinct thrill of power. But, as Shulamith Firestone and others after her have rightly pointed out, it is a deeply compromised form of power. The woman who styles herself in the role of the beauty queen risks making herself into a sort of cardboard cutout, a mannequin who becomes enslaved to her own method of assuring for herself a modicum of social prestige. Her mental energies may be sapped by constant preoccupation with her appearance, fussing endlessly over clothes, hair, and cosmetics. Agonized over bodily imperfections, the limits of her natural endowments, or the predations of age, she may even put herself under the surgeon's knife for a host of alterations.

Ironically, the woman who allows herself to be consumed by the pursuit of the beauty ideal will end up starving herself for the very thing that she most craves: the satisfaction of recognition. She may be haunted by a sense of emptiness, wounded by the suspicion that men love her only for a contrived, outer crust of attractiveness and not for her intrinsic qualities. When her capacity to re-create the desired image begins to fail, as it inevitably will, she is left with a gnawing sense of confusion and loneliness.

The Freudian perspective does not in the least deny the existence of powerful male expectations concerning women's appearance nor does it deny the (limited) usefulness to many women of sometimes fulfilling those expectations. But Freud points to an additional factor, without which the whole picture of women's willingness to conform to the image prepared for them by men cannot be fully explained: the greater tendency of the feminine personality to involve itself with the other, to experience itself from the point of view of the other, to live *for* the other. The psychoanalytic view thus puts the focus on the structure of the feminine ego, which tends to be less definitely bounded, less securely insulated from the other.

It is here that feminine masochism forms the counterpart to masculine aggression. If what characterizes the masculine disposition to aggression is a tendency to cut itself off from the other, even to the point of conceiving the other as an inanimate object, a focus of hatred and abuse, the feminine character is disposed in the opposite direction, toward an exaggerated tendency to take the part of the other, to put itself in the place of the other and to style itself in accordance with the other's demands. The masculine strategy is autonomy from the other, the feminine curse is that of being too readily bound up with the other. The feminine subject is constantly in danger of becoming the slave of the other to the extent that she cannot resist a sympathetic connection to something outside herself.

It is with this difference in mind that we can return to the sensitive question of whether women desire rape. Of course, many men would like to think so. If men can convince themselves that women desire to be used and abused, then the object-role women are asked to play for men is happily confirmed. Feminist writers have attacked Freud for aiding and abetting this notion. But if we put the emphasis on the feminine tendency to assume the position of the other, we can both reject the idea that women take any pleasure in abuse yet also affirm that the phantasy of rape can indeed be an occasion of feminine desire. It can be so *precisely because rape is a possible object of male phantasy.* If women can phantasize about being ravished by a man, it is in part because women can be drawn more readily than men into participation with the phantasies of the other.

Let's try to illustrate some of these points by taking a provocative example from popular culture: the series of episodes, riveting for millions of devotees of the daytime soap-opera blockbuster *General Hospital*, in which Laura falls in love with Luke, a man who had earlier raped her. For a certain kind of feminist critic, this twist of the plot presents the worst sort of pandering to male phantasies about women, reinforcing the idea that women secretly want to be overpowered. Such is the verdict of Susan Brownmiller. "Do women want to be raped?" she asks. "Do we crave humiliation and violation of our bodily integrity? Do we psychologically need to be seized, taken, ravished and ravaged? Must a feminist deal with this preposterous question? The sad answer is yes, it must be dealt with, because the popular culture that we inhabit, absorb, and even contribute to, has so decreed."

It is certainly not my intention to rescue the writers of *General Hospital* from the opprobrium they probably deserve. No doubt the Luke and Laura drama *does* flatter the self-justifications of male aggressors and, as such, it warrants our criticism. Nevertheless, from a psychoanalytic perspective the judgment to be made is at least one step more complicated. From the point of view that we are exploring, one that brings to light the greater liability of the feminine personality to be drawn into the orbit of the other, we can be alert to the self-excuses of masculine aggression but can also take the risk of affirming, at least in a limited sense, that there may be something attractive in the phantasy of rape. Laura finds it possible to return to the arms of her rapist not because she is a slave to pain but because she is able to conceive his rape as an index of his desire for her. What is attractive in the feminine phantasy of rape—to the extent that it can be attractive at all—is the notion that a man might be so overcome with desire that he cannot help himself. In this way, rape phantasies are *phantasies from the perspective of the other.* It is not so much rape per se that is phantasized, the painful actuality of sexual invasion, as much as it is the prospect of seduction animated by an overwhelming force of desire, the idea of being pursued by a man whose longing is so relentlessly insistent that it will stop at nothing short of satisfaction.

The point here can be enlarged upon by way of another example: the classic work of pornography, *The Story of O*, published anonymously under the pseudonym "Pauline Réage." Its appearance on the French literary scene in 1954 aroused scandal and even investigation by the Parisian authorities. Jean Paulhan, a well-known and respected figure of French letters, supplied a preface entitled "Happiness in Slavery" and was later questioned by police eager to know the true identity of the book's author. He steadfastly refused to reveal it. A decade after its publication, the book was the most widely read contemporary French novel in the world. It has since been translated into more than two dozen languages and has sold millions of copies. It is the tale of a nameless girl who allows herself to be taken prisoner in the Chateau Roissy where she is submitted to an elaborate course of humiliations and sexual violations, performed upon her by a circle of men, all overseen by her lover, René. Upon entering the Chateau, she is told that

> you are here to serve your masters. During the day, you will perform whatever domestic duties are assigned to you, such as sweeping, putting back the books, arranging flowers, or waiting on table. Nothing more difficult than that. But at the first word or sign from anyone you will drop whatever you are doing and ready yourself for what is really your one and only duty, to lend yourself. Your hands are not your own, nor are your breasts, nor, most especially, any of your bodily orifices, which we may explore or penetrate at will. You will remember at all times—or as constantly as possible—that you have lost all right to privacy or concealment, and as a reminder of this fact, in our presence you will never close your lips completely, or cross your legs, or press your knees together (you may recall that you were forbidden to do this the minute you arrived).... The whip will be used only between dusk and dawn. But besides the whipping you receive from whoever may want to whip you, you will also be flogged in the evening, as punishment for any infractions of the rules committed during the day: for having been slow to oblige, for having raised your eyes and looked at the person addressing you or taking you—you must never look any of us in the face ... at night you will have only your lips with which to honor us—and your wide-spread thighs—for your hands will be tied behind your back and you will be naked, as you were a short while ago.... both this flogging and the chain—which when attached to the ring of your collar keeps you more or less closely confined to your bed several hours a day—are intended less to make you suffer, scream, or shed tears than to make you feel, through this suffering, that you are not free but fettered, and to teach you that you are totally dedicated to something outside yourself.

So begins O's education as a pure instrument of satisfaction. An iron collar is fitted around her neck and rings are inserted into her labia, to which light chains can be attached. Her anus is penetrated by ever larger objects in order more easily to accommodate any man who wishes to use it for his gratification. As the narrative unfolds, she is subjected to ever more elaborate rituals of whipping, sodomy, and ravishment by the male inhabitants of the Chateau. All of which she does willingly.

How can we imagine a more extravagant and outrageous realization of male phantasy? Far from being conceivable as a depiction of women's desire, mustn't we conclude that no woman would find the prospect of O's sufferings to be anything but repugnant in the extreme? Susan Brownmiller, among others, found it impossible to believe that *The Story of O* could have been written by a woman. She confessed herself to be "vehemently hostile to suggestions that some known, popular sex fantasies attributed to women are indeed the product of a woman's mind, or the product of a healthy woman's mind."

But the fact remains that it was a woman who wrote it. Her true identity was finally revealed in a *New Yorker* interview in 1994. *The Story of O* was written by Dominique Aury, a Parisian journalist, editor, and translator. The French police were right to suspect that Jean Paulhan had something to do with it, though wrong in thinking that he was the author. Aury wrote *The Story of O* in the midst of her thirty-year love affair with Paulhan. She was in her mid-forties, he was approaching seventy. In effect, the book was a protracted love letter, written in an attempt to keep Paulhan's interest. "I wasn't young, I wasn't pretty," Aury said in the *New Yorker* interview, "it was necessary to find other weapons. The weapons, alas, were in the head." Her strategy worked. *The Story of O* was, Paulhan said, "the most ardent love letter any man has ever received." It was he who suggested that she publish it.

What, then, are we to conclude from these facts about the question of feminine masochism? Surely we can agree with a central element of Susan Brownmiller's view: *The Story of O* presents a florid theater of male phantasies. Moreover, Brownmiller is right to say that no woman, or no healthy woman, would enjoy the abuse heaped upon the captive of Chateau Roissy. But to stop there is unfortunately too simple. Dominique Aury, too, allows that "there is no reality here. Nobody could stand being treated like that. It's entirely fantastic." But is her novel a catalog of exclusively male phantasies? "That's what everyone says," Aury replied. "I've always been reproached for that. All I know is that they were honest fantasies—whether they were male or female, I couldn't say."

The psychoanalytic argument to be made at this point is not to deny that *The Story of O* is decisively shaped by male phantasy. It is. But an additional point can be made: Male phantasy can be, and very routinely is, taken over by women and made their own. And it is precisely in that willingness to assume the desire of the other that feminine masochism consists. Freud's contention is not that women desire mistreatment, but that they show a greater openness to what the other desires and a greater willingness to offer themselves to satisfy it, sometimes even to the point of accepting mistreatment. There are many women for whom self-defeating behavior, by no means limited to the sexual sphere, becomes the dominant rule of their lives. But what lies behind such behavior, the hidden hook on which it all hangs, is the way in which feminine desire is circuited in and through the position of the other.

This point about the feminine tendency to accommodate the desire of the other enables us to add a comment about Freud's bungled conception of female orgasm that distinguished clitoral from vaginal orgasms. Are we not now in a position to suppose that it was Freud's conviction about the greater liability of the feminine personality toward more sensitive concern for what the other is experiencing, a sensitivity that can even have the effect of allowing one's own satisfaction to take a backseat to that of the other, that led him to his otherwise unsustainable claim about the primacy of vaginal orgasm? The very notion of a vaginal orgasm, as distinct from the clitoral, appears to be based on a distinction between the sort of excitation available to a woman by masturbation and another form of stimulation that presumably requires her penetration by another.

Much has been made by Freud's critics of his expressions of puzzlement over the question, "What does a woman want?" Feminine sexuality, he confessed, presented a kind of "dark continent," impossible to understand. These passages are sometimes cited with little-disguised satisfaction, as if to say "There! You see, even Freud himself admits that he knows nothing about women!" Yet from the point of view at which we have arrived, we can say that it was precisely the roundabout circuit of feminine desire, a circuit that becomes energized only by passage through the position of the other, that Freud found so confusing. Before Freud embarked upon the strange path of psychoanalysis, his early education had impressed upon him a deep streak of common sense. His point of departure was to assume that desire is something that originates in the unique constitution of the individual human being, indeed that desire is exactly what makes each individual a distinct and separate entity. What could be more decidedly *mine* than my desire? Yet the evidence of his clinical experience forced upon him another view. The riddle of femininity in particular faced him with the mysterious prospect of a desire that is eccentric to itself, a desire that arises outside oneself—desire in and through the other.

It is at this point more than any other that the Lacanian rereading of Freud is directed, reminding us of a cardinal point of Freud's discovery of the unconscious but also of Freud's inability to fully account for it. Lacan draws from the example of feminine sexuality—the enigma of what he calls *feminine jouissance*—a general lesson about all unconscious processes. Human desire, he concludes, is always and intrinsically haunted by "the desire of the other." But this means that the crucial thing to be heard in Freud's question—what does a woman want?—is ultimately less a matter of the strange and threatening foreignness of women's desire per se than it is a matter of the foreignness of all desire. What is at stake is precisely the foreignness of the unconscious itself, the way in which the unconscious roots of desire make us all foreign to ourselves.

Questions of Conscience

The crucial prerequisite for understanding Freud's theory of feminine masochism is to see that he is offering a properly psychological definition, one that links the satisfaction of the masochist to the desire of the other. Masochism is no mere taste for pain, a quest for physical torment pure and simple, but is rather a penchant for putting oneself at the disposal of the other. It is not for nothing that we often refer to masochistic practices in tandem with sadism: "S & M." Masochism and sadism form a bonded couplet. The thrill of masochism derives less from pain per se than from the sense that it is suffered in the course of being used as an instrument of someone else's pleasure. The masochist thus needs the sadist, a truth that we glimpse in an old joke: "The masochist said 'Beat me.' The sadist said 'No!'" Masochism is *enjoyment from the place of the other*. The masochist's pleasure in pain is energized by the perception of the other's satisfaction.

It is in this way—with reference to the desire of the other—that we have defined the Freudian death drive. As an impulse to breach the boundaries of the ego, the death drive is the attraction to what is utterly other. It is the imperative of *jouissance*, the lure of the ecstatic enjoyment in feeling oneself enveloped by something larger than oneself. If Freud is correct, it is an impulse to which we are all liable. Indeed, it corresponds to the most primordial movement of human desire, a consequence of the opposition between the ego and the id. But not everyone lives this tension in the same way and the two main alternatives, embracing versus resisting the transcendence of the ego, accepting a measure of self-mortification in the name of the other versus preserving one's self by adopting a posture of competitive violence and aggression, tend to coincide with the difference between femininity and masculinity. Gender difference thus falls in line with the notion that has guided us throughout: the boundaries of the feminine ego display a greater degree of flexibility and inclusiveness, in comparison with which the masculine ego is characterized by a greater defensive rigidity and fixity.

To avoid misunderstanding, especially given the contentiousness of the questions involved here, let us quickly make three key clarifications:

1. We have constantly to remind ourselves that "feminine" cannot simply or exclusively be identified with women. In the language of psychoanalysis, femininity refers to a subjective posture that can readily be assumed by men, either momentarily, as a function of particular situations or relationships, or permanently as the defining structure of a man's identity.
2. When feminine masochism and masculine aggression are referred, as I have done, to the position of the other, it becomes possible to see that Freud's theory is by no means a cheap slander against women. On the contrary, masochism and aggression here become two means of negotiating the dynamics of connection and separation between self and other.
3. While there are surely extremes at either end, there is a continuum between the poles of masochism and sadism with complicated

> admixtures of the two in the middle. While we remember that femininity and masculinity do not perfectly align with female and male, therefore, we can also note that they need not be exclusive. Freud repeatedly insists that "all human individuals ... combine in themselves both masculine and feminine characteristics, so that pure masculinity and femininity remain theoretical constructions of uncertain content." Indeed, a psychoanalytic perspective has long recognized that a mature and well-formed personality crucially involves some balancing of feminine and masculine traits and tendencies.

We can now usefully linger in making a fourth, important point, by means of which we can open up a new avenue of discussion. It is not difficult to recognize that the masochistic tendency—in a woman or in a man—can lead to a debilitating lack of self-assertion and to the destructive consequences of habitually self-defeating behavior. It is certainly not Freud's intention to recommend it. But we must also recognize that there may in certain circumstances be something valuable in the masochistic posture. Especially when it is compared to the defensive posture of the embattled ego that preserves itself at all costs against the threat of the other's influence, the openness to what is other, the ability to submit oneself to what is foreign and dissimilar, even to the point of allowing oneself to be dominated by something outside oneself, can and should be recognized as a potentially valuable achievement of maturity. Its implications are especially important in the domain of ethics. Morally speaking, the more typically feminine openness to the experience of the other must be counted in many contexts as a significant virtue. It is the capacity, as the old saying has it, of walking a mile in the other person's shoes. It is the psychological prerequisite of sympathy, the condition of genuine understanding, the first step toward compromise. The moral sense requires putting one's own advantage aside, however provisionally, in order to appreciate the impact of one's acts upon others.

With these remarks about morality and masochism in mind, we can offer a useful corrective to another notorious claim commonly attributed to Freud: the notion that women are somehow morally defective, that they have no superego. In fact, Freud claims nothing of the sort. As happens so often, when we return to the actual text of Freud we find that things are not at all so simple. The point is not that women lack a superego, but that the feminine superego shows important differences from its masculine counterpart. What Freud actually says is the following:

> For women the level of what is ethically normal is different from what it is in men. Their super-ego is never so inexorable, so impersonal, so independent of its emotional origins as we require it to be in men. Character-traits which critics of every epoch have brought up against

> women—that they show less sense of justice than men, that they are less ready to submit to the exigencies of life, that they are more often influenced in their judgements by feelings of affection or hostility—all these would be amply accounted for by the modification in the formation of their super-ego which we have inferred above.

Freud's claim in this passage is that the moral strictures to which men hold themselves tend to be less flexible and less tolerant of ambiguity than those adhered to by women. The moral sensibility of men tends to be governed by unvarying adherence to principle "come hell or highwater." Masculine duty conceives itself to be bound by rules of conduct that must be followed to the letter. In these ways, the masculine superego follows the pattern set by the masculine ego: It is more definitely bounded and insists upon more decided separation from the other. Morality in the feminine character is not lacking but rather different in style and sensibility. It is, as Freud says, less impersonal, less independent—in short, less free of the immediate influence of others.

Freud's theory on this point can be seen, as we have seen it before in other instances, to confirm rather than contradict a significant feminist perspective. In an enormously influential book, *In a Different Voice: Psychological Theory and Women's Development*, the Harvard psychologist Carol Gilligan distinguished between two styles of moral reasoning, one more closely associated with masculinity, the other with femininity. Men, according to Gilligan, show a greater tendency to make moral judgments guided by consideration of rights and abstract principles. Obsessed with rights, masculine morality everywhere presupposes a definite line of separation between individuals. Masculine morality therefore tends to be a morality of property, which, as the old saw has it, is nine-tenths of the law. It is a morality built around careful consideration of what is *proper*, not just in the sense of what is correct and appropriate, but of what in French is called *propre*, what is *mine*. Women, on the other hand, tend to measure the consequences of their actions with greater sensitivity to responsibilities and relationships. Women remain more sensitive to context and more open to consideration of specific cases. Where men begin by assuming independence between individuals, women tend to assume connection. Masculine morality is driven by a demand for autonomy, feminine morality by a concern for mutuality. Is this distinction not exactly parallel to the structural differences between the masculine and feminine ego as we have just characterized them?

Let us pause to unfold this point a bit. The comparison to a psychoanalytic perspective here is interesting not least because Carol Gilligan herself fails to see it. Gilligan argues that traditional theories of ethical choice have overlooked the more characteristically feminine mode of moral judgment. The theory of moral development put forward by her teacher and colleague Lawrence Kohlberg is a good case in point. Kohlberg's theory puts a premium on the evolution of a capacity for autonomous judgment. To evaluate things for oneself without being swayed by the opinions of others is a key characteristic of what Kohlberg defines as the highest level of moral reasoning. Growing up, morally speaking, means making oneself increasingly independent. Such a definition of moral development, Gilligan is right to point out, uncritically takes the masculine style as the ideal.

And Kohlberg is not alone. The masculinist bias that Gilligan points out in Kohlberg's theory is rooted in a tradition of moral thought that extends all the way back to the ancient world. We see its origins with special clarity in the definition of masculine and feminine laid down by the Greek philosopher Pythagoras, the author of the famous theorem about right triangles that bears his name. Convinced that all reality is organized mathematically, Pythagoras arranged a table of opposing cosmic principles in accordance with the master antithesis of even and odd. Thinking in terms of such opposites was an enormously popular way of looking at things in the ancient world. With the Even, Pythagoras associated the Many, the Unlimited (in the sense of what is unbounded, vague, or indeterminate), the Curved, the Moving, the Dark, the Left, the Bad, and the Female. Grouped with the Odd were qualities of the One (the principle of unity), the Limited (or bounded and definite), along with the Straight, Resting, Light, Right, Good, and Male. In all, Pythagoras envisioned ten pairs of opposites:

Even	Odd
Many	One
Oblong	Square
Curved	Straight
Unlimited	Limited
Moving	Resting
Dark	Light
Left	Right
Bad	Good
Female	Male

Only a little reflection is needed to see that the moral outlook of our contemporary culture remains deeply Pythagorean some twenty-five centuries after the philosopher's death. To take just a single example, consider our behavior and expectations in a criminal courtroom. In the conduct of a trial, the first order of business is to determine the truth of what happened. And like good Pythagoreans, we assume the truth to be One, not Many. We ask witnesses to "tell the whole truth (the *one* truth) and nothing but the truth." When the truth is out, we get the story *straight.* If we want a really unvarnished account of the facts, we ask someone to tell it to us straight. The truthful person is thus a straight shooter (maybe even a *square*). The straight and upright person won't throw us any *curve* balls. He or she is not a crook, or a shifty character. Moreover, we describe the truth as coming to *light.* In fact, the truth is itself a kind of light; we *see* the truth and are enlightened by it. And once told, we don't expect the truth to change. When the evidence is in and we've got the one, full story, the case can *rest.* How appropriate, then, once we have all these Pythagorean features lined up, that the witness takes the stand with the *right* hand raised. It is from the right hand, the proper and public hand with which we greet each other, that we expect to get a fair shake. The *left* hand—"left" in Latin, we remember, is "sinister"—is placed on a Bible, as if bringing it into contact with the Good Book will help minimize its wayward tendencies. Last but certainly not least, we fully expect that the trial will issue in some definite result. The verdict will be *limited* in the Pythagorean sense. We assume that the defendant will be found either innocent or guilty, not some messy mixture of both.

Imagine for a moment what an alternative, non-Pythagorean system of justice might look like. Such a system would begin from the assumption that the truth in criminal cases is not likely to be simple or unitary, but rather complex and multilayered. Correlatively, it would recognize that there probably is no one culprit and that guilt and responsibility for most crimes, far from being attributable to a single individual, would very probably involve a considerably wider circle of other contributing persons, events, and circumstances. Such an alternative evaluation of justice would therefore refuse to see the world in terms of discrete and separate moral agents (a few "bad apples") whose crimes can be neatly separated from the rest, in favor of a greater appreciation of the interconnectedness of agents with larger communities and contexts (it takes a village to raise a criminal?). Finally, verdicts might not be simply yea or nay, either/or judgments of guilt or innocence, but would make room for more nuanced and complex judgments—assigning degrees of guilt, for example.

Such a non-Pythagorean system of moral assumptions, while there may appear to be some things to recommend it, certainly doesn't describe the codes by which we currently make moral and legal judgments. A non-Pythagorean system would surely be a morality "in a different voice." While it isn't Carol Gilligan's purpose to flesh it out explicitly, a major implication of her work is that an alternative morality of this sort would reflect a more feminine sensibility. Gilligan helps us to recognize, for example, how the logic of the Pythagorean opposites informs conceptions of gender that remain pervasively influential in our own time. They are clearly present in our most garden-variety prejudices and stereotypes. According to the persistent banalities of sexist discourse, women are frustrating because they lack the masculine traits of unity, limitedness, and unwavering stability. How familiar we are with the voices of these banalities: "Women are fickle, given to shifting caprices. They're impossible to please because they want one thing at one moment, and something else at another. You just never know! Emotion, not reason, is their guide, so there's no arguing with them. Their heads are full of vague and fuzzy notions. How can men be expected to understand them, they don't understand themselves!" Translated into Pythagorean terms, these stereotypical assessments come to the same thing: women belong to the category of the *unlimited.*

In accordance with the Pythagorean system of opposites, the distinction between feminine and masculine thus echoes other great dichotomies, such as those between illusion and truth, nature and culture, or chaos and control. In a universe guided by such dualities, moral and ethical life requires a dominance of the masculine over the feminine. Harmony between the two great categories of opposing principles depends on an ascendancy of masculine values. Man must rule over woman, correcting and containing what remains unformed and indeterminate in her changing and chaotic nature.

Against the background of the Pythagorean values that have guided Western morality for centuries, Carol Gilligan's articulation of "the different voice" of feminine moral judgment is surely something new. It points us in the direction of an ethics guided as much by relationship as by rights, as much by mutuality as by autonomy. Such a feminine morality would be oriented more sensitively to the position of the other and, as such, would invert the Pythagorean bias in favor of unity, definiteness, and stasis. So where, between these two alternatives, does Freud fit? In Gilligan's estimation, he is clearly a member of the old guard. The theory and practice of psychoanalysis, she argues, is complicit with the ethics of autonomy that still dominates our culture.

Is she right?

Going Over to the Dark Side

Is Freud an old-school Pythagorean? Some of Freud's own comments appear to argue that he is. After distinguishing in his own way between masculine and feminine styles of moral evaluation, Freud remarks that "we must not allow ourselves to be deflected from such conclusions by the denials of the feminists, who are anxious to force us to regard the two sexes as completely equal in position and worth." Freud thus appears to endorse the superiority of the masculine. At other points, too, his sympathies seem to lie with the Pythagorean ethics of unity, limit, and permanence. Didn't Freud take the point of analysis to be one of "making the unconscious conscious"? Didn't he say that "where id was, there ego shall be" (*Wo es war, soll Ich werden*), comparing this process to the way in which the Dutch reclaim dry land from the waters of the Zuider Zee? In that case, doesn't Freud commit himself to the masculine values of separation and independence? What room can there be in Freud's theories for a more feminine sensibility of accommodation to the other?

More careful consideration reveals a completely different picture. In fact, the ethic of psychoanalysis is less an endorsement of Pythagorean values than a reversal and overturning of them. The key is to see how the moral categories typified by Pythagoras's philosophy—the one and the limited versus the many and the unlimited—reflect the opposition between ego and id. The traditional conception of the good closely parallels the qualities of the ego. We therefore describe as good what is pure and inviolate, uncontaminated or even untouched. According to the moral code we have inherited, goodness is associated with uprightness, simplicity, definiteness, and permanence. Innocence, almost canonically compared metaphorically to virginity, is conceived as being unsoiled and unsullied, and is therefore well symbolized by an immaculate expanse of unbroken whiteness. Evil, on the contrary, is the crooked, the indeterminate, and the shifty. Evil compromises the perfect unity and coherence of the good. Evil is the stain that pollutes and tarnishes the unblemished purity of the good.

When we align these traditional moral categories with the terms of Freudian theory it becomes clear that Freud, whatever his occasional remarks to the contrary, is not at all a traditional moralist. By opening the ego to the unknown of the id, the underlying movement of the whole psychoanalytic experience implies a measured embrace of one's own evil, an attempt to delve into the forgotten and condemned parts of ourselves. Psychoanalysis is a science of darkness and shadow. It is a sensibility well spoken for by the motto, taken from the seventh book of Virgil's *Aeneid*, with which Freud prefaced *The Interpretation of Dreams*: *Flectere si nequeo Superos, Acheronta movebo.* "If I cannot bend the higher powers, I will move the infernal regions."

When Freud claims that the aim of analysis is to make the unconscious conscious, he doesn't mean that the obscurity of the unconscious will be somehow rendered perfectly transparent. The cardinal postulate of psychoanalysis is that consciousness can never fully illuminate the depths of the unconscious. Psychoanalysis maintains, not just that perfect self-knowledge is difficult, but that it is ultimately impossible. Analysis is therefore a profoundly paradoxical enterprise in which we become aware of the limits of awareness. What is to become conscious is precisely the inescapability of the unconscious.

Or again, by saying that "where id was, there ego shall be," Freud doesn't intend to suggest that the ego might ever fully integrate the contents of the id. If the progress of analysis is comparable to winning some parcel of dry land from the sea, there is and will always remain an ocean beyond it. The genuine spirit of analysis is that by which we are brought to realize the limits of the ego, in fact to realize that the ego is part of the problem. Psychoanalysis is indeed a paradoxical undertaking: it aims to strengthen the ego to the point of being able to tolerate a certain loss of the ego. In this respect, analysis might be likened to the gesture of Christian salvation: To find oneself requires losing oneself. Lacan makes this point with special emphasis. "The ego," he argues, "is structured exactly like a symptom. At the heart of the subject, it is only a privileged symptom, the human symptom par excellence, the mental illness of man." "What is at issue, at the end of analysis," Lacan insists, is "a twilight, an imaginary decline of the world, and even an experience at the limit of depersonalization."

Far from being committed to masculinist values of unity, coherence, stability, and control, psychoanalysis invites a deliberate suspension of them. Analysis is a gently calculated engagement with complexity, chaos, uncertainty, obscurity, and change. In turning toward the unconscious, Freud inverts the traditional requirements of truth, associated since Pythagoras with unity, definition, light, and permanence. The "truth" of the unconscious is bound up with the damnable qualities of a darker side of ourselves. The aim of analysis is one of learning how to tolerate one's own inner chaos, one's own internal otherness.

Viewed from this angle, the judgment to be made by psychoanalysis on feminine masochism is far from simply negative. It is not for nothing that Freud so closely associated morality with masochism. In fact, to the extent that the guiding values and orientation of psychoanalysis can be said to be tinged with masochism, psychoanalysis itself must be judged—who would have guessed?—to be profoundly feminist. In the course of psychoanalysis, both analyst and analysand must practice the virtues of femininity. The work of the analysand is to follow the one fundamental rule of analysis: to say whatever comes into one's head, however apparently absurd, obscene, irrelevant, or nonsensical. To follow this rule is to submit oneself to the threatening foreignness of one's own unconscious. It is to surrender to the register of the Other. Such is the law of free association, at once the method by which analysis unfolds and the objective at which it aims. To free associate is to relax the constraints that guide the everyday operation of the mind and to allow oneself to be seized by thoughts that appear arbitrary, illegitimate, or even outrageous. The patient who has genuinely mastered the ability to remain reflectively engaged while floating in the shifting currents of free association no longer needs analysis.

A complementary point can be made about the role and function of the analyst. Contrary to the popular image of analytic interpretation as a matter of forcing the patient to accept the meaning of his or her unconscious motives—contrary, too, it must be admitted, to the manner in which psychoanalysis is sometimes practiced—the primary task of the analyst is to stay out of the way. Lacan compares the analyst's position to that of the dummy hand in bridge. The analyst facilitates the unfolding of the patient's own unconscious by resisting the impulse to intervene, to explain, to cajole, or to moralize. The analyst plays the dummy. Indeed, in a certain sense, the analyst plays dead. Such is the true meaning of the analyst's famous silence. The challenge is to avoid controlling the course of analysis by the imposition of one's own complexes, and thereby to offer an open space in which the patient's own voice, as yet unrecognized, can finally be heard. For both analyst and patient, then, the progress of analysis requires a measured exercise of masochism. It requires a certain suspension of ego and a turning toward what is fearfully other to it. Psychoanalysis, as Socrates said of philosophy, is a practice of death, an art of mortality.

Anatomy Is(n't) Destiny

It has been too long since we've heard the critic's voice and I can easily imagine the skeptical question it might pose at this point: "Throughout your discussion," the critic would begin, "haven't you assumed a very particular account of gender difference, and one that is all too stereotypical? Surely some aspects of the picture you paint are familiar enough, but isn't the phenomenon of gender much more culturally and historically variable? Haven't you given us merely one version of gender difference, and a rather caricatured one at that?"

Before I can gather myself to answer, another question immediately pops up, one that gives rise to a veritable harangue: "Even if we accept some features of gender difference as you have presented it," the critic wants to know, "why do we need a psychoanalytic theory to make sense of them? After all, Freud's theory is a cumbersome architecture of concepts, at many points abusive to common sense and beggaring plausibility. Aren't there much simpler explanations more ready to hand? You have been arguing that women tend to be more attuned to others, more sensitive to the overall context or situation, more concerned with the effects of their actions on those around them. Men, by contrast, are quicker to act impulsively, more exclusively focused on the objects toward which their actions are directed, and less likely to feel thrown off balance by questions about how those actions will affect other people. Maybe so. But why be surprised by this difference? And why appeal to such an arcane theory to explain it? Freud would even have us believe that feminine deference and masculine assertiveness are to be referred to that most obscure and mysterious of psychoanalytic notions, the death drive. Isn't it much more likely that women are frequently deferential and self-effacing, that they tend to be more aware and more concerned about others around them, because they have long been accustomed to secondary status in a male-dominated world? Women have had to learn to play the role of a mere accompanist, always careful to let someone else have the lead, because they are socially and economically dependent on men. If men have the luxury of being oblivious to others, of being able to stomp and bang around without a second thought, it is because they enjoy a degree of socially sanctioned autonomy and privilege not shared by women. The underlying issue is less psychological than political, or better, the psychological reality is a mere effect of the political."

Well! The first thing to be said is that the critic has a point. In response to these questions we need once again to remind ourselves of the limits of a psychoanalytic perspective, insisting above all that psychoanalysis ought not to deny or displace the effects of other kinds of psychologically formative influences. There is no question that masculinity and femininity are formed in very large measure by the shaping forces of culture and socialization. To see how, we need only to stroll through any toy store, first down the pink aisle of little girls' dolls, tea sets, makeup kits, and lightbulb ovens; then down the boys' aisle, decked out in black, browns, and camouflage, featuring drag racers, machine guns, bows and arrows, commando outfits, and baseball bats. It's Poolside Barbie versus G.I. Joe. From their earliest experiences, little girls and little boys are bombarded with messages about the sorts of behaviors that are gender appropriate and those that are not. And these messages are inseparable from the larger social and political world in which power and prestige are unequally distributed between men and women. It is surely no surprise that the socially disadvantaged sex masters the skills of deferring her own needs and remaining hyperalert to the needs of others.

What, then, does psychoanalysis have to add? The psychoanalytic point is not to deny the pervasive effect of such social forces but to suggest that they are built upon the deeper foundation of certain psychological predispositions. What sort of predispositions? Everything we have said about the psychoanalytic characterization of gender difference can be summarized in terms of the structural difference between the masculine and feminine ego. The masculine personality tends to be characterized by a relatively more rigid and defensive crust that separates the executive functions of the ego from a deeper stratum of emotional needs and sensitivities. This more defensively crusted structure assumes the function of a "character armor" and issues in a greater tendency to adopt an aggressive and adversarial posture toward an objectified other. The boundary of the feminine ego, by contrast, is relatively more indefinite, pliant, and adaptable. It not only tends to include the other, but quite typically extends itself toward the other, even to its own detriment.

It is important to admit that this picture remains the barest sketch, outlined in very crude strokes. It exhausts neither what might be said in a general way about gender difference, nor even what might be said from a Freudian point of view. Moreover, we must remind ourselves of the difference between questions of gender and questions of sex, that no distinction between masculine and feminine can be taken to correspond perfectly to the distinction between male and female. Every human individual, male or female, is a psychological composite of masculine and feminine elements.

Keeping to these limits, however, a psychoanalytic perspective still allows us to offer some explanation of the links that tend to predispose males in the direction of masculinity and females toward femininity. In relating masculinity and femininity to differing ego structure, we've so far focused on two key factors, relevant to the different ways that men and women pass through the two great transitions of psychological development, the Oedipus complex and puberty. With respect to the Oedipus complex, we refer to the fact that a heterosexual man will come in adulthood to bind himself to a lover of the same sex as his mother. This identity between the caretaker of infancy and the lover of adulthood calls for defensive measures not required by the psychological development of women. With respect to the changes of puberty, the dramatic physical alterations undergone by the adolescent girl dispose her toward a revival of narcissistic concern for the body image that has little counterpart in the development of boys. The feminine ego thus tends to remain more intimately involved with self-consciousness of the body image. Where masculine psychology tends to revolve around an unconscious need for nurturance (and to be hamstrung by its own defensive efforts to keep that need at bay), femininity is haunted by the deep-seated hunger for recognition. He wants to be stroked, she wants to be spoken to.

To these two factors we may now add a third element of the puzzle, also relevant to the issue of body image, that will help to address the questions before us. We have already seen how the structure of the infantile ego, the psychological function that will serve to divide the internal economy of impulses and to separate self from other, is modeled most primitively on the unity of the body image. Must we not then imagine that the psychological structure of the ego is profoundly affected by the anatomical reality of sexual intercourse, the fact that one sex submits to being bodily penetrated by the other? In that case, the roots of gender difference would be brought into relation with the most obvious feature of difference between male and female sexual identity.

Whatever their social preparation to assume a future feminine role, little girls come very early to understand that their bodies are penetrable. Even if they only later learn the role of that penetrability in the sexual act, the growing girl becomes aware at an early age that the female body is occupiable by the other in the form of babies. There is nothing comparable in the experience of the little boy. To grow up male is to understand one's own body as inviolate. The male body is a means for acting rather than of being acted upon, an instrument for extending power into the world rather than a site at which the world may enter in and leave its mark. How can we not imagine these differences between male and female ways of experiencing the body don't have far-reaching effects on the formation of character and personality?

From this point of view, we can see from a new angle the meaning of Freud's quip that "anatomy is destiny." The psychoanalytic theory of the human being places the schema of the body image at the very foundation of the unconscious. This means that one's conception of one's own body and its relation to others and to the world around it, a conception that is formed and continues to operate largely beneath the level of explicit awareness, lies at the very base of that phenomenon of personal style and sensibility that we call "character." Whether the body is experienced as capable of being opened and occupied by others, or rather as being closed upon itself and inviolate, is therefore of decisive significance for the entire formation of personality.

This concern for body image can be related to another constant of Freud's theory, his tendency to align masculinity and femininity with activity and passivity. In drawing this parallel, Freud is less interested in specific behaviors than in general dispositions toward behavior that are rooted in unconscious psychical structure—precisely the sort of thing that is at stake in the assumption of one or another unconscious image of the body. On the one hand, we have the masculine sense of agency that is disposed toward operating on persons and things outside itself and that tends to imagine itself to be impervious to alteration. On the other, there is the feminine readiness to accommodate itself to persons and situations, positioning itself to respond to the other's initiative and allowing itself to be made over in the image of the other's desire. It is not difficult to imagine how these two alternative postures are rooted in differing conceptions of the body. On one side, there is the typically masculine sense of the body as the tool, perfectly unobtrusive and taken for granted without a second thought, with which things in the world are seized and manipulated. On the other, there is the more hesitant and slightly inhibited posture, borne of the subliminal sense of the body as capable of being entered, of being itself acted upon.

It is instructive to observe how activity and passivity are implied by our everyday manner of speaking about the sexual act, itself obviously bound up with questions of the wholeness and integrity of the body image. Sexual intercourse is referred to as "penetration," a term that puts the accent on the active role of the male, but also one that stresses a kind of bodily violation. How different it would be if the active part were attributed to the woman! We might then have intercourse as "envelopment" or "engulfing." Or maybe we'll need some altogether new word. How about "enwrapture"? But no, the standard view conceives of sex as dissymmetrical, with the male acting to enter the woman's body.

The point is clearly, if rather brutally, evident in the word "fuck." While it ostensibly designates an act that requires two people, the word implies an unequal relation between them. As it is usually used, "fuck" belongs to the class of verbs such as "hit," "grab," "rob," or "punish"—terms that refer to something done by one person to another. This transitivity of the verb is obviously part of what outfits the word to be used as a term of abuse, as in "Fuck you," "Get fucked," or even "Fuck yourself." The insult is directed to the passive position, the one who is fucked, as someone to whom something is done. Implicit in this transitivity and its power to insult is the idea of a bodily violation, of having something thrust into the body against one's will. A series of related insults call up a whole range of bodily violations: "Up yours!" "Shove it!" "Get bent!" "Blow me!" or, as the English have it, "Bugger off!"

To grasp the real point at stake in the link Freud makes between ego structure and body image, to understand what he meant by saying that "anatomy is destiny," it is crucial to recognize that anatomy—the morphology of the body objectively considered—is not really the issue. "Body image" doesn't refer here to the structure and functions of the biological organism, but to the way the body feels to the person who lives in and through it, and above all to the way that the body *looks*. Considered on the level of the biological organism, for example, it is not possible to neatly separate the body from its environment. In truth, the body is not at all the sort of self-contained packet that we carelessly imagine it to be. On the contrary, it is more like a system of exchanges in which a variety of substances are constantly being taken in and given off. The unity of the body is continually traversed by a range of materials: gases are continually being inhaled and exhaled, fluids are being passed off in the evaporation of sweat, particles of skin and hair unceasingly rain from the body laying down a veritable path of micro-wreckage the way a slug weaving its way along the porch railing leaves behind a trail of slime, a continual stream of digesting food is constantly moved through the gastrointestinal tract prior to being expelled by the rhythmic squeezings of peristalsis.

But none of this is apparent in our everyday apprehension of bodies. We take the body of the person sitting across the room, as we take our own, to be a perfectly unitary object that is discretely outlined and bounded. We conveniently forget the many ways in which the contours of the body unity are constantly shifting. Body image—as the word *image* should tell us—refers less to the biological reality of the body than to a mere *picture* of it. What is at stake in the psychoanalytic sense of body image is less a matter of anatomy than of *imaginary anatomy*.

This point about the fictional character of body image is crucial, in its turn, for clarifying how Freud's conception is to be compared with other theories of gender. Theorizing about gender has very often come down to a matter of deciding between nature and nurture. On one extreme, there are the biological essentialists who want to assert that masculinity and femininity are ultimately derived from biology. There is a fixed and definite essence of gender that is rooted in organic determinants. At the other extreme are those—call them cultural relativists or social constructivists—who deny that there is any inherent and unchangeable essence of gender and who see differences of masculinity and femininity as learned behaviors shaped by varying influences of culture and society. To which camp does Freud belong?

To neither. And therein resides the most valuable and interesting thing about the Freudian theory of gender. On the one hand, Freud rejects the idea that gender is a simple function of biology. Just as the Freudian drive is no mere expression of animal instinct, the formations of gender are no mere products of biology. There is in the phenomenon of gender a significant margin of variability in which the effects of culture and socialization play themselves out. From a Freudian point of view, there is therefore something quite right in the skeptical hesitation with which we began this section. Gender is by no means fixed and immutable. No serious discussion of masculinity and femininity can wholly ignore the cultural and historical relativity of gender.

Yet—and here we come to the most distinctive Freudian contribution—neither does Freud accept the idea that gender is merely a product of cultural pressures and socialization. Beneath the play of variation in the definition of gender, differences of body images between male and female predispose men in the direction of masculinity and women toward femininity. Predispose without predetermining. The influence of body image can always be overridden by other factors arising in the course of psychological development. Indeed, there is nothing absolutely determinative even about body image itself. It is perfectly possible for a man to offer his body for penetration, just as a woman may refuse it.

By referring the problem of gender to the effects of body image, psychoanalysis escapes from the deadlock of the nature-nurture debate and seizes upon a third factor which is neither simply biological nor simply social, yet allows for the influence of both. In the process, a psychoanalytic perspective is able to provide an elegant answer to the most basic question faced by any theorist of gender, a question that neither essentialists nor constructivists are well equipped to deal with. The problem is to explain how gender difference, if it is not simply determined by biology, nevertheless occurs with such regularity across different cultures and epochs of history. If gender differences were merely a matter of culture, if they were merely products of socialization, we would presumably see a greater range of variation. There would be cultures in which women clearly dominate, or others in which there is little or no difference between masculine and feminine. Perhaps there would be cultures in which the elaborate system of distinctions that we call "gender" doesn't exist at all. The fact, however, is that no such cultures exist, and, moreover, that most cultures throughout history have displayed a conspicuously patriarchal and masculinist bias. We are therefore prompted to seek an additional factor. There must be something that tends to align sex (maleness and femaleness) with gender (masculinity and femininity) while at the same time allowing a limited margin of free play and variation. In addition to its central concern for the formative dynamics of the Oedipus complex, psychoanalysis discovers such a factor in the psychological influence of body image. By serving to form the unconscious foundations of the ego, body image *favors* an alignment of sex and gender without making it absolutely necessary or unavoidable.

But if reference to the unconscious influence of body image helps to complete the psychoanalytic explanation of the origin and meaning of gender difference, in the process providing an alternative in the debate between biological essentialism and social constructivism, I have yet to respond fully to the critic's other question about the historical relativity of gender. I have posed the opposition between masculine and feminine as an opposition of assertion versus deference, aggressiveness versus accommodation, exaggerated need for autonomy versus mutuality. To what extent can this account be taken as valid across different cultures and epochs of history? In the remaining chapters, we will take some steps toward an answer. The aim will be to illuminate the historical relativity of sex and gender. What is needed is to place Freud himself in a historical perspective, to understand in what sense Freud is a child of his times, and to reevaluate his theories in the light of what is distinctive about sexuality in the modern age.

Part III
Histories

6
Inventing the Intimate

The first week in December 1933 was a big one for shaping the future of American popular culture. By sunset on the 5th, Utah became the thirty-sixth state to ratify repeal of the Eighteenth Amendment. The legal right to booze was back. Prohibition was over. The next day, Judge John Woolsey, ruling in the District Court of New York, denied the claim of the United States Attorney that James Joyce's book *Ulysses* be deemed obscene and, as such, "subject to seizure, forfeiture, confiscation, and destruction." The counsel for the defense, Morris Ernst, might be forgiven a little gushing over the verdict: "The New Deal in the law of letters is here.... The *Ulysses* case marks a turning point. It is a body blow for the censors. The necessity for hypocrisy and circumlocution in literature has been eliminated. Writers need no longer seek refuge in euphemisms. They may now describe basic human functions without fear of the law." Judge Woolsey's opinion, something of a milestone toward more open expression in matters of sexuality, marked the end of another kind of prohibition.

The flashpoint in *Ulysses* was Joyce's use—sparing, to be sure, but printed for all to see—of the word *fuck*. As Woolsey delicately put it, Joyce's "objective has required him incidentally to use certain words which are generally considered dirty words and has led at times to what many think is a too poignant preoccupation with sex in the thoughts of his characters." The judge then added, quite straight-facedly, that "the words which are criticized are old Saxon words known to almost all men and, I venture, to many women, and are such words as would be naturally and habitually used, I believe, by the types of folk whose life, physical and mental, Joyce is seeking to describe." Woolsey also apparently found it in Joyce's favor that "in respect of the recurrent theme of sex in the minds of his characters, it must always be remembered that his locale was Celtic and his season Spring."

For us, what is most remarkable about Woolsey's decision is that, in the larger scheme of things, it is so recent. Looking around ourselves now, who would think that a mere three or four generations ago, the printed appearance of the word *fuck* was, quite literally, a federal case? Yet the contentiousness of the *Ulysses* affair seems very far away indeed when we turn to James Kelman's novel *How Late It Was, How Late*, the book that won the Booker Prize in 1996. To sample a random, but very representative, passage:

> And when he made it up to Helen's, christ, he would be fucking knackered, he would sleep for a fucking week. Unless he collapsed on the fucking road man he was fucking exhausted, right fucking now, it was a hands and knees game, that was what he felt like, getting down on the ground and crawling his way up the road. Fuck sake man. Fucking hell! What like was it at all? A fucking nightmare ye kidding! A fucking nightmare was like a fucking Walt Disney cartoon man compared to this jesus christ almighty fucking Bugs Bunny man know what I'm talking about!

We've come a long way, baby! But, of course, not only in print. The trajectory from Joyce to Kelman is but a tiny indication of a gigantic transformation of attitudes toward sexuality and its markers that has swept across much of the world in the last century. For a combination of reasons—the relaxation of social and religious barriers to sexual expression, the invention of photography and film, the proliferation of mass media communications, the expanded protection of privacy rights in modern democratic societies, the relative anonymity of contemporary urban cultures—the public presence of sex has exploded in recent years. That public presence and the sea-change of attitudes and behaviors betokened by it cry out for thoughtful reflection. What's happened here?

Perhaps the most conspicuous feature of this modern transformation is the sheer *visibility* of sex. The contemporary urban landscape displays sexual images in unprecedented quantity and modern sexual sensibilities appear to be more and more driven by those images. We are well familiar with the indicators of these changes. The explosion of the multibillion dollar pornography industry is only its most direct and obvious commercial exploitation. Sex has also become a staple reference of magazine, newspaper, and billboard advertising, the sales-pitch trope par excellence. More or less explicitly sexual images now pervade films, music videos, and television advertising. In the modern Western world, skin seems to be just about everywhere. As a result, the pulse of Eros that was confined in a bygone time to the private sphere now ranges freely over the public domain. Viewed globally, this mushrooming presence of sexual imagery has become in itself one of the most contested social issues of our time, forming a battle line between social progressives and fundamentalists of various stripes. But how well have we understood these developments? And what might be said about them from a psychoanalytic point of view? What, furthermore, does the modern sexual explosion have to teach us about psychoanalysis itself?

In the three chapters that follow, we'll take a stab at these questions, of necessity questions of history. Our earlier discussions have touched on some of the major concepts of psychoanalysis—the phallus and the drive, repression and sublimation, narcissism and masochism. Running through it all like a red thread has been the dynamics of the Oedipus complex, allowing us to see anew why the Oedipal drama remained for Freud the central and indispensable axis of his psychology. And we have continually sharpened the inner meaning of that complex, especially relevant to questions of gender and sexuality: the masculine personality is defensively postured in relation to woman. Yet along the way, we have had little occasion to place the battery of Freudian concepts in any historical perspective. It is now high time we did.

Lack of attention to questions of history has been a frequent complaint against psychoanalysis and it is not difficult to see why. The very choice of Oedipus as the emblem of Freud's central discovery appears to imply that, psychologically speaking, nothing much has changed from the time of the Greeks. Then again, while Freud devoted several of his most famous and far-reaching papers to questions of the historical unfolding of civilization, those studies readily give the impression of a thinker more eager to trace lines of continuity than cleavages of historical difference. Relevant in this connection, too, is Freud's critique of the Marxist dream of revolutionary transformation, a reflection of Freud's skepticism that the fundamentals of human nature could be altered by any mere tinkering with the structures of political economy. Yet a crucial question remains: Is the unconscious discovered by Freud impervious to the shifting winds of history or should we expect it to evolve and change over the course of time? Mustn't any adequate theory of the mind take some account of history? These questions are particularly pressing when the topic is sexuality, for which the advent of the modern era has ushered in such enormous transformations. We will find in what follows that those transformations have been a long time in the making. In fact, the roots of the contemporary situation of sexuality must be traced to the dawn of modernity in the seventeenth century.

Behind the Wall

We've already cast the question of sex in the modern world in terms of its public imagery. It remains to be seen whether this provisional approach will be a fruitful one. But even in order to put it to the test, it is useful first to reflect on the history of the distinction between public and private. If the philosopher Hannah Arendt is correct, the very essence of modernity is centered on a revolution in relations between public and private life.[1] To understand what she means, we must transport ourselves back to the very different sensibility of the ancient world.

Getting a feel for the culture of ancient Greece is difficult for a person of modern temper, especially for an American, in part because the classical culture of the Golden Age was dominated by a vastly different sense of the

---

[1]It is important to note that I am using the term *modern* in the broad sense to name the period from roughly 1600 to the present. As we will have occasion to see in some detail in what follows, the shape of life in the twentieth century—what many people have in mind when they hear the word *modern*—owes its existence to changes that began several centuries earlier.

meaning and value of politics. Far from being the dirty word that it has become in our time, *politics* named the sphere of the noblest activity. It was, said Aristotle, the master science of the good for human beings, the science that must organize all others in the service of justice and happiness. As such, politics was inseparable from the public space in which the citizens of the *polis* sought to display the greatest achievement of virtue. It was above all a realm of speech, a domain in which the arts of rhetoric and persuasion were deployed in the service of matters of paramount importance. The space of the ancient forum thus offered a man the opportunity to assume the stature of greatness by commanding the attention and respect of his fellows in the arena of political discourse. In this way, the public realm was the realm of civic virtue, but also of freedom. Here, the great man became truly an individual, distinguished from the common herd, by extraordinary words and deeds. The public domain was the realm in which human beings transcended the level of mere animal existence and became fully human.

This tradition of grand politics that characterized the Greek city-state later inspired the civic values of the Roman republic. The premium placed on public life by those great civilizations is visible to us in the towering monuments of public architecture that, even as ruins, still humble everything built ever since. Indeed, it was for reason of the value placed by the ancients on the culture of public virtue that architecture was the queen of the arts, followed closely by sculpture. Architecture defined the public space in which civic excellence could be achieved, and sculpture displayed the great figures, of both gods and men, whose example was a stimulus to every virtuous aspiration. Music and drama, too, served the celebration of public greatness, even in those depictions of tragic dereliction in which heroic personalities were seen to struggle with the dark forces of catastrophic fate.

In stark contrast to the public domain that held out the promise of freedom and uniqueness, the private world of the ancient household, what was called in Greek *oikos*, was a closed and hidden realm in which a man was bent to the ends of brute necessity, the sustaining of the body and the fulfillment of its basic needs. Although private ownership was surely a prerequisite for participation in the public life of the city, in and by itself, without the redeeming value of serving as a platform from which a public role could be launched, a man's private existence was considered to be a thing of relatively little worth. Not until Roman times would the domestic hearth be regarded as a refuge, a comforting space of temporary withdrawal from the rigors of public performance. For the Greeks, private life was judged a good deal more negatively. In his private life, a man could be master in a limited sense only, for his efforts were aimed ultimately only at maintaining the conditions of survival. His labors were harnessed to the wheel of a dreary repetition: the provision of shelter and sustenance, the cycle of daily work and nightly rest, the begetting of children and the burial of the dead. The domestic sphere was therefore a relatively secret space, in which management of the mere material requirements of life was discreetly accomplished outside the public eye. Indeed, to the extent that the domestic sphere was positively cut off from the larger public world, life in private could assume, as the very word suggests, a *privative* character, the sense of being deprived of something.

Of course, for the man of means in the ancient world, the actual labor of household maintenance was performed by wives, children, and slaves. Yet because the domestic enclave of the *oikos* implied a bondage to the iron rule of material necessity, private life, even that of the wealthy man, was thought to be akin to a kind of slavery. Though exempt from the more demeaning forms of physical exertion, every *paterfamilias* was harnessed to the tasks of management and oversight demanded by the household routine.

In this way, even the head of the house was subject to the domination of a power outside himself. The ultimate master within the private sphere was the relentless necessity of service to the body's needs and to the protection of its vulnerabilities. It was for this reason that the father's absolute authority over others within the private domain, an authority that we would today judge to be arbitrary and tyrannical, was thought to be fully justified. Private life meant subjection for everyone to the unvarying toil of subsistence. A hierarchy of power, tantamount to an entire regime of enslavement, not only of slaves proper, but also of wives and children, was therefore taken to be perfectly appropriate. Responsible for the smooth operation of the whole, the father, too, was subject to a kind of bondage to the unrelenting demands of domestic life. For the same reason, a measure of domestic violence was taken to be perfectly defensible, even necessary, to ensure the security and efficient conduct of the household. For slaves, women, and children to suffer at times under the blows of the family patriarch was to be expected, for he, too, was forced by the whip of practical necessity.

For the ancients, then, the private world was emphatically a world apart, an enclosure within whose confines the requirements of bodily survival were serviced. This sense of private containment was perfectly expressed in the architectural convention of the atrium, the inner space of the household that was securely contained within the household walls. To be sure, this internal space constituted a certain precinct of sacredness, overseen by household gods and animated by reverence for family ancestors. Yet contrasted to the sphere of freedom and accomplishment offered by the public domain, the hidden preserve of the private realm was tinged with a degree of shame. Private affairs were kept strictly sequestered, cordoned off from the arena of civic life.

From this point of view, we can understand the sense in which the Greek concept of law was centered on a notion of containment and separation. Law functioned as a boundary between domains. "The people," says a fragment from Heraclitus, "must fight on behalf of the law as though for the city wall." The wall of the law served to separate one man's property from another's (one ancient Greek law prohibited houses from touching one another), but it also enforced the all-important separation of private and public domains. We still recognize this sense of law in the contemporary world to the extent that we expect public officials to put private concerns aside in the administration of statecraft. Yet the separation of private from public life has shrunk from its status in the ancient world as the organizing principle that defined an entire social and moral ethos. The modern sense of propriety in the conduct of public business is often limited to the minimal expectation that officers of the public trust keep their hands out of the till, resisting the temptation to use public funds for private uses.

Greek Sex

Mindful of Hannah Arendt's depiction of ancient attitudes about the division between public and private, we can shed a good deal of light on Greek attitudes toward sexuality. It allows us, for example, to correct a common misconception. Perhaps as a spin-off of popular images of debauched Roman orgies complete with wild romps of fornication and spectacular perversions, or perhaps as a conclusion drawn from acquaintance with the fact of Greek homosexuality, or maybe just from seeing one too many randy scenes of Attic vase painting, there is a tendency among many people to suppose that the Greeks were a sort of anything-goes, no-holds-barred crowd in sexual matters. One might even get the impression that the Greeks were, of all civilizations, the freest and most sexually over-indulgent. Alas, nothing of the sort. On the contrary, moderation was the watchword for sexual ethics in Greece, as it was in all questions of virtue. And moderation was a matter of self-control, the very opposite of self-indulgence. In this way, sexual ethics among the Greeks were continuous with the attitudes toward private life that we have been exploring. As the most private of private things, sexuality was approached cautiously as a potential source of shame.

The crucial thing to remember, however, is what sort of shame we are dealing with here. For the Greeks had nothing of the guilt-ridden self-consciousness about sexuality that has fermented for centuries in the Judeo-Christian tradition. The Greeks did not demonize the flesh as sinful in itself, nor did they conceive of erotic desire as a fall from divine grace. The problem, rather, was precisely the privacy of sex. As we have seen, too great an attachment to private life kept a man from assuming his proper role in the public world of action and virtue. And what greater bondage to the private domain can there be than over-attachment to erotic enjoyment? The over-lascivious man shows himself to be a slave of bodily pleasure. Unable to tear himself away from the soft embrace of Eros, the man with a weakness for sexual pleasure fatally compromises his own self-possession. He loses the respect of others by displaying a deficiency of self-respect. He is unfit to be master of any other man because, unable to resist a slavish bondage to his own body, he has failed to be master to himself.

The Greeks' sense of shame about sexuality was therefore deeply rooted in their jaundiced view of private life in general. There was nothing intrinsically wrong with the pleasures of home, hearth, and marriage bed. Surely no man would have been faulted for arranging his domestic affairs with care. The private sphere served the needs of the body and its appetites, and who does not have such needs? Yet there was something shameful in becoming a slave to such needs. Unable to resist the siren call of fleshly pleasure, the lust-driven man becomes base and pathetic, not because he is in revolt against divine law or because he relishes the taste of forbidden fruits, but because he shows himself to be the puppet of forces other than himself. Such a slave of bodily cravings is unworthy and unable to participate in the larger world of public life. True greatness of soul—true courage, virtue, and self-possession—can be achieved only in rising above the level of merely private satisfactions and assuming one's place in the public domain in which honor can be won.

From the perspective that we have opened up, we also gain a new insight into the ancient conception of gender. The separation of public and private corresponded almost exactly to that between masculine and feminine. Only men were privileged to participate fully in the public affairs of the *polis.* Women were consigned to the domestic sphere, safely contained within the walls of the private household. And like everything private, everything having to do with the servicing of bodily need, the concerns of the feminine were associated with a certain shame. In Sanskrit, the word for shame is the same as the word for the female genitalia. For a man to remain too closely tied to the private, feminine world was disgraceful.[2]

Midway through Homer's *Iliad*, we see this shame visited upon Paris. Lounging with the lovely Helen, far from the dust and danger of battle, Paris is harangued by his brother Hector for hanging back, comfy among the love pillows, while his comrades fight. We glimpse a similar attitude in Sophocles's *Antigone.* When Antigone violates the edict of Creon by burying the body of her brother Polynices, she sets in motion a fatal collision between public duty and private kinship. It is a collision not just between a man and a woman, but between the domain and prerogatives of the masculine and those of the feminine. Creon's son, in love with Antigone, is then caught in the middle. For Creon, the result is unambiguous: His son Haemon has been co-opted by the feminine. Over and over again, Creon derides his hapless son for acting like a woman or for being dominated by one.

Under the right conditions, the cloud of shame that hung over the feminine enclave of ancient domesticity could erupt into an outright storm of horror. We witness such explosions in more than one of the great Attic tragedies, but none so poignantly as *Oedipus Rex.* The main focus of interest,

[2]A distant echo of this ancient attitude is still readily audible in contemporary street language when the man who chooses to head home to his wife or girlfriend rather than accompany his male friends for a night on the town is derided for being "pussy whipped."

signaled by the play's title, is of course the drama of the unfortunate Oedipus, who in the blindness of ignorance murders his father and marries his mother. Aside from the sheer atrociousness of the crimes with which he pollutes himself, the tragic figure of Oedipus horrifies us by the way in which he fulfills the dictates of fate while in the very act of trying to avoid them. (Oedipus, it will be remembered, hears the terrible prophecy of his patricide while he is still living in Corinth with Polybus and Merope, the adoptive couple he takes to be his true parents. It is then precisely in his haste to get away from Corinth that he attacks and kills a man on the road—none other than his real father, Laius.) At the same time, however, Oedipus brings about a collision between the public and private realms. In the appalling discovery of his true identity, Oedipus effects a catastrophic short circuit between public and private. When his public duty to find Laius's murderer finally leads to Oedipus himself as the perpetrator, his public role as king collapses sickeningly onto the level of private transgressor.

Yet there is a second layer of outrage in *Oedipus Rex,* often overlooked by commentators, that is even more directly relevant to Greek ambivalence about the private domain—this time to its specifically feminine character. This second dimension of atrocity, equally or even more disturbing than the unwitting crimes of Oedipus, is centered on his mother Jocasta, the enigmatic queen of Thebes, wife of the murdered Laius. And here the sense of horror is generated not by ignorance but by knowledge. As the drama unfolds and as the dreadful realization of his past dawns upon poor Oedipus, it becomes increasingly clear that Jocasta has known the truth all along. And how could she not? Of course, we are naturally inclined to expect any mother to recognize her own child, even after a long separation. Moreover, recognition of this sort was a theme familiar among the Greeks, perhaps the most venerable and touching example being that of Odysseus's faithful dog who instantly recognizes his old master, even after his absence of twenty years. Yet Jocasta needn't have relied solely on maternal intuition. It was because Jocasta knew the terrible prophecy from the start that she gave the infant Oedipus into the arms of her herdsman, the man who, later moved by pity, gave the child to a passing shepherd instead of leaving it to die on the barren mountainside. Moreover, it was this very man, Jocasta's particular servant, who was the only witness to Laius's murder and thus the only one who could answer the crucial question about whether Laius's train was attacked by a roving band or by a single man. As Oedipus presses closer and closer to the loathsome truth, insisting that he interview the mysterious herdsman, Jocasta begs him to "ask no more questions. I have suffered enough," she groans, "I pray you may never find out who you are." When the awful facts have at last come out, the chorus leaves little doubt about the conclusion they have drawn about Jocasta's knowledge: "How," they ask in horror, "could the furrows your father sowed have endured you so long in silence?"

She knew all along? The shock of this idea gains its full measure of force when we remember that Oedipus sets out to solve his father's murder almost twenty years after the fact—twenty years, that is, after becoming his mother's husband. Over that period, Oedipus and Jocasta have produced at least four children, including, of course, the ill-starred Antigone. When the truth is finally out, therefore, the traumatic effect is partly a function of devastating retroaction, an effect not unlike that suffered by the spouse of an adulterer who, after having been told of a love affair, must then brace for the second, potentially even more destructive revelation: the answer to the question, "How long has this been going on?" Looked at in this way, *Oedipus Rex* presents us with a kind of double-whammy. It is, on the one hand, a harrowing spectacle of unwitting parricide and incest, but it is also, and perhaps even more appallingly, a tale of knowing complicity.

It's not easy to say which of these horrible faces of the tragedy the original audience would have found most bloodcurdling. Yet in view of ancient attitudes toward the private, feminine domain, we can be sure that the Greek audience would have recognized something all too familiar in the travesty of Jocasta's terrible knowledge. They would have seen it as an instance, distinguished only by its extremity, of a secret knowledge available only to women. Such occult knowledge, the source of "women's wiles," was, quite literally, the savvy of "insiders," the special possession not only of those in a position to pass it around a closed circle but even more importantly of those who live sequestered in a hidden space; their sensibilities profoundly shaped their participation in private mysteries. The special arts of the midwife, for example, would have formed part of such a specifically feminine knowledge, inaccessible and forever vaguely threatening to men.

If women are privy to a special knowledge, incubated in a hidden and enclosed space, perhaps it is in part because they are themselves enclosures, containing an inner "room" in which we have all at one time been in residence, yet which remains beyond the eyes and control of men. At least among the ancients, masculine fear and distrust of the feminine was very much related to the mysterious functions of the womb. Ultimately, however, it was not only the hiddenness of the womb but its connection to the occult powers of the natural world that made it, and the woman who possesses it, objects of fear. How dreadful that this feminine organ appears regularly to rupture and bleed, as if it were a wound impossible of healing! And how much more terrifying that the rhythm of this uncanny self-laceration is synchronized with the ebb and flow of the oceanic tides and with the waxing and waning of the moon! The ancients were deeply impressed, as Simone de Beauvoir has remarked, that "woman is a part of that fearsome machinery which turns the planets and the sun in their courses, she is the prey of cosmic energies that rule the destiny of the stars and the tides, and of which men must undergo the disturbing radiations." In accordance with woman's inner nature, the ancients concluded, there is something dark, animal, and ultimately deadly at the heart of the feminine. It is a notion that has had a long and dramatic career, not least in the history of witch-hunting. Through the centuries, those accused of being witches, very predominantly women, were thought to possess secret and dangerous knowledge, typically derived from sexual liaisons with the devil or from intimate relationship with one or another animal, the witches' so-called familiar.

Right to Privacy

It is in order to shed some light on the emergence of modern sexuality that we have been pursuing the theme of public and private. To prepare the next crucial step, we need to return to Hannah Arendt's argument as she traces the modern transformation of the public and private spheres. How did attitudes toward public and private life change at the dawn of the modern epoch?

We are fond of thinking of ourselves as the proud inheritors of Athenian democracy. And, of course, there are some ways in which modern politics still echoes the ancient value on public life. The founding principles of the modern democracies, enshrined for Americans in the Declaration of Independence and the Constitution, bear traces of the ancient concern for service to the republic that transcends all private interests. Yet the fact remains that somewhere along the path to modernity the entire conception of private and public life got turned completely upside-down. Indeed, between ancient and modern we find an almost complete reversal of values. Where the ancients regarded the public domain as the arena of freedom and individuality, for us moderns it is precisely the opposite. Only in private life, on our own time and in our own space, are we truly free. Only as a private person, free to express our idiosyncratic tastes, do we become genuine individuals. Far from providing the occasion for assuming our true identity and exercising our freedom, the public realm of the modern world demands submission to rules and routines that often feel arbitrary, alienating, or even enslaving.

What happened?

This epochal transformation was rooted in multiple social and economic changes during the early modern period and it does not lie in the path of our purposes to go into them too deeply. We do, however, need to get a grasp on the radically new sensibility that emerged from them. We see that new outlook blossoming forth in the work of the seventeenth-century English philosopher Thomas Hobbes, a thinker whose influence upon American political traditions, and by extension virtually all modern democratic institutions, is hard to overestimate. Hobbes's great book, *Leviathan*, was an attempt to establish the legitimacy of centralized political power, a project given urgency by the bloody spectacle of the English civil war of 1648. Hobbes's basic assumptions, the battery of concepts that informed his view of human nature, were drawn not from classical thought but from the revolutionary, mechanistic physics of

Galileo. Human beings, Hobbes proposed, can be likened to material bodies in motion. Like billiard balls that, once struck, will continue moving in a straight line until they strike or are struck by something else, all individual humans are motivated by their own, independent inertia, the force of their individual desires and appetites, and will restlessly seek the fulfillment of those desires unless impeded by some compelling force outside themselves.

Such a mechanistic conception of human nature utterly overturned the age-old notion, derived from Aristotle, that related the human being to its proper end or *telos*, an overarching aim that both orients individual lives and unifies the political community. Hobbes put forward a conception of human life devoid of any other final purpose than the satisfaction of private desires. This change of perspective had revolutionary implications for political life. In the classical vision, politics served the good life for the human community as a whole. If the human being is by nature—in accordance with its *telos*—a political animal, my welfare is inseparably bound up with that of my neighbors. We are all in it together. The watchword for Hobbes, by contrast, is unavoidable conflict between competing individuals. The function of politics thus becomes merely that of guaranteeing the security of individuals against murderous conflicts with others who are themselves seeking the gratification of their own interests. To be sure, Hobbes insists that the survival of the state depends on the existence of a central, sovereign power, and he explains how granting authority to such a central authority will require each individual citizen to give up a portion of his or her natural liberty. But the only reason to come together into political association of any sort is for protection of private rights. The political commonwealth is thus based on an implicit covenant or social contract in which individuals bind themselves to a limited political unity only to the extent that it serves their advantage to do so. The ultimate goal of Hobbesian politics is the protection of private interests.

In this way, Hobbes introduced a notion of freedom almost exactly the reverse of the classical one. For Hobbes, freedom becomes solely a matter of the private individual's freedom from external interference or constraint. This new, modern sense of freedom is rooted in precisely those private needs that the ancients deemed to be the very antithesis of autonomy and independence. Gone was the idea of freedom exercised in the public realm, a freedom for the pursuit of public virtue that was predicated on a transcendence of private life. After Hobbes, freedom is the freedom of and for privacy.

These changes prepared for the unfolding of the most characteristic features of modern life. The way was open, for example, for the development of the modern culture of commodity consumption. To the extent that people express their freedom in the sphere of private appetite rather than that of public achievement, they come to define their individual identity in the pattern of their private tastes. They come to feel that their personal character and worth are reflected in what and how they consume. Personal identity is mirrored in the idiosyncratic particulars of private choice—in habits and hobbies, likes and dislikes, and above all in possessions. Once this new regime of freedom and identity is established, nearly limitless possibilities of advertising manipulation suddenly yawn open, possibilities in which the underlying pitch is always fundamentally the same: own this (*buy this!*) and you will feel more free, more fulfilled, more truly yourself.

In this brave new world of private rights, the public realm so valued by the ancients tends to become emptied of its original content. Public life becomes increasingly taken up with the task of merely protecting and extending private satisfactions. The ancient reverence for noble sacrifice is eclipsed by dreams of personal gratification. The function of government becomes, in the words we all know by heart, that of securing "life, liberty, and the pursuit of happiness." This shift in the nature and function of politics is summed up in the modern idea of "political economy." For the ancient ear, the very phrase would have sounded like a contradiction in terms. Derived from the word *oikos* (for house or dwelling), "economy" among the ancients was an entirely private matter, the management of the household. In the modern age, however, the entire state becomes in itself nothing but a gigantic household. Politics then becomes a matter of mere administration, an overseeing of economic efficiency and productivity. It's not for nothing that we now refer to the government simply as "the administration." The rallying cry that swept Bill Clinton into the American presidency speaks eloquently for the political reality of the whole modern world: "It's the economy, stupid!" Aside from threats from outside adversaries, the greatest, indeed perhaps the only, danger to the modern becomes malfunction of the economy.

With the emerging dominance of political economy, the classical ideals of public life in the *polis* are overtaken by concern for the material welfare of the brute mass of individuals that we now call "society." The ancient arena of civic life, the sphere of public virtue and action, is replaced by a mere statistical collective, the bare aggregate of individuals each pursuing private designs with the sole proviso that the individual's strivings do not overly infringe on those of others. The structures of efficient management and administration of society then proliferate in the emergence of that familiar scourge of modern life: bureaucracy. The domination of an anonymous system of administration by forms, rules, and records becomes an almost inevitable development when public life is bent to the service of innumerable private ends. The irony, of course, is that while private wealth and comfort now rule as the highest values, bureaucratized public life becomes increasingly distant and impersonal.

Arendt now comes to a point that is crucial to her overall argument, and even more so for the use we will make of it. Faced with the progressive emptying out of the public realm and its replacement by a faceless system of social management, the modern individual stages a rebellion against the more alienating aspects of society at large by taking refuge in an increasingly insular and atomized existence. Modern Western culture thus witnesses the invention of what Arendt calls the "intimate." In the intimate, the modern individual seeks to drink deeply at the well of strictly personal experience. The intimate is the baptism of the absolutely particular, a celebration of the miniature. One of its great, early champions was the French philosopher Rousseau, author of *Confessions of a Solitary Walker* and quite fittingly the only Western thinker of any consequence commonly referred to by his first name: Jean-Jacques. Under the halo of the intimate, the details of the private world assume an unprecedented confidence to overcome the ancient modesty about material concerns in general and about bodily functions in particular. Private life steps shamelessly into the light of day.

The diminished importance of the public realm and the newfound taste for the intimate are directly reflected in the arts of modernity. The privilege accorded by the ancients to architecture and sculpture, for example, gives way to the modern triumph of oil painting. Of all the fine arts, painting most perfectly fits the bill for the emerging modern celebration of private life. Discrete and portable, paintings offer themselves as convenient decorations for private residences and are eminently suitable as commodities for a culture driven by personal acquisitiveness. Moreover, after the Renaissance, the characteristic themes of painting increasingly shift from treatment of religious and mythic subjects to depiction of details from everyday private life: still lifes, nudes, and domestic scenes. It is no accident that the first self-portrait, that of Albrecht Dürer in 1504, appears precisely at the dawn of the modern age. Oil painting becomes the mirror in which modern appreciation of the intimate sees itself reflected.

Few paintings better emblematize this private turn than Eduard Manet's *Déjeuner sur l'herbe* of 1863, with its foregrounded trio of anonymous people, an unclothed woman and two men, chatting over a picnic in a grassy glade. In the past, these figures would have been identifiable personages of religion or myth and their activity interpretable symbolically or allegorically. Yet as Manet gives them to us, they could be anyone and their lunch, while charged rather tantalizingly with the unanswered question posed by the woman's nakedness, remains simply, unapologetically, resolutely … *lunch*. The naked woman stares out at us, the viewers, with a careless but focused gaze that seems almost provocative, as if it responds beforehand to any objection on the part of the viewer: "You gotta problem with this?"

Elsewhere in the arts, the quest for the intimate underlies the rise of the modernist art form par excellence, the novel. In the novel, the reader is invited into the interior of private lives as into a deep and winding cave passage. Privy to the most intimate thoughts of characters by means of first-person or omniscient narration, the reader is able to identify with the protagonists of the novel in a fashion completely unprecedented in the history of human culture. The reader vicariously follows every sigh, winces at every pang of pain, blushes from every embarrassment, and thrills to every transport of ecstasy. The result is that the novel becomes a kind of particle accelerator of the intimate life, a machine for the intensification of interior experience in which modern subjectivity is spun at ever greater speeds around its own axis. With very few exceptions, the modern novel tends to relegate the forces and events of public life to the status of mere backdrops against which the private struggles of individual characters are more charmingly depicted.

In music, too, the modern taste for the intimate in rebellion against the cold and impersonal form of the social world has had decisive effects. While the piano can justifiably lay claim to special status as the modern instrument of all instruments, perhaps mostly for the completeness of its range and its power to reveal the structure of music (the piano, for good reasons, is the composer's choice), the queen of the modern instruments is unquestionably the violin. Of all the orchestral instruments the most like a human voice, the violin is the instrument most charged with the expression of emotion. Bursting upon the scene at precisely the dawn of the modern age—the first violins appear right around 1600—the violin was ideally suited to express the modern fascination with the inner life of the intimate. Flaubert perfectly evokes the emotive power of the violin in a description of Emma Bovary. In a swoon of passionate transport at the opera with her lover Leon, "she felt a vibration pass through her whole being, as if the bows of the violins were being drawn across her own nerves."

Our Bodies, Our Selves

When Flaubert said of his character, "*Emma Bovary, c'est moi!*", he was speaking for all of us. Emma is a poster child of the modern sensibility. At least she is the perfect embodiment of the modern quest for the intimate as Hannah Arendt describes it. Emma's imagination is inflamed by the reading of romantic novels, an activity pursued in solitude that surrounds her with a virtual world of persons and events infinitely more fascinating than the pallid circumstances of her actual life. In fact, Emma is utterly bored by life in the provincial town in which her new husband, a doting but hapless country doctor, has deposited her. The pettiness and banality of this little world soon become suffocating to her and Charles comes to represent everything that Emma detests, everything that stands in the way of her dreams of passion and romance. The path to her first adulterous relationship is thus opened up by a desperate need to get away, to escape, to involve herself with *anything but this*! She flings herself into the arms, first of Rudolphe, and later of Leon, driven by a relentless hunger for emotional transport.

So obsessed is she with breaking free from the odious monotony of her life that Emma seems oblivious to the risks entailed by her adulterous liaisons. Not until just before the final, fatal *dénouement* does she appear to be aware of the impending catastrophe. Up to that point, she is able to think only of the next rendezvous, the next stolen kiss. The web of social ties and expectations that define her as a doctor's wife appears to her merely as a loathsome trap into which she has fallen, a prison house from which she must at all costs free herself. In this context, the secrecy required by her adultery, far from being an onerous or anxiety-producing impediment to her enjoyment, is a positive means of its enlargement. And here we glimpse the degree of Emma's enthrallment with the intimate. The concealment and isolation of Emma's love affairs provide the ideal conditions for the deepening experience of the intimate. Emma dreams of the bright lights and dazzling *soirées* of Paris, yet her longing for the big city has nothing at all to do with the public space of the ancient world, the stage upon which civic accomplishment was recognized. On the contrary, as Emma yearns for the banality of everyday life to be swept away by the wild passion of an all-consuming romance, she appreciates the metropolis mostly for its anonymity. Lost in the hustle of the city crowd, Emma is able to sink blissfully into the intoxicating pillow of the intimate.

The social world is horizontal, a skein of relationships and mutual responsibilities that spreads out in all directions, sustaining the individual in a stable network. The intimate, by contrast, is vertical. Pursuit of the intimate deliberately turns away from the broad expanse of the social and seeks to twist its augur into the recesses of a purely private existence. This aspect of the intimate, too, is perfectly realized in the figure of Emma Bovary. All of Emma's exploits, all of her hopes, fears, and dreams, are ultimately self-referential. Her life becomes consumed by a kind of malignancy of the private domain. The danger of such self-absorption, however, for Emma Bovary or for anyone who follows the same path, is a growing sense of emptiness. As Emma descends into the vortex of the intimate, she is more and more threatened with being unable to find any compelling content there. She rushes from one man to another, from one romantic scenario to another, desperately trying to inflate a continually collapsing sense of meaning. How can the project of the intimate save itself from this gathering void? Having withdrawn from the public world and unable to draw sustenance from the social nexus that knits that world together, the intimate seeks to fashion its own substance by the only means available to it: it tries to bloat itself with emotional and perceptual immediacy. A sense of convincing and authentic aliveness is sought in the mere registration of powerful feeling and sensation. Bring out the violins!

The master analyst of this restless hunger of the modern spirit, constantly threatened by its own inner vacuity and thus constantly driven to jack up the intensities of emotional experience, was the great Danish existentialist, Søren Kierkegaard. The prime danger for the alienated modern individual, Kierkegaard astutely points out, is boredom. The cure is pursuit of "the interesting." Thus we get Kierkegaard's category of the aesthetic personality, devoted to cultivating the piquant experiences of the moment. In seeking to validate its own substantiality, to convince itself of its own reality, the aesthetic personality will accept only the evidence of sensuous immediacy. Unpersuaded by rational consideration and unmoved by ethical commitment, the aesthete turns to feeling as the sole criterion of authenticity. For this reason, the aesthetic type—the type, Kierkegaard argues, that describes the basic tendency of modernity—is driven almost by necessity toward sexuality as one of the surest means of giving meaning and measure to existence. Sexuality is a virtually inexhaustible source of the interesting. The aesthetic personality is thus epitomized by the seducer.[3]

Kierkegaard would have well recognized the yearnings of Emma Bovary. It is no accident that Emma's quest for the intimate leads her to adultery. Indeed, adultery is a perfect field for the cultivation of the intimate. It is a kind of double exploitation of the private. On the one hand, of course, adultery is sex. As such, it provides a ready spring of feeling and sensing from which the seeker of the intimate can imbibe. Sexuality immerses the lover in the immediacy of the body and does so in its most privy functions. In sex, the quest for the intimate discovers a treasure trove of intensely compelling experience. In this respect, too, Manet's *Déjeuner sur l'herbe* is a perfect emblem of the modern project of the intimate, as if the enigmatic nakedness at the center of it all betokens the preference of the intimate for absorption in the erotic. At the same time, however, by being forced to hide an illicit relation from the spouse and family, adultery carves out for itself a secret space within the privacy of the household, a kind of hidden annex in which the privacy of sex is raised to another power. If sex is the goldmine of the intimate, adultery is its richest vein.

The example of Emma Bovary thus enables us to draw out the consequences of Hannah Arendt's analysis of public and private life for sexuality in the modern world. Emma is a kind of tragic heroine of modernity precisely because she is a frenzied pursuer of the intimate. The engine of that frenzy is a pervasive sense of alienation that leads her to reject the public world of social roles, duties, and relations. Unsure of exactly what she wants or needs to replace it, she desires only to be delivered from the flat and tiresome world of petty bourgeois society. She attempts to escape into a purely private world, modeled on the romances she has read and reread. She bores deeper and deeper into the heart of what is most private, as if she might magically burst out upon some other plane, some other world, in which she would finally be the woman she longs to be, loved by the man who truly deserves her.

By virtue of being enlisted in the modern pursuit of the intimate, sexuality has in our time become the bearer of values and expectations that would have been unthinkable for anyone in the ancient world. The stakes are nothing less than the definition of personal identity. For the ancients, the worth and status of a man, the measure of his very being, was inseparable from speech and action in the public realm. For us moderns, by contrast, personal identity has taken refuge in the private domain and is decisively defined by its most private

[3]Kierkegaard's conception of the aesthetic is developed in the first volume of his masterwork, *Either/Or*, the culminating portion of which is "The Diary of the Seducer."

expression. Sex, more than any other single dimension of our being, has become the touchstone of personal identity, the privileged domain of freedom and individuality, the space within which we find what we most consider to be our inner selves.

This change, in which private life has become centered on the sexual and the sexual has become the index of personal identity, is reflected in our use of language. The word *intimate* itself, for example, has come to be strongly associated with the sexual. So, too, the word *private.* By our *privates* we refer most of all to the organs of sex. Even the word *identity* has been drawn into the sphere of the sexual, as we moderns increasingly categorize ourselves according to the possession of differing "sexual identities." This sort of talk has now risen to such dominance that it is hard to imagine that things might ever have been otherwise.

But things *were* otherwise. In fact, the whole lexicon of sexual identity is a very recent invention. The words *homosexual* and *heterosexual,* for example, though they draw upon Greek roots, came into circulation only in the late nineteenth century. Apparently coined in 1868 by Karl Maria Kertbeny, a German sex-law reformer, *homosexuality* and *heterosexuality* were originally intended to form a quartet with two other terms, *monosexual* (masturbators) and *heterogenit* (those who indulge in sexual acts with other species). In the United States, the word *heterosexuality* appeared in print for the first time in a medical journal article by Dr. James Kiernan, published in 1892. For the ancients, indeed even for the majority of people just a couple of centuries ago, none of this would have made any sense. The sexual pigeonholing implied by our notions of "sexual orientation," for example, would have been strange to them. It isn't that they didn't recognize a range of tastes—"different strokes for different folks," as we might say these days—but it would never have occurred to them to make such differences in any way exclusive of one another, much less to pin a person's individual status and uniqueness upon them.

From the point of view of the ancient world, the modern coupling of sex and identity is a contradiction in terms. Far from considering sexual desire as a source of individuating identity, the ancients regarded the activity of that mischievous god Eros to be precisely what makes us unrecognizable to ourselves, leading us to do crazy things we would never do otherwise. Sexual desire is a disorienting maelstrom. This ancient sensibility still resonates in the modern poetics of love, revived (though somewhat sanitized) by the romantic tradition. Love is still supposed to sweep us off our feet, leave us blind and foolish, dazed and breathless. "Love is the ocean," croons Stevie Nicks, "in which we all want to drown." According to this classical conception of Eros as a mighty—and mightily confusing—power, sex is obviously unsuited to be a source of personal identity. On the contrary, sex is what we have most in common, not just with one another, but with every grunting, panting animal in rut. Sex is the great umbilical cord that connects us to the primal pulse of universal Nature.

But modernity has amended the rules of the game, forcing sex to bear the burden of being a marker of personal uniqueness. Pressure-cooked in the litigious atmosphere of contemporary society, the latent contradiction in all of this has been brought into full blossom. Thus while we still evoke loss of control as a sure sign of being truly bowled over by love, we insist at the same time that sex be fully consensual, fully responsible, fully controlled. Sex thus becomes like driving a car, something that should be engaged in only by sober, responsible, licensed (that is to say, married) adults. The extreme form of this contradiction is obvious in those guidelines now given to college students in an attempt to address the growing problem of date rape. Fully correct sexual behavior means not only avoiding sex with anyone who is intoxicated (and therefore not fully responsible) but getting permission from one's partner for each increment of sexual advance. This "Simon says," step-by-step procedure makes sex seem like playing doctor in a new sense: the participants are under constant threat of suit for malpractice.

We can readily extend this analysis to the role of sexuality in the identity politics that are now so decisive for modern social life. Along with nationality and religion, issues of sexuality are the focus of the most inflammatory political debates of our time. It is no accident that the present age of identity anxiety, the era of culture wars and struggles for national, local, and personal self-determination, is also the age of seemingly endless disputes over questions related to sexuality: abortion, homosexuality, in vitro fertilization and cloning, gay marriage and adoption, marriage and divorce rates, sexual harassment, sexual content in media, and so forth. If it can now plausibly be said that "the personal is the political," it is above all because of the centrality of sex in many of the most pressing questions of modern culture. Viewed from this perspective, it should not really surprise us that Supreme Court nominees are grilled by Senate committees about their tastes in porno films, or that presidents are impeached for their extramarital follies.

We can usefully linger a moment longer on the case against Bill Clinton, as it offers a telling illustration of the inversion of public and private realms that we have been tracing. On the most general level, the whole Lewinsky affair had the effect of turning the attention of the country away from issues of public policy and wholly absorbing it in what would not so very long ago have been considered a purely private matter. This result was clearly a stunning victory for Clinton's political enemies, most of them people who had campaigned on issues of private morality (abortion, school prayer, family values, etc.) and who viewed the public policy agenda of the New Democrats, led by a popular, charismatic president, as a distinctly threatening prospect. By means of preoccupying the national consciousness with President Clinton's flaws of personal character, his public agenda was thoroughly eclipsed. Indeed, for

Clinton's neo-conservative opponents a more satisfactory turning of the tables could hardly have been invented. Or maybe it *was* invented. One need not be a wide-eyed conspiracy theorist to suspect that Monicagate was the product of a calculated strategy for which the Paula Jones imbroglio was a dress (or undress) rehearsal.

Whatever the machinations of conservative operatives, sleaze mongers, and mass-mail moguls, the single greatest factor in Clinton's downfall, aside from Clinton's own reckless behavior, was the American public's insatiable hunger for the ultra-public consumption of private scandal, preferably well saturated with sexual overtones (for which the dress rehearsal was less Paula Jones than the O.J. Simpson trial). Yet even such mass zeal for exposing the private lives of public persons could not by itself have led to Clinton's impeachment. For that an additional factor was required. And it is instructive to see exactly how an impeachable offense was obtained from what would otherwise have been an embarrassing but not fatal peccadillo. The mechanism was itself a very precisely engineered short-circuit between the public and private realms. By maneuvering Clinton into a Grand Jury deposition concerning his relationship with Monica Lewinsky, the Independent Counsel succeeded in staging a perfect collision of public and private law. According to the unwritten law of private behavior, a man who is asked about an extramarital dalliance is naturally expected to lie about it. In fact, to speak too freely about a love affair would rightly be regarded as shameful, even culpable: Having cheated on his wife, a public confession of it would only add insult to injury. In this situation, a decent man (if he could still be decent at all) must lie, if only to protect his wife from public humiliation. Yet in the context of a formal deposition, governed by public law, for Clinton to obey this code of private conduct inevitably meant perjuring himself. To obey the private law was to violate the public one. *Et voilà!* Grounds for impeachment.

The larger lesson to be learned from the Clinton impeachment is less about sexual conduct per se than it is about the accelerating disappearance of the dividing line between public and private concerns. We are well familiar with one aspect of this collapse of distinction, though we have another name for it. We call it "the character issue." And by "character" we refer to something admittedly intangible, an inner quality of the person that is thought to animate his or her actions and judgments but is never visible in itself. Even in its invisibility—or rather precisely *because* of its invisibility—the issue of character can trump all other considerations. Thus even many of Clinton's most ardent supporters, people who had cheered him through the tough times of his two terms in office because they believed in the political objectives that he had fought for, found themselves at a loss to defend him against the stain of the Lewinsky affair. The character question seemed somehow to disqualify Clinton's record, retroactively erasing all of his accomplishments. Two years later, it would do the opposite for George W. Bush. While a majority of voters found him to be lacking in almost all tangible qualities—intelligence, experience, ideas, articulateness, even policy positions—he was nevertheless preferred to Al Gore largely for reasons of his more wholesome and appealing "character."

As a way of making private life a public issue, the character question in contemporary politics reminds us that, if the modern sensibility has invested itself deeply in pursuit of the intimate, it has also turned the lining of intimate life inside out and spread it before the public domain. What is this but the modern phenomenon of celebrity? At least since the advent of the motion picture industry and the star cults propagated by it, the public eye has fed voraciously on the presumably private lives of celebrities. The fact that these "private lives" are largely manufactured by press agents and PR men is less germane for our purposes at the moment than the hunger of the viewing public to become fascinated with their stories. Indeed, the cult of celebrity has become a means of having our cake and eating it: We are able to turn away from public life in the classical sense in favor of immersion in the intimate, yet at the same time are able to recover a certain kind of public life—a life that is at least very much "in public"—provided by the lives of the celebrities. The figure of the modern media celebrity thus short-circuits the distinction of public and private altogether.

The extreme case of this short-circuit, taking the incessant tabloid intrusion into the private lives of celebrities to its logical conclusion, was Madonna's experiment in *Truth or Dare*, in which she agreed to have every moment of her private existence recorded on film and displayed before the world. This "bare-all" game was touted as an attempt to subvert the image system of celebrity, showing us the real human being beneath the air-brushed artifice of the media-icon. From the perspective we've adopted, on the contrary, the conclusion to be drawn is exactly the opposite. Far from being a subversion of celebrity, the private-become-public trick of *Truth or Dare* was its most perfect expression.

It is along similar lines that we can explain one of the deep motivations for the appearance of sexual images in the public domain. The public presence of sex, like the celebrity culture with which it is closely related, serves to fill the public space with enormously compelling content that is, in the last analysis, not truly public at all, but merely lifted from the domain of the intimate and broadcast at large. The result is a profound contradiction that we tend not to notice as such, perhaps because it has already become so routine. Driving along the highway, for example, we float by billboard advertisements many of which feature erotically provocative content. Bare skin, fine lace, over-puffed lips, and languorous looks thus combine to address us on the most private level of sexual arousal but do so in the context of an emphatically public place.

Freud's Science of Intimacy

The preceding history of attitudes toward public and private life is obviously an extremely rough sketch of an immense set of problems. I've put forward a sweeping comparison of ancient and modern sensibilities, skipping altogether any mention of the Christian Middle Ages, and I have offered only the barest tidbits of evidence for my claims. Yet I have chosen to run the risk of such oversimplification in order to highlight Hannah Arendt's conception of the modern pursuit of the intimate. Against that background, it was possible to draw some preliminary conclusions about the distinctively modern meaning of sexuality. On the same basis, it is now possible to see how the historically altered situation I've described is related to the emergence of Freudian psychoanalysis.

The absolute core of Freud's theory, the point on which he never budged over the course of his career, the point upon which he continued to insist in spite of bitter struggles among the members of his inner circle, is that issues of sexuality lie at the heart of the personality. Indeed, Freud asserts that the personality is constructed around sexuality. Sex is the trellis for the unfolding of psychological development, the skeleton on which the flesh of personal character is hung. But, we can now assert, this focus on sexuality was itself historically determined. Whatever the applications of Freud's theories to the premodern era, they are nowhere more relevant than to the present period of history. In putting the erotic at the center of his psychology, Freud was responding to the emerging shape of modern culture, putting his finger on the pulse of a radical transformation in modern subjectivity that invests itself in the intimate, and in sex as the very heart of the intimate. The crux of Freud's theories is thus a response to the conditions of modernity; indeed, it is a theoretically elaborated description of them. Freud is the theorist of the intimate par excellence.

In the same stroke, we can see how Freud's theory, centered on questions of sexuality, was almost inevitably bound to become widely influential. Focused upon the intimate, inner life in general and upon questions of sexuality in particular, psychoanalysis mirrored the emergent tendency of Western culture. This is not to deny the resistance that met Freud's theories at the turn of the century. The early psychoanalytic movement frequently triggered reactions of pitched outrage, expressed both by members of the psychiatric establishment and by the popular press. Freud's sense of himself as an embattled, even heretical innovator, persecuted for openly discussing matters of sexuality that most people energetically refused to acknowledge, was in many respects quite justified. Nor is this to deny that psychoanalysis was itself a major influence in the evolution of more open and tolerant attitudes toward sex. Contemporary culture unmistakably bears the impress of that influence. Yet the fact remains that Freud was less a creator of his times than he was a product of them. Freud's discovery of the rootedness of personality in the dynamics of sexual life was, after all, the product of observation. And what he observed were the consequences of an epochal shift in European culture. Freud began looking under the covers of sexual life at a time when Western culture was becoming obsessed with lifting the covers.

Viewed from this angle, there is something partly false about the received image of Freud as a solitary subversive pitted heroically against a prudish Victorian establishment, an image that is rehearsed yet again as a major guiding theme of Peter Gay's biography of Freud (indeed, it would be interesting merely to count the number of times Gay uses the word *subversive* in his account of Freud's career). There is no doubt that Freud encountered energetic opposition to his sexual theories and no doubt that he saw himself as threatened and isolated. But puritanical resistance to Freudianism was ultimately a sideshow. Far more decisive for the future history of psychoanalysis was the incoming tide of interest in sexuality that was already flowing at the turn of the century, a tide that helped enormously to spread the influence of Freudian psychoanalysis into the mainstream of cultural life in Europe and America. Ironically, Freud's focus on sexuality, the very thing that Freud himself regarded as the greatest threat to psychoanalysis, was in fact one of the most potent sources of its enormous success.

To which we can add a more general comment about the reception of Freud's theories. One way to summarize the shift traced by Hannah Arendt between ancient and modern sensibilities is to distinguish between an ethics of sacrifice and an ethics of satisfaction. The ancient world was characterized by an ethics of sacrifice. One can say the same, though for quite different reasons, appropriate to a very different cultural context, of medieval Christendom. Premodern society positioned the individual securely within the larger matrix of family, clan, and kingdom in such a way that the affairs of private life were almost entirely overshadowed and subsumed by matters that transcended merely private concern. Personal identity and allegiance were determined by the skein of relationships that knit individuals together in some shared, public existence. Of course, this doesn't mean that self-indulgence and private excess are exclusively modern inventions. The point is rather that the framework of values in which people understood their needs and struggles was decisively oriented toward some larger social whole in which the individual was caught up. Compared with the duties and affiliations by which the individual was linked to a larger world beyond himself or herself, the exigencies and gratifications of private life were decidedly secondary.

Such a guiding sense of participation in a larger community has increasingly eroded during the modern period as life has become focused on more purely private concerns. In contemporary society, the extended family has more and more disintegrated. The place and purposes of work have become less and less connected with home and hearth. The activities and involvements of children have become separated from the lives of their parents by a widening gulf. In short, the social world has become progressively more atomized and the private individual has accordingly become steadily more sovereign. Shakespeare's Romeo and Juliet, sidestepping family allegiances to Montagues and Capulets for the sake of a secret romance, are in this sense a distinctly modern couple. In fact, they provide a handy emblem of the modern sensibility, not only for the way that they embody the quintessential modern romantic duo, cutting themselves free of the family web to pursue an exclusive intimacy, but even more so for the fact that we, the audience, would be enormously disappointed had they done otherwise. The modern ideal of romance is a phantasy of erotic exclusivity in the face of which everything else is secondary. Give me love above all else!

Of course, these changes have not left the modern individual entirely bereft of community. Significant vestiges of the old order remain and are augmented by new forms of alliance and affiliation. Think, for instance, of the way in which the latest fad passes through the teen population like a virus. These fads reflect a hunger for belonging that, while being typically adolescent, also reflect a typically modern deficit of social connectedness. Thus we get the paradox of conspicuous conformity alongside every attempt at radical individualism. In the black leather, steel studded, and spiked hair of the punk style, for example, the posture of rebellion that flaunts its rejection of everything conventional becomes at the same time a kind of uniform for a new, close-knit tribalism. What is really crucial, however, is that the citizen of modern society feels less and less compelled to subordinate his or her own gratifications to the good of a larger collective. Personal satisfaction is the bottom line, the compass by which the individual navigates the choices available. In fact, those very choices are more and more presented to us—directly by advertising or indirectly by the general atmosphere in which we all live and work—in terms of their potential for individual gratification. The dilemma of the modern individual becomes less a matter of feeling torn between private gratification and public service than of deciding between one gratification and another that competes with it. Satisfaction, not sacrifice, is the order of the day.

It is in this context that Freud put forward the psychoanalytic theory of the unconscious, a theory centered on the question of desire and its satisfaction, or lack of it. And it is with the same context in mind that we can see both the aptness and the appeal of that theory. On the one hand, Freud's theory is in large measure a description of the historical moment it inhabits. The psychical individual envisioned by psychoanalysis, seeking above all to discharge the tensions of its own needs yet beset by the constraining influence of inhibition and repression, accurately mirrors the modern subject of satisfaction. Mirror indeed!—for even as Freud's thought can be said to reflect the circumstances of modern subjectivity, elaborating theoretically key aspects of the modern condition, so too the modern spirit has in Freud's theories enjoyed contemplation of its own image. Broadly considered, Freud's legacy not only theorized the modern subject but also encouraged and enlarged it. Probably no other piece of scholarly abstraction, psychological or otherwise, has so powerfully underwritten, even justified, the tendency that we are calling the modern ethics of satisfaction.

The qualification "broadly considered" is crucial here. Especially with respect to its popular reception (though not only there), Freud's thought has been sacked for specific purposes. Like those rapacious frontiersmen who took only the tongues of the buffalo they shot, leaving the carcasses to rot in the Western sun, the popular imagination has fed very selectively upon the Freudian corpus. The portion that has been most readily assimilated is Freud's earlier work, dominated by the notion of the pleasure principle. And we can now see very clearly why this is so: It is this part of Freud's theory that comes closest to really mirroring the situation of the modern individual, devoted to the ethics of satisfaction. Freud initially conceived mental illness as the result, quite literally, of insufficient satisfaction. Freud's 1897 recommendation for one of his female hysterics, confided in a letter to his friend Wilhelm Fliess, was a prescription offered only half in jest—*Rx: Penis Dossitur.* Infinitely less palatable, though far more significant to Freud himself, was the theory developed after 1920 in which the dualism of the pleasure and reality principles was replaced by the conflict, far more mysterious and far more disturbing, between the fundamental drives of Life and Death. With the publication of *Beyond the Pleasure Principle*, the book that introduced the hypothesis of the death drive, Freud's thought took a much darker, much more genuinely subversive turn. It is a darkness, perhaps not surprisingly, into which few people have chosen to follow him, including many of Freud's closest adherents.

Think Again

"It seems to me that you've overshot the mark," pipes up the critic. "You talk as though sex had become perfectly acceptable to us, as if, ever since we blew off the dusty cloud of Victorian stuffiness, it's been nothing but halcyon days of sexual liberation. It doesn't look that way to me! We may have come a long way, as you say, but we still have a long way to go before most people are very comfortable talking about sex. We may be able to read *Ulysses* without a censor but most people still can't say the word *penis* without stuttering. We still rate movies far more carefully for sexual content than for violence. People still have fits about porn on the Internet or about adult shops moving into the better parts of town. It wasn't so very long ago that the board of an Ohio art museum was almost ridden out of town on a rail for mounting a show of Robert Mapplethorpe's photographic nudes. You would have us believe that Freud's success was a result of our contemporary obsession with sex. In this case, I think Freud himself got it right: it was an uphill battle all the way, and the battle ain't over yet!"

Which picture is right? Are we more than ever preoccupied with sex, surrounded by sexual images and messages, and apparently quite happy to be that way? Or are we as tightly defended against sex as ever, unwilling to allow the slimy stuff of sex to leak out of the familiar containers in which we've had it bottled up for centuries? Are we sexually obsessed or sexually repressed?

Isn't it both? Isn't the correct description of our contemporary situation precisely that we are at the same time fascinated with sex yet also deeply fearful and inhibited about it? The examples the critic raises are perfect illustrations. We do still rate movies—in fact, we rate them more carefully than ever. But how keenly movie producers fight for "R" ratings! It's the two extremes that need to be avoided. The PG rating is almost as deadly as the dreaded NC-17. Moviemakers know that to sell movies there needs to be some sex, just not too much, and they are well skilled at finding the middle ground of a deeply split public attitude. The example of the Internet also displays this two-sidedness very well. On the one hand, the creation of the Internet almost immediately led to a veritable nuclear explosion of pornography. In fact, it can be hard to navigate on the Net without being inundated by porn. One horrified parent recounted the experience of his sixth-grade daughter when, gathering material for her school paper on Louisa May Alcott, she started a search for "Little Women." And once contacted, many porn sites erupt like oil gushers with a stream of automatically activated and increasingly dirty "pop-up" windows. The screen is suddenly thronged with forms of sexual behavior that may rattle even the most liberal of consenting adults. For that very reason, we are especially anxious to control the smut spigot. Internet usage is thus subjected to elaborate filters and screening devices. Congress is pressured to pass laws. Nor is the offense taken by many people at the public presence of sex merely a matter of the protection of children. The fact is that we remain in many ways deeply threatened by sexuality.

What are we to make of this Janus-faced attitude? How well have we understood the way in which, on the topic of sex, our contemporary society appears to be so conspicuously both hot and cold? I can imagine my critic taking these questions as another opportunity to give me a jab. "There you go again," he will say, "making things more complicated than they need to be. The whole thing is really pretty simple. Sure there's a lot of sex around these days—sex sells!—but people don't want their nose rubbed in it all the time. And you, of all people, shouldn't be surprised that we're hot and cold about sex. Haven't you been telling us all this time about Freud's notion of 'ambivalence'? You've been going on and on about how sexuality, in tension with the unity and stability of the ego, is an occasion for ambivalence, indeed that sex is the ambivalent experience par excellence. You've already answered your own question!"

Not so fast! Perhaps things really *are* somewhat more complicated. The critic is quite right to bring up ambivalence, but we need to go further. For Freud, ambivalence was more than just a matter of mixed feelings. It was also a key aspect of the structure of the symptom. Freud's concept of the symptom was among his most original and useful ideas. Why? Because by means of the symptom, he could explain some of the most contradictory things people do. In the symptom, the opposing strands of ambivalent feelings are knotted together in a single, internally complex figure.

An example from Camus' classic novel *The Stranger* gives us a good preliminary idea of this aspect of the symptom. The protagonist of the novel shares his apartment building with Salamano, a curmudgeonly old man who is inseparable from a rather pathetic, apparently equally aged little dog. At first glance, the striking thing is the way that the man continually insults and berates the hapless little beast: "Salaud!" "Charogne!"—"Swine!" "Filth!" Yet things eventually appear more complicated when, evidently having slipped his collar, the dog disappears. Salamano claims that he won't waste a centime trying to find the little cur. Yet he is later heard weeping bitterly over his loss. Can we not immediately sense that this dog is Salamano's symptom? And can we not also see that the dog is a symptom precisely because he is something more than a mere object of ambivalence? To be sure, Salamano's dog embodies opposing emotions of love and hate, but as a symptom he entwines those currents of love and hate in a particularly intimate and enigmatic way. For reasons that remain obscure to us, this little animal has been loaded with a cargo of deeply conflicting emotions drawn from some dark recesses of his master's soul. The dog must be continually abused and humiliated *because* he is so loved, just as he is loved *because* he focuses the force of a virulent hatred.

The function of the symptom is to fuse completely contrary currents of feeling into a kind of miraculous unity. Symptoms are thus like the quilting points at which two planes of very different material have been stitched together. Freud therefore refers to the symptom as a "compromise formation." It is a truce drawn up between opposing camps. Between the two conflicting sides there ranges the force of repression; indeed, repression is what sets up the separation and conflict between the two sides in the first place. What makes the symptom such an ingenious solution is that it simultaneously gives something to each. Freud compared it to the way in which nineteenth century tourists were hauled to the top of the pyramids, with one crew of sweating locals pulling from above and another group pushing from below. The symptom therefore functions to enact repression, but also to partially suspend its force. The symptom *both represses and expresses.* It is this double function of the symptom, giving to each side of a psychological conflict some portion of what is wanted, that accounts for its tenacity. We are loath to give up our neurotic symptoms because they deliver a precious quantum of satisfaction where there might otherwise be none at all.

Take compulsive nail-biting as an illustration. We can be pretty sure that we are in the presence of a garden-variety symptom both because of the forced, compulsive character of the habit (the fact that one does it unconsciously and often uncontrollably), and because the tendency to bite one's nails increases with every increase in the level of anxiety. In fact, nail-biting is very typically a means of coping with anxiety. What anxiety? As we know, Freud traces anxiety back to the surfacing of a repressed impulse. Well! In this case, the source of anxiety would appear to be especially clear, for it is an impulse that has left its telltale vestiges symbolically legible in the symptom itself. Nail-biting, after all, is a form of biting. Nail-biting thus allows one to manage—or repress—aggressiveness. Instead of biting someone else (or hitting, or kicking them), I bite *myself*. While nervously biting my nails (say, while I anxiously await my evaluation interview with the boss) I am able to resist the temptation to lash out aggressively (what I would really like to do is go in there and scratch the bastard's face off). And how perfectly appropriate is the specific object of my biting. Quite literally, I bite off my own claws. Yet the repressive aspect is only half the story. The really ingenious part of the symptom shows itself when we realize that, in the very act of repressing my aggression, I am nevertheless partially expressing and satisfying it. I am, after all, *biting*! And gnawing, and ripping, and tearing …

With this bi-fold structure of the symptom in mind, we can return to the topic of sex and pose a crucial question: Does the deeply divided attitude of contemporary society toward sexuality betoken the dynamics of the Freudian symptom? Are we dealing here with a more definitely structured formation than any mere play of mixed feelings? Are we not more than just ambivalent about sex? Are we not deeply torn apart by it, continually drawn to it but unable to live with it comfortably? Let us take this question forward into the next chapter: Is sexuality in the modern world somehow the focus of a collective neurosis?

Is sex the prime symptom of our epoch?

7
Oedipal Modernity

We've posed the modern meaning of sex in Freudian terms, asking whether our conspicuously mixed attitude toward sex might be symptomatic in the precise Freudian sense of that word. If this comparison to the psychoanalytic symptom is a fair one, based on something more than a superficial likeness, it should be possible to work out its meaning by rigorously applying the essential categories of psychoanalytic theory. But doesn't that mean that the question we face here about modern sexuality would have to be posed in terms of the Oedipus complex? Freud remained adamant to the end of his life about the centrality of the Oedipus complex in the theory of psychoanalysis, even to the point of losing several of his closest followers who departed from his teaching on this point. How, then, are we to gauge the relevance of the Oedipus complex to the situation of modernity?

In seeking an answer to this question, what better place to begin than New York's Museum of Modern Art? I well remember the day when, strolling through that museum, I first happened upon Charles Ray's sculpture, *Family Romance.* It immediately struck me as a riveting and deeply unsettling work, though it took me some time to understand why. Ray's sculpture is a "life-size" depiction of a family of four—a father, mother, grade-school boy and baby girl—rendered ultra-realistically in meticulously painted, molded plastic. Posed side by side in a line, each standing straight with eyes ahead and arms hanging down, opened slightly to each side as if in a gesture of clinical revealment, all four figures are completely naked. "Life-size" requires some quotation marks because the really arresting feature of this ensemble is that all four figures are exactly the same height. By means of this manipulation of height, denying us the most obvious marker of differentiation between child and parent, Ray achieves a positively uncanny effect. The sculpture continually generates a profound dissonance, as if we can never make up our minds between what we know (parents are bigger than kids) and what we see (this toddler is as tall as her father). The nakedness of the four figures appears only to underscore this violation of expectation, making it impossible for us to avoid the uncomfortable tension it sets up.

In what follows, I will argue that Ray's sculpture is an apt emblem of the modern situation. Its stunning effect is partly a shock of recognition. In our time, the distance between adult and child has markedly diminished. A visit to the local science museum on any given weekend gives a quick indication: The

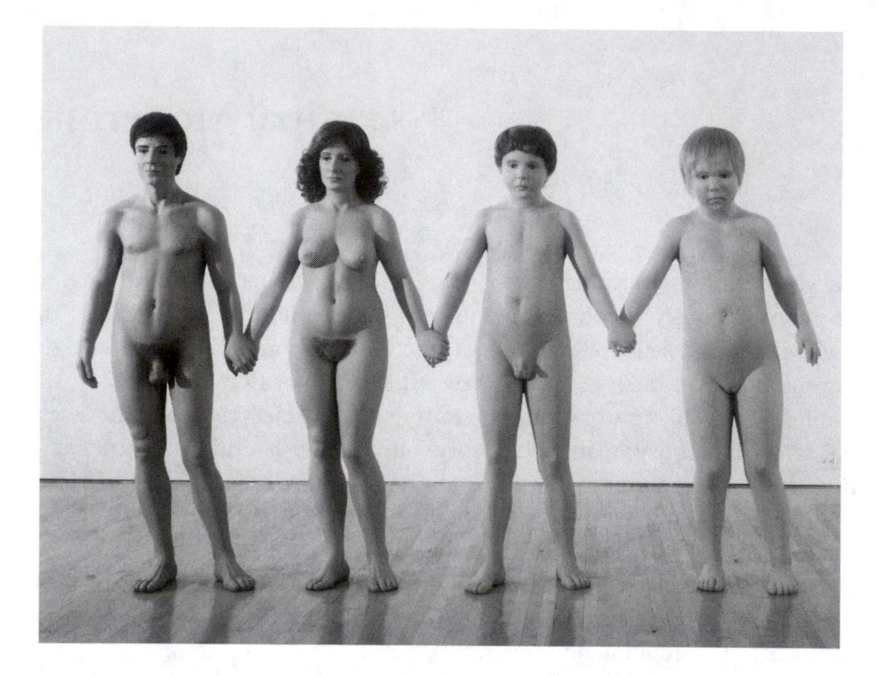

Fig. 7.1 *Family Romance* by Charles Ray.

dress code for fathers—T-shirt, baggy shorts, sneakers, ball cap—is strikingly similar to that of their six-year-old sons. The little boy's T-shirt may sport a smiling Barney while Dad's advertises Bud Lite, but the effect is the same. It will be my thesis that this situation represents one of the most profoundly significant features of modern culture: a diminishment of the status, authority, and prerogative of the father. In fact, this change in the father's role and influence is a key part of what defines the modern age. I will argue, further, that few theorists put us in a better position to understand the effects of this change than Freud. It will be the business of this chapter to sketch some main features of this modern situation and to survey some of those effects. But first, what do we mean by saying that the modern epoch involves an eclipse of the father?

In the last chapter, I posed modernity as an inversion of ancient attitudes toward public and private life, an inversion that led to the modern discovery of the intimate. My purpose in doing so was to provide a background for understanding the unique situation of sexuality in the modern era and also for seeing how that situation was related to the invention of Freudian psychoanalysis and to its rise to such prominence in the intellectual imagination of our time. But there are other ways of looking at the distinctive character of the modern age that bear significantly on the historical situation of both sexuality and psychoanalysis. In fact, far more obvious than what we've so far had to say about the public and private is the way in which the modern world represents a transformation of *authority*. Modernity is the death throes of monarchy. To play on Jefferson's famous remark about the tree of liberty, we can say that the blossoming of modernity, itself above all else a dream of freedom, is watered by the blood of kings. Yet what is this but an assertion that the modern epoch is made possible by the waning of paternal authority? Indeed, what are we to conclude but that the modern era is the Oedipal age par excellence? To see what I mean, we need to dive once more into questions of history. The effort to do so will pay big dividends in allowing us to see the current situation of sexuality in a completely new light.

Every Man a King

Finding the traces of Oedipal struggle between rebellious sons and tyrannical fathers is not difficult to do for any epoch of history. The colorful, almost cartoon-like character of ancient myth makes for especially good hunting. We find a veritable bonanza of Oedipal themes, for example, in Hesiod's *Theogony*, the marvelous catalog of Greek myth from the eighth century B.C.E., in which the poet recounts the origin of gods and men in descent from the primal parents, Gaia and Ouranos (Earth and Sky). The drama is set in motion by the cruelty of the first father, Ouranos, who refuses to allow the spawn of his union with Mother Earth to be born. Groaning in desperation from the pressure of her overloaded belly, Gaia at last gives to her son Chronos (somehow spared being buried in the earth along with his siblings) a flinty blade with which to castrate his overbearing father. Stealing in upon the drowsy sire, Chronos slices off his father's genitals and flings them into the sea, from whence they immediately reemerge as beings of monstrous power. Among them, arising from the bloodied sea foam, is the goddess of love, Aphrodite, whose Greek name means "foam-born." (As for the gleaming sickle with which Chronos attacked his father, do we not see it reappear each month in the sky with perfect regularity—in the form of the crescent moon—a symbol of the submission of Sky's awesome power to the even mightier authority of Time?) But Chronos in his turn wreaks violence upon his own progeny. Father Time—the mythic image makes perfect sense!—eats his children. Eventually, time devours everything. It then falls to the son of Chronos, wily Zeus, to overthrow his despotic father by tricking him into swallowing a stone wrapped in a swaddling blanket.

Evidently enough, there is no shortage of Oedipal thematics throughout history. Nevertheless, the modern period rightly lays claim to being the most profoundly and pervasively Oedipal epoch of all. To demonstrate this point, let us take the four features that most distinguish the modern period: Natural Science, Protestantism, Enlightenment, and Capitalism. To be sure, none of these developments is immune from the enduring influence of traditional masculine privilege, a fact that has been pointed out repeatedly by many scholars. All the same, it is crucial to recognize the extent to which all four developments, the defining movements of modernity, are deeply inimical to the power and prestige of traditional patriarchy. All four are inherently corrosive to the authority of the father. Consider for a moment how this is so for each of the four.

Natural Science

The rise of natural science, coalescing in the seventeenth century and accelerating ever since, was predicted upon the elevation of observed evidence over traditional authority. Before the dawn of the modern age, the role played by the oldest members of the community was a crucial one, and in several respects. In the first place, knowledge of nature and of the processes of art and craft with which the materials and cycles of nature could be fit to human purposes were passed down from generation to generation, the received wisdom of collective experience. The elders of the community, those who had been steeped longest in such traditional know-how, were therefore indispensable to the ongoing life of the community. They were the repositories of knowledge who tutored the young in the conduct of practices that had evolved from centuries of trial and error.

If such old wise ones were important in showing how nature could be made to serve human purposes, their role became even more important when it couldn't be. The power of premodern societies to manipulate nature was, after all, very limited. Survival was a chancy business, threatened by the disappearance of game and forage or by the failure of crops, by the caprices of drought, flood, fire, disease, and pestilence, and by the possibility of devastating attacks by other human groups. When hard-pressed by such calamities, people turned to the elders for spiritual guidance, less to escape from sufferings than to find a way to live with them a little less painfully by inserting them into some web of cosmic meaning. The old shamans and medicine men then stepped in to provide knowledge of myth and ritual by means of which a human community could make some peace, at least symbolically, with a world of forces it couldn't control.

The emergence of natural science radically undermined these functions of traditional authority. Science meant, first of all, a different way of gathering and keeping knowledge. For the scientist, unlocking the secrets of nature owes less to the memory of tradition than to the observation of experiment. And for that, age is far from being an unqualified advantage. Even more decisive than the invention of one or another new gadget of observation was the radical idea that, once the experimental conditions are set up correctly, pretty much anyone can do the observing. In fact, the interchangeability of observers was and remains absolutely crucial to the conduct of science. Gone is the idea of a privileged observer who, by dint of long experience and subtle cultivation of soul, could see things that would escape the notice of less-seasoned practitioners. In the brave new world of science, appeal to old and venerable authorities has become not only unnecessary but in many cases positively undesirable. For the march of science, the wisdom of the forefathers, the intellectual inheritance of the patriarchs, has become less an enabling resource than a crippling obstacle.

This revolutionary shift, overturning the age-old respect for the testimony of elders simply because they were elders, was among the most potent factors henceforth dividing science from religion. So, too, it divided emerging technology, relying increasingly on purely mechanical manipulation, from traditional craftwork, which depended on the employment of enormously subtle skills whose acquisition required long apprenticeship to an experienced master. But we can see the tension between science and religion from another point of view as well. In finding themselves at the limits of their capacity to control nature, premodern communities turned to religious elders for guidance and consolation. Increasingly during the last two centuries, however, sufferings that would have driven our forebears to the altar simply lead us back to the laboratory. We more and more look to science and technology to deliver us from evil. Judging less on the basis of what we may say on the Sabbath than on the way we act during the other six days of the week—judging, that is, by the way that we look forward to a new genetically altered, pest-resistant crop, the way we expect development of new and more efficient engines, or the way we eagerly await the next breakthrough treatment for cancer—science has become for us the Mind of God and technology the New Providence.

These changes have meant an enormous diminution of our veneration for the old among us. Science is in many ways a young person's game. It is not accidental that really innovative discoveries are often the work of people in their twenties and thirties. To be sure, these young bucks first receive instruction by those older than themselves. But it is not long before the mind-set of the older generation is rightly regarded as an inhibiting influence that stunts imagination and innovation. The most exciting discoveries in science thus often fall to those intrepid youngsters who are the first to break the mold of the old thinking.

Protestantism

The undermining of inherited authority by the emergence of natural science had its analogue inside the religious tradition in the form of the Protestant reformation. Luther's revolutionary translation of scripture into the language of the vernacular was motivated less by the presumption of an intrinsic superiority of German over Latin than by the insistence that every worshipper be authorized to read the word of God for himself or herself. True, Luther's raging against the hypocrisies and corruptions of the Papacy, the sort of thing that led him to compare the Pope to Satan's butt-licker, was a potent ingredient in the rhetorical appeal of the Protestant insurgency against Rome. But vilifying the iniquities of the Pope and his minions was ultimately of secondary importance. The core of Luther's rebellion against the Pontificate was the conviction that the relationship of the human being to the divine should brook no intermediary. For Luther, the hierarchy of the Church, the immense network of priests and prelates, was less a mode of access to God than a hedge of thorns separating us from him. Nothing must get in the way of the direct communication between God and the devout person who worships him.

The central paradox discovered by Protestantism was that, while the distance between the worshipper and God might be infinite, it is nevertheless the distance of a single step. It is, moreover, a step that must be taken only by a solitary, unaided individual. Three centuries after Luther's death, Kierkegaard would call this single step the "leap of faith." In this way, Protestantism contributed mightily to the modern respect for the sovereign individual and, in the same stroke, to the deterioration of the bonds that had traditionally tied the individual so firmly within a network of relationships, both within the family and in society at large. When Luther nailed his ninety-five theses on the church door at Wittenberg, the inflated authority of the traditional father suffered another gigantic puncture.

The Enlightenment

The sensibility that emerged during the eighteenth-century Enlightenment was closely linked to the rise of natural science and Protestantism, but passed beyond them by distilling their intellectual essence and rigorously following their implications. The Enlightenment championed the values of the individual, free from the influence of outside forces and guided by the light of his or her own reason. The Enlightenment was therefore to politics what natural science was to the investigation of nature: an insistence upon appeal to individual reason as the only valid court of judgment. The result was a series of earthquakes in the political sphere that sought to overturn the entrenched and established order of power, earthquakes that began with the American and French Revolutions and have continued to rumble through Tiananmen Square and beyond.

The essence of the enlightened spirit is well spoken for by Immanuel Kant's famous essay, written in 1786 and devoted to the question: "What is Enlightenment?" The definition of enlightenment, Kant begins, is the refusal of "our self-imposed immaturity." The German word for such immaturity—*Unmündigkeit*—is a telling one. Its meaning derives from the root word *Mund* or "mouth." To be enlightened means overcoming the state of being *unmündig*, the state, literally speaking, of having no mouth. Enlightenment is thus a matter of finding one's own voice, of being able to speak for oneself, where speaking for oneself is the fruit of thinking for oneself.

Kant's definition conceives of Enlightenment in terms casting off *immaturity*. Becoming enlightened thus is a form of growing up. This conclusion is perfectly consistent with the metaphor of finding one's own voice. Enlightenment depends crucially on refusing to accept the voice of external authorities in the place of one's own. What is required is the courage of independent thought. The challenge for the intrepid spirit of Enlightenment, according to Kant's motto, is *Sapere Aude*—"dare to know." But the metaphor of maturity also makes it clear that the primary authority against which the Enlightenment must assert itself is the authority of the previous generation. Enlightenment is a declaration of war on the false privilege and prestige of the old and a celebration of the promise of the new. The legacy of the Enlightenment has thus left a taint of suspicion upon everything belonging to the past. It is a sensibility that continues very powerfully to animate the modern dream of progress.

In all of these ways, Enlightenment is essentially an Oedipal struggle. By its very nature, the battle of Enlightenment is a battle against the established authority of the patriarch. Nowhere do we see this force of rebellion against patriarchy erupt more violently or spectacularly than in the French Revolution. One can hardly imagine a more powerful demonstration of the will to overturn traditional authority than the severed heads of Bourbon royalty gathering flies atop the bristle of iron pikes that surrounded the ruins of the Bastille. And how profoundly appropriate, Freud might add, that these horrible fruits of independence were harvested by means of the guillotine, a mechanized realization of castration phantasies if ever there was one. Chronos would have loved it.

Capitalism

Perhaps the most potent of the four anti-patriarchal dimensions of modernity that we've taken to examine is that of capitalist economy. Why? In large part because capitalism, in its endless voraciousness, its capacity to absorb nearly everything into itself and transform it into a new opportunity for generating profit, has developed in almost perfect tandem with each of the other three developments we have surveyed. The fruits of natural scientific inquiry have fueled its engines of production, the Protestant spirit of individual salvation prepared for the emergence of the sovereign producer-consumer, and the Enlightenment celebration of freedom has provided capital with its charter of legitimacy (so long as freedom is first and foremost understood in the form of free markets). Karl Marx, whose analysis of the nature and functions of capitalism remains in many key respects undiminished by the failure of the communist societies constructed in his name, was exquisitely aware of this adaptive capacity of capital, its never-ending hunger for growth. But Marx also recognized its destructive side. Relentlessly expanding, capitalist economy inevitably transforms any society into which it is introduced. Marx described this tendency in one of the most famous passages of the *Communist Manifesto*:

> The bourgeoisie cannot exist without constantly revolutionizing the instruments of production, and thereby the relations of production,

> and with them the whole relations of society. Conservation of the old modes of production in unaltered form was, on the contrary, the first condition of existence for all earlier industrial classes. Constant revolutionizing of production, uninterrupted disturbance of all social conditions, everlasting uncertainty and agitation distinguish the bourgeois epoch from all earlier ones. All fixed, fast-frozen relations, with their train of ancient and venerable prejudices and opinions, are swept away, all new-formed ones become antiquated before they can ossify. All that is solid melts into air, all that is holy is profaned.

From the perspective opened up by this passage, the advertisers' incessant chant that such and such a product is "New! New! New!" is more than a mere huckster's gimmick. Rather, it represents on the level of individual commodities the far vaster tendency of capitalism itself to continually regenerate an endless demand for growth. It is a tendency toward continual change that not only affects the processes of production but also the forms of social life, including that of the family. Capitalism, like the other developments we've examined, thus tends to transform family structure and, in the process, to corrode the power and status of the traditional father.

Let us look at this corrosive effect more closely. The core of capitalist economy, the innovation in human affairs that provides its inner dynamo, is deceptively contained in the single word that Marx reserves for it: *labor.* The idea of capitalist labor, as revolutionary as any idea in the history of the human race, is that a human being might rent the pure force of his or her bodily exertions for a given period of time in exchange for a wage. The real meaning of this sort of labor, a phenomenon that deserves to be called a distinctly modern invention, appears only when we compare it to work in premodern societies. For the denizens of all cultures up to the dawn of the modern period, work was fully integrated into the warp and woof of life as a whole. Hunting, farming, weaving, the husbanding of animals, the construction of shelters and clothing, the preparation of foods—the whole range of activities—were seamlessly joined to the overall pattern of life. Work—if that word can even be used to describe such activity—meaningfully reflected that order and character of life both in the objects produced and in the manner of their production. In traditional society, to be engaged in work, far from requiring separation from the family or community, further deepened and enriched those relationships. The sowing or gathering of the harvest, for example, was a shared enterprise in which whole communities took part. The main exception to this rule was the work of slaves, though even slaves were often linked in lifelong association with a particular community.

Work in a modern economy—work, as Marx would put it, in the context of the division between bourgeois owners and proletarian wage-laborers—is something completely different. To punch the time clock at the factory is to initiate a period of body rental in which the employee agrees to provide his or her pure labor power in exchange for cash payment. Quite typically, the objects of manufacture and the purposes to which those objects will be put have little or nothing to do with the laborer's own life context—the circumstance Marx referred to as "alienation." Nor do the conditions of employment include in any essential way the participation of other members of the worker's family. The contract of capitalist employment is wholly individualized. The bourgeois owner hires the worker on a wholly separate basis, without being bound in any way to hire brothers, sisters, husbands, or wives. Indeed, in the absence of governmental controls, the capitalist is not even bound to consider the worker's own employment in the future. All obligation to the worker is fulfilled when the day's wages are paid.

In a certain sense, then, capital economy brings about a kind of perverse democracy of labor, at least to the extent that anyone capable of providing the required labor power is equally satisfactory as a worker. In fact, for the factory owner who obeys the pure logic of capital, the only relevant discrimination to be made between equally capable workers is the willingness of one to accept lower wages than another. A man, a woman, or, as we well know from the history of capitalism, even a child will do. It is for these reasons that Marx claims that "the bourgeoisie has torn away from the family its sentimental veil, and has reduced the family relation to a mere money relation." Capitalism tends to atomize the family, not from any ill-will or malice, but simply as a function of the equal liability of all to labor.

All of which brings us back to Charles Ray's *Family*. In the perspective we've unfolded, we can recognize Ray's sculpture as a fitting depiction of the basic situation of the modern social world. It is a world in which the population tends to be splintered into discrete individuals and subjected to a leveling, equalizing effect. It is a world in which, at least in principle, everyone enjoys a fundamental parity before the truth, the divine, the law, and the marketplace of labor. Ray's sculpture is a lineup of autonomous individuals devoid of hierarchy. It represents the ideal community of scientists, the company of the (potentially) faithful, the body politic of all those "created equal," no less than the labor pool of capitalist economy. Ray's work presents a world in which the wife, the son, and the daughter are all fully the equals of the father—a world after the death of patriarchy.

Who Wears the Pants

By now the critic who has been the terrier at my heels from the start will be unable to contain an explosion of protest. "What modern world have you been living in? In fact, your thesis appears to be the very height of naïveté! In the first place, isn't it perfectly obvious that, despite a lot of pious talk about universal human rights, the modern world is as definitely, even viciously, hierarchical as it ever was? And isn't it also obvious that the hierarchy of power is still pervasively tilted in favor of men? Corporate boardrooms are still filled by men, the Senate is still over 90% male, Protestant evangelicals are as deeply sexist as anyone or more so, and the majority of foundation grants for scientific research still go to male researchers whose underpaid and overworked secretarial staff is mostly female. Where exactly do you see evidence of the leveling effect you're talking about? Moreover, with little more than a wave of the hand, you dispense with the masses of scholarly work devoted to exposing the masculinist bias built into the very movements you describe as fundamentally egalitarian and anti-patriarchal. Far from being the end of patriarchy, the modern 'enlightened' age of science and capitalism appears to have left the privilege of masculinity very much alive and well. The passing of monarchy makes 'every man a king' you say!—an obviously false proposition in any case, but even as a rhetorical flourish it flies in the face of the still glaring lack of equality between men and women. I've had problems with your pronouncements before, but this time you've gone completely over the edge!"

To which I have to respond that *the critic is precisely correct.* The vestiges of patriarchy remain pervasively present all over the world, indeed so pervasively that it is already misleading to call them mere vestiges.

What? The critic is right? Then what is the point of the preceding section?

Let's take this a little more slowly. There are no doubt important arguments to be made in answer to the critic. We cannot forget, for instance, that the modern era and the twentieth century in particular have seen unprecedented transformations in the relations between gender and power. To take some examples from the American experience: While the levers of corporate power are still wielded largely by men, women now head a growing number of multinational corporate giants. While the Senate remains dominated by men, the percentage of women has been steadily rising, both there and in other areas of government. While Protestantism surely has its deeply sexist moments, Protestants are clearly ahead of their Catholic brethren in the ordination of women and homosexuals to the ministry and in other issues related to sexuality and gender equality. And while the number of Ph.D.s in the sciences remains weighted toward men, women now outnumber men in the American undergraduate population. I would submit that these changes, while not wholly conclusive, are enormously significant. Moreover, I would argue that they are changes that have been produced by the four historical movements I described above, indeed, that they are well nigh unthinkable without those movements. In spite of these arguments, however, and a good deal else that could be added to them, I want to grant that the critic is quite right to say that in the contemporary world traditionally male power and privilege remain largely intact.

But in that case, the question repeats: what exactly am I claiming about the anti-patriarchal tendencies of Science, Protestantism, Enlightenment, and Capitalism? The point I want to make is not that these four defining features of modern life have wholly swept patriarchy aside. Far from it! The point, rather, is that all four palpably *threaten it.* For reasons that belong in different ways to each of these epochal movements, they each favor a deepening of modern individualism. Each tends in its own way to undermine the traditional authority of the father and the family network over which he presided. The prerogative of the patriarch is not dead, but it is increasingly destabilized by a fundamentally altered situation. In some places, revolutionary changes of modern history have actually unseated the patriarchs (or at least some of them), but significant changes of attitude have affected the way that power sees itself virtually everywhere.

I want to argue that in order to understand the modern era, and particularly to understand the modern status of sexuality, it is crucial to recognize this underlying destabilization and to take it seriously into account. Forces have been set in motion by the four historical movements I've described that, while they are still far from changing everything, have changed enough to create a definitely new state of affairs. The really decisive point might be put this way: what hasn't been changed in *fact* has been altered by the *perception* that change might be on the way. It is for reason of this perceived possibility of change that being a man in today's world—in fact still very much a man's world—means something very different from what it did two or three hundred years ago.

A trivial but telling example offers a hint of what I'm driving at: the surprise hit film of the nineties, *The Full Monty*. In this film, things actually have changed for a close-knit group of British men who struggle to keep their heads above water when they get laid off from the only factory in town. Increasingly desperate for income, they finally seize upon the idea of making a little cash the way desperate women have done for centuries: They'll strip for money. This role reversal has its charming and comical side, as when the initial euphoria of their breakthrough idea begins to fade and they realize, sobered by an inspection of themselves in the mirror, that gangs of drink-emboldened, fully clothed women will actually be giving their naked male bodies a good, long look. And to think that they'll be exposing a good deal more than just some flabby love handles—they're going to do the Full Monty! So this is what women have had to deal with all this time!

But the comic relief of *The Full Monty* cannot wholly conceal a more somber dimension of the film, which, if it could be distilled from the dominant feel-good mood, might be very much like the effect produced by Charles Ray's sculpture. These are men who are fighting to adjust to a world in which the rules have somehow changed in threatening and confusing ways, a world in which men have been cut down to size. The crucial point, however, is that it's not just the guys on stage who are affected. In the contemporary marketplace, no one is wholly free from the anxiety of being laid off, replaced by a machine, or downsized. In the work world of capitalist economy, employees become as interchangeable as the mechanical parts on the assembly line. Part of the impact of *The Full Monty* resides in the audience's realization that, in a certain very palpable sense, the globalized free market system is already well on its way to stripping us all naked.

In fact, the chummy humor of *The Full Monty* lets us off the hook far too easily. The film presents us with a circle of men who are caught in the riptide of a rapidly changing world and ultimately respond to it with a creative and extremely good-natured solution. Faced with the cruel fact that they can no longer succeed as men are expected to, the blokes of *The Full Monty* seem happy to indulge in a little gender-bending. But if we look around the world, it is not difficult to see enormously larger numbers of men, indeed whole populations of them, who find themselves threatened by the disruptions and dislocations of modernity and react by sandbagging themselves in an anxious and aggressive reassertion of masculinity. The most visible evidence of this trend is to be found in the two dark brothers of modern democratic enlightenment: fascism and religious fundamentalism. The emergence of these two distinctly modern phenomena provides an indirect proof of the profoundly anti-patriarchal character of the key movements of modernity. Fascism and fundamentalism are essentially reactions to the modern erosion of traditionally patriarchal culture. They each represent defensive countermeasures—one secular and overtly militarist, the other theocratic and more covertly militarist. They each recognize the "degenerate" aspects of modern culture, most of them precisely the products of science, enlightenment, and capitalism, and seek to stem their encroaching tide by a erecting a sturdy bulwark of aggressively reaffirmed patriarchal values and institutions.

I am aware that this is a sweeping claim and that to demonstrate it with any adequacy would require (at least) a volume of its own—a volume I won't be providing here. I take the risk of leaving it in this crudely sketched form because I think I can show in what follows how it provides an especially powerful key for opening up the meaning of sexuality in our modern world. Even in the very briefest compass, however, it is not difficult to suggest how fascism and fundamentalism are both intimately related to questions of paternal authority and to questions of sexual license. Indeed, the problem for a brief treatment of this topic is the vast quantity of suggestive material that rushes forward. I will limit myself to commenting on three main features.

1. Both fascism and fundamentalism are deeply devoted to establishing an unambiguous and unshakable authority. Moreover, the character of that authority is unmistakably masculine—not only, it should quickly be added, because their leaders, Führers or Ayatollahs, happen themselves to be men, but because of the demand for rigid clarity and inflexibility that characterizes their governing regimes.[1] In addition (and linked with their call for strong central authority), both fascism and fundamentalism seek to legitimate themselves by

[1]The possibility of a fascist state ruled by a woman should not be ruled out too quickly. In fact, there is some reason to predict that such an eventuality might prove even more virulent than the consistently male-led versions that history has so far given us.

appeal to a notion of fidelity to a lost and more glorious past, and both tend to employ one or another rhetoric to identify the ways in which the forces of the present threaten a further degeneration or perversion of that past. Both make a virtue of provincialism. For both, the enemy is cosmopolitanism, whether it be the Jews, homosexuals, communists, and degenerate artists for the Nazis or the great American Satan for Islamic militants. Both indulge in a kind of "circle the wagons" mentality that, even if it develops fantasies of outward expansion and conquest, strives toward reclaiming and protecting a sense of intact community and tradition. There is, then, a deep paranoid streak in both fascism and fundamentalism, and this underlying paranoia is a good indicator of the inner psychological reality of these reactionary movements. Both are essentially defensive, rearguard actions that seek to mitigate the decline of patriarchal influence by advancing an overwrought caricature of paternal power.

2. If the rhetoric of purity so central to fascism and fundamentalism has tended to assume the form of racial and religious intolerance—the motive origin of "ethnic cleansing"—so, too, it typically displays a conspicuously sexual dimension. The only thing even more predictable about these movements than their militarism is their exaggerated concern for feminine chastity, virtue, and sacrifice. Both are centrally concerned with promoting images of morally upright masculinity and morally pure femininity. The Islamic veil is the perfect symbol of this fanatical insistence on the sequestering of the feminine. In countries controlled by militant Islamic clerics, violations of laws concerning sexual conduct are particularly harsh, especially for women. A woman caught in adultery may be stoned. An unwed mother may also be executed. The Nazis, too, were deeply committed to the ethics of feminine sexual purity and virtue. Indeed, the Nazi celebration of pure Aryan maidenhood was a perfect fusion of their racial mania with their idealization of morally immaculate femininity. In the persecution of the Jews, this ethics of sexual purity led to some near contradictions, as when the Jews were alternately condemned for being sexual aggressors and for being effeminate. The Nazi campaign against homosexuals, on the other hand, can be seen as the application of a more consistent principle. In effect, it reveals the inner secret of the cult of pure and perfect femininity: in order to maintain the ideal of perfect womanhood, men must hold themselves to an ever more exaggerated standard of perfect manhood.
3. Both fascism and fundamentalism recall the distinction we made toward the end of the last chapter: They both very explicitly promote

> an ethics of sacrifice. Of course, such an appeal to sacrifice is a virtual necessity for any regime that has invested itself in an aggressive and militarist posture. Every young man must be prepared to die for the fatherland; indeed, he must be made to realize that there is no greater glory. But the reactionary appeal to the ethics of sacrifice must also be recognized in its connection with the deeper agenda of a revivified patriarchy, and here we can stitch the discussion of Oedipal modernity of this chapter to our treatment of the intimate in the preceding one. In their own ways, the reactionary movements of fascism and fundamentalism are both acutely alert to the corruptive influence of the modern turn to privacy, its indulgence in the intimate, and to the ethics of unrestrained satisfaction that has resulted from it. Both fascism and fundamentalism tend to launch critiques of soft and flabby consumer culture in favor of a rigid, self-denying (and also self-congratulating) masculinity. Both stand four-square against the modern ethics of satisfaction.

I need quickly to add two cautionary notes. First, an immediate danger of this discussion, especially given some of my examples just now, is to think that "fascism" refers only to the Third Reich and "fundamentalism" only to Iranian or Taliban-style Islamic radicals. Not at all. Both these forms of reaction are now discernible to some degree in almost every nation in the world and are abundantly present in the United States. By "fascism" and "fundamentalism" I mean to refer to two kindred styles of political and religious thinking that we need to be able to recognize even in the absence of jack-booted storm troopers or bearded clerics in flowing caftans. Right-wing movements everywhere can be heard to mouth the rhetoric of a sort of "fascism lite," identifiable by the way that it combines condemnation of moral lassitude, militarist insistence on law and order, and scapegoating of minority groups (homosexuals, immigrants, etc.). Fundamentalism is now as much a feature of American Protestantism as it is a part of radical Islam. Both insist on the most literal reading of holy scripture, both feel themselves to be surrounded by forces of moral degeneracy, both are obsessed with the paramount need to safeguard the structure of the traditional family from the menace of modernity.

Members of the U.S. Senate are well capable of sounding clarion calls for moral recovery by means of good old law and order that are essentially fascist and/or fundamentalist in nature. The rhetoric of "family values" is a good case in point. Rarely are appeals to family values given much real content, unless it is to contrast them, as Dan Quayle famously did in the late eighties, with single-mom television characters such as Murphy Brown. Just under the surface (and sometimes not so hidden) are many of the earmark tendencies of the fascist–fundamentalist style: the nostalgic appeal to traditional values, the anti-cosmopolitanism (before 9/11, New York City was a favorite target of politicians who wanted to get down-home appeal by showing themselves to be critics of the big city's moral sinkhole), the insistence that all social problems can be solved by a "get tough" approach, the call for closing borders to keep out foreigners. There is a deep strain of contemporary American life that longs for a bygone order of things, a longing, whether it is able to articulate it or not, for the regime of "father knows best."

The irony of the neo-conservative right, at least in the United States, is that the very people who most vociferously champion family values are also often the most vigorous supporters of big capital interests. What these cultural conservatives fail to recognize is that the most virulent enemy of the old-fashioned values they hold dear is the very free market economy they worship. Oblivious to the predations of big business and to the culturally corrosive influence of the culture of advertising and consumption, they are instead obsessed with the sinister specter of big government. In fact, "traditional values" are eroded far more decisively by media-driven multinational capitalism than by welfare state government. Yet many right-minded ideologues act as if the family values agenda were perfectly compatible with unregulated free marketism.

A second note of caution is in order as well, lest we think that fascism and fundamentalism, even in their more temperate expressions, exhaust the influence of the modern crisis of patriarchal authority we've been examining. The underlying pressures of destabilized authority that give rise to fascism and fundamentalism also have far broader effects, shaping the behavior of people and institutions in the mainstream of social life. To find an example, we need only to go back to our point of departure in the necktie. In fact, the analysis that we made of the neckwear code, centered on the phallic necktie, can now be seen with renewed clarity. I suggested at the time that the appearance of the necktie just a century or so ago was related to the entry of women into the public space of the working world. The necktie served to mark gender difference in very graphic terms, using the relatively primitive but very powerful symbolic vocabulary of iconic resemblance. It is now possible to extend that hypothesis by putting it into a larger perspective.

The emergence of women into a fuller participation in public life has been a direct result of the four movements we've posed as determinative of the modern situation. At least as early as Marie Curie and in ever-increasing numbers, women have entered the lecture halls and laboratories of modern science. Women now routinely oversee the liturgy in Protestant churches, often as fully ordained ministers. An increasingly open labor market has included more and more women, even in physically demanding professions once thought to be manageable only by men. And through it all, the Enlightenment spirit of equality among all individuals, engraved in the founding documents of modern democracies, has assured the moral and political legitimacy of women's claim to parity of status with men. Can we not suspect that the phallic code of neckwear as we traced it in the first chapter is itself a reflection of the crisis of patriarchal authority in the contemporary world? Though surely far more benign than the twin menaces of fascism or fundamentalism (and even more unconscious of itself than they), the necktie represents on the level of a fashion standard an effort to sandbag the same erosion of paternal authority.

Symptoms of the Times

Let me try to summarize my point. I want to advance a two-stage hypothesis about our modern situation, both stages of which are especially well illuminated by a psychoanalytic perspective. The first stage asserts that each of the four distinguishing features of modernity that I have identified functions to undermine the traditional structure of family life in general and the authority of the patriarchal father in particular.[2] Science, Protestantism, Enlightenment, and Capitalism all contribute, each for its own reasons, to the modern culture of the sovereign individual and, to that extent, help to bring about a slow but steady deterioration of the centuries-old power and prestige of paternal authority. In Freudian terms, therefore, the situation of modernity is fundamentally Oedipal. While it is quite true that the reality of modern social, economic, and political life has been neither wholly nor consistently altered by the epochal forces at work upon it, modernity is nevertheless virtually definable as a cracking of the foundations of traditional authority and privilege.

To draw out the implications of this analysis for psychoanalysis itself, we can now make for the Oedipus complex a point parallel to the one that we made earlier about the emerging centrality of sex in the modern pursuit of the intimate. Freud's theory of the Oedipus complex was no mere happenstance. It was neither the result of an over-fevered reading of Sophocles, nor merely an effect of Freud's own biography, the product of tensions with his own father. Freud's notion of the Oedipus complex was, on the contrary, a discovery in the best sense of the word, an insight into the underlying dynamics of the social world we inhabit. Psychoanalysis was indeed, as Freud insisted, a kind of microscope. It enabled him to see into the deep workings of the modern mind and to recognize there the outline of a crisis of the traditional father.

This is not to say that Freud grasped the meaning of the Oedipus complex in the historical fashion that I am seeking to highlight. He didn't. On the contrary, Freud constantly sought to draw the lessons of his clinical observations beyond the horizon of his historical situation. He was generally much more interested in the universal character of the Oedipus complex than in its historical specificity. In *Totem and Taboo*, for example, he made the speculative leap

[2]Right-wing ideologues are therefore partly correct in decrying the way that "secular humanism" is destructive of traditional values. What they have done, we might say, is to grasp the anti-traditional influence of two of the four movements we've identified—Science and Enlightenment—while giving the other two a free pass.

of projecting the murder of the father back into prehistory and supposing primal patricide to be the origin of morality. Despite his own hesitations about its validity, it was an argument to which he returned more than once. There's no question, therefore, that I am adding a historical dimension to Freud's thought that Freud himself did not consider. All the same, I take myself to be making a basically Freudian argument. I am saying that the basic dynamics of the Oedipus complex, while certainly not limited to the modern age, are specially intensified by the Oedipal rebellion that virtually defines the modern temper.

It is absolutely crucial, however, to recognize how the first stage of my hypothesis is inseparable from a second: Patriarchy, though under fire, is by no means dead. Indeed, precisely because it is under fire, new assertions of patriarchy are more strident than ever. Far from it being the case that the essential movements of modernity have brought about the elimination of patriarchy, the influence of those movements has given rise to forms of social and political reaction that seek to install a renewed and transformed dominion of paternal authority. I've so far identified two main currents of such reaction, fascism and fundamentalism, and I pointed to the primary features that link them to rule of the father. I've also tried to warn against the error of thinking that the basic dynamics that give rise to these social and political forms can be limited to their most spectacular manifestations. The longing for lost authority that motivates fascism and fundamentalism shows itself in a whole range of expressions from the most apparently benign to the most obviously brutalizing.

I am arguing, therefore, that beneath the surface of social and political turbulence that roils the modern world there is a deep root-problem that remains largely unrecognized: the problem of the father. In all essentials, it is the problem to which Nietzsche enigmatically pointed in his shattering diagnosis of the modern predicament: God is dead. The result of this underlying crisis is that the contemporary social and political world is stretched between two opposing camps, one more or less enthusiastically promoting the end of traditional authority, the other seeking to revivify it. These contending forces are in a very rough way parallel to left- and right-wing politics. And both have had considerable success. The overall picture, if we size things up from a global point of view, is thus a decidedly mixed one. My thesis, in fact, is that modernity is itself precisely this mixture of opposites. We thus arrive at this paradoxical conclusion: the contemporary world is *both less and more patriarchal than ever before.*

Both less and more patriarchal at the same time. Is that possible? If Freud provides a theoretical reference point for the first stage of my hypothesis—in the very notion of the Oedipus complex—his perspective is even more valuable for helping us to make sense of the second—in the Freudian theory of the symptom. As we saw at the close of the last chapter, the symptom is always a two-sided structure, or "compromise formation," in which two opposing trends are simultaneously engaged. The symptom, we said, simultaneously represses and expresses some impulse. It is this model that we can now rely upon to make sense of the historical situation in which we find ourselves. In doing so, we are comparing the collective situation of the modern world to the psychological dynamics of an individual. The four currents of historical forces that we have identified with the emergence of modernity are comparable to the force of a destabilizing impulse. The result is the pressure to overthrow the rule of traditional authority. But the upsurge of this impulse is met with the counterforce of repression, in the form of a reassertion of the threatened authority. Confronted with an unprecedented situation, this counterforce by necessity takes new forms. Though fascism and fundamentalism have roots in social and political forms of the past, they both represent uniquely modern social and political developments.

I've said that fascism and fundamentalism ought not to be limited to their most obvious manifestations. Nor should the forces of patriarchal reaction be limited to fascism and fundamentalism, even broadly conceived. In fact, the symptomatic character of the situation I'm describing—its "both sides now" character—is even more clearly illustrated by other examples. The history of the French Revolution is one. The Revolution and its aftermath provide a superb illustration of the modern crisis of authority and a symptomatic reaction to it. Following the anti-patriarchal explosion of the Revolution and the Terror, the symptomatic reaction was not far behind—in the form of Napoleon Bonaparte's meteoric rise to power. And in the rule of Napoleon, we find an especially striking mixture of opposites—a mix that bears the markings of symptomatic ambivalence. Napoleon's imperium was a potent and paradoxical mix of ever more extravagant submission to a single male authority, combined with an unprecedented sense of citizen equality and participation. Implausibly enough, Napoleon's battalions lunged into battle flushed with equal enthusiasm for Emperor and for Liberty.

Let us try to clarify things further by way of another example, that of the socialist revolutions of the twentieth century. Far from being exceptions to my basic thesis, the Marxist revolutions in Russia and China serve to demonstrate it ever more decisively. This is so, first, because the revolutions inspired by Marxism were even more explicitly anti-patriarchal in character than the upheavals of the late eighteenth and mid-nineteenth centuries. Marx and Engels were absolutely clear from very early in their thinking that the taproot of oppression is deeply embedded in the structure of the family and that traditional political institutions share that underlying structure. Socialist revolution is therefore unavoidably revolution against paternal authority in all of its forms. After the revolution, no one, not even the oldest and most venerable, will be addressed as "Mon-sieur" (my sire) but only as "Comrade." In the socialist state, itself destined to wither away in the fullness of time, there is to be no parent at all. There will be only a perfect equality of brothers and sisters.

If the anti-patriarchal program of socialist revolution was even more pointed and unambiguous than that of earlier, Enlightenment revolutions, so, too, was the symptomatic reaction that it triggered. The prestige and authority of the dead father was reinstalled in the form of the Party Leader. What makes this situation unique, differentiating it from the fascist and fundamentalism reactions that occurred elsewhere, is that the anti-patriarchal force and the symptomatic reaction against it *were embodied in one and the same revolutionary movement*. For this reason, the symptomatic reaction was bound to be even more intense, if only because the force of internal contradiction was so much more enormous. The result of this rebound, this "return of the repressed," was the emergence of father cults of unprecedented proportions. In effect, the figure of the patriarch loomed larger than ever. The rules of Stalin and Mao, probably the two most powerful human beings who have ever lived, bear eloquent witness to the enormous force of these father identifications.

In Stalin's case, the association with the patriarch could hardly have been more explicit, as he came to be called the "little father of the people." What is most fascinating and important in this phrase requires a bit of unpacking. Of first interest is that the phrase was previously reserved for the czar. One wonders whether this echo of an endearing appellation for the czar wasn't especially appreciated by those who were most deeply threatened by the upheaval of the revolution. To call Stalin the "little father of the people" is to suggest that nothing essential has changed. At the same time, there was something deeply and perversely obfuscating about its new usage. There was, of course, nothing little about Josef Stalin, either in the immensity of his lust for power, the depth of his paranoia about losing it, or the murderousness of the methods by which he ensured its continuance. Stalin was in fact much more powerful than the Czar ever was. To refer to Stalin as the "little father of the people" therefore functioned as a double contradiction of reality. It was a perfect crystallization of the symptom that Stalin himself embodied, simultaneously an overturning and restoration of patriarchal values.[3]

I said in passing a moment ago that the two sides of the modern situation I'm describing can be roughly equated with left and right politics. It is a parallel that I don't want to overstate. No doubt things are not so simple. All the same, it is very tempting to interpret the so-called culture wars of the moment as a result of an ongoing conflict: on one side, feminists, gay rights advocates, socialists, Greens, and other countercultural progressivists, united by a deep animus against the established order of traditional authority; on the other, a range of conservative forces of reaction, eager to renew the power and prestige

[3]Cf. Andrei Zagdansky's extraordinary film, made in Russia just before the breakup of the Soviet Union, *The Interpretation of Dreams*.

of that very authority. In between these left and right flanks, one finds relatively small groups that stir the two underlying forces together in strange, virtually contradictory blends. The American militia movements, for example, the movements that spawned Timothy McVeigh and Randy Weaver, fuse a deep social conservatism (the father is god in his home) with a semi-paranoid rejection of the federal government (centralized political authority is the enemy).

Love Stories

But what has any of this to do with the subject of sex? The answer is that sexuality has absorbed into itself the historical tensions I have been describing. As we will see in what follows, sexuality has become both part of the modern revolt against patriarchy but also, at the same time, the most significant field in which a revivified patriarchal tendency makes its play for a reassertion of masculine privilege. It is along these lines that we will be able to answer the question posed at the end of the last chapter about sex as the symptom of our times. In posing the question, it was the conspicuous ambivalence toward sex, what seems to be an attitude that is by turns yes and no, hot and cold, obsessed and repressed, that hinted at its symptomatic character. The foregoing discussion of the historical crisis of modernity provides a background against which we will be able to see more deeply into the symptomatic two-sidedness of the modern attitude toward sexuality.

The aim, then, is to put sexuality into the context of what is distinctive about the modern age. Of course, it makes perfect sense that the historical forces at work in modernity would show themselves in the field of sexuality. If it is true that the role and function of paternal authority is now caught up in an ongoing crisis, if modernity is in its essence very closely bound up with that crisis, then we might very reasonably expect to see some corresponding effects in the nature and function of sexual life. To see how, let us take our clue from what I suspect is a relatively little known book, now out of print, Murray S. Davis's *Smut: Erotic Reality and Obscene Ideology*. Davis's book, while not without its weak points, provides a very handy and suggestive classification of contemporary attitudes toward sex. Borrowing his scheme will give us the tools to put the modern meaning of sex together with the historical situation we've described.

As the subtitle indicates, Davis's book has two main parts, the first describing the peculiarities of "erotic reality" and the second laying out what Davis calls the three ideologies of the obscene. While it is that second part that will most interest us, the first is an important preparation and we can usefully make a few remarks about it.

Davis begins by setting himself the task of understanding why sex becomes taboo at all. What is it about sex that requires, in virtually every human society, an elaborate series of restrictions and controls? What's so dangerous about sex? The key to this riddle, Davis believes, is to recognize the distinction, very palpable on the level of our lived experience, between two largely separate realities, the everyday and the erotic. Caught up in the swirl of sexual excitement, the world we seem to inhabit, or the way that we inhabit it, undergoes a series of dramatic changes. Time condenses, as future and past recede from the focus of awareness and the present more and more consumes our interest. Consciousness of space, too, tends to shrink as we become increasingly absorbed in what is most immediately around us. Indeed, when the force of Eros has most completely claimed us, attention becomes wholly occupied by the body of the beloved, or even by mere parts of that body. At the height of arousal, we become completely oblivious to our surroundings. Blissful—and maybe dangerous!—ignorance.

Perhaps most significant, the passage from everyday to erotic reality involves an erasure of boundaries and definition. Articulate speech disintegrates into mere spasms of breath—sighs, moans, and gasps. Consciousness of objects and relations to them tend to fade into a haze of irrelevance. Our very being appears more and more defined by a driving, pulsing rhythm of pure carnality. Whirling down into this chasm of indistinction, we feel ourselves to be less and less separate from our lovers. At the moment of climax, if not already before then, the line of separation between lovers completely disappears. We are aswim in the river of passion. No, we are nothing but that river.

It is in this loss of definition, a loss that shakes the foundations of everyday reality, that Davis locates the threatening aspect of sex. Sex destabilizes the boundaries that separate one individual from another and that define the space and time of a rationally structured world. It is in order to contain and control this potentially destructive power, Davis argues, that sex becomes subject to a range of social and cultural constraints. On this basis, he then goes on to provide an interesting and useful classification of sexual taboos. Even what might be called "normal" sex must be carefully controlled, for the way that it blurs the line between self and other. The varieties of perversion, challenging not just to the definition of self but to the very order of the social world—challenging, that is, not just the boundary between self and other, but that between the clean and the polluted, the human and the animal, the living and the dead—become subject to even more severe restrictions.

Most of this should sound very familiar. Davis's guiding question about sexual repression is essentially identical to the question I pursued in Chapter 3. His answer, too, is virtually the same, except that from the very outset he dismisses Freud as completely unhelpful. The reason for this dismissal is the usual one. In fact, Davis's book is a perfect example of the way that Freud and his legacy are routinely misunderstood by a great number of thoughtful and otherwise informed people. Davis has uncritically absorbed the popular vision of Freud as a theorist of instinct. "Freudians," he says, "see sex as basically biological." For his own part, Davis wants to investigate the more properly psychological and phenomenological dimensions of sex, the ways in which sex is actually experienced. The result is that Davis fails to see how the underlying tension that he identifies between everyday and erotic reality is almost exactly parallel to that drawn by Freud between ego and id. Davis reinvents significant portions of psychoanalytic theory without knowing it.

But let us leave that criticism aside in favor of the material in the second half of Davis's book that will be of use to us. There, he identifies three so-called ideologies of sex, the three main lenses through which we define what sex is and what it means to us. The purpose of these ideologies is to help their adherents to manage the discomforting split between erotic and everyday reality. The three dominant ideologies of sexuality, Davis argues, are the Jehovanist, the Gnostic, and the Naturalist.

Davis starts with the Jehovanist because it describes the most traditional posture toward sex and sexuality. While Davis no doubt has Judeo-Christianity primarily in mind, he calls this attitude "Jehovanist" less to identify it with any particular religious tradition than to signify an essentially defensive posture toward sex that marshals the resources of religion as the first line of resistance to it. The Jehovanist regards sexuality as intrinsically threatening and insists on its strict containment. The Jehovanist therefore treats sex the way we deal with fire: We recognize its necessity and usefulness, but we are also wary of its destructive power and take care to contain it safely in specially built, heavily insulated enclosures. Sex, too, has its uses, but in the absence of proper containment it will burn down the house. The defensive posture of the Jehovanist is thus supported by a litany of sexual prohibitions: rules against masturbation, premarital and extramarital sex, as well as homosexuality, sodomy, bestiality and other "unnatural" forms of gratification. In short, for the Jehovanist, sex is only permissible within the secure confines of a religiously sanctified bond of marriage, and even then it needs to be indulged in with cautious moderation or perhaps even restricted to the purposes of procreation alone.

While the Jehovanist outlook is closest to traditionally dominant attitudes toward sex, the other two ideologies identified by Davis, the Gnostic and the Naturalist, represent more modern developments. By "Gnostic," he wants to name the near opposite of the Jehovanist. Where the Jehovanist condemns sex as a font of evil and seeks to suppress and contain it, the Gnostic delights in the obscene and celebrates sexual transgression. Davis borrows the term *Gnostic* from the now-vanished heretical Christian sects who, in the eyes of the Church, took the other-worldly appeal of heaven too far, declaring this earthly existence to be hopelessly tainted and fallen, a mere trial that must be endured until the pure beatitude of the beyond can be attained. And, in fact, some Gnostic cults apparently used sexuality, the more licentious the better, as a means of showing their contempt for the false standards of this world and of getting some taste of the divine ecstasy that awaits in the next.

As an attitude toward sexuality, what Davis is calling Gnostic exploits the obscene as a form of rebellion against the everyday. The Gnostic is bored and disgusted with the empty banality and downright hypocrisy of social life and looks to sex as the touchstone of a greater authenticity. What was horror for the Jehovanist is therefore redemptive for the Gnostic. The lewd and lascivious, the indecent, even the degraded, hold out promise of deliverance from the flat and vapid world of the quotidian. This Gnostic flaunting of the obscene is particularly visible in some currents of pop music. The hip-pumping rock star, the dark and vaguely sadistic punk style, the in-your-face profanity of gangsta rap, all participate in the Gnostic program of rebellion tinged with erotic provocation. As Davis rightly points out, the Gnostic sensibility has been elaborated in a considerable literature, much of it a direct inheritance from the Marquis de Sade, that revels in ecstatic sexual excess. As Davis points out,

> the influence of de Sade's brand of Gnostic sexuality has been subterranean but tenacious. All but forgotten for nearly seventy-five years, it resurfaced toward the end of the nineteenth century in the French authors Joris Karl Huysmans (*Against Nature*) and Charles Baudelaire (*Flowers of Evil*), and in the English authors Algernon Swinburne (*The Whippingham Papers*) and Oscar Wilde (*The Picture of Dorian Gray*). It became more widely disseminated during the twentieth century, especially in France by Georges Bataille (*Story of the Eye*), Jean Genet (*Our Lady of the Flowers*), and Pauline Réage (*The Story of O*); and in America by Norman Mailer ("The Time of Her Time"), Lenny Bruce (*How To Talk Dirty and Influence People*), William Burroughs (*Naked Lunch*), John Rechy (*City of Night*), and Marco Vassi (*The Saline Solution*).

The Jehovanist and the Gnostic agree about one thing: Sex is something dirty and dangerous. They only disagree on how to deal with it. Where the Jehovanist reacts to an anxious horror of sex by insisting on a litany of sexual prohibitions, the Gnostic counters with a spirit of exuberant transgression that revels in violating them. For the Naturalist, on the other hand, sex is neither dirty nor dangerous. It is simply a bodily function, perfectly comparable to eating, breathing, and sleeping. The Naturalist therefore chooses the language of science over that of religion, removing sex from the sphere of the sacred in which questions of sexual behavior assume moral or even cosmic significance and placing it in the domain of biology for which satisfaction of natural impulses becomes a matter of health and wellness. The Naturalist therefore adopts an attitude of scientific neutrality in the questions of sexual morality. Alfred Kinsey, appropriately enough, was trained as a zoologist before turning to the scientific investigation of human sexuality. What were perversions or abominations for the Jehovanist become in the eyes of the Naturalist mere "variations." At the same time, many Jehovanist beliefs about the dangerous and destructive aspects of sex, drawn upon to enforce a repressive agenda, are revealed to be "myths"—the myth that masturbation causes blindness, the myth that homosexuality is wholly unnatural, and so on. For the Naturalist, if there is anything unhealthy and dangerous about sex it is precisely the prevalence of such myths and the cramping influence of the over-rigid sexual mores based on them. What is needed is a frank and open attitude toward sexuality that dispels the cloud of fear, superstition, and prejudice that has hung over sex for so many centuries.

Davis observes that each of the three ideologies of the sexual presupposes and supports a particular conception of self or identity. The Jehovanist envisions a stable and coherent identity that must be protected from the corrosive influence of sex. The sexual morality promulgated by Jehovanists, expressed in metaphors of pollution and the stain of sin, is therefore centered on what are essentially threats to the integrity of the self. Maintaining a separation and distinctness of identity is the basic desideratum. This underlying agenda is also visible in other kinds of cultic restriction aimed at the treatment of food (some classes of food may not touch each other, others may not be eaten at all, etc.). The Gnostic, by contrast, views the self as a kind of prison-house in which a divine spark has been trapped. The aim is thus not preservation but ecstatic destruction of self. The path to redemption consists in blasting apart a false and alienating identity in order to release the divine reflection that has been constrained by it. Sexual transgression, even of the most outrageous sort, can therefore become the very means of Gnostic transfiguration.

Yet another conception of self is assumed by the Naturalist, for whom notions of moral contamination are virtually nonsensical. The Naturalist self is, or should be, infinitely plastic and adaptable. It is less a fixed form or structure (to be either protected or destroyed) than a sensate surface that, like the skin itself, is forever renewable. This is the self of the empiricists, a pure mirror of the world lacking all quality in itself other than its own reflectivity. Davis calls it a rubber- or Teflon-self. For the Naturalist, there can be no real corruption of self, unless it be a diminishment of the self's receptivity to experience. But in that case, we would have a deterioration not of holiness but of health. The tendency of the Naturalist perspective is to take sex out of the domain of morals and put it squarely in that of medicine.

The relevance of the three categories proposed by Davis to my sketch of the historical situation of modernity is not far to seek, at least in its primary features. The Jehovanist is essentially representative of the traditional order of patriarchy. To illustrate the sexual ethics of the Jehovanist, Davis can readily draw upon biblical texts, beginning with expulsion of Adam and Eve, shamed and fig-leafed, from the Garden of Eden, and continuing through Leviticus all the way to the letters of Paul. The Gnostic outlook, on the other hand, is very much a blossom of modernity. The literature of what Davis calls Gnostic sexuality clearly partakes of the modern spirit of revolt against the established order. In this way, the Jehovanist–Gnostic opposition parallels the tension we have been exploring between traditional patriarchy and the modern forces arrayed against it.

From one point of view, of course, the tension between the Jehovanist and the Gnostic corresponds to an obvious psychological dynamic. Indeed, where would the Gnostic be without the Jehovanist to rebel against? The Gnostic needs the Jehovanist's kill-joy spirit of pious renunciation as the foil for launching a program of naughty indulgence. In this respect, the Gnostic's wicked excess is actually parasitical upon Jehovanist severity. The Gnostic savors the fruits that Jehovanists have sweetened with prohibition. The Jehovanist needs to be there in the background, playing the straight man, so to speak, for the Gnostic project of delicious depravity. But the lovers' quarrel of Gnostics and Jehovanists is also very clearly a historical episode. This historical dimension becomes especially clear when we recognize that what Murray Davis calls Gnostic sexuality is intimately related to the rise of pornography. In fact, the two can seem at times to be so closely linked as to be almost two different words for the same thing.

Pornographic Revolutions

Pornography has become an object of scholarly interest only fairly recently.[4] When the Meese Commission issued its report on pornography for the Reagan administration in 1986, only 16 of its almost 2,000 pages were devoted to the history of pornography, a reflection in part of the paucity of literature on the subject. Since then, however, that history has gotten more attention and it has become increasingly clear that, at least in the Western world, pornography emerged with the dawn of modernity itself. The word *pornographe* (from the Greek *graphé* of the *pornae*, or whore's writings) first appeared in 1769 in a treatise by the French author Restif de la Bretonne and referred to writing about prostitution. Only in the first half of the nineteenth century did the term enter more general usage in its contemporary sense, designating any obscene writings or images. The *Oxford English Dictionary* listed the word *pornography* for the first time in 1857. To be sure, by that time pornographic texts in the modern sense had been around for quite a while. The first such texts date from the sixteenth and seventeenth centuries, among them the sonnets of the Italian Pietro Aretino, famously illustrated with erotic engravings that depicted various positions for lovemaking (1527), and the notorious French classics *L'Ecole des filles* (1655) and *L'Academie des dames* (1660). It was the eighteenth century, however, especially in France and England, that saw the first real explosion of pornographic writings.

[4]An especially valuable fruit of this new interest, from which I draw heavily in the following section, is the collection of essays entitled *The Invention of Pornography: Obscenity and the Origins of Modernity, 1500–1800,* edited by Lynn Hunt and published by Zone Books.

The interesting thing for our purposes, centered on the historical destiny of patriarchy, is that a significant portion of eighteenth-century pornography was explicitly political in character. Explicit depiction of the sexual debauchery of the royal court or even of the king himself became a standard means of attacking the established order of power. The following extract from *Poems on the Affairs of State*, published in England in 1697, gives a good example. It recounts the labors of the mistress of Charles II, Nell Gwynn, to coax her liege to erection.

> This you'd believe, had I but time to tell ye
> The pains it cost to poor laborious Nelly
> While she employs hands, fingers, lips and things
> E'er she can raise the member she enjoys.

Another ditty expands further upon the same theme:

> his pintle and his sceptre are of a length
> and she may sway the one who plays with the other.

The prevalence of pornography in England was second only to its popularity in France. In fact, nowhere was the emergence of pornography more dramatic and extensive than in France and nowhere were its political dimensions more striking. This rising tide of politically motivated pornography reached its high-water mark in the decades just before and after the French Revolution. Some 200 or more illicit pamphlets and books were published in France between 1789 and 1792 alone. Among the most famous titles, many of which have been discreetly preserved on the shelves of the so-called Collection d'Enfer (or Collection of Hell) at the Bibliothèque Nationale in Paris, were *Histoire de Dom Bougre, portier des Chartreux* (1741), *Thérèse Philosophe* (1748), *Vie privée, libertine, et scandaleuse de Marie-Antoinette*, and *La Messaline française*, as well, of course, as the writings of the Marquis de Sade. Other, lesser titles give a good indication of the targets and tone of attack: *Les Enfans de Sodome à l'Assemblée Nationale* (The National Assembly's Children of Sodom; 1790), *Bord—R—* (The Queen's Bordello; 1789), *Le Godmiché Royal* (The Royal Dildo; 1789).

Most such politically charged pornography was published in the form of pamphlets, very often with explicit illustrations accompanied by derisive captions. No doubt these engraved illustrations were the most explosive elements of these pamphlet torpedoes. Here, if anywhere, were pictures worth a thousand words. Their power to agitate pubic opinion was observed by a contemporary commentator, Boyer de Nîmes, a royalist sympathizer who in 1792 published a two-volume treatment of revolutionary engravings. Of specifically obscene engravings, he remarked that "if we should note that caricatures are the thermometer which tells the temperature of the public opinion, we should also note that those who know how to master its variations know also how to master public opinion itself." He went on to record that the prevalence of anti-royalist engravings vastly increased in the weeks before the collapse of the monarchy. "A year before, some of these engravings had been shown by print merchants in the streets and along the quais of the capital, but since then, their number has so prodigiously grown and has become so considerable that one can find various of them in almost every window of the shops."

Among the prime targets of political pornography were figures of the Church. Lewd depictions of clergy engaged in all imaginable forms of perversion and debauchery became a staple of pornographic pamphleteering. But particularly around the time of the Revolution, such attacks on ecclesiastical power tended to be at the same time attacks on the State. Sade was especially incisive in linking the authority of the Church to the scourge of monarchy and used his extravagant depictions of sexual excess to undermine them both. "Religions are the cradles of despotism," he declared in *Philosophy in the Bedroom* (1795). "Let us not be content with breaking the scepters; we will pulverize the idols forever: there is never more than a single step from superstition to royalism.... Let us treat every Christian image as we have the tokens of monarchy."

With regard to assaults on royalty in particular, the figure of Marie-Antoinette was an especially conspicuous object of attack. The queen's sexual antics were a standard subject of obscene descriptions and the paternity of her children was derisively questioned. In *L'Autrichienne en goguettes*, for example, the queen throws herself into an orgy with the king's brother, the Count D'Artois, and with the Duchesse de Polignac. At one point the duchess, feeling somewhat left out of the frenzied couplings of the queen and her brother-in-law, tries to satisfy herself by masturbating while reading *Histoire de Dom Bougre, portier des Chartreux*, a famous pornographic text of the day.

Of course, to cast doubt upon the paternity of the queen's offspring was a very direct means of undermining the authority of the king, implying both a pollution of the royal lineage and the king's inability to control his own wife. But pornographic attacks on church and state figures also had politically revolutionary effects for more general reasons having to do with the very nature of pornographic representations. Pornography is profoundly anti-hierarchal in the sense that it tends to put all persons, royal or common, on the same level of a kind of physical interchangeability. To graphically depict the sexual exploits of the queen is to invite every man to imagine himself in bed with her. When pageboys are lusted after by countesses and peasant girls are sodomized by cardinals, the effect is immediately destructive of the aura and mystique of traditional power. In the language of the pamphleteers, well calculated to shock, the queen with her clothes off is just another cunt, the king another prick. By its very nature, therefore, the materialist world of pornography invites a degree of democratic leveling.

The revolutionary career of eighteenth-century pornography was relatively brief. By the 1800s and ever after, pornography settled into its now familiar function of purely erotic titillation. But lack of a revolutionary agenda doesn't make pornography politically neutral. Even after the collapse of monarchy, the consumer of pornography continues to rehearse an implicit theme of underlying equality. Andréa de Nerciat's classic pornographic novel *Le Diable au corps*, published in 1803, provides a good example. While de Nerciat's book still features libertine escapades of the libidinous aristocracy, the sharp edge of political attack is gone. Thus when De Nerciat gives us a randy marquise who goes to bed with a peddler of some especially promising English dildos while a lascivious abbé watches from the closet, or when he depicts a small circle of court ladies discovering with a donkey "all the attractions that can make an ass interesting," his concern is wholly occupied with the arousing and titillating aspects of his subject. Nevertheless, the reader of these scenes is inevitably drawn once again into the democracy of the pornographic, a world in which all are equally subjects of sexual desire. The only sovereign power in the pornographic universe is that of sex itself.

The Universal Brothel

What Murray Davis calls the Gnostic strand of modern sexuality, the tradition of transgressive excess for which the Marquis de Sade was such a key representative, was thus an integral part of the political upheavals of modernity—indeed, in its own way, it contributed to those very upheavals. In the case of the French Revolution in particular, this Gnostic sensibility, expressed in politically charged pornography, exerted a potent anti-establishment force. In its most immediate effects, this force was anti-patriarchal and democratic, and was so in a double sense, political but also sexual. In helping to undermine patriarchal legitimacy, Gnostic pornography also helped to unchain sexuality from its anchorage in traditional forms of authority. Bypassing the customary paternal gatekeeper of sexuality, this anti-patriarchal trend promised to open up an unprecedented availability of sex. Traces of this promise are audible in documents from the period. One tract from 1790, for example, using a string of double entendres, announces to the citizens of the infant republic a new access to sexuality. "Vigorous patriots, amiable fellow citizens, a new FIELD which though more NARROW than that of MARS[5] is nonetheless agreeable, is now OPEN to you; hasten to ENTER there." Elsewhere in the same pamphlet is a poem in which a prostitute offers cut rates for patriots: "Eighteen sous, instead of twenty-four; It's to that that my national cunt has been reduced."

---

[5]The poem refers here to the "Champ de Mars," or "field of Mars," the vast open space that stretches south from the current site of the Eiffel Tower.

The Gnostic sensibility, so closely allied with the pornographic, can thus be shown to be an anti-patriarchal, democratizing force. But where in all of this is the symptomatic reaction as I sketched it earlier, the counter movement of a renewed assertion of patriarchal privilege? Do we see such a reaction? Indeed, we do, and it is a dramatic one. It may be quite true that pornography depicts a profoundly materialist world in which distinctions of social hierarchy and privilege are collapsed onto the level of pure physicality. Differences of social status tend to be erased by pornography and replaced by a rollicking carnival of flesh saturated by promiscuous desire. Unrestrained lust emerges as the great equalizer. But there is another side to this story. If pornography has its democratizing effect, we must quickly add that it is a democracy that admits of a very significant qualification: the division between men and women.

Of course, the fact that the pornographic imagination is cut through by a deep, gender-related division should hardly be surprising. Pornography traditionally has been and still is very predominantly consumed by men.[6] The consequences of that fact for shaping the typical themes and implicit assumptions of pornography, what might be called the "masculinist worldview of pornography," have been explored by an extensive literature over the past few decades. We can now accept some of the key results of those explorations and fit them to the thesis that we've been unfolding. To get a start, we can return to the historical origins of pornography and note a remarkable detail. A striking number of early modern pornographic texts, while written by men, presented themselves as written by women. The most famous was John Cleland's English classic *Memoirs of a Woman of Pleasure* (more commonly known as *Fanny Hill*), probably the all-time pornographic bestseller. An even greater number featured a woman as narrator. It is a tradition that goes back at least to Aretino's *Ragionamenti*, and includes many other classic titles, among them *L'Ecole des filles*, *Thérèse philosophe*, *Félicia*, and *Margot la ravaudeuse*.

Why were women appointed in this way to be the mouthpieces of pornographic sexuality? There was, of course, a good reason for a male author of scandalous obscenity to conceal his identity behind a false name. But why a woman's name? Judging by its origins, pornography appears to be sexy stories told to men by women. Why women?

One very tempting answer to this question is to conclude that the image of sexuality presented to men by pornography was and remains one in which women are depicted as not only perfectly willing, but downright eager to participate. Pornography can very happily be sexy stories told by women because the primary theme that is rehearsed by pornography is that of the unlimited availability of women for sex, either because they themselves want it so much,

[6]Predominantly but by no means exclusively. A good antidote to the stereotype of the exclusively masculine consumer of pornography is Sally Tisdale's book *Talk Dirty to Me: An Intimate Philosophy of Sex*.

or because they aren't in a position to say no. The pornographic phantasy continually rehearses, both directly and indirectly, the infinite sexual accessibility of women.

This view helps to explain not only why pornography might be pseudonymously attributed to and/or narrated by women but also why those women are so frequently prostitutes. From *Fanny Hill* to *The Happy Hooker*, the 1977 bestseller that actually was authored by a woman, the tell-all whore has been a favorite pornographic device. Part of the reason, we can readily suppose, is that a prostitute's account of her sexual adventures enables a reader who might never actually do so to visit a whore vicariously. But even more importantly, the whore-narrator of pornography contributes mightily to the reader conceiving of all women as readily available for sexual use.

There are a number of ways in which this end is accomplished—a number of ways, that is, in which the class of libertine women is broadened beyond the author/narrator who is at present speaking. First, we very frequently find the female narrator tutoring other, younger women in the pleasure-craft of Eros. The purpose of this education is almost always a matter of graduating from prudery and constraint. "Speak plainly," instructs the prostitute Antonia in Aretino's *Ragionamenti*, "and say 'fuck,' 'prick,' 'cunt,' and 'ass.'" This sort of tutelage by the more sexually savvy older woman, suggesting the way that new recruits might be groomed for service by the madame in a brothel, calls up the idea that all women might eventually be properly educated. Consider, too, the way in which the device of the whore-narrator effects a short-circuit between high and low society. These spectacularly wanton women also tend to be highly intelligent, witty, and perceptive, often discoursing at some length about "philosophy." They thus fuse opposite extremes in a way that implicitly unites all women in a single figure. Again the reader is led to think that maybe all women are, or could be, as sexually open and available as this one!

More decisive than what the prostitute-narrators of pornography say is what they do. And what they do, setting a standard for every woman to follow, is offer themselves to men with absolute abandon. There seems to be no end to their appetites and no limit to their willingness to gratify the desires of the men who want them. The heroine of *Margot la ravaudeuse*, for example, recalls finding herself alone in a brothel and compelled to satisfy a regiment of musketeers. "I was forced," she says, "to suffer thirty assaults in the space of two hours." The only problem with this treatment, she claims, is that it was just too much of a good thing. "Too much is too much. I was stuffed with so much pleasure that I had a kind of indigestion." When a similar challenge confronts Marguerite, the niece of Dom Bourge, she is more fully up to the task. Taking on five soldiers at once and allowing them the enjoyment of all of her orifices, she achieves orgasm herself in unison with all five. "This new type of debauchery," she exclaims, "gave me a taste for more récherché pleasures."

The prostitute-narrator of classic pornography, a figure that becomes a perennial fixture of the porn imagination, constitutes a masculine ideal for all women—perpetually ready for sex. (Has she not also become an ideal for women themselves? Do we not see, especially in the past few decades, a very striking tendency for women's fashions to resemble more and more a kind of "whore chic"—stiletto heels, fishnet stockings, push-up bras and corsets, exaggerated makeup and lip gloss, etc.—that people of a not-so-very-bygone time would have regarded as outrageously trashy?) Equally significant, however, is the way that the female denizen of the porn world demonstrates her willingness to grant her favors equally to all men. The intrepid heroine of *Julie philosophe, ou Le Bon patriote* (1791), as if to prove the aptness of the book's title, pursues a course of successive affairs that is conspicuous for spanning the entire social hierarchy. After coupling with a hack writer, a doctor, a Belgian revolutionary, an English exile, a clergyman, and an aristocrat, she finally winds up flush with money from her aristocrat but married to a peasant. The implication is clearly that the women who populate the pornographic imagination are equally available to all men of every nation and every social status.

This every-woman-for-all-men feature of pornography, like so many other characteristics of porn, is shown in exaggerated relief by that arch-Gnostic, the Marquis de Sade. The two most famous women of Sade's invention, Juliette and Justine, are no doubt the twin record holders for the sheer number and variety of men to whom they have loaned their orifices. Indeed, it is a record that transcends mere sexual stamina in the direction of miraculous survival. But Sade is not content merely to demonstrate the infinite accessibility of women for sex; he also provides an elaborate theoretical argument for it. In the long social and political treatise that forms the centerpiece of "Philosophy in the Bedroom," itself a part of the gigantic novel *Justine*, Sade proposes the institution of new laws, logical extensions of the newly won revolutionary rights of man. Henceforth, he declares, every man should be guaranteed an unlimited right to use any woman for the purposes of his sexual gratification.

> A man who would like to enjoy whatever woman or girl will henceforth be able, if the laws you promulgate are just, to have her summoned at once to duty at one of the houses; and there, under the supervision of the matrons of that temple of Venus, she will be surrendered to him, to satisfy, humbly and with submission, all the fancies in which he will be pleased to indulge with her, however strange and irregular they may be.... There remains but to fix the woman's age; now, I maintain it cannot be fixed without restricting the freedom of a man who desires a girl of any given age. He who has the right to eat the fruit of a tree may assuredly pluck it ripe or green, according to the inspiration of his taste.

Sade is very explicit in offering this proposal as not only consistent with the guiding principles of the revolution, which he fully endorses, but as necessary to bring the revolutionary agenda to completion. He collects them under the title, "Yet another effort, Frenchmen, if you would become Republicans!" Sade's idea is therefore that the female sex be henceforth established as a universal brothel. And consistent with the conduct of a brothel, women should be compensated. How compensated? In view of the natural sexual insatiability of women, they should be guaranteed the absolute right to as much sex as they wish, conducted with any man who strikes their fancy, and utilizing any part of the body to achieve satisfaction. What is not included in this amendment to the original program of men's access to women, it should be noted, is any woman's right of refusal.

> I say then that women, having been endowed with considerably more violent penchants for carnal pleasure than we, will be able to give themselves over to it wholeheartedly, absolutely free of all encumbering hymeneal ties, of all false notions of modesty, absolutely restored to a state of Nature; I want laws permitting them to give themselves to as many men as they see fit; I would have them accorded the enjoyment of all sexes and, as in the case of men, the enjoyment of all parts of the body; and under the special clause prescribing their surrender to all who desire them, there must be subjoined another guaranteeing them a similar freedom to enjoy all they deem worthy to satisfy them.

Extreme though it is, indeed extreme to the point of absolute caricature, Sade's proposal nevertheless highlights a central feature of the pornographic imagination, which is to make all women objects and subjects of unlimited desire. The idea continually rehearsed for the male consumer of pornography is that all women are sexually available to him, and that they desire nothing more than that very availability.

His and Hers

With this conclusion, briefly sketched as it is, we get a deeper insight into the symptomatic character of modern sexuality I have been aiming at, relevant at least to its Gnostic strand. We've seen how and why that Gnostic sensibility, reveling in the obscene and insisting upon the erotic democracy of bodies, exerted a significantly anti-patriarchal force. But at the same time, as if to make up for the damage it had done to the legacy of patriarchal privilege, Gnostic-pornographic sexuality provided a compensation in the form of a reinforcement and exaggeration of gender difference. Having contributed to the overturning of patriarchal authority, the emerging strain of Gnostic sexuality held out the promise of continued, even improved, sexual access to women.

The result, as it might be put in the terms of Freud's *Totem and Taboo*, is that after the murder of the father, power over women was taken over by the band of brothers who had committed the deed. And what could be more appropriate? In the traditional order of things, sexual access to women was a prerogative of the patriarch. The hopeful suitor asked the father's leave for his daughter's hand. In the modern context, it is a custom that is increasingly outmoded. Yet control over women and their bodies continues. Indeed, in the phantasy domain of the pornographic, things are better than ever. Her father might have said no, but clearly every woman can only say yes, yes, yes!

My thesis, then, is that pornography, born with the Enlightenment and itself a contributor to emerging democratic sensibilities, has also functioned to erect a crucial limit to post-revolutionary democracy. It does so by pervasively reinforcing an exaggerated sense of sexual difference tilted decisively in favor of men. The picture is one of patriarchal power overthrown in fact, yet reinstated in phantasy. A rebellion against traditional social order in the form of an attack on a specific, centralized authority in the political sphere led to an intensification of masculine privilege in the domain of gender and sexuality. To properly understand what I mean, it is necessary to add three important comments.

1. I'm pointing to a change that was by no means brought about solely by the modern explosion of pornography. The shadow world of pornography helps give the clue to recognizing this transformation, but we can readily see its effects elsewhere in the clear light of day. The reason is that the pornographic depiction of sex difference reflects in its own sphere a more general exaggeration of sex difference in culture at large. Thus we see in the century following the anti-monarchic revolutions of the eighteenth century the advent of a period of especially conspicuous differentiation between masculinity and femininity. The most obvious emblem of this intensified culture of gender distinction was the moral and aesthetic ideal of the nineteenth-century Victorian lady, along with the fantastically elaborate trappings—in clothes, carriages, furnishings, and manners—that were needed to stage the impression she was required to make.

   Ultimately, however, it is necessary to see that the Victorian lady represented in a language of moral poise and purity what the pornographic prostitute does in that of debauchery: both served to mark the chasm between masculinity and femininity. The demure bourgeois lady and the brazen gutter strumpet were thus flip sides of the same coin. Both served a single, underlying dynamic. Not only did they mutually support and define each other, each providing a perfect negation of her opposite counterpart, but they both functioned to inscribe the masculine–feminine fault line that formed the most important axis of the social world in the fledgling democracies. However glaring the contrast between high women and low, the really effective and significant division in Victorian society remained that between all women and the men who controlled them.

Mention of the Victorian Lady gives me the occasion quickly to add a further note that might reduce some confusion. Of course, I am not saying that gender differentiation is a modern invention. Premodern societies were very conspicuously cleaved by sexual difference. I am, however, claiming that the distinction of genders has in the past two centuries been specially intensified and exaggerated. The point can be seen in the sphere of clothing and costume. Especially when we take the long view, looking back for example to the robes worn by men and women in antiquity and even into the Middle Ages, the suits and dresses of the modern period—especially the corsets, bustles, hooped skirts, and crinoline of Victorian women's drawing room attire—stand out as particularly exaggerated forms of gender-typed clothing. Here, we can think again for a last time of our point of departure, trivial though it may have seemed at the time, with the modern man's necktie. Gender-differentiated clothing obviously didn't get invented with the necktie, but it got a big boost.

2. It is important to emphasize the role of phantasy in all of this. By saying that the regime of kings was replaced by a brotherhood of men distinct from women, I am pointing to a passage from an order of real power, backed up by force of the sword, to a power based on phantasy. By that I mean that the social order of premodern patriarchy was ultimately based on the force of law. In contemporary democratic societies, by contrast, women have progressively won a variety of rights—rights of property ownership, of divorce, of voting, of holding public office, and so on—that were legally denied to them in the past. What then maintains the structure and stability of masculine privilege? To a far larger extent than ever before, that privilege is maintained by forces of attitude and perception. The stability of social order is compelled by means that are less legal than merely ideological.

This is not to say that the reign of premodern patriarchy was not itself to a very considerable extent phantasmatic. The power of the monarch was a power that existed largely in the minds of his subjects. The immense theater of regal pomp and circumstance, the gigantic architectural staging, the whole phantasmagoria of royal majesty, served to reinforce that psychology of subjection. Nor is it to deny that the phantasmatic regime of modern sexuality is without very real effects in the material world, not least in the ways that it shapes the actual lives of men and women. Nevertheless, the new form of domination I am trying to point to in highlighting the symptomatic dimension of modern sexuality, this "rule of the king after the fact," has as its core source of power a regime of pure perception.

If the thesis I am proposing is valid, then we can draw from it an important implication for our understanding of the relationship between the sexual revolution of the modern period and the emergence of twentieth-century media culture. It helps us avoid the mistake of assuming that the relatively recent explosion of diverse photographic media—from art to advertising—was responsible for the transformation of sexual attitudes so characteristic of late-twentieth-century urban society. The explosion of modern media technology didn't create a new sexual regime but rather brought an unprecedented means of visual expression to an already fundamentally altered situation in which the meaning of sexuality was already well on its way to a new formation.

3. I am proposing that modern pornography both emerged during a period of anti-patriarchal tension and contributed to its expansion. At the same time, pornography served to help frame a masculinist reaction that sought to consolidate a new form of social power along lines of sex difference. I am not claiming, however, that there is anything intrinsically sexist about pornography. We can easily imagine a highly developed art of sexual arousal that does not somehow privilege the masculine position or degrade the feminine one. Indeed, a great deal of existing pornography is already used for purposes of arousal and satisfaction by both men and women, gay and straight. Some writers have tried to make this point by separating pornography that is degrading to women from eroticism, in which sexual difference doesn't mean sexual disadvantage.

I therefore do not agree with critics of pornography such as Catherine MacKinnon and Andrea Dworkin, who argue that porn is sexist by its very nature. Their claim that explicit portrayal of sexual organs or acts is unavoidably masculinist strikes me as ultimately unconvincing. Porn is not intrinsically sexist. But it has been historically so. Indeed, one of the advantages of the thesis I am proposing is that it helps to explain why pornography, which is at least conceivable in a nonchauvinist form, has as a matter of historical fact evolved with a very conspicuous sexist streak. Modern pornography has been shaped by the exigencies of its historical context. Arising precisely with the onset of the modern crisis of patriarchy, pornography has lent its resources very readily to the reconstruction of a kind of secondary formation of masculine privilege. In terms of its effects, shoring up an injured sense of masculine prerogative by exaggerating key features of the relations between the sexes, pornographic chauvinism is a consolation prize for the modern diminishment of monarchal patriarchy.

The aim of this chapter has been to pose the emergence of the Gnostic current of Western sexuality in the context of the political upheavals of the modern period and to suggest how it played a double role, indeed a role that is virtually contradictory, at once undermining patriarchal authority (in its political form) and rebuttressing patriarchal privilege (in its social-sexual form). The key lesson concerns the way in which sex has become the privileged field in which the essential antagonists of the modern age—anti-patriarchal forces in conflict with the traditional order of patriarchal authority—contest against each other. Faced with significantly anti-hierarchal trends in the fields of science, religion, politics, and economics, masculine prerogative reinforced its dominance in the sexual sphere, a sphere in which, obviously enough, it had long ago established the upper hand.

Presenting this thesis has required a good deal of background preparation and even now, having devoted a long chapter to it, I have at best sketched it only in the barest outline. Another book would be required to give it anything like adequate treatment. It is, moreover, a thesis that is not susceptible of any simple proof. Nevertheless, while it cannot count as proof, it ought to be taken as highly significant that during the period of the past two centuries, as if in response to the Gnostic challenge, the Jehovanist sensibility so readily identifiable with the order of traditional patriarchy has in many ways increased the rigor and stridency of its stance toward sexual morality. It is a trend that is strikingly visible in the distinctly modern developments of fascism and fundamentalism, but is also discernible in many currents of more mainstream culture. It is clearly present, for example, in the development and elaboration of doctrines on sexual morality in the Catholic Church. The number of officially articulated Church positions on matters touching upon sex has dramatically increased during the past two hundred years. Indeed, judging by the written codex of Catholic doctrines on sex and sexuality, we are justified in concluding, in stark contradiction to a common misconception about the repressiveness of the dark ages of the past, that the Church is significantly more repressive today than ever before. The impression one gets is that of an ongoing response to an increasing challenge, a continuing effort to hold the line against the corrosive influence of modernity itself.

8
Empire of Fetishes

"Okay," the critic breaks in for a last time, "I think I see the point you're trying to make. I was going to object a moment ago that the modern history of England foils your case: the monarchy survived perfectly well, but the cult of the proper bourgeois lady was as strong there as anywhere. I now imagine that your answer would be that while England has preserved a vestige of its monarchy, its real power was long ago gradually but drastically diminished as the underlying anti-traditional forces you point to have had their effects in England as they have elsewhere. I can even imagine you adding a discussion about the sex scandals that have rocked the House of Windsor in recent years, fitting them to your thesis. When pornography doesn't succeed in toppling royalty, royalty turns into pornography anyway. Something like that!

"I can also see that you intend the two accounts of modernity that you've given (the anti-patriarchal rebellion against monarchy and the intimate rebellion against bureaucracy) to be perfectly compatible with one another. Indeed, you would probably argue that they are both deeply bound up with the modern supremacy of the individual. But what ever happened to the other modern ideology of the sexual, the Naturalist? Though you have yet to deal with it, I suppose that it, too, is part of the symptomatic complex, both rebellious and restabilizing, that you are describing. In fact, I assume that you now plan to complete the picture you've been trying to sketch with reference to the Naturalist perspective."

We do indeed have to consider the role of the Naturalist ideology. No doubt, the sexual field of contemporary life is very deeply inscribed with the assumptions of a Naturalist perspective. And, yes, tracing its underlying dynamics will help to fill out the picture of the symptomatic status of modern sexuality. In the end, however, to grasp more fully the nature and functions of sexuality in our time, we will need to add to our analysis of the three ideologies another crucial consideration that will return us ever more decisively to the theoretical formulations of Freud. The final destination of our explorations, for which our discussions of the historical meaning of the three ideologies will have been a necessary preparation, is the modern significance of Freud's concept of fetishism.

From Sade to Sex Ed

In many ways, the Naturalist perspective appears increasingly to be the dominant ideology of sexuality in our time. Indeed, the very term *sexuality* is essentially a Naturalist invention. "Sexuality" is part of the jargon of the modern social and biological sciences and refers to the reproductive functions of the human being in analogy to the reproductive behavior of animals. No wonder so many sex education programs introduce the mechanics of sex by way of some comparison to animal reproduction—sex becomes truly a matter of "the birds and the bees." Yet a naturalist perspective is rarely to be found in its pure state, but is rather mixed, happily or unhappily, with the other two ideologies. That may be the reason sex education classes are so often called courses in "*Human* sexuality"—I remember taking a particularly good one as an undergraduate called the "Yale Course in Human Sexuality." The qualifier "human" doesn't get added because people might make a mistake about which species will be examined. The problem is that by itself the word *sexuality* may sound a little too brutely biological, materialist, or even mechanical. Calling it "human" sexuality softens the blow. It is as if, viewing our sexual behavior from a strictly scientific point of view—saying, in effect, that what we do is essentially no different from animal copulation—such courses still want to reassure us that there is after all something distinctly human about it. "Human sexuality" therefore becomes a kind of code phrase, a fig leaf for predominantly medical and scientific treatments of sex, and represents an uneasy truce between a predominantly naturalist treatment and more traditional sensibilities.

The fragility of this truce was illustrated for me when I was involved some years ago in helping to organize an extracurricular course in sexuality for undergraduates at a Catholic college. The Jesuits on the large organizing committee (one from the faculty of Management and Law, another from Theology, and a third from Pastoral Counseling) readily agreed with the rest of the committee that the first sessions of the course should be devoted to the biology of reproduction. Predictably enough, the Jesuits were also enthusiastic supporters of calling the course "The *Human* Sexuality Seminar." As if the qualifier "human" were not enough to signal sufficient distance from mere biology, however, they also insisted that the course contain a prominent section devoted to questions of "Ethical and Religious Perspectives" and suggested that the session might best be taught by a priest.

The ultimate fate of the course was in its own way a telling witness to the crossfire of emotions that now troubles questions of sex. Two professors from the psychology department, a woman and a man, both specialists in topics of sexuality and relationships, taught the course for three years to rave reviews from the hundred-odd students who enrolled each year. In its third year, however, the course ran afoul of a kind of Jehovanist revenge in the form of an embarrassing media campaign, whipped up by a small cell of conservative students and faculty who "discovered" that masturbation, homosexuality, and abortion were being discussed in morally neutral terms. The college president, blindsided by this unwelcome fracas, ordered that the course be discontinued "pending further study."

While Jehovanists may react with horror to finding a Naturalist outlook encroaching too far upon their domain, the Gnostic attitude toward sex has always been close to Naturalism. The reason is that the Gnostic tends to use the appeal to nature as one of its primary weapons in its fight against Jehovanist repression. In this respect, the sexual Gnostic may be a faithful child of the Enlightenment who shares a kinship with those Enlightenment thinkers like Rousseau who prefer the authenticity of nature to the artifice of civilized convention. We see this tendency with particular clarity in the writings of Sade. When Sade wants to defend the most outrageous violations of decency he often turns to Nature as his warrant. Our desires for violence and debauchery, he claims, are placed in us by Nature herself ("there is no extravagance which is not in Nature, none which she does not acknowledge as her own") and nothing could be more defensible than to act in accord with the dictates of Nature ("there can exist no evil in obedience to Nature's promptings").

If the Gnostic has always been part Naturalist, the Naturalist is very often, at least in one respect, a closet Gnostic. For the Naturalist, too, regards the repressive regime of Jehovanist morality as an unnatural censure of urges that ought to be embraced as perfectly healthy and normal. For the Naturalist, as for the Gnostic, the Jehovanist is a stodgy old killjoy who would like to impose upon others the same regimen of self-flagellation, inflated with metaphysical hocus-pocus and stiffened with dogmatism, that he has imposed upon himself. The big difference between the Naturalist and the Gnostic is not the degree to which they criticize Jehovanists, but the degree to which they enjoy it. Where the Gnostic offends and outrages the Jehovanist with undisguised glee, the Naturalist soberly continues collecting statistics. Where the Gnostic smacks his lips over the prospect of debauching another virgin, this time dressed in vestments he has stolen from the priory, the Naturalist presents another study of the well-adjusted personality.

Indeed, enjoyment would seem to be the real problem for the Naturalist altogether. The Naturalist attitude toward sex resembles that of militant health food enthusiasts whose approach to cooking dismisses presentation or even taste in favor of fanatical devotion to sound nutrition. The dish they offer is scientifically unassailable, but who would want to eat it? The Naturalist gives us sex without Eros. The nudist movement is a good example. The underlying motivation of nudism is a revolt against Jehovanist conventions of shame and guilt. Modesty, proclaims the nudist, is a wholly unnatural response, instilled in us by the constraining and distorting influence of centuries of myth and superstition. Animals don't hide their nakedness, why should we? Yet the pleasure of nudism often appears to be limited to casting aside such artificial constraints. To enjoy the naked bodies in the nudist camp for their erotic potential—to the point, say, of getting an erection in the middle of the shuffleboard game—would be in extremely bad taste. Naturalists seem to want to make sex a bodily function like any other, but only so long as it remains as unexciting as any other.

Viewed in relation to the other two ideologies we've identified, the Naturalist faces us with an odd paradox. By that I mean that the Naturalist appears to revolt against the repressive regime of Jehovanist tradition, yet also to achieve some of the Jehovanist's basic objectives by other means. The Naturalist is very far indeed from sharing the Gnostic program of subversion by unrestrained indulgence, the ferocious anarchy of pleasure that Sade raised to such a fevered pitch. The Naturalist seems oddly to have forgotten pleasure, or worse, to have submitted it to a new form of denial. In the scientific literature of the Naturalist perspective, the living pulse of sexual pleasure often appears to be strangled beneath a heavy layer of technical language, not infrequently expressed in Latin. In a Preface to his classic *Psychopathia Sexualis*, a groundbreaking work in the Naturalist perspective, Richard von Krafft-Ebing remarked that

> in order that unqualified persons should not become readers, the author saw himself compelled to choose a title understood only by the learned, and also, where possible, to express himself in *terminis technicis*. It seemed necessary to give certain particularly revolting portions in Latin.

Krafft-Ebing's comment is interesting in part for what it doesn't say but clearly implies. The reason that "unqualified persons" are to be kept away from his book is presumably to avoid giving them fodder for prurient interest. "The learned," we may presume, are already above such things. Nevertheless, Krafft-Ebing refers to himself in the third person, as if he wants very definitely to reassure his audience that he, surely one of the very learned, has securely split his sexual from his intellectual self and that it is the voice of pure intellect that will be speaking in his account of the perversions. The point is an important one—worthy of Krafft-Ebing's efforts to clarify it—because his recounting the perversions very probably *was* a source of a certain enjoyment. But of what sort? Certainly, he assures us, not a sexual one.

Freud, too, himself a great contributor to the Naturalist perspective on sex, availed himself of similar devices when it came to describing the most intimate of sexual secrets, especially when they were his own. He thus famously reverted to Latin in recounting an electrifying childhood memory of seeing his mother naked: I saw, he said, *matrem nudam*. In fact it is not difficult to gather from Naturalist accounts of sex the impression of a kind of stolen, quasi-voyeuristic enjoyment that, once tasted, is both disavowed for oneself and denied to others. The Naturalist picture of sexual behavior tends to be decidedly, studiously, emphatically un-pornographic. As a result, one can reasonably wonder whether the effect of statistic-crunching sexologists is ultimately even more pleasure-denying, if more subtly so, than that of Bible-thumping Jehovanists. As the Gnostic example has taught us, Jehovanist repression can be a positive incitement to lasciviousness. The prurient hungers for nothing more than the prohibited. To what exactly is Naturalism an incitement? Only, it seems, to more Naturalism.

Are we to conclude that the Naturalist ideology of sex, too, is a symptomatic fusion that simultaneously rebels against repression, yet reinstitutes a new form of control in which the sheer pleasure-value of sex is once again refused?

Victoria's Secret

The question of the symptomatic character of modern sex, at once liberating and repressing, the question that we now pose in terms of the pleasure-refusing effects of the scientific systematization of sex, recalls the argument made by Michel Foucault in the first volume of his *History of Sexuality.* In this book, Foucault proposes that our contemporary understanding of ourselves as sexually "liberated" is largely an illusion. It is an illusion that is fed from two main sources: (1) the picture we have of the proper ladies and gentlemen of the bygone Victorian age, who we imagine to have suffered from a crushing burden of sexual repression, and (2) the ease and frequency with which we now talk about sex as part of health and hygiene. We end up congratulating ourselves for our sexual openness while looking down our noses at our nineteenth-century forebears with a mixture of pity and contempt.

Foucault first sets his critical sights on Victorian attitudes toward sex in order to expose the myth of what he calls the "repressive hypothesis." According to this widely accepted notion, the stiff-collared prudery of the nineteenth century virtually forbade all utterance about sex and, having driven sex into the most cramped containment of denial, suffered its absence with stony resignation. Whatever its source (Foucault counts Freud as a major culprit), this view has become a near dogma, both in the academy and in the popular imagination.

Foucault overturns this image of Victorian repression by insisting that the Victorians, far from being unable to speak of sex, were downright obsessed with it. In fact, the nineteenth century was the culmination of a modern trend toward ceaselessly confessing the secrets of the flesh. This compulsion to speak of sex, Foucault claims, is what lay behind the elaboration of a whole range of emerging scientific discourses in which the varieties of sexual behavior were meticulously surveyed and cataloged by physicians, psychiatrists, educators, and hygienists. Freud, however distinctive his theories, was therefore not at all alone in turning the lens of scientific observation toward the subject of sex. Indeed, the incessant inspection and scientific systematization of sex was a key part of the whole spirit of the Victorian age. This frenzy for scientific study of the details of sexual life resembled the obsessive rigor and exhaustiveness with which the pioneers of natural history had only a century before set about cataloging the varieties of living organisms. The result, Foucault asserts, is that "we must therefore abandon the hypothesis that modern industrial societies ushered in an age of increased sexual repression." "What is peculiar to modern societies," he concludes, "is not that they consigned sex to a shadow existence, but that they dedicated themselves to speaking of it *ad infinitum*, while exploiting it as the secret." Foucault then arrives at his conclusion: the hidden purpose of this burgeoning science of sex is a kind of domestication of the erotic, a submission of sex-pleasure to a rational scheme. The modern compulsion to talk endlessly about sex conceals the unfolding of a new technics of power.

As he does in many of his books, Foucault supplies an especially vivid example to illustrate his basic thesis. In this case, it is the example of a simple-minded farmhand from the French village of Lapcourt who, one day in 1867, "obtained a few caresses from a little girl, just as he had done before and seen done by the village urchins around about him; for, at the edge of the wood, or in the ditch by the road leading to Saint-Nicholas, they would play the familiar game called 'curdled milk.'" Once the village authorities were apprised of these goings-on, however, they regarded them as anything but mere fun and games. What is significant about this story, Foucault suggests, is the crushing weight of deadly seriousness, the gravity of scientific inquiry and certification, that suddenly descended upon the hapless peasant whose sexual pleasure had attracted official attention. The striking thing, Foucault insists, is

> the fact that this everyday occurrence in the life of village sexuality, these inconsequential bucolic pleasures, could become, from a certain time, the object not only of a collective intolerance but of a judicial action, a medical intervention, a careful clinical examination, and an entire theoretical elaboration. The thing to note is that they went so far as to measure the brainpan, study the facial bone structure, and inspect for possible signs of degenerescence the anatomy of this personage who up to that moment had been an integral part of village life; that they made him talk; that they questioned him concerning his thoughts, inclinations, habits, sensations, and opinions. And then, acquitting him of any crime, they decided finally to make him into a pure object of medicine and knowledge—an object to be shut away till the end of his days in the hospital at Maréville, but also one to be made known to the world of learning through a detailed analysis.... So it was that our society—and it was doubtless the first in history to take such measures—assembled around these timeless gestures, these barely furtive pleasures between simple-minded adults and alert children, a whole machinery for speechifying, analyzing, and investigating.

With vignettes like this one in mind, it is tempting to think of Foucault's picture of modern sexuality as one of a lost innocence in which sexual pleasure is submitted to the regularizing and rationalizing influence of scientific scrutiny. Does Foucault mean to suggest that sex in the premodern era—say, in the Middle Ages—was free from the dominating influence of a scrutinizing power? Not at all. Sex was then subject to a regime of moral-religious oversight that enforced its own "confession of the flesh." But in the modern context, such regulatory scrutiny has become ever more pervasive and microscopic, albeit under the auspices of new and different authorities. The picture, then, is of one controlling authority replaced by another that is subtler, more organized, more invasive. And far more deceptive. By condemning the past for its repressive excesses while trumpeting its own openness and volubility about sex, modern sexual science institutes a regime of control that is all the more effective for being able to give the appearance of a liberation.

In this way, Foucault's argument in the *History of Sexuality* parallels my discussion of the symptomatic character of the Naturalist treatment of sex that poses as a liberating trend but has quasi-repressive effects of its own. His argument also echoes my contention that these changes have occurred as part of the transition from monarchic power to a new form of social domination that takes sex as a privileged means of effecting control. The two-part title of his final chapter, "Right of Death and Power Over Life," indicates precisely the shift from the autocratic rule of a monarchic sovereign to the decentralized ordering of scientific rationality. It is the traditional threat of the sword to wreak death versus the controlling discourses of modern sexuality that yield the technics of what Foucault calls "bio-power." As Foucault summarizes this point:

> Power would no longer be dealing simply with legal subjects over whom the ultimate dominion was death, but with living beings, and the mastery it would be able to exercise over them would have to be applied at the level of life itself; it was the taking charge of life, more than the threat of death, that gave power its access even to the body.

As Foucault sees it, the hold of authority over the lives of individuals in the modern age has become increasingly related not to the factual link between generations, the blood lines of ancestry, but rather to the ceaseless interrogation of sexuality, an analytic tracing and retracing of the vectors of desire. We have passed, as Foucault puts it, "from a *symbolics of blood* to an *analytics of sexuality*." Here, too, there is a connection with a major point of our previous discussions. The underlying issue concerns the definition of individual identity, the answer to the question of who and what one is. In this way, Foucault's perspective recalls our earlier discussions of modern identity invested in pursuit of the intimate. In the passage into modernity, identity becomes a matter less of the paternity of one's birth than of the pattern of one's desire.

Foucault's claim in the *History of Sexuality* is powerfully argued and has been deservedly influential. I am happy to think that my own argument here converges with it. Nevertheless, Foucault's outlook seems to me to fall short in two respects. The first is that Foucault tends to overstate the case, as if modernity were only to be characterized by the controlling and regulating aspects of the scientific systematization of sex that he calls "the deployment of sexuality." Said otherwise, I suspect that he fails to appreciate what I have been here calling the double-edged, symptomatic character of sex in our time.

It may be true, as Foucault claims, that the modern scientific discourses of sexuality submit the forces of Eros to a kind of domestication, as if sex were a wild vine that has been trellised by scientific rationality and forced to grow along prescribed pathways, always subject to inspection and improvement. But it seems to me at the same time undeniable that, at least in some places, sex has undergone a degree of genuine liberation, particularly during the past century and especially in the last half of that century. I remember hearing this point made very movingly in a radio interview with the poet Stephen Spender not long before his death. Speaking of the terrible scourge of AIDS, Spender went on to remark upon the awful irony, a kind of fateful twist worthy of a truly demonic imagination, that this new plague has arrived in the world at precisely the time when, emerging from under the weight of centuries of suppression, misunderstanding, and persecution, the sexual life of human beings at last appeared to be taking wing, tentatively yet hopefully, into a new sphere of freedom. It is as if, sticking its head out from under the shell of age-old constraints, sex was immediately whacked by the calamity of an ultra-deadly virus. Spender's comments touch upon an essential point that cannot be forgotten, even as we appreciate the impact of the counter-movement described by Foucault: in some very significant respects—qualified and compromised to be sure—sex in the post-Enlightenment period of Western culture *has* undergone a very real degree of liberation.

The truth of the matter is that we must admit both sides of the argument. In fact, we don't face a forced choice between Foucault and Spender. They are both right. And the reason is that the reality of modern sexuality is itself profoundly divided. The situation of sexuality in our time is a story of unprecedented liberation *and* of new and more subtle forms of control and refusal, a situation of greater authenticity *and* greater alienation. Moreover, these opposing tendencies are in many ways consequences of the same changed conditions. In partially wresting sex from the grip of religion, science has unleashed greater freedom of expression and experience yet also produced new effects of constraint and control. It is this two-sided character of our current situation—both expressive and repressive—that I have characterized as the symptomatic dimension of modern sexuality.

My second criticism is that Foucault focuses too exclusively on the *discursive* dimension of modern sexuality. He is surely correct that sex has in the past two centuries been the subject of an immense elaboration of rationalizing discourses—biological, medical, psychiatric, criminal, hygienic, pedagogic—and he is certainly right to ask about the effects of that massive insertion of Eros into a regularizing discourse. But if the question before us concerns the specifically modern meaning of sexuality, the ways in which sex has undergone transformations that belong in essential ways to the conditions of modernity, then we must take account not only of the word but also of the image. For here, too, there has been an enormous revolution. If sexuality has been transformed by its entry into language, equally or even more conspicuous has been its explosion in painting, photography, and film. It is a process that has obviously accelerated dramatically in the second half of the twentieth century but which has deep roots in the early modern period, precisely the period in which painting turned from its traditional subject matter of religious and mythic themes to an ever-intensifying focus on the details of private life. The nude thus emerged for the first time since antiquity as an object of aesthetic interest in its own right, unregulated by placement in a religious or mythic context. Oil painting, the techniques of which were revolutionized in the late Renaissance, was the perfect medium in which to represent the particular luminosity and subtleties of color and depth so characteristic of human skin. "Flesh," as Wilhelm de Kooning aptly remarked, "was the reason why oil painting was invented."

By failing to address the register of the image, Foucault limits the force of his own point. The basic idea of the first volume of his *History of Sexuality*, the notion that modern sexual "liberation" conceals the workings of new and subtle forms of domination, is arguably even more applicable to nonlinguistic representations of sex than to the elaboration of sexuality in discourse. Isn't it above all the burgeoning of sexual *images* that seems to announce a liberation, a revolutionary overturning of the prudishness of the past? And if there is a darker side of this modern sexual liberation, a way in which sex itself becomes a means for establishing new and subtler forms of control, might we not reasonably expect that it is precisely the sphere of sexual imagery, the sphere in which the power to arouse and manipulate desire is greatest, that would offer the most potent resources for those new effects of control?

With this question, we reconnect with our point of departure in Chapter 6 concerning the public *visibility* of sex in the contemporary world. We can now regrasp that point of departure in a new way by asking whether the modern blossoming forth of sexual imagery is symptomatic in the specific sense that we have been giving to that term. Can we discover the double-sided structure of the symptom, at once expressive and repressive, in the modern proliferation of sexual images? Indeed, I think we can. In fact, it is with respect to the imagery of sex in our time that its symptomatic character is most pronounced.

The clue to seeing how resides in Freud's concept of fetishism. The fetish, itself an aspect of desire made *visible*, is among the quintessential expressions of modern sexuality. Fetishism increasingly appears to be the very heartbeat of modern sex.

The Consolation of the Fetish

Freud's analysis of fetishism confronts us once again with a theory that initially sounds pretty outlandish. The fetish, Freud claims, supplies the missing phallus of the mother. Desire for the fetish is motivated by the child's fear of castration. If the mother has been castrated, thinks the child, what is there to prevent my own castration? The presence of the fetish allays that fear. The fetish says, in effect, she is not castrated after all—her phallus is right here!

The first step to understanding Freud's theory of the fetish is to put sufficient emphasis on its purpose of managing anxiety. The fetish functions like a good luck charm, that little something to hold on to in the hope of warding off evil. The rabbit's foot, the lucky horseshoe, and the charm bracelet are essentially nonsexual fetishes. The same could be said for many of the objects of religious ritual and veneration. Prayer stones, rosary beads, crucifixes, and so on function to provide a still point in a swirling universe, a steady and dependable focus that by its very sameness and simplicity reassures the anxious spirit.

We might even risk a note about the Madonna in this connection. If the power of the fetish consists partly in its capacity to console, are we not invited to recognize in the figure of Mary an especially potent religious fetish? Particularly for Christians in the Catholic tradition, the cloaked figure of Mary, itself a vaguely phallic outline, holds out a special hope of deliverance from earthly burdens of care and suffering. It may be too late to prevent some readers from taking offense at this suggestion. Nevertheless, the judgment to be passed from a Freudian perspective remains insistent. Any singling out of a special object or token of luck and protection shares to some degree in the psychology of fetishism. It must be admitted, moreover, the figure of the Virgin Mother offers to that psychology an abundance of symbolic material that is particularly suggestive. If the fetish is essentially a substitute for the missing phallus of the mother, then what better fetish-object than a woman who conceived without contact with a man?

Comparing the fetish to familiar good luck talismans may soften the blow, but Freud's theory of the fetish, like so many of his speculations, will nonetheless strike many readers as farfetched to the point of absurdity. First, there is the near-reflex of general incredulity that attaches to the very notion of the phallus, to say nothing of a maternal phallus. But there is also the familiar weakness that the theory can be less easily applied to little girls than to boys, who presumably have more to fear from the realization that the mother is missing the organ that they so highly prize. Is this asymmetry between the sexes a fatal problem for Freud's approach? On the contrary, at least from one point of view, it is an advantage. By tracing the origin of fetishism to fears of castration, Freud's account makes some sense of the clinical fact that fetishism is far more prevalent among men than among women. Sexual fetishism, it appears, is pretty much a male thing. Any successful theory of fetishism must recognize this gender-typed difference and include some important distinction between masculine and feminine psychology in relation to fetishism.

Freud's theory also provides a clever account of some of the most common choices of fetish objects. Freud links them to the way in which the roving eye, approaching the site of the maternal phallus, is arrested just short of the fearful revelation of its absence. Fetishistic interest becomes fixated upon what it finds there. Thus Freud remarks that "fur and velvet—as has long been suspected—are a fixation of the sight of the pubic hair, which should have been followed by the longed-for sight of the female member; pieces of underclothing, which are so often chosen as a fetish, crystallize the moment of undressing, the last moment in which the woman could still be regarded as phallic."

In like fashion, women's legs or feet may become fetishized, along with the lingerie or shoes that adorn them. In effect, the fetishist seizes upon these objects as substitutes for what is missing further up the female body. Following this line of explanation, we can understand why thigh-high stockings, with their garter belts and other frilly attachments, tend to be recognized by many people as sexier than knee socks (thigh-highs form a virtual uniform for the streetwalker or the porn star). Knee-highs actually bare more leg and thigh. So why are they so much less exciting? The erotic tension is heightened by high stockings because their lacy upper edge delivers the viewer so much closer to the brink of the vaguely distressing spectacle of the missing phallus. The result is an unconscious thrill a little like the anxious excitement of stepping to the edge of a sheer cliff. Arriving at the delicate underclothes that mark the perimeter of the genital area functions as an erotic stimulant, we can say, because it serves to emphasize sexual difference.

Freud's theory of the fetish receives a further, if indirect, confirmation if we return for a moment to the spectacularly phallic culture of ancient Greece. Among the most striking features of the Greek civilization at the zenith of its development was the erotic cult of the beautiful boy. The art and literature of the ancient world provide ample testimony to the power of this object of erotic phantasy. Greek homosexuality found in the figure of the barely pubescent boy an electrifying stimulant. Plato and others record the frequency with which many a grown man was reduced to a lovesick fool under the spell of a pretty boy. In the right circumstances, a comely boy could spoil the self-control of even the most restrained character. Greek sculpture immortalized his magnificent allure in the *kouroi* statues of the archaic period and even more sublimely during the Golden Age in the naked boys sculpted by Phidias and Praxiteles.

Viewed in the context of Greek culture as a whole, the figure of the boy readily appears as a fetish object, not only for the way in which it presents to male desire an object of such incandescent attractiveness, but also, as Freud defines the general principle of fetishism, for the way that the craze for boys can be understood in relation to Greek attitudes toward women. Love of boys was a perfect counterpart to the very conspicuous Greek fear and hatred of the feminine. Greek myth, literature, and philosophy provide ample evidence of a profound mistrust of women. From Pandora and the Sirens to Helen and Medea, Greek women were held to be the ruination of men. In relation to that mistrust, the eroticized boy appears as a kind of antidote to the anxious tension surrounding everything womanly. The boy represented a welcome redirection of sexual interest toward an object that conveniently sidestepped the dangerous specter of the feminine.

The specifically Freudian character of the fetishized Greek boy becomes even clearer in the light of a second consideration: the way in which the figure of the boy comes as close as possible to the feminine while retaining the crucial thing that distinguishes male from female. While Greek homosexuality was by no means confined to the cult of boys, the erotic mania for the boy was strictly limited by a crucial condition: the appearance of facial hair. What triggered the most intense erotic charge was the virginal hairlessness of the preadolescent boy. With the sprouting of manly body hair, the spell cast by the boy's physique was significantly deflated. What other conclusion can be drawn from this very specific requirement, but that the boy's allure was a function of his *androgyny*? The comely boy was almost a woman, but not quite. Like the fetish object in Freud's theory, which draws its fascination from its position on the very edge of sex difference, the way it is located at the moment just before the woman is recognized to lack the phallus, the Greek boy exerted an erotic power that derived from his occupying a place on the slimmest dividing line between the masculine and the feminine.

In the second chapter, we had occasion to remark upon the vaginal "spread shot" that virtually defines a whole genre of pornographic images. We noted how, from a psychoanalytic standpoint, the spread shot derives its special power not from the way that it "bares all," but, quite the opposite, from the way in which it leaves something perpetually unshown, something still to be discovered. It is this evocation of something as-yet-to-be-seen that continually feeds the restless drive to view yet another image, and another, and so on. We can now draw upon the Freudian theory of the fetish to specify what exactly this unseen "something more" might be. It is nothing other than the phallus. The logic of Freud's view forces us to suppose that the real object of this sort of pornography is precisely what is not shown: the phallus. On the level of the unconscious, what the open vulva of the vaginal spread shot really evokes is the male member that will fill it.

I can imagine that this conclusion might raise in some readers a new wave of disbelief. Yet before rejecting the idea out of hand, consider how it makes sense of some of the primary features of mainstream heterosexual pornography. It implies, for example, that the greatest satisfaction of straight porn derives less from any mere display of female anatomy than from the way in which that display flatters the viewer's feeling of masculine potency. Among the men who are its primary consumers, pornography serves to bolster a reassuring sense of "having what it takes." Is it not for this reason that the women depicted by pornography typically appear in a state of wanton desire? By presenting a woman who very obviously "wants it," and wants it from any and all men whose gaze she attracts, pornography invites the viewer to imagine that it is he (the only one around at the moment) who will satisfy her. If she lies back on silky sheets, it is to beckon him to fall into her arms. If she teasingly presents her backside, it is to solicit him to mount her. It is along the same lines that we can interpret that other staple of the pornographic photo-layout in which the model throws her head back in ecstatic swoon, her eyes closed and her lipstick-besmeared mouth yawning open in breathless abandon. How can this effect of pleasure-swoon fail to evoke its unseen cause? In all of these ways, pornography stimulates male desire by means of stroking the masculine ego. Said otherwise, porn is typically less about the women it parades for the viewer than about the phallus they crave to be given by him. Pornography is a magical mirror in which the male viewer sees reflected an ideal image of his own phallic power.

I realize, of course, that the varieties of pornography are legion and my comments here are by no means relevant to all of it. I'm most concerned here with the form of mass-market heterosexual porn known as the "girlie magazine." While it occupies only a particular niche in larger market, it is all the same the most visible and widely accepted form of pornography. The basic approach I've taken seems confirmed by that moment of its history when the vaginal spread shot first burst on the scene. Throughout the 1960s and into the 1970s, the twin flagships of soft-core porn, *Playboy* and *Penthouse*, discreetly avoided any such flagrant display of genitalia. It fell to Larry Flynt's *Hustler* magazine to break the barrier and, having done so, the brazenly opened vulva (made visible not just by the legs spread apart but by being pulled open with the fingers) immediately became the hallmark of the *Hustler* style.

The interesting thing is that *Hustler* simultaneously became powerfully identified as the working man's magazine. Moreover, it did so at a time—the mid-1970s—when high inflation and shrinking numbers of skilled jobs left blue-collar American males particularly hard-pressed. It was a certain form of class appeal that the editors of *Hustler* gleefully exploited, going out of their way to mock the hoity-toity *Playboy* mansion, populated by buxom bunnies serving martinis to upper-crust types in tuxedos and smoking jackets. For this project of deflating high-class pretension, the vaginal spread shot was a perfect weapon. It appeared to tear aside the veils of stuffy, upper-class hypocrisy and give real men what they were really looking for. But it also did something else. From the psychoanalytic viewpoint we have adopted, the "wide open beaver shot" enabled *Hustler* readers simultaneously to thumb their noses at the stuffed shirts who read *Playboy* and to allay their anxieties about a deeper sense of masculine potency. The women of *Hustler* not only stripped for the working man but pulled themselves agape as if to show him the size of the tool with which he would thrill them. Once again, the vaginal spread shot is less about the feminine anatomy that it lays open to view than it is about the phallic pride of the man before whom it is displayed.

But perhaps there is a last objection to be lodged against the perspective I have adopted, an objection that takes note of the fact that *Hustler* and other magazines like it increasingly feature layouts in which women are paired with men in a state of full erection. How are these images of couples to be squared with my thesis that the pornographic images of solitary women prop up the male viewer's sense of masculine prerogative by subliminally evoking the missing phallus? It is not difficult to imagine an answer when we notice the worshipful attitude in which the women are typically posed. The viewer is invited to identify with the man who is adoringly serviced by these women. On their knees before their partner's engorged member, reverently clasping it in their hands, or poised on the verge of taking it in their mouths, the women of these sex scenarios demonstrate even more decisively than their solo counterparts that they exist for the sake of gratifying men's desire and of buttressing their masculine confidence. Alone or in tandem with a partner, the women of the porn world are routinely enlisted in a project of masculine promotion.

Lonely Bliss

So far we have followed the clue of Freud's classical theory of the fetish. Can we now enlarge the question of fetishism to address a broader field of problems?

We can indeed, if we turn again to the angle of view adopted by Jacques Lacan. Just as Lacan extends the notion of castration anxiety beyond the little boy's fear of a particular dismemberment in the direction of a much more general fear of loss,[1] a Lacanian perspective also enables us to recognize a more global function of fetishism. For Lacan, the fetish is not merely a means to relieve fear of castration by providing a substitute for the missing maternal phallus. The reason is that castration is not merely a matter of losing the penis. As Lacan thinks of it, castration is a specific phantasy that represents a much more encompassing possibility of loss. The consoling power of the fetish thus derives from its capacity to hide from the subject its own sense of lack. The fetish is an attempt to sandbag the overflow of anxiety. It defends the subject from an overwhelming loss of control. We have already glimpsed this point in comparing the fetish to the good luck charm. It now remains to understand more specifically what is at stake.

The key point for Lacan—his way of acknowledging the correctness of Freud's intuition that the fetish is related to the child's anxiety about the mother's body—is that fetishism cannot be understood apart from the human

[1]For this point, see the section on "The Prime Cut" in Chapter 2.

being's relations to other people. By means of his magical object, the fetishist conceals from himself his dependence on others. Clinging to the beloved fetish enables him to imagine that it is only *this little object* that he desires. The other person becomes a mere add-on, part of the staging that enhances the allure of the fetish itself.

This view is well illustrated by the example of the Greek boy. If the mania for boys represented a fetishistic escape from the Hellenic fear and distrust of the feminine, the underlying problem was that dependence on women could not be altogether avoided. What was feared and hated was that very dependence itself. Against the background of that detestable bond to the feminine, the sexual aura of the beautiful boy served to focus a dream of masculine autonomy and independence. The boy became the erotic linchpin for an exclusively male circle of society.

This strategy of substitution was not without its paradoxes. In effect, one form of slavery (desire for the mother/woman) was replaced by another (in which the grown man turns his adoration toward the comely boy). But the love of boys mitigated the risks of erotic passion by anchoring it securely within the sphere of things male and masculine. How fitting, then, that the primary danger posed by the sexual fascination of the boy was recognized to be that of losing one's manly self-control. As the famous discussion in Plato's *Symposium* shows, the refined ethic governing the love of boys stressed above all the necessity of maintaining restraint and decorum. While a taste for boys is surely understandable, Pausanias explains, the man who makes a fool of himself in his craving for a boy creates a shameful and pathetic spectacle. For his older male lover, the beautiful Greek boy radiated a dazzling power of attraction, compelling enough to conceal men's troubling dependence on women. In this way, the boy fulfilled the basic function of the fetish object, that of creating an illusion of autonomy and self-sufficiency.

A similar point can be made with respect to the companion theme of the last section, the dynamics of the pornographic imagination. We need only to remind ourselves that the prime use of pornography is its role as a stimulant for masturbation. Most pornography functions to provide sex minus another person. From a psychoanalytic point of view, this bypassing of the living, breathing other is no mere effect of convenience, as if one has sex with a magazine or a video merely because at the moment there isn't anyone else around. On the contrary, one turns to pornography precisely to avoid the other. Porn helps realize the dream of being entirely self-contained.

It is a dream that is perfectly achieved in the video booth of the adult bookstore or sex shop. Here the viewer enters his own tiny room, a darkened, completely autonomous cell, in which a parade of erotic images will fire his imagination but no actually present human being need ever disturb his private satisfactions. In the video-porn peep booth, the sexual voyeur is not so much looking *through* the keyhole as he is completely *inside* the keyhole, looking out at the entire sexual world. He enjoys the image of others but is completely exempt from their reality. Pornography thus severs the tie that binds us to dependency on the other and thereby allows us to cheat the innermost longing of Eros for ecstatic fusion with another being. Porn is sex without the possibility of rejection. The masturbatory consumer of pornography is a solitary monarch who rules over an empty kingdom.

We can summarize these points in a terse formula: In pornography, sex itself is fetishized. To a greater or lesser degree, all pornography disembeds the sexual act from the larger context of everyday human lives and presents it as an isolated and free-floating event. The camera's field of view is drawn in tightly to focus on mere body parts—breasts, buttocks, belly, genitalia. The press of erotic urgency reduces awareness of time to an absorption in the moment. In all of these ways, pornography shares the essential structure of fetishism, the purpose of which, as Freud observed, is to restrict the field of awareness and suspend an anxiously awaited future.

It is for this reason—or at least most deeply for this reason—that pornography is so conspicuously lacking in plot. In porn videos, as well as in those tell-all "readers' letters" featured by magazines such as *Penthouse*, sex tends to happen suddenly and unexpectedly between people with little or no connection with each other—the bored housewife couples with the lawn boy, the junior executive gropes the cleaning lady after hours, and so on. Pornography continually dreams of sex that has been purified of every encumbering connection to practical concerns of everyday life. It dreams of what Erica Jong famously dubbed "the zipless fuck," an utterly spontaneous sexual coupling as might happen, according to Jong's description of it, between two complete strangers on a train who fall, wordlessly and breathlessly, into one another's arms.

> The zipless fuck was more than a fuck. It was a platonic ideal. Zipless because when you came together zippers fell away like rose petals, underwear blew off in one breath like dandelion fluff. Tongues intertwined and turned liquid. Your whole soul flowed out through your tongue and into the mouth of your lover.
>
> For the true, ultimate zipless A-1 fuck, it was necessary that you never get to know the man very well. I had noticed, for example, how all my infatuations dissolved as soon as I really became friends with a man, became sympathetic to his problems, listened to him kvetch about his wife, or ex-wives, his mother, his children. After that I would like him, perhaps even love him—but without passion. And it was passion that I wanted.
>
> ... another condition for the zipless fuck was brevity. And anonymity made it even better.

The sex act depicted by pornography is not really an "act" at all, if by a genuine act we mean conduct that emerges from a web of intentions rooted more or less globally in one's real-life situation. By this definition, porn sex is not genuinely enacted. It merely happens. Like the lovers in Erica Jong's zipless fuck, porn sex is routinely portrayed as a kind of swoon in which the participants feel themselves suddenly overwhelmed by sex the way a wearied swimmer is sucked out to sea by a riptide. Of course, this sense of being passively overcome is essential to the most intensely erotic experience. It is why we compare love to falling or to being swept away. It is why we call love a "passion." But it is worth noting how often suddenness and anonymity become for pornography the sole, defining features of sexual experience. And it is these aspects of disconnectedness (from time, from space, from other people—even, in anonymity, from the partner) that gives pornographic sex its fetishistic character. With the accent on this lack of connection and relationship, the zipless fuck, far from having the character of an act, is more like an object. It is a phantasy object in contemplation of which the ties that bind ongoing human relationships are dissolved. In the zipless fuck, the sex act has itself become a fetish.

The point of this analysis should not be mistaken for a new form of moralizing about the evils of pornography. There may be some delicious and very primitive attraction to erotic anonymity, and therefore something quasi-fetishistic and pornographic, that lies at the very heart of the sexual impulse in the human being. I wouldn't be surprised that there is. My interest here is rather in highlighting the structure of interpersonal relationship—or lack of it—that underlies the fetishistic attitude, and I do so in order to clarify the meaning of Freud's theory of the fetish as an attempt to supply the missing maternal phallus. For the mother to remain phallic means that the third point of the Oedipal triangle, the position occupied by the father, is cut out of the picture. By means of that occlusion, the fetishist succeeds in concealing the open-ended character of human desire, the way in which desire may move along a succession of objects. The fetishist seeks to remove the contingency of desire, the dependence of his longings on factors beyond his control. Fetishism is the dream of becoming master of desire by virtue of possessing a sort of magic key with which satisfaction can be achieved at will.

Defined in this way, the psychological function of the fetish can be recognized in its relation to modern individualism. The dream of modernity, the dream of the free and sovereign individual fully in control of his or her satisfaction, is perfectly realized in the fetish. It is no accident, then, that fetishism makes a special appearance in Marx's analysis of capitalist economy. It is a linkage that we are now better equipped to appreciate.

Shop 'Til You Drop

Though developed by Marx in a relatively brief passage of his monumental work, *Capital*, the notion of commodity fetishism has had a long and significant career among Marxist critics of capitalist economy and bourgeois culture. The basic idea is that commodities become placeholders of value that far exceeds their practical worth. The exotic flowers of the seventeenth-century Dutch tulip craze is a good case in point. Caught up in a speculative fever that had as much to do with social status and prestige as with investment value, frenzied enthusiasts would bid the equivalent of a working man's annual wages for a single flower bulb. As fetishized commodities, tulips became an extreme example of what we now call "status symbols."

In the postmodern, media-driven culture of the "new world order," Marx's idea is more relevant than ever. It concerns the way in which the commodities of the contemporary marketplace take on a particular aura of desirability, a kind of quasi-mystical halo, derived from the way that they *do not* appear to be products of human labor. In this way, manufactured goods appear to violate the basic law of value as Marx defines it: rather than owing their worth to the quantity of labor that went into them, fetishized commodities seem to be valuable in and of themselves, as if they had fallen from heaven.

Advertising often seeks to heighten this appearance of magical, almost otherworldly value. Indeed, if the lust for commodities is a kind of fetishism, then advertising deserves to be called the pornography of commodities. Think, for example, of those ads for cars in which the latest model is posed atop a rotating pedestal, photographed against a neutrally textured backdrop, or made to appear as if it were floating on a shimmering surface of water. The mirror-like automobile finish, perhaps accentuated by rolling a silvery ball bearing along the joints of the door panels and hood, only serves to underscore a fetishizing effect. The result is an epiphany of uncanny fascination. Far from appearing as if they are the work of human hands (belonging to real-life people who struggle to make ends meet on the wages they are paid for their labor), these magical objects seem to belong to another realm altogether. Such is exactly the impression that advertisers want to create. Automobile advertisers make cars appear as if they were magically dropped from another world because the underlying message is always about how you, the potential owner, will be utterly transformed, virtually transported to that other world, if only you would buy one.

The example of the car perfectly illustrates the primary purpose of the fetishized commodity. In our society, the car is the most popular and most highly valued big-ticket commodity fetish, and the reason becomes perfectly clear in the light of the foregoing discussion. Cars are privileged objects of desire, perhaps the most compellingly desirable objects in the ever-burgeoning theater of consumption that surrounds us. But their desirability stems in large part from the way in which the car liberates us from others. The car is a second skin, a mobile image-unit of ourselves, in which we are separated from other people and able to move independently of them. As such, the car is a perfect embodiment of the fetish-object that helps establish an illusion of disconnection and autonomy. The automobile, as its very name suggests, is the greatest-ever incarnation of the dream of self-sufficiency. It is the twentieth-century realization of Aristotle's definition of god as self-moved mover, now made available to every denizen of industrial society. The car objectifies for every driver the American ideal of rugged individualism. It is a steel-rubber-and-glass Declaration of Independence. The car is thus not only an object of desire but also a staging of identity, a means by which we seek to signal our boundaries to others, a primary source of confirmation of who and what we are.

The current craze for sport utility vehicles only amplifies these points. Of course, a considerable part of the appeal of SUVs is bound up with a wish to escape the hectic crush of traffic, as if the very possibility of dropping it into four-wheel drive and going off-road were a partial antidote to the maddening sense of helplessness inflicted upon us by the grind of the daily commute. (Never mind that only a tiny fraction of SUV owners ever drive them across the rugged landscapes in which advertisers display them.) There is also the way in which the SUV appeals to baby boomers who spent their rebellious youth bucking the establishment. For them, the idea of toting the family about town in a station wagon or a minivan comes dangerously close to re-creating the dreaded image of their parents' lifestyle. Behind the wheel of a rough-and-ready SUV, millions of now successful thirty- and forty-somethings can pretend that they are still bushwhacking their own path in life in spite of the fact that they have become just as firmly establishment as their parents ever were.

Notwithstanding these other source of appeal, one of the most potent satisfactions promised by an SUV lies in the defensive and even aggressive statement it implicitly makes to other drivers. Not so much outdoorsy as simply outsized, less nature-loving than muscle-flexing, the real selling point of most SUVs is their assertive heft and bulk. A Honda ad touts its latest model as "King of the Concrete Jungle." Lexus poses its SUV on a suburban driveway—everyone else on the block has an armored tank parked out front, but Lexus stills claims an advantage. Ford's colossal Excursion (bigger even than the Explorer or the Expedition) is so absurdly oversized as to need little hyperbolic advertising; its imposing, road-hogging enormity speaks for itself. Even the much more modestly-sized Subaru Outback has been sold as the perfect defense for a threatening world. In one series of ads, the Outback is piloted by Paul Hogan (aka "Crocodile Dundee") and is seen nimbly outpacing a pack of mayhem-minded, wild-west desperados.

For the SUV to have risen to its current status as the king of all car fetishes is deeply appropriate in the sense that SUVs have been designed and marketed to achieve the psychological goal of all fetishes: that keeping at a distance the other person upon whom I might otherwise depend. An advertisement for the

HumVee, larger and more imposing even than the Ford Excursion, the vehicle of choice for invaders of Iraq, makes this theme brutally clear. Implying a damning comparison with its wimpier competitors, one HumVee ad warns, "Don't take a knife to a gun fight."

Freudian theory, with its otherwise improbable reference to the missing maternal phallus, helps us to enlarge and enhance the commonplace understanding of commodities as "status symbols," as it allows us to recognize in commodity hunger the fetishistic project of self-sufficient autonomy. The primary aim of this form of fetishism has been very usefully described by John Berger as the pursuit of glamour.[2] Fetishized commodities make their owner appear glamorous. A svelte Polo jacket, stylish Ray-Ban sunglasses, a pair of Gucci shoes, and a sleek BMW coupe—an ensemble of high-fashion commodities creates an alluring aura of glamour. But as Berger rightly points out, the inner secret of glamour, its real essence, is the way in which it incites the envy of others. The glamour seeker wants to be the object of other people's covetousness. Berger's point fits neatly with the main thrust of the preceding pages: Glamour achieves the fetishists' dream of assuring a separation from other people, or better, of simultaneously attracting their attention while refusing all connection with them. Glamour works the trick of constantly announcing itself to others while denying that it has the slightest interest in them. Confronted with the glamorous person, other people are reduced to an envying audience. Glamour is thus intimately bound up with the psychological dynamics of fetishism. Indeed, glamour is nothing but the social effect of a certain kind of public fetishism.

To the extent that commodity fetishism is a quest for glamour and glamour is based on the incitement of social envy, we suddenly realize that our discussion of fetishism has returned us to penis envy. The envy of glamour is ultimately yet another form of penis envy. The key point throughout our earlier discussions of penis envy (see pp. 50–55) was to see that what is really at stake in the unconscious symbolism of the phallus is much less the male organ than the lure of desirability in general. By means of the Freudian theory of the fetish, the link between them is made palpable. Freud allows us to see how our longing for objects is to be traced back to the emotional system of the family and to a need for love that has come to grief.

To which we can add a final note that helps to complete the linkage between Freud and Marx. The core of Marx's critique of capitalist economy can be traced to two basic propositions: (1) that all increase of value is ultimately rooted in the expenditure of labor and (2) that disproportionate accumulation of wealth by one individual (the capitalist) is derived from siphoning off the value created by someone else's labor (the worker). The most basic function of commodity fetishism is to conceal the truth of both of these

[2]I refer here to Berger's copiously illustrated and insightful little book, companion to a BBC miniseries by the same name, *Ways of Seeing*.

propositions. To the extent that they appear to be magical objects that carry their value wholly within themselves, unrelated to a network of labor that produced them, commodities ground the illusion that the enviable wealth, power, and status of their owners is equally *sui generis.* Ownership of certain highly fetishized commodities therefore presents a paradox that is essential to the maintenance of capitalism: The commodity serves to conceal the labor that brought the commodity into being and also conceals the source of wealth that made acquisition of the commodity possible in the first place. Put in the most general terms: The fetishism of commodities continually generates a misrecognition of social relations. The commodity fetish therefore accomplishes a social task that is perfectly parallel in structure to that of the psychological function of the sexual fetish: both serve to conceal key aspects of the dependence of one person upon another.

In illustration of this point, consider the example of the diamond wedding ring, a conspicuous instance of value that is as utterly useless as it is highly prized. Intended to symbolize the enormity of a man's love for his bride, the proud wife's massive diamond also broadcasts to her envious friends a sure signal of her husband's financial prowess. A moment's reflection might well reveal a painful paradox: The bigger the diamond, the more likely it is that the wife who flaunts it is in fact dependent on a man. But this hint of dependence is concealed behind the mesmerizing sparkle of a really dazzling rock. Or perhaps we should say that this dependence on a man is not so much simply concealed as it is transformed into something positive, a measure not of her dependence on him but of his adoration for her. Yet this is not the only way in which the wedding ring accomplishes the little miracle of all commodity fetishes—that of allowing us to misrecognize the reality of social relations. As in the case of so many fetishized commodities, the allure of the diamond ring depends on our remaining oblivious to the labor power that produced it. Once again, it renders invisible the dependence of one person or class of persons on another. Imagine a gaggle of breathless admirers, ooohing and aaahing over a friend's engagement ring in a thrall of diamond envy. This swell of enthusiasm might be sadly deflated were the circle of friends reminded that gold and diamond mining remain among the world's most viciously oppressive slave industries.

The Triumph of Sexiness

Let us venture a final series of remarks about the role of fetishism in contemporary life. I earlier made the suggestion that in pornography sex itself is fetishized. This notion obviously has something a little strange about it inasmuch as fetishes are usually thought to be something like tools or instruments of sex. One has sex with the help of a fetish. In the extreme, the fetish becomes itself the object of sexual arousal and satisfaction. In either case, the fetish serves the interest of having sex. What, then, can it mean that sex itself is fetishized? In the service of what can sex be a fetish?

To answer we need only to regrasp the meaning of the fetish as mediating the relation with the Other. That sex itself becomes objectified as a fetish means that sex in some measure loses its character as a mode of intimacy with the other and is redeployed as the very opposite: a mode of distancing oneself from real intimacy and controlling it. Sex becomes a strategy of being in the presence of the other, but exempt from real connection. In fact, we approached this point much earlier, in the concluding discussion of Chapter 3 (see pp. 83–88). It is now possible to specify the point with reference to a prominent phenomenon of our age, one with which every citizen of our media-driven society is familiar, though perhaps without ever having thought much about it. I have in mind the phenomenon of "sexiness."

By "sexiness" I mean something very particular, though very ubiquitous. Sexiness is the distinctive effect generated by a certain class of images, above all advertising images, whose power derives from their palpably erotic charge. Thumbing through the pages of any high-class glossy magazine—*Vogue, Cosmopolitan, GQ, Vanity Fair*—will readily yield no shortage of examples. The sexy image has even made some limited inroads in the pages of the (up to now) notoriously stodgy *New Yorker*. As one might expect, sexiness appears most abundantly in ads for high-fashion clothing, cosmetics, perfumes, and jewelry—Prada, Dior, Ralph Lauren, Calvin Klein, Armani, and so on. Yet it is also clearly present in ads for a host of other products less directly associated with the body and its adornment, even ads for completely inanimate objects, everything from cars to cruises, luggage to liquor. In some cases, an unmistakable tincture of sexiness can be powerfully evoked even in the absence of a model. Sexiness is an ambient atmosphere; less an object than mode of illumination of objects, less a specific content than a stylized presentation of content.

It is not easy to say exactly what features constitute the sexy. No doubt the markers of sexiness are sensitive to subtle variations in cultural microclimates. Its defining attributes vary somewhat from decade to decade. Still, there are a few readily predictable characteristics. Penetrating eye contact is probably the most typical property of sexiness, though it is by no means a requirement. Particular manipulations of posture, gesture, or expression are also standard means of pumping up a sense of the sexy; indeed, many of the traits by which we recognize the sexy are highly stereotypical. A seated or lounging woman with legs slightly apart is a stock trope, as are open lips, head and hair thrown languidly back, or slightly downcast, sidelong glances. For female models, the prime object-stimuli of the sexy, copious quantities of makeup are a near necessity. Particular lighting is also a hallmark, often to the end of creating the most dramatic effects less with highlight than with shadow. All of which indicates that the image-language of sexiness that now surrounds us has absorbed and reprocessed the vocabulary of glamour photography pioneered in the first half of the twentieth century.

More important than any specific content, however, are the general forms and functions of sexiness. A number of nearly universal aspects can be discerned. Immediately striking, beyond one or another suggestion of seductiveness, is a sense of *provocation.* Most often communicated by a model's gaze and bearing, a provocative note can also be generated by objects or situations, especially those that intimate risk or danger. In one way or another, the tableau of the sexy is calculated to produce a kind of micro-shock; it confronts the viewer with a vague but palpable sense of something physically or morally jarring. The sexy needs a certain grittiness. It is intrinsically edgy. But provocation alone is not enough to produce sexiness. What is needed is a hint of provocation in the midst of luxury. The sexy is thus produced most readily when a situation defined by conspicuous comfort (sumptuous materials, fine furnishings, rare and exotic objects) is set on edge by some detail that challenges or even violates the serenity of luxury. The result is a sense of charming transgression, something slightly dangerous that disturbs a relaxed security, something sassy and devil-may-care amid reposed elegance.

Said otherwise: Sexiness is generally enhanced by an intimation of conflict. It therefore very typically plays on the communication of mixed messages. Especially successful are carefully orchestrated collisions between innocence and sultriness, decorum and naughtiness, public propriety and private pleasures. In an advertisement for lingerie, a conspicuously young girl is surrounded by grade school trappings, yet gazes out at us over an outsized bloom of incandescent lip gloss. In a perfume ad, a gorgeously delicate neck and throat, stretching like a field of snow from the ruby lips above to the hint of cleavage below, is draped about, necklace-like, by an exotic snake. The erotic voltage is heightened by such contradictions.

But we now come to the crucial point: Perhaps the mixed message most essential to the phenomenology of the sexy image, the axis of the most significant conflict, is that between sexiness and sex itself. Although an erotic prospect appears to be the central preoccupation of sexiness, although erotic electricity is its essential element, the sexual involvement of the viewer remains strangely suspended. It is this suspension of the erotic charge, as if a quantity of lascivious energy is generated but then curiously held in reserve, that distinguishes the image of sexiness from pornography. It is as if the trajectory of desire, once initiated by sexiness, is then oddly abandoned. Sexiness continually presents a sexual come-on that fails to materialize.

It would be interesting to make a systematic study of the precise means by which this effect of erotic suspension is achieved. The means are themselves frequently traces of conflict or tension. The captivating gaze of an alluring model often appears to communicate an arresting challenge: not just "Come on, baby" but "Come on … I dare you." Objects and bodies presented in the magic sphere of the sexy, photographed with an almost hallucinogenic clarity, are often startlingly lucid, hyper-saturated with color and highlights, yet with the strange result that the viewer finds those very objects and bodies even more distant and untouchable. The figure of a woman lounging languidly before us seems almost impossibly relaxed and confident, so much so that the viewer is oddly discomforted and put on edge. In these and a thousand other ways, the imagery of sexiness succeeds in producing a curious push–pull or rip-saw effect reminiscent of the essential gesture of the hysteric. A sexual message is being simultaneously extended and retracted. Sexiness continually gets us going and leaves us hanging.

This effect of erotic incitement–suspension produced by the sexy perfectly embodies the symptomatic character of sexuality in the modern period that I have been at pains to describe. Sexiness both is and is not something sexual. Like the boorish dinner companion who continually drops the name of a famous friend, sexiness perpetually refers to sex yet never produces it. Indeed, the enduring effect is that sexiness can seem virtually repressive of real sexual arousal. In the sexy, the actually erotic dimension drops out, leaving only a strangely alluring husk, a bewitching sheen that is, quite literally, only skin deep.

Is it not for precisely this reason that sexiness sells? The subtle dialectic of incitement and suspension that we here discern in the sexy, its dynamic of erotic seduction and reduction, is marvelously suited to the underlying intention of all advertising: that of awakening a force of desire that can be reassigned to a range of objects. In sexiness, the voltage is ratcheted up, then deprived of the circuit most ready to hand. Inevitably, a spark will jump the gap in the direction of the next closest object—precisely the object being sold by the ad. Sexiness is the original bait-and-switch technique. To make the same point from another angle: It would be almost impossible to use pornography to peddle consumer goods. Unlike the titillating power of sexiness that divides the sexy from the truly sexual, pornography is pure sexual stimulus. The only thing peddled by pornography is more of itself.

Against the background of these considerations, we can now add a final point that will allow us to gather and integrate everything we've said: the emotional tone of sexiness is frequently tinged with a distinct hint of aggressiveness. The erotic allure of the sexy, we might say, is rarely offered to the viewer for free. On the contrary, sexiness very typically communicates a distinct note of challenge and confrontation. It is as if the implicit invitation extended to the viewer by sexiness is accompanied by a certain throwing down of the gauntlet. Experiment for yourself. Collect a few examples of Madison Avenue sexiness from your favorite glossy magazines and look into the eyes of the models who stare out at you. In many instances, only a slight shift in perspective is needed to recognize that the intensity of these gazes communicates something more than erotic fascination. The eyes also broadcast a vague but discernible note of defiance or hostility. The message is no mere "Come on," nor even "Come on ... I dare you," but more something like "Come on ... I know I intimidate you (and I enjoy it)." The emotional impact of sexiness, far from being compromised by an undercurrent of aggression, seems only to be enhanced by it.

In this hint of the aggressive, the advertising image of sexiness again shows its distance from pornography. The pornographic image offers an erotic smorgasbord to the viewer's delectation. When porn indulges in aggression (actually such instances are a good deal less prevalent in pornography than many people suppose) the exercise of threat or force is generally situated between the actors. By contrast, advertising sexiness deliberately aims its aggressiveness at the viewer.

Now, it is crucial to avoid a misunderstanding at this point. This dimension of aggressive tension, far from being obvious and overt, is generally very subtle and measured. The objective is to create in the viewer a barely palpable sense of unease that doesn't rise to the level that would trigger real defensiveness. The level and kind of aggression involved in the sexy are those required by the posture of being "cool." Sexiness is an eroticized form of ultra-cool. In fact, maintaining an attitude of cool generally means that direct or over-obvious aggressiveness has to be avoided, if only because engaging the viewer too directly is to abandon the preferred position of the sexy, that of supreme indifference and self-sufficiency. It is for this reason that the aggressive tonality of sexiness is very often limited to conveying a sense of elitism. The image of sexiness doesn't hesitate to communicate to the viewer that "what you see here—it's definitely not you!" Even in those instances in which models don't assume a direct and insouciant look at the viewer, therefore, instances in which a languid gaze is cast off to the side or the eyes are closed altogether, the image of advertising sexiness typically implies a clear sense of exclusiveness. While not directly aggressive or confrontational, the viewer's sense is that of looking through a window upon another world—that world of provocative luxury—in which the viewer is not (at least not yet) included.

At first glance, it's hard to imagine how the aggressive undertone that so frequently saturates the image of sexiness can serve the interests of advertising. Can we be threatened into buying things? What's the function of this aggressive subtext? We have already begun to sketch the solution to this little riddle and can present it in two interrelated points. The first returns us to the theme of envy. Sexiness is very typically calculated to incite envy and a subtle hint of aggressiveness only intensifies the effect. The in-your-face character of sexiness is fully intended to induce social rivalry. What better means could be imagined if the larger purpose of sexiness is that of turning up the pressure to buy something? The aggressive manipulation of envy creates a problem for which buying something—new clothes, new perfumes, new cars, new anything—becomes the solution.

The second point serves to integrate the main themes of the preceding discussion. One of the most characteristic features of the sexy, we've said, is the way in which it succeeds in splitting off an image of sexiness from any actual sexual arousal. Said otherwise, sexiness divorces sex from intimacy. It is this feature that links sexiness most clearly to the dynamics of fetishism, inasmuch as the underlying function of the fetish is to drive a wedge into the heart of the relation between self and other. Fetishism manages the threat of intimacy by means of an intervening object that puts the other at a distance. But in that case, a measured prospect of threat or aggression is the perfect expedient of the fetishistic effect. Indeed, from this angle of view, we glimpse the deep affinity between fetishism and sadism. We also see more readily the main conclusion to be drawn about the true nature of the sexy. Sexiness is less about sex than it is about power. Rather than creating and enhancing intimacy, the sexy tends to create distance and differentials of power.

Sexiness is essentially a fantasy of power. No wonder, then, that sexiness becomes so readily bound up with class distinction. The provocative luxury of the sexy becomes the perfect marker of what separates the upper crust from the lower classes. To appreciate the full measure of its power, however, we need to take full account of the erotic dimension. Sexiness is the perfect weapon of class warfare, a kind of stealth bomber of social status, because it depicts class distinction in a way that is difficult for lower-class people to recognize or mobilize against. Indeed, even the bottom rungs of the social ladder are powerfully susceptible to its appeal. Why? Precisely because the siren song of sexiness is articulated in the register of sexual allure, a register in which virtually everyone is participant. Sexiness is thus deeply mystifying. It is fundamentally about power and property but presents itself as a matter of physical attraction. Somewhat ironically, what makes the advertising appeal of sexiness so confusing is the way in which it restores the fetishism of commodities to the sexual sphere in which all fetishism has its roots.

This brief reference to the class relevance of sexiness brings to mind a final question about its potency as a political factor. How far can we trace the influence of this particularly powerful form of seductive manipulation? What role does it now play in the burgeoning hegemony of the new world order of global capital? Should we not consider the language of sexiness to be one of the prime exports of Western economies? The "velvet revolutions" in which the Soviet Union collapsed were striking for their lack of violence but also for the way in which they were motivated by the spectacle of Western luxury from which the East was excluded. More than anything else, the Berlin Wall symbolized to East Germans the barrier between them and the great sea of consumer goods that lay just beyond it. The desirability of capitalism was shown above all in its fruits—the svelte and sexy commodities that crowded the billboards and glossy magazines of the West. This envy of Western products went much further than a mere longing for the bare necessities or the demand for "a chicken in every pot." It represented the dream of a magically transformed existence effected by the commodities themselves, a kind of transcendence by means of ownership. Are we not tempted to see in this remarkable transformation an increasingly worldwide triumph of commodity fetishism? One wonders, to what extent should the end of the Cold War be chalked up to the triumph of sexiness?

Conclusion: The Freudian Prospect

More than a hundred years have passed since the publication in 1900 of Freud's masterwork *The Interpretation of Dreams.* In fact, although the book actually appeared late in 1899, Freud was careful to adjust the date of publication so that his first great articulation of psychoanalysis would be born with the new century. In fulfillment of his most fervent wish, his influence upon the twentieth century was prodigious indeed. But what are his prospects in the twenty-first?

It has been my contention that Freud's theories have been subject to a deepening misunderstanding, both inside and outside the academy. I've tried to show that a key part of that misunderstanding centers on the concept of "drive," what Freud called *Trieb.* Encouraged by a mistranslation of the word into English, undergraduate psychology textbooks routinely present Freud as an "instinct theorist." The picture, as the title of an influential book would have it, becomes that of Freud as a "biologist of the mind." The unconscious is thus thought to be the animal in us, the unruly beast that is held in check by the repressive strictures of civilized propriety.

The irony in all of this is that the now common prejudice that offers biology as the preferred mode of explanation in matters of sexuality, the same prejudice that champions psychopharmacology over any cure by mere talking and therefore tends to discount the value of psychoanalysis as a mode of therapy, has also been largely responsible for the widespread misconception of psychoanalysis as a theory. In fact, the Freudian notion of the sexual drive is anything but a matter of simple biology.

To be sure, Freud's intention is not to deny altogether the relevance of biology in matters of sex. Trained as an anatomist and having made his first contributions to science in researching such things as the gonads of eels and the nerve cells of crayfish, Freud appreciated the rootedness of sexuality in biology at least as much as his contemporaries. Indeed, maybe more so. Freud was clearly convinced of the important role played by organic factors in sexual life and he felt safe in predicting that much more would come to be known about them in the future. Nevertheless, while sex is always subject to the influence of biology, that influence is by no means wholly determinative. As we have seen in some detail, a crucial dimension of the drive as Freud thinks of it resides precisely in its distance from any natural, biological function. Far from being what we have in common with animals, the plasticity of the drive, its capacity to assume a wide range of forms, is the primary factor separating the human from the animal. The variability of the drive is the point at which the human being is most distinctively human.

Let us lean upon this corrected notion of the drive to ask a final question. In the last three chapters, I have sketched the outline of a Freudian reading of the distinctively modern situation of sexuality, a reading for which the theory of the Oedipus complex provided the primary clue. From this point of view, the essence of the modern age appears as a contestation of patriarchy. That contestation, bound up in different ways with each of the four great underlying movements of modernity—natural science, Protestantism, Enlightenment, and capitalism—has energized the sexual field with special tensions. Sex has become the pivotal point of intersection for the contending forces that now stress and strain the social fabric of the modern world. Sex has assumed the function of a cultural symptom, indeed perhaps the privileged symptom of our epoch. It might now be asked, in the light of this perspective, what exactly are we saying about nature, status, and destiny of sexuality? Are we to conclude, for instance, that the pressures of modern, industrial culture have somehow distorted sexual life, alienating it from the simpler, truer, more natural sexuality of a bygone time? Must we now look back on some "good old days" of sexuality that have given way to a contemporary deformation of sex in which the natural order of things has been perverted? Does my argument here imply that the essential nature of sexuality, somehow at home in the structure of traditional patriarchal society, has now become displaced and alienated?

On the contrary! If the question is put as to the essential nature of sex, the Freudian answer, though mysterious in itself and far-reaching in its implications, can at least be clearly stated. There isn't any. Freud's conception of the open and indeterminate character of the drive enables us to assert the radical plasticity of sex. The whole upshot of Freud's understanding of libido, the very reason why he resurrects a strange sounding Latin term to name it, is that the sexual drive in the human being has no essential form given to it by nature. There is no "true" sexuality; no pure, simple, or natural reality of sex. This is the deeper meaning of Freud's assertion that sexuality is the key to personality: Sex is, of all dimensions of psychical life, the point at which the human being is least determined by nature. Sex is the least animal thing about us.

We should pause to understand this point correctly. In addition to his acknowledgment of the partial rootedness of the drive in biological processes, Freud well recognizes that the sexual desires of most mature human beings are quite highly specific and do not easily admit to change. Along a number of parameters (the preferred choice of objects, acts, etc.), the force and direction of the drive is usually pretty firmly established by early adulthood. Indeed, Freud doesn't hesitate to relate such established channeling of the drive to the psychical phenomenon that he calls "fixation."

When Freud continues to insist upon the fluid and indeterminate character of libido, therefore, he is making a theoretical point with a definite purpose. He means to indicate that the structured and relatively stable character of the average person's sexual drive is to a considerable extent a product of psychical development, the outcome of a particular psychological history, and that in this domain of psychical structure *things might have turned out otherwise.* It is this margin of what might have developed otherwise (in another time, another place, with another family, under the influence of other events and circumstances) that accounts for cultural and historical variations in sexual norms. It is in that margin of variability that social and cultural influences routinely play themselves out. We've returned more than once to a prime case in point: the classical Greek attitude toward homosexuality that contrasts so markedly to our own.

In the analysis of modernity that I have sketched, we see the shape of the drive undergoing another historical-cultural variation. Yet far from it being the case that sex in the modern period is perverted from its natural essence, it would be more true to say that with modernity sex comes more fully into its own. How? By assuming a greater measure of its own intrinsic indeterminacy. From the standpoint of our current sensibility, what is sex? Is it not above all something that cannot be defined neatly? Contemporary discussions of sex are marked by a conspicuous refusal to universalize, by an almost exaggerated scrupulousness about exceptional cases, by an insistent regard for the diversity of sexual identities. Increasingly, the singular form of the noun appears inadequate and we opt for the plural: *sexualities.* Sex now seems to overflow every conceptual containment; it is precisely what is not merely natural, not merely binary, not ordered in ways that can be universalized. Looking around ourselves today, how can we avoid the judgment that contemporary sexuality stubbornly insists on its plurality, its polymorphousness, its multivocity?

Rapidly changing attitudes toward homosexuality are among the most palpable indications of the contemporary fluidity of sex. Is it not obvious that popular culture in America has for long time been flirting very happily with gay identity? The runaway success of the TV serial *Queer Eye for the Straight Guy* (the show in which a platoon of deliciously glib and gleeful gay guys invade the apartment of some hapless heterosexual and transform his flophouse into something simply *fabulous*) really shouldn't have been so surprising. To take only one, very particular example, the tip of an iceberg of other evidence that could be offered, it is not for nothing that the American Academy of Film's listing of the one hundred greatest movies of all time is topped by the gender-bending "Some Like It Hot" from 1959. In the delightful final scene of that movie, when the tycoon learns that Daphne (Jack Lemmon) is really a man, he responds with a blithe and breezy "I don't care!"[1] Spoken with an irresistible, winking charm by means of which an undeniable naughtiness is made thoroughly innocent, the words also speak for a growing segment of American culture for whom the lines of traditional sexual identity have been losing their hard edges. Only a couple of short years after its unexpected triumph, *Queer Eye* was speedily one-upped by another show, *He's a Lady*, in which a gang of heavily masculine guys undergo a burly-to-girly transformation, emerging at the climax of the hour decked out in drag getups that are both comical and disconcertingly convincing.

Putting the focus on TV shows and movies is appropriate in this instance because the changes I'm pointing to are less changes in behavior than shifts of ideology, less issues of fact than of value. It is not so much a matter of what people do (the sexual acts they actually engage in) than what they think about it. People have indulged in a wide variety of sexual practices during nearly every epoch of history. What is striking about our most recent history is a greater degree of public acknowledgment of those practices and an expansion of tolerance toward them.

But, of course, not everyone has been willing to say "I don't care." If the modern period, for reasons that have to do with the most profound features and tendencies of modern life, has ushered in a destabilizing multiplication of sexual identities, a kind of freeing of the drive from traditional constraints upon it, we need immediately to recall the counterpoint of conservative reaction. While *He's a Lady* was in production on the West Coast, a constitutional amendment prohibiting gay marriage was in preparation on the East. Only the two movements taken together can adequately describe the current situation of sexuality. In fact, my thesis has been that the force and passion of the fundamentalist reaction among one segment of the population is roughly proportional to the liberating change in attitudes among another segment. The more open and tolerant the posture of one group, the more shrill and sanctimonious is the battle cry of the other. If one segment of the population has been willing to blur the boundaries of sexual identity, another segment has thrown itself energetically into the effort of stamping out all ambiguity.

I have tried to show that Freud offers a unique resource for the interpretation of these trends and does so in at least two senses. The first draws on his theory of the Oedipus complex. We have leaned upon that theory to draw the link between the slow-melt of modern sexuality identities and the decline of

---

[1]In fact, the actual script is even more charming:
Daphne: "I'm not a blonde."
Osgood: "Doesn't matter."
Daphne: "I smoke."
Osgood: "I don't care."
Daphne: "I'm a terrible mess. For the past three years I've been living with a saxophone player."
Osgood: "I forgive you."
Daphne: "I can never have children."
Osgood: "We can adopt some."
Daphne: "I'm a man!"
Osgood: "Well, nobody's perfect."

patriarchal authority. It is as if the patriarchal matrix of traditional society provided the containment chamber for the polymorphous potential of Eros that now appears to be enjoying a striking expansion and proliferation. To draw this conclusion is merely to apply to a certain historical development the scheme attributed by Freud to the psychical maturation of the individual. A containment and regularizing of sexuality, effected by the establishment of emotional structure and stabilization by a network of repressions and identifications, was thought by Freud to be the psychological function of the Oedipus complex in personal development. For that reason, disturbances of the Oedipal triangle yield effects in the sexual sphere. The question then becomes: Are long-established patterns of repression and identification associated with patriarchal order now undergoing gradual alterations in response to the modern crisis of patriarchy?

The second way in which Freud makes an indispensable contribution to deciphering the truth of our historical moment is by means of his concept of the symptom. As we have seen, the structure of the symptom is intrinsically manifold. In the symptom, what may initially appear to be completely contrary forces become recognizable as the two sides of a particularly stubborn and stable unity. It is not for nothing that the watchword of psychoanalytic theory is "complex." By means of the notion of symptom and its intrinsically complex structure, Freud allows us to see beneath the welter of surface phenomena and to discern the interaction of underlying forces that are knotted in conflict with one another. That sexuality in the modern world has assumed the function of a symptom helps to explain why questions of sexual morality now focus our most intense social, political, religious debates. Sex is the privileged field in which the underlying tensions of the modern era are most intensely fraught. At the most elemental level, the deep tensions bound up in this symptomatic knot can be readily indicated. As the most potent and intimate mode of connection between human beings, sex quite naturally undergoes a kind of hyperventilation in an atmosphere of deepening social atomism and alienation. With the increasing isolation of the modern individual, sex becomes freed from traditional restraints but also becomes freighted with the emotional energy of lost affiliations.

The value of the Freudian notion of the symptom for allowing us to see beyond superficialities and grasp the deeper, determinative conflicts at stake is well illustrated by the American election of 2004. As I write this conclusion, George W. Bush has won a second term as president in an election widely supposed to have been decisively influenced by voters' concern about "moral values." While the vagueness of the term no doubt allows it to function as a catchall for a variety of obscure fears and loathings, there is also little doubt that issues of sexual identity and norms are uppermost in many people's understanding of what "moral values" means, not least because of the prominence of the gay marriage debate in the buildup to the election. It would be a serious mistake, however, to think that the underlying motive forces behind the appeal of "moral values" are merely phenomena of the moment. On the contrary, if the argument I have pursued is even roughly correct, the battle lines of the 2004 election have been centuries in the making and may well take some further centuries to resolve. With the emphasis on the symptomatic character of modern sexuality, we can recognize how the much-touted division of the country between progressives and conservatives is to be seen dialectically, that is, as two sides of a single historical complex. The currents of liberation and reaction that now split the electorate, like the positive and negative poles of a single battery, are in fact the two sides, as inseparable as they are mutually enhancing, of a single process of epochal transformation.

Putting modern sexuality into the category of the psychoanalytic symptom helps us to understand the paradoxical situation in which we find ourselves: a world in which the blurring of gender marches side by side with insistent retrenchments of traditional canons of sex difference. If the perspective of the symptom helps to clarify this paradox, allowing us to see the way in which liberationist and conservative attitudes toward sex form an almost necessary couplet, it also allows us to see beneath merely apparent differences on either side and to grasp their underlying identity. We are able, for example, to recognize how, viewed in the largest perspective that takes account of the epochal movements of the modern era, George W. Bush and Osama bin Laden have more in common than they have differences. One hears a good deal of talk these days about the clash of civilizations, as if the battle lines of the contemporary situation are to be located on the boundary between West and East. The deeper tension, however, is that between the forces of modernity itself and those who oppose it.

With that deeper tension in mind, Bush and bin Laden must be recognized, despite the sworn enmity between them, as deeply akin to one another. It is a kinship most readily evident in their shared appeal to traditional values. In their own very different spheres, each leader sounds the call to protect time-worn cultural forms, including the traditional distinction between the sexes and the institutions based upon it, against the corrosive and confusing influence of modernity. Of course, it would be perfectly correct to remind ourselves that things are not quite so simple. As a faithful friend of global free market capitalism, George W. Bush, apparently unknown to himself, is a champion of the most powerfully destabilizing forces of modernization. And yet, as if positioning himself precisely on the fault-line that defines the symptomatic structure of contemporary society, Bush continually reemphasizes his unwavering commitment to old-fashioned standards. Explicitly or implicitly, Bush constantly repeats a vow to protect time-honored mores from the encroachments of modernity. Simultaneously the champion of freedom and of traditional values, Bush himself is therefore the perfect embodiment of the symptomatic split. In fact, one wonders to what extent his power derives from this very capacity to work both sides of the symptomatic dichotomy at once.

How, then, do these reflections bear upon the question of Freud and his future? Among the more damning contemporary judgments about Freud, ingredient in many attacks on his legacy but perhaps none more so than those of his feminist detractors, is the charge that Freud now deserves our opprobrium because his views are woefully traditional. The mantra is that Freud is an old-guard masculinist, an apologist of patriarchy. I hope to have shown the error of this verdict and to have demonstrated how Freud, far from being a defender of traditional male privilege, supplies to us the theoretical tools with which to recognize the psychological roots of patriarchy and to analyze its modern crisis.

In concluding, we can offer a final observation about the deep reasons for Freud's current disfavor, an observation that gathers the threads of our reflections about the symptomatic situation of modernity. For if Freud is accused by some people of being in league with traditional sexism, others attack him for being the very opposite. For every progressive enemy of patriarchy who shrinks back from Freud's alleged misogyny, there is a conservative who is outraged by Freud's focus on sex, a focus that commits, if nothing else, the travesty of continually mentioning the unmentionable. Even today, many dyed-in-the-wool social conservatives will roll their eyes at the mere mention of Freud. It is difficult not to conclude that the real reason for all their teeth-gnashing is usually left unspoken: they detest Freud for being the prime culprit who legitimated all the contemporary talk about sexuality. Freud is, above all others, the one who let the cat out of the bag. The crucial thing is to recognize is that Freud tends to get it from both sides. He is the *bête noir* of radicals and reactionaries alike. The irony, however, is not just that Freud really belongs to neither side, but that it is Freud, perhaps more than any other thinker, who enables us to recognize the two sides for what they are and to discern the meaning of the dynamics at play between them.

What are the prospects for Freud's continued relevance in the twenty-first century? Will his complex vision of our sexual selves become even more widely misconstrued and distorted? Will it be simply ignored? Or might Freud's theories enjoy a future revival and expansion, allowing the nature and destiny of sexuality to be seen more clearly—perhaps seen for the first time—in their relation to the dynamics of the unconscious that he discovered? The answer to these questions may depend on the degree to which we remain caught in the vice grip of the symptomatic deadlock that Freud best allows us to recognize.

Endnotes

Chapter 1

"put thy hand under my thigh."

Genesis, 24:2.

"*men act* and *women appear*"

John Berger, *Ways of Seeing*, (London: Penguin Books, 1981), 47.

"a crackpot religion that would never have got off the ground ..."

Gore Vidal, Preface to Jonathasn Ned Katz, *The Invention of Heterosexuality* (New York: Dutton, 1995), viii.

Chapter 2

"exalted a certain shine on the nose ..."

Sigmund Freud, *The Standard Edition of the Complete Works of Sigmund Freud*, edited & translated by James Strachey, et al. 24 Vols. (London: Hogarth Press, 1958), 21:152.

"a kiss is a secret ..."

Edmond Rostand, *Cyrano de Bergerac: Comédie héroïque en cinq actes*, edited with introduction, notes, and vocabulary by Oscar Kuhns and Henry Ward Church (New York: Henry Holt and Company, 1939), Act III, Scene 9, 101 (my translation).

"some people would never have fall in love ..."

La Rochefoucauld, *Maxims*, translated by Leonard Tancock (Harmondsworth, England: Penguin Books, 1959), 54.

"mythical entities ..."

Freud, *Standard Edition*, 22:95.

"no one who has seen a baby ..."

Freud, *Standard Edition*, 7:182.

"in recalling Satan's attacks ..."

William Manchester, *A World Lit Only by Fire: The Medieval Mind and the Renaissance, Portrait of an Age*. (Boston: Little, Brown & Company, 1993), 139–40.

"who, then, is this other …"

Jacques Lacan, *Écrits, A Selection*, translated by Alan Sheridan (New York: Norton, 1977), 172.

"no one has to this point seriously enough considered …"

Hans Bellmer, quoted by Gilles Néret in *Twentieth Century Erotic Art*, edited by Angelika Muthesius and Burkhard Biemschneider (Köln: Taschen Verlag, 1998), 21.

Chapter 3

"will only permit …"

Freud, *Standard Edition*, 21:105.

"sometimes one seems to perceive …"

Freud, *Standard Edition*, 21:105.

"civilization is obeying the laws of economic necessity …"

Freud, *Standard Edition*, 21:104.

"I get up, everything spins …"

Jean-Paul Sartre, *Nausea*, translated by Lloyd Alexander (New York: New Directions, 1964), 177–78.

"the ego is first and foremost a bodily ego …"

Freud, *Standard Edition*, 19:26.

Chapter 4

"why, that's myself: S.P …"

Freud, *Standard Edition*, 17:94.

"women, especially if they grow up with good looks …"

Freud, *Standard Edition*, 14: 88–89.

"Strictly speaking …," "this description …," "differences are of course …," "there are quite a number of women.…"

Freud, *Standard Edition*, 14:89.

"man finds it repugnant …"

Simone de Beauvoir, *The Second Sex*, translated and edited by H. M. Parshley (New York: Vintage Books, 1989), 150.

"the Oedipus Complex [is] considered …"

de Beauvoir, *Second Sex*, 195.

"when a man stands in the midst …"

Friedrich Nietzsche, *The Gay Science*, translated by Walter Kaufmann (New York: Random House, 1974), 123–24.

"someone took a youth to a sage …"
Nietzsche, *Gay Science,* 126.

"where they love they do not desire …"
Freud, *Standard Edition,* 11:179.

"woman is a temple …," "if she agrees to deny her animality.…"
quoted by de Beauvoir, *Second Sex,* 170.

"phantasies of being seduced …"
Freud, *Standard Edition,* 16:370.

"the sexual abuse …" etc.
Freud, *Standard Edition,* 23:187.

"a little girl …"
Freud, *Standard Edition,* 23:75–76.

"a number of parents and child-care providers …"
Frederick Crews, "The Unknown Freud," *The New York Review of Books,* Vol. 40, No. 19. November 18, 1993, 65.

"Although the therapists in question …"
Crews, "The Unknown Freud," 65.

Chapter 5

"Only by the concurrent or mutually opposing action …"
Freud, *Standard Edition,* 23:243.

"mysterious masochistic trends of the ego …"
Freud, *Standard Edition,* 18:14.

"a pure culture of the death drive …"
Freud, *Standard Edition,* 19:53.

"the superego is always close to the id …"
Freud, *Standard Edition,* 19:48.

"With wide staring eyes …"
Plato, *Collected Dialogues of Plato,* translated by Edith Hamilton and Huntington Cairns (Princeton, N.J.: Bollingen Press, 1961), 642.

"What pleasure can there be …"
St. Augustine, *Confessions,* translated by R. S. Pine-Coffin (Harmondsworth, England: Penguin Books, 1961), 242.

"Camil: The main thing was …"
Susan Brownmiller, *Against Our Will: Men, Women, and Rape* (New York: Simon and Schuster, 1975), 108–9.

"That's an everyday affair …"
Brownmiller, *Against Our Will*, 104–5.

"battle-test that brings honor to men …"
Homer, *Iliad*, translated by Robert Fitzgerald (New York: Anchor Books, 1974), 95.

"they only do it when there are a lot of guys around.…"
Brownmiller, *Against Our Will*, 107.

"I hate gooks …"
Quoted by Anthony Wilden, "In the Penal Colony: The Body as the Discourse of the Other," *Semiotica*, Vol. 54-1/2 (1985), 40.

"It was a woman …"
Brownmiller, *Against Our Will*, 105.

"In El Salvador women tortured and then murdered …"
Wilden, "In the Penal Colony," 41.

"[rape] is a conscious process of intimidation …"
Brownmiller, *Against Our Will*, 15.

"Do women want to be raped?…"
Brownmiller, *Against Our Will*, 313.

"you are here to serve your masters …"
Pauline Réage, *The Story of O* (New York: Grove Press, 1965), 15–17.

"vehemently hostile to suggestions …"
Brownmiller, *Against Our Will*, 323.

"I wasn't young, I wasn't pretty …"
John De St. Jorre, "The Unmasking of O." *New Yorker*, August 1, 1994, 43.

"the most ardent love letter any man has ever received …"
De St. Jorre, "The Unmasking of O," 43.

"there is no reality here …"
De St. Jorre, "The Unmasking of O," 45.

"That's what everyone says,"
De St. Jorre, "The Unmasking of O," 45.

"For women the level of what is ethically normal …"
Freud, *Standard Edition*, 19:257–58.

"all human individuals ... combine in themselves both masculine and feminine ..."

Freud, *Standard Edition*, 19:258.

"we must not allow ourselves to be deflected ..."

Freud, *Standard Edition*, 19:258.

"making the unconscious conscious ..."

In these or similar words, Freud makes this point in many places. See, for instance, Freud, *Standard Edition*, 7:12, 49, 112–14, 189, 228.

"where id was, there ego shall be ..."

Freud, *Standard Edition*, 22:80.

"The ego is structured exactly like a symptom ..."

Lacan, *Écrits, A Selection*, 16.

"What is at issue, at the end of analysis ..."

Jacques Lacan, *The Seminar of Jacques Lacan, Book I, Freud's Papers on Technique*, edited by Jacques-Alain Miller, translated by John Forrester (New York: W. W. Norton & Co., 1988), 232.

"anatomy is destiny"

Freud, *Standard Edition*, 19:178.

Chapter 6

"the New Deal in the law of letters ..."

James Joyce, *Ulysses* (New York: Vintage Books, 1961), v.

"[Joyce's] objective has required him ..."

Joyce, *Ulysses*, ix–x.

"the words which are criticized ..."

Joyce, *Ulysses*, x.

"in respect of the theme of sex ..."

Joyce, *Ulysses*, x.

"And when he made it up to Helen's ..."

James Kelman, *How Late It Was, How Late* (New York: Dell Publishing, 1994), 55.

"The people must fight on behalf of the law ..."

Heraclitus, Fragment #44, quoted in G. S. Kirk and J. E. Raven, *The Presocratic Philosophers* (Cambridge: Cambridge University Press, 1957), 213.

"ask no more questions ...," "I have suffered enough"
Sophocles, *Oedipus The King and Antigone*, translated by Peter Arnott (Arlington Heights, Ill.: Harlan Davidson, 1960), lines 1027 and 1034, 40.

"How could the furrows your father sowed ..."
Sophocles, *Oedipus the King*, lines 1172–73, 46.

"woman is a part of that fearsome machinery ..."
de Beauvoir, *The Second Sex*, 149–50.

"she felt a vibration pass through her whole being ..."
Gustave Flaubert, *Madame Bovary*, translated by Geoffrey Wall (Harmondsworth, England: Penguin Books, 1992), 180.

Chapter 7

"our self-imposed immaturity."
Immanuel Kant, *Perpetual Peace and Other Essays*, translated by Ted Humphrey (Indianapolis: Hackett Publishing Company, 1985), 41.

"The bourgeoisie cannot exist without constantly revolutionizing ..."
Karl Marx and Frederick Engels, *The Communist Manifesto* (London: Verso, 1998), 38.

"the bourgeoisie has torn away from the family its sentimental veil ..."
Marx and Engels, *The Communist Manifesto*, 38.

"Freudians see sex as basically biological."
Murray Davis, *Smut: Erotic Reality and Obscene Ideology* (Chicago: University of Chicago Press, 1983), 9xv.

"the influence of de Sade's brand of Gnostic sexuality ..."
Davis, *Smut*, 178–79.

"This you'd believe, had I but time to tell ye ..."
Quoted by Rachel Weil, "Sometimes a Scepter Is Only a Scepter: Pornography and Politics in Restoration England," in Lynn Hunt, editor, *The Invention of Pornography: Obscenity and the Origins of Modernity, 1500–1800* (New York: Zone Books, 1993), 125.

"his pintle and his sceptre are of a length ..."
Quoted by Rachel Weil, "Sometimes a Scepter ..." in Hunt, *The Invention of Pornography*, 143.

"if we should note that caricatures are the thermometer ..."
Quoted by Lynn Hunt, "Pornography and the French Revolution," in *The Invention of Pornography*, 321.

"A year before, some of these engravings ..."
Quoted by Hunt, "Pornography and the French Revolution," 324.

"Religions are the cradles of despotism." "Let us not be content ..."
Marquis de Sade, *The Complete Justine, Philosophy in the Bedroom, and Other Writings*, translated by Richard Seaver & Austryn Wainhouse (New York: Grove Press, 1965), 305, 300.

"all the attractions that can make an ass interesting ..."
Quoted by Hunt, "Pornography and the French Revolution," 335.

"Vigorous patriots, amiable fellow citizens, a new FIELD ..."
Quoted by Hunt, "Pornography and the French Revolution," 326–27.

"Eighteen sous, instead of twenty-four ..."
Quoted by Hunt, "Pornography and the French Revolution," 327.

"Speak plainly, and say 'fuck,' ..."
Quoted by Lynn Hunt, "Introduction: Obscenity and the Origins of Modernity," in Hunt, *The Invention of Pornography*, 37.

"I was forced to suffer thirty assaults...." "Too much is too much ..."
Quoted by Kathryn Norberg, "The Libertine Whore: Prostitution in French Pornography From Margot to Juliette," in Hunt, *The Invention of Pornography*, 231.

"This new type of debauchery ..."
Quoted by Norberg, "The Libertine Whore...," 231.

"A man who would like to enjoy whatever woman or girl ..."
Sade, *Justine*, 320.

"I say then that women, having been endowed ..."
Sade, *Justine*, 321.

Chapter 8

"there is no extravagance ..."
Sade, *Justine*, 320.

"there can exist no evil in obedience ..."
Sade, *Justine*, 323.

"in order that unqualified persons should not become readers ..."
Richard von Krafft-Ebing, quoted by H. Ruitenbeek, *The New Sexuality* (New York: New Viewpoints, 1974), 36.

"we must therefore abandon the hypothesis ..."
Michel Foucault, *History of Sexuality, Volume I, Introduction,* translated by Robert Hurley (New York: Vintage Books, 1990), 49.

"What is peculiar to modern societies ..."
Foucault, *History of Sexuality,* 35.

"obtained a few caresses,..." "the fact that this everyday occurrence ..."
Foucault, *History of Sexuality,* 31–32.

Power would no longer be dealing simply with legal subjects ..."
Foucault, *History of Sexuality,* 142–43.

"from a symbolics of blood to an analytics of sexuality ..."
Foucault, *History of Sexuality,* 141.

"Flesh was the reason why oil painting was invented."
Quoted in *Willem de Kooning Paintings,* Essays by David Sylvester and Richard Shiff, catalog by Marla Prather (New Haven: Yale University Press, 1994), 16.

"fur and velvet—as has long been suspected—are a fixation ..."
Freud, *Standard Edition,* 21:155.

"The zipless fuck was more than a fuck...."
Erica Jong, *Fear of Flying* (New York: Signet, 1973), 11.

Bibliography

Arendt, Hannah. *The Human Condition*. Chicago: University of Chicago Press, 1958.

Barthes, Roland. *The Fashion System*. Translated by Matthew Ward and Richard Howard. New York: Hill and Wang, 1983.

Berger, John. *Ways of Seeing*. London: Penguin Books, 1981.

Bergler, Edmund. *Fashion and the Unconscious*. Madison, WI: International Universities Press, 1987.

Blankenhorn, David. *Fatherless America: Confronting Our Most Urgent Social Problem*. New York: Harper Perennial, 1996.

Boothby, Richard. *Death and Desire: Psychoanalytic Theory in Lacan's Return to Freud*. New York: Routledge, 1991.

———. *Freud as Philosopher: Metapsychology after Lacan*. New York: Routledge, 2001.

Brennan, Teresa, Editor. *Between Psychoanalysis and Feminism*. London: Routledge, 1989.

———. *History after Lacan*. London: Routledge, 1993.

———. *The Interpretation of the Flesh: Freud and Femininity*. London: Routledge, 1992.

Brownmiller, Susan. *Against Our Will: Men, Women, and Rape*. New York: Simon & Schuster, 1975.

Brundage, James. *Law, Sex, and Christian Society in Medieval Europe*. Chicago: University of Chicago Press, 1987.

Butler, Judith. *Bodies That Matter: On the Discursive Limits of Sex*. New York: Routledge, 1993.

Camus, Albert. *The Stranger*. Translated by Stuart Gilbert. New York: Vintage Books, 1954.

Capellanus, Andreas. *The Art of Courtly Love*. Introduction, translation, and notes by John Jay Parry. New York: Columbia University Press, 1960.

Chassequet-Smirgel, Janine. *Female Sexuality: New Psychoanalytic Views*. Ann Arbor: University of Michigan Press, 1970.

Chodorow, Nancy. *The Reproduction of Mothering: Psychoanalysis and the Sociology of Gender*. Berkeley and Los Angeles: University of California Press, 1978.

Crews, Frederick. "The Unknown Freud," in *The New York Review of Books*, Vol. 40 No. 19. November 18, 1993.

———. Editor. *Unauthorized Freud: Doubters Confront a Legend*. Harmondsworth, England: Penguin Books, 1998.

Davis, Fred. *Fashion, Culture, and Identity*. Chicago: University of Chicago Press, 1992.

Davis, Murray. *Smut: Erotic Reality and Obscene Ideology*. Chicago: University of Chicago Press, 1983.

Dean, Tim. *Beyond Sexuality*. Chicago: University of Chicago Press, 2000.

Dean, Tim, and Christopher Lane, Editors. *Homosexuality and Psychoanalysis*. Chicago: University of Chicago Press, 2001.

De Beauvoir, Simone. *The Second Sex*. Translated and edited by H. M. Parshley. New York: Vintage Books, 1989.

Debord, Guy. *The Society of the Spectacle*. Translated by Donald Nicholson Smith. New York: Zone Books, 1995.

De St. Jorre, John. "The Unmasking of O." *New Yorker*, August 1, 1994.

De Waal, Frans. *Peacemaking among Primates*. Cambridge, Mass.: Harvard University Press, 1989.

Dinnerstein, Dorothy. *The Mermaid and the Minotaur: Sexual Arrangements and the Human Malaise*. New York: Other Press, 1999.

Dworkin, Andrea. *Pornography: Men Possessing Women*. New York: Dutton, 1989.

Ehrenreich, Barbara. *The Hearts of Men: American Dreams and the Flight from Commitment*. New York: Anchor Books, 1983.

Firestone, Shulamith. *The Dialectic of Sex: The Case for Feminist Revolution*. New York: Bantam, 1972.

Flaubert, Gustave. *Madame Bovary*. Translated by Geoffrey Wall. Harmondsworth, England: Penguin Books, 1992.

Flügel, J. C. *The Psychology of Clothes.* London: Hogarth Press and The Institute of Psycho-analysis, 1930.

Foucault, Michel. *The History of Sexuality, Volume I, Introduction.* Translated by Robert Hurley. New York: Vintage Books, 1990.

Freud, Sigmund. "Analysis Terminable and Interminable." *Standard Edition,* Vol. 23, pp. 209–54.

———. "Anxiety and Instinctual Life." *Standard Edition,* Vol. 22, pp. 81–111.

———. "Beyond the Pleasure Principle." *Standard Edition,* Vol. 18, pp. 1–64.

———. "Civilization and Its Discontents." *Standard Edition,* Vol. 21, pp. 57–146.

———. "Dissection of the Personality." *Standard Edition,* Vol. 22, pp. 57–80.

———. "The Dissolution of the Oedipus Complex." *Standard Edition,* Vol. 19, pp. 173–79.

———. "The Ego and the Id." *Standard Edition,* Vol. 19, pp. 1–66.

———. "Femininity." *Standard Edition,* Vol. 22, pp. 112–35.

———. "Fetishism." *Standard Edition,* Vol. 21, pp. 147–58.

———. "Group Psychology and the Analysis of the Ego." *Standard Edition,* Vol. 18, pp. 65–144.

———. "The Infantile Genital Organization: An Interpolation into the Theory of Sexuality." *Standard Edition,* Vol. 19, pp. 141–48.

———. "An Infantile Neurosis." *Standard Edition,* Vol. 17, pp. 1–133.

———. "Inhibitions, Symptoms, and Anxiety." *Standard Edition,* Vol. 20, pp. 71–176.

———. "Instincts and Their Vicissitudes." *Standard Edition,* Vol. 14, pp. 109–40.

———. "The Interpretation of Dreams." *The Standard Edition of the Complete Works of Sigmund Freud.* Edited and translated by James Strachey, et al. 24 Vols. London: Hogarth Press, 1958, Vols. 4 & 5.

———. "Jokes and Their Relation to the Unconscious." *Standard Edition,* Vol. 8.

———. "Notes Upon a Case of Obsessional Neurosis." *Standard Edition,* Vol. 10, pp. 152–318.

———. "On Narcissism: An Introduction." *Standard Edition,* Vol. 14, pp. 67–104.

———. "On the Universal Tendency to Debasement in the Sphere of Love." *Standard Edition,* Vol. 11, pp. 179–90.

———. "An Outline of Psycho-analysis." *Standard Edition,* Vol. 23, pp. 144–207.

———. "The Paths to the Formation of Symptoms." *Standard Edition,* Vol. 14, pp. 358–77.

———. "Some Psychical Consequences of the Anatomical Distinction between the Sexes." *Standard Edition,* Vol. 19, pp. 248–58.

———. "Three Essays on the Theory of Sexuality." *Standard Edition,* Vol. 7, pp. 123–246.

———. "Totem and Taboo." *Standard Edition,* Vol. 13, pp. 1–161.

Fromm, Erik. *The Art of Loving: An Enquiry into the Nature of Love.* New York: Harper Colophon, 1956.

Gay, Peter. *The Tender Passion: The Bourgeois Experience from Victoria to Freud.* Oxford: Oxford University Press, 1986.

———. *Freud: A Life for Our Time.* New York: Anchor Books, 1988.

Gilligan, Carol. *In a Different Voice: Psychological Theory and Women's Development.* Cambridge, Mass.: Harvard University Press, 1982.

Hobbes, Thomas. *Leviathan.* Edited by C. B. Macpherson. Harmondsworth, England: Penguin Classics, 1981.

Hollander, Anne. *Sex and Suits.* New York: Alfred H. Knopf, 1994.

Hollander, Xaviera. *The Happy Hooker.* New York: Dell Publishing, 1972.

Homer. *Iliad.* Translated by Robert Fitzgerald. New York: Anchor Books, 1974.

Horney, Karen. *Feminine Psychology.* New York: W. W. Norton & Co., 1967.

Hunt, Lynn, Editor. *The Invention of Pornography: Obscenity and the Origins of Modernity, 1500–1800.* New York: Zone Books, 1993.

Hyde, H. Montgomery. *A History of Pornography.* New York: Dell, 1966.

Illouz, Eva. *Consuming the Romantic Utopia: Love and the Cultural Contradictions of Capitalism.* Berkeley: University of California Press, 1997.

Jong, Erica. *Fear of Flying.* New York: Signet, 1973.

Joyce, James. *Ulysses.* New York: Vintage Books, 1961.

Kaiser, Susan. *Social Psychology of Clothing: Symbolic Appearances in Context.* New York: Macmillan, 1990.

Kant, Immanuel. *Perpetual Peace and Other Essays.* Translated by Ted Humphrey. Indianapolis: Hackett Publishing, 1985.

Katz, Jonathan Ned. *The Invention of Heterosexuality.* New York: Dutton, 1995.

Kelman, James. *How Late It Was, How Late.* New York: Dell Publishing, 1994.

Kierkegaard, Soren. *Either/Or.* Translated by David F. Swenson and Lillian Marvin Swenson. Princeton, N.J.: Princeton University Press, 1971.

Kinsey, A. C., W. B. Pomeroy, and C. E. Martin. *Sexual Behavior in the Human Male.* Philadelphia: W. B. Saunders, 1948.

Kirk, G. S., and J. E. Raven. *The Presocratic Philosophers.* Cambridge: Cambridge University Press, 1957.

Krafft-Ebing, Richard von. *Psychopathia Sexualis.* Translated by Franklin S. Klaf. New York: Stein and Day, 1965.

Lacan, Jacques. *Les Complexes Familiaux.* Dijon: Navarin Editeur, 1984.

———. *Écrits, A Selection.* Translated by Alan Sheridan. New York: Norton, 1977.

———. *Feminine Sexuality.* Edited by Jacqueline Rose and Juliette Mitchell. New York: W. W. Norton & Co., 1982.

———. *The Four Fundamental Concepts of Psycho-analysis.* Edited by J.-A. Miller, translated by A. Sheridan. New York: Norton Press, 1981.

———. *Le Séminaire, Livre XX, Encore.* Edited by J.-A. Miller. Paris: Editions du Seuil, 1981.

———. *The Seminar of Jacques Lacan, Book I, Freud's Papers on Technique.* Edited by Jacques-Alain Miller. Translated by John Forrester. New York: W. W. Norton & Co., 1988.

———. *The Seminar of Jacques Lacan, Book II, The Ego in Freud's Theory and in the Technique of Psychoanalysis.* Edited by Jacques-Alain Miller. Translated by Sylvana Tomaselli. New York: W. W. Norton & Co., 1988.

———. *The Seminar of Jacques Lacan, Book VII, The Ethics of Psychoanalysis.* Edited by Jacques-Alain Miller. Translated by Dennis Porter. New York: M. W. Norton & Co., 1992.

———. "Some Reflections on the Ego." *International Journal of Psycho-Analysis,* Vol. 34, 1953.

———. *Television.* Translated by Denis Hollier, Rosalind Krauss, and Annette Michelson, *October,* Vol. 40, Spring 1987.

Lacan, Jacques, and Wladimir Granoff,. "Fetishism: The Symbolic, the Imaginary, and the Real," in *Perversions: Psychodynamics and Psychotherapy,* edited by S. Lorand and M. Balint. New York: Gramercy Press, 1956.

Lane, Christopher. *The Burdens of Intimacy: Psychoanalysis and Victorian Masculinity.* Chicago: University of Chicago Press, 1999.

Laqueur, Thomas. *Making Sex: Body and Gender from the Greeks to Freud.* Cambridge, Mass.: Harvard University Press, 1992.

La Rochfoucauld. *Maxims.* Translated by Leonard Tancock. Harmondsworth, England: Penguin Books, 1959.

Lewis, Helen Block. *Shame and Guilt in Neurosis.* New York: International Universities Press, 1974.

Lurie, Alison. *The Language of Clothes.* New York: Random House, 1981.

MacCannell, Juliet Flower. *The Regime of the Brother: After the Patriarchy.* London: Routledge, 1991.

Manchester, William. *A World Lit Only by Fire: The Medieval Mind and the Renaissance, Portrait of an Age.* Boston: Little, Brown, 1993.

Marx, Karl. *Captial: A Critical Analysis of Capitalist Production.* Translated by Samuel Moore and Edward Aveling. Edited by Frederick Engels. New York: International Publishers, 1947.

Marx, Karl, and Frederick Engels. *The Communist Manifesto.* London: Verso, 1998.

Masson, Jeffrey Moussaieff. *The Assault on Truth: Freud's Suppression of the Seduction Theory.* New York: Farrar Straus and Giroux, 1984.

Mitchell, Juliette. *Psychoanalysis and Feminism.* New York: Vintage Books, 1975.

Mitscherlich, Alexander. *Society Without the Father: A Contribution to Social Psychology.* Translated by Eric Mosbacher. New York: Harcourt, Brace, & World, 1969.

Muthesius, Angelika and Burkhard Biemschneider, Editors. *Twentieth Century Erotic Art.* Köln: Taschen Verlag, 1998.

Nietzsche, Friedrich. *The Gay Science.* Translated by Walter Kaufmann. New York: Random House, 1974.

O'Toole, Laurence. *Pornocopia: Porn, Sex, Technology, and Desire.* London: Serpent's Tail, 1998.

Paglia, Camille. *Sexual Personae: Art and Decadence from Nefertiti to Emily Dickinson.* New York: Vintage Books, 1991.

Pateman, Carole. *The Sexual Contract.* Stanford, Calif.: Stanford University Press, 1988.

Pavord, Anna. *The Tulip: The Story of a Flower That Has Made Men Mad.* New York: Bloomsbury Publishing, 2001.

Phillips, Kim, and Barry Reay. Editors. *Sexualities in History: A Reader.* New York: Routledge, 2002.

Plato. *Collected Dialogues of Plato.* Translated by Edith Hamilton and Huntington Cairns. Princeton, N.J.: Bollingen Press, 1961.

Prather, Marla. Editor. *Willem de Kooning Paintings.* Essays by David Sylvester and Richard Shiff New Haven: Yale University Press, 1994.

Réage, Pauline. *The Story of O.* New York: Grove Press, 1965.

Rostand, Edmund. *Cyrano de Bergerac: Comédie héroïque en cinq actes.* Edited with introduction, notes, and vocabulary by Oscar Kuhns and Henry Ward Church. New York: Henry Holt, 1939.

Rousseau, Jean-Jacques. *Reveries of the Solitary Walker.* Translated by Peter France. Harmondsworth, England: Penguin Books, 1986.

Ruitenbeek, Hendrick. *The New Sexuality.* New York: New Viewpoints, 1974.

Sade, Marquis de. *The Complete Justine, Philosophy in the Bedroom, and Other Writings.* Translated by Richard Seaver and Austryn Wainhouse. New York: Grove Press, 1966.

———. *Juliette.* Translated by Austryn Wainhouse. New York: Grove Press, 1978.

Sartre, Jean-Paul. *Nausea.* Translated by Lloyd Alexander. New York: New Directions, 1964.

Slater, Philip. *The Glory of Hera: Greek Mythology and the Greek Family.* Boston: Beacon Press, 1971.

Sophocles. *Oedipus the King and Antigone.* Translated by Peter Arnott. Arlington Heights, Ill.: Harlan Davidson, 1960.

St. Augustine. *Confessions.* Translated by R. S. Pine-Coffin. Harmondsworth, England: Penguin Books, 1961.

St. John of the Cross. *The Dark Night of the Soul.* Translated by E. Allison Peers. New York: Image Books, 1959.

Steinem, Gloria. *Moving beyond Words.* New York: Simon & Schuster, 1994.

Sulloway, Frank. *Freud: Biologist of the Mind.* New York: Basic Books, 1979.

Tisdale, Sally. *Talk Dirty to Me: An Intimate Philosophy of Sex.* New York: Anchor Books, 1994.

Weber, Max. *The Protestant Ethic and the Spirit of Capitalism.* Translated by Talcott Parsons. New York: Routledge. 1992.

Weeks, Jeffrey. *Invented Moralities: Sexual Values in an Age of Uncertainty.* Cambridge: Polity Press, 1995.

———. *Sex, Politics, and Society: The Regulation of Sexuality Since 1800.* London: Longman, 1989.

Wilden, Anthony. "In the Penal Colony: The Body as the Discourse of the Other." *Semiotica,* Vol. 54-1/2 (1985), pp. 33–85.

Wolf, Naomi. *The Beauty Myth: How Images of Beauty Are Used against Women.* New York: Anchor Books, 1991.

Zaretsky, Eli. *Capitalism, the Family, and Personal Life.* New York: Harper & Row, 1986.

———. *Secrets of the Soul: A Social and Cultural History of Psychoanalysis.* New York: Knopf, 2004.

Zizek, Slavoj. *The Plague of Fantasies.* London: Verso, 1997.

———. *The Sublime Object of Ideology.* London: Verso, 1989.

Index

R

S

T

U

V

W

Z